Chinook by
C10 Sqn, '23-

Ian Laughran
Sqn. Ldr. Ian S. Loughran, VM.
CO. No. 37 Squadron, IAF.
Noland
Flg. Off. M.T. Leland.
Pete Wilson
16 Sqdn

THE INDIA-PAKISTAN
AIR WAR OF 1965

The India-Pakistan Air War of 1965

P.V.S. JAGAN MOHAN
SAMIR CHOPRA

MANOHAR
2006

First published 2005
Reprinted 2006

© Authors, 2005

All rights reserved. No part of this publication may be reproduced or transmitted, in any form or by any means, without prior permission of authors and the publisher

ISBN 81-7304-641-7

Published by
Ajay Kumar Jain for
Manohar Publishers & Distributors
4753/23 Ansari Road, Daryaganj
New Delhi 110002

Typeset by
A J Software Publishing Co. Pvt. Ltd.
New Delhi 110005

Printed at
Lordson Publishers Pvt. Ltd.
Delhi 110007

Distributed in South Asia by
FOUNDATION
BOOKS
4381/4 Ansari Road,
Daryaganj, New Delhi 110002
and its branches at Mumbai, Hyderabad,
Bangalore, Chennai, Kolkata

Contents

Preface		7
Acknowledgements		11
List of Abbreviations		15
1.	Indian Air Force in its Preliminary Years	19
2.	The Adversaries Prior to War	34
3.	From the Kutch to Chamb: From Skirmishes to War	60
4.	The Challenge: Flare up on 6 September	94
5.	The Sargodha Raids and the Air Battles of 7 September	124
6.	Missed Opportunity: The War in the Eastern Sector	161
7.	The Second Week of the Air War	204
8.	The End of the War: 15-23 September	252
9.	Ceasefire and Post-mortem	286
10.	Epilogue	318

Appendices

Appendix A:	PAF Air Combat Claims *versus* Actual IAF Losses	341
Appendix B:	Official List of Indian Armed Forces Aircraft Losses	343
Appendix C:	IAF Claims *versus* Official List of Pakistani Losses	348

Appendix D:	Gallantry Award Winners (IAF) in the 1965 Air War	351
Appendix E:	IAF Order of Battle in the 1965 War	354
Appendix F:	IAF Canberra Operations	356
Appendix G:	IAF Strength: Reported *versus* Actual	358
Appendix H:	List of Interviewees	360
Bibliography		363
Index		367

Preface

The India-Pakistan Air War of 1965 is a book that aims to fill in the gaps regarding a military conflict that took place almost four decades ago. Why is a book about an air war that took place four decades ago being written now? Perhaps this is best answered indirectly. In 1999, a military conflict broke out in Kashmir. The world read about a war that threatened to reach a nuclear flashpoint. In fact, earlier too, the world has read about wars fought over the same region. In this book we describe the air component of a war that was triggered by the issue of Kashmir in 1965; we believe that the air war has not been documented adequately. While the Pakistani side of the story has been told, the Indian story has not.

The book begins with a brief historical background to the Indian Air Force (IAF) and discusses the events that drove the IAF's developments in the years leading up to the war. These chapters enable some appreciation of the challenges that faced the IAF as it strove to develop the aviation component of its military. The political circumstances of India and Pakistan drove their purchasing policies: American aces from the Korean War had trained the Pakistan Air Force (PAF) whose main strike force consisted of F 86 Sabres—the stars of the Korean War—and B 57 Canberras; the IAF flew a mixture of British, Russian and French jets. With some brief technical detail, we examine the orders of battle in 1965. India was often using untried and untested aircraft beyond their designated performance profiles. India persisted in attempting self-reliance in military matters. This process continues to this day and can be witnessed in its manufacture of nuclear weapons and the development of an indigenous aviation and space programme.

After a brief look at the events that eventually triggered the war in September 1965—the battles in the disputed Rann of Kutch territory and the Pakistani intrusion into Kashmir by

Operation Gibraltar—we move on to a day by day recounting of the war, from the Pakistani attack in Jammu to the Indian retaliation across the Punjab border, to a blow by blow account of the escalation of the air war on the western front. It is a sobering thought that the Kargil conflict in 1999 began in almost exactly the same fashion. We also provide a detailed description of events in the Eastern Sector, i.e. on the border between India and the erstwhile East Pakistan, something that no book on the conflict has ever attempted. Our account is unique in providing Indian eyewitness accounts of the major incidents of the air war. Subsequent chapters deal with the air component of the three-week long, inconclusive slugging battle on the ground that employed tanks and artillery, and which was only brought to a halt after intense international pressure for a ceasefire involving all the major superpowers (the US, the USSR and China) and the United Nations. We conclude with an evaluation of the performance of the respective air forces and an epilogue on the men who fought the war.

Our main source of information has been the interviews with IAF personnel who fought in the war. We were able to procure war diaries of squadrons, with the material being made available from both Indian and Pakistani sources, including magazine articles, dramatized accounts and other books—mainly by army personnel on both sides of the border—that chiefly addressed the conflict on the ground. As a result of conducting interviews—in the USA, the United Kingdom, Australia and India—we were able to get a unique perspective on the war. We faced challenges: some IAF personnel simply could not be located; some had migrated and left the country to settle abroad; some were reluctant to talk about a subject that could often evoke painful memories; some had passed away before we began the book; and, others sadly left us as the book was being written. Lastly, the IAF itself has not made public its records of the war. Still, our contact with ex-IAF personnel provided us with unique information: pilot's logbook scans, never before published photographs, including gun camera photos and personal details of the men who fought the war. We also conducted interviews via e-mail, by sending questionnaires to the veterans involved. We used the Indian Government's *Official History of the 1965 War* to cross-check details and verify claims. We did not, however, have access to the Indian Air Force's history cell. We have received no funding from the Indian Government or the IAF. We did receive support from serving IAF officers in an unofficial capacity.

The book is of value in understanding the deployment of airpower of the twentieth century. Furthermore, the 1965 war represents a turning point in Indo-Pakistan relations. India had already realized its military vulnerability after the 1962 war with China. This war took it further down the path of military modernization and re-equipment. Its air force was rapidly undergoing an expansion programme in the mid 1960s; it took the lessons from this war into its next campaign, the highly successful war to liberate East Pakistan in 1971. The lessons learned from the 1965 war still drive military aviation in India, which has embarked on the Light Combat Aircraft project and recently inducted the Sukhoi 30MKI, the most advanced jet aircraft in the world today in active service. Understanding this war will help dispel some notions the West has about the countries that find themselves still locked in battle over Kashmir. One of these is the misconception that the countries are not militarily sophisticated. On the contrary, as this book will show, the two have had practice in developing military tactics over a period of time, which are unique to the theaters that they will fight in. The two countries have fought fiercely, with no quarter given and certainly none asked for. The armoured battles in the Sialkot sector in 1965 were the most intense since the Second World War, rivaled only by Israeli-Egyptian battles in the Sinai in 1973, and the air battles often took place at low-altitudes in high performance aircraft.

Each country appointed heroes; this book recounts some of the Indian stories. We tell for the first time the story of Alfred Cooke, the Indian pilot who tangled with four PAF Sabres and shot down two of them. Cooke is peacefully retired in Australia, this being the first time his story has been recorded. Some legendary raids that have made their way into the aviation lore of the Indian subcontinent are described for the first time in print, such as Pete Wilson's raid on Badin, the Pakistani pilot admiringly dubbed '8-Pass Charlie' by Indian pilots and the story of the daring, clandestine reconnaissance missions flown in broad daylight by Jaggi Nath, at low level over Pakistan, prior to the outbreak of hostilities.

The war had a unique edge to it. Prior to the creation of India and Pakistan, men who had served together in air academies were now in a war against each other. The Air Chiefs in the war—Arjan Singh and Nur Khan—were friends before the war and remain friends to this day. Indian pilots flew across the border and over the villages that their grandparents and parents had lived in. More than one Indian pilot was to comment on the incongruity of fighting against men who might have been his squadron mates had the history of the subcontinent been even marginally different.

With the publication of this book, the history of the 1965 war will be complete. We do not spend much time on political details, commentary or historical background that is non-aviation related. Much has already been written on these matters. For the interested reader we provide a bibliography for further reading that will provide adequate background on the land war and on the politics of Indo-Pak relations in 1965. We started this project with a certain boyish enthusiasm and have used that as a balance to the seriousness of the project. Still, in writing this book, we strive to do justice to the facts, to present history with respect for its players and with the fervent hope that the future history of the subcontinent will not require the kind of cost that appears to be imminent in these grim days.

Contact e-mail addresses of the authors:
P.V.S. Jagan Mohan: jagan@warbirdsofindia.com
Samir Chopra: schopra@sci.brooklyn.cuny.edu

Acknowledgements

In 1989, I came across Air Chief Marshal P.C. Lal's *My Years with the IAF*. I read with fascination a blow-by-blow account of the Indian Air Force's contribution in the 1971 war and how it shaped the history of the subcontinent. Since then I have waited in vain for an authoritative account of the 1965 conflict. There were numerous accounts of the 1965 conflict, though none was specific to the air war and most of them were vague or contradictory to each other. Something had to be done to fill the void. Thus, this story of the 1965 Indo-Pak air war basically started off as an amateurish venture to satisfy my own curiosity.

The initial chapters and write-ups were done for my own consumption. It was when I saw Rupak Chattopadhyay's Indian Air Force site, that I thought about putting the information on the Web. Rupak helped me out in this matter, offering valuable advice and support. Rupak's co-webmasters at the Bharat Rakshak site (www.bharat-rakshak.com), L.N. Subramanian and Rakesh Koshy too extended their support and shared much information.

When I thought about putting the story of 1965 together, I never imagined I would enjoy the benefit of hearing the stories from the people who fought in the frontline. Somewhere along the line, I started tracing out and interviewing retired officers and men of the IAF who had taken part in these operations. Meeting these officers provided me with a tremendous amount of satisfaction. Not only at sharing their experiences, but also at ensuring the accuracy of events depicted in the book.

Halfway through the effort, I was fortunate in establishing contact with Samir Chopra. He had gone through the initial draft and made an offer to edit the document. But Samir's contribution went beyond the editing of the document; he became involved in tracking down many veterans of the conflict and interviewing them. He managed to accumulate numerous first-person accounts, unofficial wartime documents from veterans' collections and a number of rare photographs. Soon, the quantum of work he put in the book was enough to warrant his inclusion as the co-author; anything less would not have done justice to his contribution. Samir's personal interest in the war came through his desire to find out more about his father's role in the war (Squadron Leader P.C. Chopra was awarded the VrC).

Pushpindar Singh Chopra, Anandeep Pannu, Seetal Patel, Dr. Shivshankar Sastry, Polly Singh, VP, Hemraj, Nakul Shah, Sanjeev K. Sharma, Gus Sheridan, Linda Sheridan and Sree Krishan Kumar were instrumental in shaping this account into its final form.

Besides the list of officers who are acknowledged in the list of Interviewees, I would also like to acknowledge the help of Group Captain Kapil Bhargava (Retd.), Group Captain Anant Bewoor (Retd.) and Air Marshal S. Raghavendran (Retd.).

Thanks also to several Pakistani websites that provide information about the conflict. Mr. Ikram Sehgal's *Defence Journal* is an indispensable website for anyone looking towards information from the other side. Pushpindar Singh Chopra is bringing out a comprehensive three-volume history of the Indian Air Force. Till then we hope this book will fill the void as far as the air war of 1965 is concerned.

This is not the final word on the 1965 air war; new facts will come to light and mistakes in existing accounts and versions will be discovered. We hope to update the book constantly by enhancing it with more personal experiences of the people who fought in the war and more details and pictures from that era.

30 November 2003   P.V.S. JAGAN MOHAN
Hyderabad

In 1998, while working as a System Administrator for an online brokerage, I browsed the Web looking for information on the Indian Air Force. I'd been an aviation history enthusiast since childhood; growing up in air force bases will do that to you. I found Jagan's site on the Web and was fascinated to see an

ACKNOWLEDGMENTS

entire site dedicated to the 1965 conflict. I made an entry in Jagan's guestbook, supplying some information and carried on. Jagan wrote back, sparking off a correspondence between us on matters of air force history. Two years later, Jagan sent me the first draft of this book, requesting comments. By that time I had finished my doctoral work in the US and had moved to Australia on a postdoctoral fellowship. I read the draft with great interest and offered my editing help. As I continued to work on the book, I fell deeper into the task of getting the history right, of accumulating more details, of contacting veterans and conducting interviews. Soon I found myself co-author of the book, and truly I don't think I've ever engaged in a more pleasurable and rewarding collaboration. Jagan and I would exchange e-mails frequently, checking with each other, clearing each change, sending each other snippets of information as and when they became available. We collaborated on the writing of the book in purely electronic fashion. To date, we have not met each other in person but hope to do so someday.

I would like to thank Sree Krishan Kumar for his careful readings of the manuscript and for his marvelously detailed commentary and discussions over e-mail. He has been an inspiration in more ways than one. I would like to thank all the pilots I interviewed for their hospitality and generosity and for transporting me back to a considerably more innocent time of my life. I would like to thank Desmond Peters for arranging the interview with Alfred Cooke and for his wonderful meals; Alfred Cooke and Fred Josephs for their hospitality in Australia; Madhabendra Banerji, Jimmy Bhatia and Vinod Patney for their hospitality in Delhi; those that offered their memories of my father and his days in the IAF: P. D. Bapat, V. G. Kumar, Mike McMahon, Philip Rajkumar, Peter Brown, Paddy Earle, Manna Murdeshwar, Pratap Rao; my brother Ashutosh Chopra for being an IAF pilot—his flying lets me remain a boy at heart. My sincere apologies to anyone that I have missed.

30 November 2003　　　　　　　　　　　　　　　SAMIR CHOPRA
New York City

Abbreviations

AA	Anti Aircraft
AAM	Air to Air Missile
AC	Ashoka Chakra
AD	Air Defence
ADC	Air Defence Centre / Air Defence Control
ADGES	Air Defence Ground Environment System
AEB	Aircrew Examination Board
AEW	Airborne Early Warning
AFS	Air Force Station
AFSD	Air Force Storage Depot
AGL	Above Ground Level
AHQ	Air Head Quarters
AOC	Air Officer Commanding
AOC-in-C	Air Officer Commanding in Chief
AOP	Airborne Observation Post
ASI	Air Speed Indicator
ATC	Air Traffic Control / Air Traffic Controller
AVSM	Ati Vishisht Seva Medal
AWACS	Airborne Warning And Control Systems
BAF	Bangladesh Air Force
BPI	Bulk Petroleum Installation
C-in-C	Commander in Chief
CAC	Central Air Command
CAP	Combat Air Patrol
CAS	Chief of Air Staff
CDF	Coastal Defence Flight
CFL	Ceasefire Line
CIA	Central Intelligence Agency
CO	Commanding Officer
COAS	Chief of Army Staff
CQMH	Company Quarter Master Havildar
DCAS	Deputy Chief of Air Staff

LIST OF ABBREVIATIONS

DFC	Distinguished Flying Cross
DSO	Distinguished Service Order
EAC	Eastern Air Command
ECC	Emergency Coordination Committee
ELINT	Electronic Intelligence
EME	Electrical and Mechanical Engineers
FFAR	Folding Fin Aerial Rocket
FIS	Flying Instructors School
FOD	Foreign Object Damage
FTW	Fighter Training Wing
GCI	Ground Controlled Interception
GLO	Ground Liasion Officer
GOC	General Officer Commanding
GOC-in-C	General Officer Commanding in Chief
HAL	Hindustan Aeronautics Limited
HJ	Hilal-e-Juraat
HQ	Headquarters
HU	Helicopter Unit
IAF	Indian Air Force
IAFVR	Indian Air Force Volunteer Reserve
IIT	Indian Institute of Technology
IN	Indian Navy
INS	Indian Naval Ship / Station
IR	Infra Red
IST	Indian Standard Time
JBCU	Jet Bomber Conversion Unit
KC	Kirti Chakra
LAC	Leading Aircraftsman
LAS	Light Air Support
LOC	Line of Control
MC	Maintenance Command
MC	Military Cross
MinD	Mentioned in Dispatches
MVC	Maha Vir Chakra
NATO	North Atlantic Treaty Organisation
NCC	National Cadet Corps
NCO	Non Commissioned Officer
NEFA	North East Frontier Agency

LIST OF ABBREVIATIONS

NWFP	North West Frontier Province
OC	Officer Commanding
OCU	Operational Conversion Unit
ORP	Operational Readiness Platform
PAF	Pakistan Air Force
PN	Pakistan Navy
POK	Pakistan Occupied Kashmir
POW	Prisoner of War
PR	Photo Reconnaissance
PST	Pakistani Standard Time
PVC	Param Vir Chakra
PVSM	Param Vishisht Seva Medal
QFI	Qualified Flying Instructors
R/T	Radio Telephony
RAF	Royal Air Force
RCL	Recoilless (Gun)
RIAF	Royal Indian Air Force
RPAF	Royal Pakistan Air Force
SAM	Surface to Air Missile
SASO	Senior Air Staff Officer
SC	Shaurya Chakra
SEATO	South East Asian Treaty Organisation
SJ	Sitara-e-Juraat
SPR	Strategic Photo Reconnaissance
SSG	Special Services Group
STOL	Short Take Off and Landing
SU	Signal Unit
SWAC	South Western Air Command
SYSM	Sarvottam Yudh Seva Medal
TAC	Tactical Air Centre
TC	Training Command
TI	Target Indicator
TJ	Tamgha-e-Juraat
TOT	Time over Target
UE	Unit Establishment
UN	United Nations
UNSC	United Nations Security Council
USAAF	United States Army Air Force

LIST OF ABBREVIATIONS

USAF	United States Air Force
UYSM	Uttam Yudh Seva Medal
VCAS	Vice-Chief of Air Staff
VM	Vayusena Medal
VrC	Vir Chakra
VSM	Vishisht Seva Medal Class I, II and III
WAC	Western Air Command
YSM	Yudh Seva Medal

CHAPTER 1

The Indian Air Force in its Preliminary Years

The Indian Air Force (IAF) was officially born on 8 October 1932, the day the Indian Air Force Act became effective. Six Indian cadets were granted the King's Commission on graduation from Royal Air Force College, Cranwell. Sent in 1930, five of these became pilots, the sixth a ground duty officer. Among them were Subroto Mukherjee, later the first Indian Chief of Air Staff, and A.B. Awan, the IAF's first Muslim pilot, later to opt for the Pakistan Air Force (PAF).[1]

Plate 1: The pioneer batch of Indian pilots—with a Westland 'what-a-pity' Wapiti in the late 1930s. Subroto Mukherjee (*standing fourth from right*) later became the first Indian Chief of Air Staff.

1 Squadron of the IAF came into being on 1 April 1933 at Drigh Road, Karachi, with the five RAF Cranwell pilot graduates—and the first batch of Hawai Sepoys—commanded by a RAF officer. The squadron's complement consisted of four Westland Wapiti biplanes, which made up Flight 'A'.

After three years of training, during which time more pilots enlisted, the squadron left for its first tour of duty, in the Northwest Frontier Province. Its primary task was to support the RAF and the British Army in operations against restive frontier tribesmen. Stationed at Miranshah, the pilots flew their rickety aircraft, often suffering casualties through forced landings, engine failures and hostile fire from tribesmen. One of the pilots to crash-land after being hit by rifle fire was a young Sikh pilot named Arjan Singh, who was on a sortie from Miranshah to Razmak. During this period, with five to six new pilots being trained each year, two more flights were raised. By 1939, 1 Squadron had undergone its baptism by fire at the frontier and was well versed in its role of cooperation with the army.

THE SECOND WORLD WAR

At the outbreak of the Second World War, the IAF executed expansion plans to raise more squadrons. An RAF squadron at Risalpur was assigned responsibility for training of air crew and invitations were sent to commercial pilot license holders to join the newly created Indian Air Force Volunteer Reserve (IAFVR). A hundred such pilots joined the IAFVR; among them were P.C. Lal and Ramaswamy Rajaram, who went on to occupy senior posts in the IAF after the war. After a short conversion course, the pilots were posted to the newly raised Coastal Defence Flights (CDF) where they flew the Wapiti, Hart, Audax and other types requisitioned from civil owners. Their duties consisted of long surveillance missions over coastal waters and, occasionally, the escort of ship convoys through maritime trade lanes.

Japan's entry into the war in 1941 accelerated the expansion of the IAF. Flying schools were set up at Walton near Lahore and at Ambala. Two Operational Training Units came up at Risalpur (fighters) and Peshawar (ground attack) and the number of squadrons grew from one to ten. A total of 3,000 officers and 25,000 servicemen were trained between 1942 and 1945. Approximately 600 pilots flew with the ten squadrons, all seeing action against the Japanese in Burma. Some pilots attached to the RAF saw action against the Germans and Italians in North Africa and England.

On the Burma front, the IAF flew aircraft inferior to the Japanese ones. The RAF had relegated these, the Hawker Hurricanes and Vultee Vengeances, to second line duty. Throughout the war the IAF made do with aircraft discarded by the RAF as inferior. Only at war's end did the IAF acquire the latest versions of the Spitfire. In spite of this handicap it fared well. Field Marshal Slim in praising 6 Squadron wrote:[2] I was impressed with the conduct of a reconnaissance squadron of the Indian Air Force. Flying in pairs the Indian pilots in their outmoded Hurricanes went out, time and again, in the face of overwhelming enemy fighter superiority. . . . [T]hey were a happy, efficient, and a very gallant squadron.'

Coming from one of the greatest generals of Second World War, this testimonial was proof indeed of the bravery of the pilots.

When the war ended, Indian pilots had earned 1 DSO, 22 DFCs (with 1 bar) and a host of other awards. The gallantry awards came at a cost: the IAF lost 60 pilots, who were killed in action. These figures seem small compared to losses suffered by the RAF or the land armies but the IAF's small size should be kept in mind. The Indian Air Force's contribution to the Commonwealth's victory was recognized by King George VI, who conferred upon its title the prefix 'Royal' making it the Royal Indian Air Force (RIAF) in 1945. The IAF was referred to as the RIAF till January 1950, when the prefix was discarded in keeping with India's newly declared status as an independent sovereign republic.

At the end of the war, the IAF had nine fighter squadrons flying Hawker Hurricanes and Supermarine Spitfire XIVs. It had sent one squadron (No. 4) with the British Commonwealth

Occupation Force to Japan. At this time it was thought necessary to raise a transport squadron. A few pilots had had some experience flying transport aircraft during the war but no special transport unit existed. Accordingly, 12 Squadron was raised with ten Dakotas in 1946. Before training could commence, a tropical storm wrote-off half the aircraft. Despite this inauspicious start, 12 Squadron trained on Oxfords till replacement Dakotas arrived.

In phasing out Hurricanes, IAF squadrons re-equipped with Spitfires and new Hawker Tempest IIs, as they became available. In the training role Harvards and Tigermoths—supplemented by Percival Prentice and Cornell trainers—remained the mainstay.

PARTITION AND THE 1947-1948 KASHMIR CONFLICT

As the Partition of India became inevitable, so did the division of the armed forces. India's share of the air force came to one transport and seven fighter squadrons. Pakistan received one (newly raised) transport and two fighter squadrons. The IAF lost its permanent training establishments and major bases—they were all located in Pakistani territory—and had to rebuild these from scratch.

The first Chief of Air Staff of the IAF was Air Marshal Sir Thomas Elmhirst of the RAF. Air Marshal Sir Ronald Ivelaw Chapman later succeeded him. The last British Chief of Air Staff was Air Marshal Sir Gerald Ernest Gibbs. All three British Chiefs of Staff served the IAF well during their tenures, a period that saw the drawing up of the IAF's expansion plans and its first war duty for an independent India.

Free India's air force had its first taste of action when frontier tribesmen armed and aided by Pakistan, and led by army deserters, poured into Kashmir on 20 October 1947, and went into a frenzy of killing, ransacking and pillaging through Kashmiri villages. In reply to the Maharaja's plea for help, and the signing of the documents of accession to the Indian Union, India sent troops to Srinagar by air. 12 Squadron's Dakotas, along with those supplied by private airlines, carried out a remarkable airlift at short notice. Taking off from Palam, the first Indian troops landed at Srinagar airfield at 0930 hours on 27 October.[3] The decision to do so was not without risk, since it was unclear whether the airfield was secure or already in the hands of the intruders. By the end of the day, IAF and civilian Dakotas had airlifted the 1st Battalion, Sikh Regiment and secured the airfield's safety.

On 28 October, Tempests from the IAF airbase at Ambala attacked intruder positions at Patan.[4] Two days later Spitfires were flown to Srinagar, joining the Harvards that had already flown there. Fuel to keep these aircraft flying was hard to come by, but the air force developed ingenious methods to provide the necessary supplies. As a supply Dakota landed, a jeep with a drum in its back would approach the aircraft, and with the pilot's consent, any extra fuel that the aircraft could spare would be siphoned off.[5] The fuel thus collected kept IAF Spitfires flying for the crucial battles of Badgam and Shalateng. On 3 November, the decisive battle of Badgam was fought in the vicinity of the Srinagar airfield, where Pakistani forces had launched a surprise attack. For his role in this battle, Major Somnath Sharma of the Indian Army was posthumously awarded the Param Vir Chakra, the country's highest gallantry award. Two IAF Spitfires came to the aid of the Indian Army by strafing attackers. The combined army-air force onslaught beat back the attack and four days later, on 7 November, the Pakistani invasion was terminated at the Battle of Shalateng.[6] In the face of constant attacks from the air by 7 Squadron's Tempests the tribesmen kept retreating till Uri; 147 dead bodies from the tribal forces were counted between Srinagar and Baramula, almost all due to air action.[7]

Later, IAF Tempests provided much needed air support to the Indian Army in the area of the Uri bowl, where fighting had stabilized. Tempests strafed and rocketed enemy concentrations at Kot, helped in the advance to Tithwal and dropped vital ammunition and food supplies to the beleaguered Skardu garrison. They destroyed enemy field guns at Poonch and, in a daring and spectacular low-level air raid, destroyed the bridges over the Domel and Kishenganga rivers in the face of heavy anti-aircraft fire.

The lone transport squadron, No. 12, was not to be left behind. In the course of its regular casualty evacuation and transport duties, it airlifted 25-pounder field guns to Poonch and flew the first troops to Leh. The Dakota was the first aircraft to land at Leh, and even bombing sorties in support of the army were carried out with bombs being rolled out of the cargo bay by the air crew. The driving force behind this effort was Air Commodore Mehar Singh, the head of the operational group in Jammu and Kashmir. Singh himself led many of the pioneering flights including the ones to Leh and Poonch. For leading and guiding air operations in Jammu and Kashmir, Singh received the Maha Vir Chakra (MVC). Wing Commander K.L. Bhatia, Commanding Officer of 12 Squadron, was awarded the Vir Chakra (VrC), as were several other squadron pilots.[8]

The fighting ended on 31 December 1948, with a UN mediated ceasefire. The IAF had acquitted itself well, earning 4 MVCs and 23 VrCs. An imprecise estimate of its losses is that more than five aircraft were lost to hostile AA fire; several others were lost to accidents. In one incident, a Tempest was shot down over the Tithwal area by anti-aircraft fire. The pilot, Flying Officer U.G. Wright baled out and had a harrowing parachute descent.[9] He was fired at by rifles, light machine-guns and even 3-inch mortars but made it back to Indian lines after landing. An IAF Dakota engaged in airlift duties went missing on the second day of the conflict. Its pilot Flight Lieutenant C.J. Mendoza, and the twenty passengers on board, disappeared without a trace. More than 30 years later, in 1980, the aircraft's wreckage was stumbled upon and the remains of the crew members laid to rest.[10]

No air-to-air encounters took place between the Royal Pakistani Air Force (RPAF) and the IAF but, on one occasion, a lone RPAF Dakota was intercepted by two Tempests flown by Squadron Leader E.D. Masilamani and Flight Lieutenant B.D. Dogra over Chilas. By the time the Tempests gave their warnings and fired shots, the Dakota slipped back into Pakistani airspace.[11] The pilot was awarded a well-deserved Sitara-E-Juraat[12] for the escape.

Meanwhile, in south India, the Hyderabad police action was

in progress. Here too the IAF lent a hand to the army. Tempests and Dakotas saw plenty of action, strafing, bombing and dropping leaflets against the Nizam's forces. The scale of operations, however, was minuscule compared to the Kashmir operations.

THE AGE OF EXPANSION

The end of hostilities gave the IAF some breathing space. It went ahead with its re-equipment and expansion plans to build a 20-squadron force. One hundred Spitfires and Tempests were acquired from Britain. For its bomber fleet, the IAF salvaged 40 B 24 Liberator bombers from the USAAF scrapyard at Kanpur and put these relics into the air,[13] a marvel of engineering ingenuity.[14] Britain had offered Lancaster bombers, but the IAF decided to acquire fighters with the allocated funds and to build the required bomber force with salvaged aircraft.

In November 1948, the IAF became the first Asian air arm to acquire jet fighters. 7 Squadron began the induction of British De Havilland Vampires and, eventually, some 400 were acquired by the IAF. These were to see action as late as 23 years later, in the 1971 war. To reduce its dependency on Great Britain for arms purchases, the IAF purchased aircraft from other sources. In 1953, the Dassault Ouragan (rechristened *Toofani*) was inducted. Belonging to the same generation as the Vampire, 104 of these straight-winged fighters were acquired by the IAF.

On 1 April 1954, Air Marshal Subroto Mukherjee took over as the first Indian Chief of Air Staff. Mukherjee, the first Indian to command a squadron in the IAF, utilized his good relationship with the Indian Prime Minister, Jawaharlal Nehru to facilitate the allocation of finances for the IAF's expansion plans.[15] During this period the air force received privileged treatment compared to the army, when it came to purchasing equipment. When the PAF inducted F 86 Sabres, efforts were made to acquire the Hunter FMk 6. But Britain did not release the Mk 6 for export and offered only the Mk 4. So, French Mystere IVA fighter-bombers were acquired. It was with the

Mysteres that IAF pilots broke the sound barrier for the first time. Later in 1957, when the Hunter Mk 6 was cleared for export, the IAF acquired them too.

The IAF's offensive capability received a boost with the procurement of Canberra bombers and Gnat fighters, which supplemented the strike and interceptor forces respectively. Besides India, Finland was the only country to operate the diminutive Gnat in an operational role; Britain operated trainer versions.

The transport fleet was increased to meet the demands of India's geographical size. Besides inducting more of the trustworthy Dakotas, Devons and Viscounts were acquired, as was one squadron of Ilyushin 14s. American Fairchild C 119 Packets joined the transport fleet. These aircraft could carry twice the cargo load of a Dakota and were a welcome addition. A decision to manufacture the new HS 748 (Avro) was taken and an agreement with Britain signed in 1958. In 1960, 44 Squadron was raised on Antonov 12s, the Russian equivalent of the American C 130 Hercules already in service with Pakistan. In spite of these additions, India's transport force was stretched to its limits by increasing geographical and strategic demands.

The IAF's helicopter wing was born with the Bell 47 two-seaters forming the initial equipment; these were supplemented with Sikorsky 55s. To cope with high altitude operations in the north, the Russian Mi 4 was tested, found suitable and inducted in large numbers.

There is no doubt that the IAF was never starved for money. Its expansion plans proceeded uninterrupted, without much canvassing on its part. What made the government favour the IAF over the army? One theory is that the government was keen to develop a visible military force as part of its political diplomacy, and the IAF fitted the part. It was a lopsided policy. The IAF had the best transport aircraft that money could buy but inadequate parachutes to drop supplies at forward posts. The government was eager to buy shiny new fighters but miserly in purchasing spares for them. Aircraft like the Spitfire and Tempest continued in service till 1956, the Dakota was in service till the 1980s and the Liberator till 1967. It was difficult for the

IAF to manage an effective air arm but it managed somehow, thanks to the men who led it.

Air Marshal Mukherjee died an untimely and tragic death in Japan, while still in service and was succeeded by Air Marshal Aspy Merwan Engineer, a DFC from Burma and one of the four Engineer brothers famous for flying for the RIAF in the Second World War. The Indo-China conflict flared up during his tenure. Before describing this conflict, let us take a quick look at how the IAF did in other limited encounters.

THE CONGO AND GOA OPERATIONS

The IAF first saw combat in a foreign land, when six Canberras from 5 Squadron were sent to support United Nations (UN) Forces operations in the Congo. India also sent a brigade of troops. On 6 December 1961, after fighting broke out between UN forces and the Katangan rebels, Canberras operating from Leopoldville attacked the Katangan airbase at Kolwezi, destroying one Fouga Magister jet and half a dozen miscellaneous transport aircraft, a fuel dump and a bridge at Lufira.[16] The Canberras flew close support sorties for the UN ground troops as well as escort missions for USAF transport aircraft bringing in supplies. This was the first time that IAF jets saw action and the force acquitted itself well.

In the same month back in India Operation Vijay, the liberation of Goa, took place. The Goa operations turned into an exercise for the IAF to test itself. There was no Portuguese air opposition and Canberras, Hunters, Ouragans and Vampires operated with impunity.[17] Dabolim airport and the Diu airstrip were put out of commission and Portuguese strongholds attacked to smoothen up the army's advance. However, operating from Belgaum once, having been summoned by 2nd Sikh Light Infantry to soften up Portuguese positions at Mapusa, Vampires of 45 Squadron bombed positions manned by the Indian 17th Para Field Regiment, injuring two. Throughout the action no Portuguese anti-aircraft fire was encountered.

NEFA OPERATIONS AND THE 1962 WAR

The next year brought forth new threats to the borders in the form of a confrontation with China. The army had established posts in remote corners of Ladakh and NEFA; it became the IAF's responsibility to supply these. The IAF had for some years carried out supply dropping in the jungles of Assam, and it continued doing so in Ladakh and NEFA. On most supply drops, parachutes carrying the supplies would drift away into inaccessible valleys and gorges. The policy of reusing recovered parachutes, frayed and weakened from exposure to the elements, resulted in supplies falling to the ground with unopened parachutes. The army estimated that it recovered only 40 per cent of the supplies airdropped by the air force, barely sufficient to maintain its posts.[18]

The Indo-China war started on 20 October 1962, with Chinese troops launching a heavy attack on Indian positions at the Tsangdhar area in NEFA. On that day, the IAF lost two Bell helicopters in quick succession to Chinese groundfire. Previously, as battle raged for the posts below, a lone Dakota had come over lazily on its usual supply-dropping run. Its crew was shocked at being fired upon by the Chinese, the first indication that the IAF had of hostilities on the ground. No one had informed the IAF of the battle that had started hours before.[19]

Throughout the hostilities, IAF helicopters were primarily engaged in evacuating casualties and, after the Chinese ceasefire, in picking up numerous stragglers of the broken up 4th Infantry Division making their way back to the plains. Most were forced to trek back across the country, suffering severe mental and physical strain. Helicopters picked up scores of them, including the Divisional Commander. One Mi 4 helicopter was lost to groundfire in November; another was abandoned at Zimithaung and fell into Chinese hands intact. The latter was returned after the ceasefire as a 'goodwill' gesture.[20]

On the Walong front, the IAF was the only means of supply and reinforcement for the Indian troops. The only aircraft capable of operating from Walong's airstrip was the Otter. These flew supply and casualty evacuation missions till Walong fell. One Otter, made unserviceable by the Chinese shelling, was abandoned. The Chinese returned this too later, as a 'goodwill' gesture. While the destruction of aircraft to prevent their capture by the enemy is an accepted procedure, no such measures were undertaken in the race to retreat[21] because of the lack of specific instructions/standard operating procedures. Exactly the same would occur in 1971, when the newly created Bangladesh Air Force was able to repair and fly five Sabres left behind by the fleeing PAF.

The IAF's performance in Aksai Chin in Ladakh was exemplary. Its only An 12 squadron operated in this sector and flew reinforcements in the form of troops and AMX 13 tanks to many positions, from Daulet Beg Oldi to Chushul. The perforated steel plate runway at Chushul almost disintegrated under the daily landings of these aircraft. At Leh, after the ceasefire, pilots from a visiting detachment of American C 130s were amazed at the tough and backward infrastructure with which the IAF operated on a regular basis.[22]

Two questions remain about the 1962 conflict. Why was the air force not used in an offensive role? Would it have made any difference if it had been so used? The decision not to use the IAF seems to have been a purely political one and displayed a lack of trust in its ability. It was thought at the time that the Chinese Air Force would retaliate if the IAF were used. However, what was not known at that time was that the Chinese Air Force was grounded due to shortage of fuel. Had it tried to bomb Indian cities, the IAF would certainly have had the upper hand, as its pilots and aircraft were superior in terms of training and equipment respectively.

The answer to the second question is not so straightforward. In Ladakh the Chinese attacked *en masse*, and in open areas and in broad daylight, employing field and rocket artillery. In a terrain free of vegetation, the IAF would have had a field day attacking ground targets: the battles of Rezang La, Gurung Hill and Chushul would have had different outcomes. But India suffered its main reverses in NEFA, where the Chinese had extensive forest cover, They employed no artillery, no road transport and, most importantly, fought by outflanking moves, never using roads, but jungle tracks instead. Air power could only have been used during the day while the Chinese mounted night attacks at most times, nullifying most of the airpower advantage held by India.

The IAF might have won a victory in the air but it would not have altered the situation in NEFA. Air superiority was meaningless if it was not exploited to wreck the attacking ground forces, and especially if Indian ground forces lacked the ability to defend themselves, which was precisely the situation in the 1962 war. Being ascendant in the air was no insulation against the incompetence of generals on the ground.

If it were not for the China war, India would have been caught off balance in 1965. The consequences would have been far worse than the loss of barren uninhabited territory, and the 6,000 men killed, missing or taken prisoner of war in the Chinese invasion. The IAF came through the war with a bitter sense of disappointment. It was not allowed to have a crack at the enemy, and its pride was not improved by the news that Prime Minister Jawaharlal Nehru had asked for protection for Indian cities from American planes. 1962 was not the defeat of the armed forces but of false political dreams.

After the war, aid came from many quarters. Canada supplied Caribou STOL transports, France speeded up the delivery of Allouette III helicopters, while the US loaned the services of a C 130 squadron and supplied some used Fairchild Packets. A squadron of Otters was procured from Canada. The Indian government entered into an agreement for the purchase of MiG 21s from the Soviet Union and preparations were made to undertake production of the fighter. Disused airfields in the north-east were reactivated. As a result in the 1971 Bangladesh war, the IAF had no shortage of airfields to operate from in the east. To beef up radar and communications networks the IAF procured some old radar units from the United States, called the Air Defence Ground Environment System (ADGES).[23] A plan was agreed upon to set up a troposcatter communication system. One unit was being set up when the 1965 war started and further work was stopped.

To help the IAF assess and rectify its weaknesses, an exercise was conducted jointly with the USAF and RAF in 1963. A military show of strength, with the presence of the US Navy Fleet in the Bay of Bengal and an air exercise aptly named *Shiksha* (Education), brought together fighter and bomber units from the USAF, RAF and the IAF for war simulation activities along the northern ring of bases from Baghdogra and Kalaikunda in the east to Pathankot in the west. For the first time, IAF Hunters operated alongside RAF Javelins and USAF F 100 Super Sabres. The IAF gained invaluable experience[24] in aircombat and operational tactics. Though the object was to learn to meet the Chinese threat, it helped in assessing the Pakistani threat too. Visiting USAF pilots were impressed by the performance of the Gnat, then making its presence felt in the IAF. Its turning performance against the F 100 Sabres earned it the nickname 'G-Bird'.

Following up on this, two batches of IAF fighter pilots flew Sabres with the USAF's 4521 Tiger Squadron, Nellis AFB, between September 1963 and June 1964. The visit of the IAF fighter pilots to the USA was occasioned by invitation of the Secretary of Defence of the USA. At that time, November 1963, John Kenneth Galbraith was the US Ambassador to India and had just sponsored the United States Military Supply Mission India (USMSMI) initiative, in response to the 1962 Chinese military incursion. The IAF pilots earned high grades in the flying and gunnery meets staged during their training.[25]

Perhaps the most important development was the approval of the government for the IAF to expand to a 45-squadron force. The implementation of this plan demanded a tremendous effort from all those in the service. The expansion would be a long-term one, setting into motion a chain of events that would result in a powerful, modern air force. But before that, many troubles awaited.

On 1 August 1964, Air Marshal Arjan Singh DFC took over as the Chief of Air Staff from Air Marshal Aspy Engineer. A tall and well-built Sikh, according to P.C. Lal he was, 'a man of courage, no flamboyance, a rare combination of dignity, modesty, firmness and decision'. Singh, a distinguished pilot,

Plate 2: IAF pilots weren't total strangers to the F 86. In the early 1960s three batches of IAF pilots went to the USA to train on the F 86 Sabre. Flying Officer Mike McMahon (*left*) and Flight Lieutenant Russ De Montes (*centre*) pose by a Sabre in this undated colour photo. Strangely, most of the pilots who returned from the training were assigned to Mystere ground attack squadrons where their knowledge of the Sabre's aircombat capabilities was less likely to be used as compared to the Hunter and Gnat squadrons.

had seen action in Burma and was the first Air Chief to be medically and operationally fit to fly all types of aircraft, including the latest jets. He had kept himself flying trim by flying with *operational* squadrons. As a flier to the end of his term, he could have led a squadron into battle if the need ever rose. On him fell the responsibility to supervise the expansion of the air force and to train it in the shortest possible time. Air Marshal Engineer had been doing that for a year and seven months and it was now Singh's job to complete what his predecessor had started: to forge the IAF into a formidable fighting machine. Little did Singh know that before that was to happen, both he and his command would be put to a severe test in less than a year.

NOTES

1. Air Chief Marshal P.C. Lal, *My Years with the IAF*, New Delhi: Lancer International, 1986, p. 12.

2. Field Marshal W.J. Slim, *Defeat into Victory*, New York: Cooper Square Press, 2000.
3. Pushpinder Singh, *Aircraft of the Indian Air Force 1933-1973*, New Delhi: English Book Depot, 1973, p. 70.
4. Lieutenant General L.P. Sen, *Slender was the Thread*, New Delhi: Orient Longman, 1969.
5. Ibid.
6. Ibid.
7. Ibid.
8. Air Chief Marshal P.C. Lal, op. cit., p. 62.
9. Government of India, *Defending Kashmir*, 1949.
10. *Asian Recorder*, 1981, p. 16128.
11. Government of India, *Defending Kashmir*, 1949.
12. The Sitara-e-Juraat is the Pakistani equivalent of the Maha Vir Chakra of the Indian Armed Forces.
13. Air Chief Marshal P.C. Lal, op. cit., pp. 72-3.
14. http://www.rquirk.com/fail/article/Failsurv.htm
15. Major General Sukhwant Singh, *Defence of the Western Border*, New Delhi: Vikas Publishing House, 1981, p. 292.
16. Pushpindar Singh, 'Canberras in the Congo', in Singh et al., *The IAF and its Aircraft 1932-1982*, London: Ducimus Books, 1982.
17. Government of India, *Official History of the Indian Armed Forces: Op Vijay, The Liberation of Goa*, 1974.
18. J.P. Dalvi, *Himalayan Blunder*, Bombay: Thacker & Company, 1969.
19. Ibid.
20. Pushpinder Singh, *Aircraft of the Indian Air Force 1933-1973*, op. cit., pp. 130, 195.
21. Ibid.
22. Air Chief Marshal P.C. Lal, op. cit., p. 115.
23. Major General Sukhwant Singh, op. cit., p. 297.
24. Ibid.
25. Flight Lieutenants Vinod Kumar Bhatia and Darshan Singh Brar came first and second respectively. The only trophy not to be won by an Indian pilot was awarded to a Pakistani pilot.

CHAPTER 2

The Adversaries Prior to War

Arjan Singh was commissioned in 1939 as a member of the last batch of Indians to graduate from RAF Cranwell and went on to serve with the IAF in the Second World War. After flying Wapitis and Lysanders, he took over 1 Squadron—then flying the Hawker Hurricane—from Subroto Mukherjee and led it on the Burma front. The squadron saw plenty of action against the Japanese; Singh was awarded the DFC for his leadership in leading the squadron in the battle of Imphal. During the course of operations, 1 Squadron became the most decorated squadron in the IAF, with 14 DFC awards to its members. Among its stalwarts were the Engineer brothers, M.M. Engineer and Rony Engineer, Ramaswamy Rajaram and A.R. Pandit, all of whom were awarded the DFC. After his tour of duty, Singh took over the No. 1 IAF Exhibition Flight, with the rank of Wing Commander.

The honour of leading the first fly-past on Independence Day went to Singh, who led a 100+ aircraft formation over Delhi on 15 August 1947. Immediately thereafter he took over as Officer Commanding (OC) Ambala Air Force Station. In 1949 he commanded Operations Command (later Western Air Command) as an Air Commodore. Always a flyer, Singh led the 26 January Republic Day fly-past for seven years straight. In 1957, Singh took over Operations Command again as an Air Vice-Marshal, before becoming the Vice Chief of Air Staff (VCAS) in 1963. Much respected and loved by IAF personnel, he took over as the IAF emerged from its hectic expansion process post-1962. The IAF, a 25-Squadron force that flew a motley crew of aircraft of British, French, American and Russian origins, had a large number of newly commissioned pilots trained under the emergency commission rules post-1962.

IAF COMMAND STRUCTURE

In the 1960s, the IAF was divided into regional and functional commands. The former comprised the Western, Central and Eastern Commands. Western Air Command (WAC)—formerly Operations Command—was the most important of the three; its location and size made this obvious. WAC's area of responsibility extended from Ladakh to Jamnagar. It received its present designation in 1963, when Central Air Command (CAC) was raised. Eastern Air Command (EAC) had been raised in 1959.

When Arjan Singh left Operations Command, his post was taken over by Air Vice-Marshal Erlic Pinto. A rising star who was thought likely to be Air Chief, Pinto unfortunately died in an Alouette crash in Jammu & Kashmir, and Air Vice-Marshal P.C. Lal was posted to WAC in his stead. Before long, Lal moved on to the VCAS position (vacated by Arjan Singh when he became chief) and Air Vice-Marshal Ramaswamy Rajaram DFC, who had previously served as the Deputy Chief of Air Staff and AOC-in-C of Eastern Air Command took over command of WAC. Rajaram had served in 1 Squadron in the Second World War—during Singh's tenure as CO—and had gone on to succeed him as Commanding Officer of 1 RIAF Squadron in the Burma operations.

WAC had to deal with two Army Commands. Besides the Western Command led by Lieutenant General Harbaksh Singh, WAC also had to cater to the Southern Command in charge of army operations in Rajasthan and Gujarat. Lieutenant General Moti Sagar, who commanded a solitary army division, then led Southern Command.

WAC's force was limited to a few major airbases in the Punjab. Pathankot, the northernmost, which was the nearest air base to Jammu & Kashmir, was 20 miles and a minutes flying time from the international border. Air bases at Adampur, Halwara (fighters) and Chandigarh (transport) supported the central airbase at Ambala. In the event of war, Adampur, Halwara and Pathankot would see the most action. The mainstay squadrons—its strike and air defense capability—flew Hunters, Gnats and Mysteres from these bases in Punjab. Ambala was deep inside Punjab but still within range of Pakistani attack aircraft. Moving south, air cover dwindled. Coverage of the Delhi area was provided by Hindon airbase, which also took care of Agra—home of the Canberras—situated deep in Uttar Pradesh. Agra was under the operational command of CAC. No other active air force stations were entrusted with offensive duties in case of war. A solitary unit, 230 Signal Unit (SU), raised in 1965 and based at Amritsar, provided air defence radar coverage for WAC. It was equipped with Russian Mobile P 35 radar, with three-dimensional capabilities. A low power radar sans GCI capabilities was based at Ferozepur.

The Indian border south of the plains of Punjab runs for 1,300 km till it reaches the Arabian Sea. It skirts the Thar Desert, the tail end of which touches the Rann of Kutch. The area is generally referred to as the south-western sector. Today, the South-Western Air Command (SWAC) provides air cover to Rajasthan and Gujarat and ranks only below WAC in terms of operational importance. Now, aircraft like the MiG 27M, MiG 23BN and the faithful MiG 21 are a familiar sight in the desert skies as they operate from bases like Uttarlai, Jodhpur, Nal, Jamnagar and Bhuj. For subcontinental strategists, this is the sector to watch in future conflicts as it is expected to be the zone of major moves and gains. But before 1981, the year of SWAC's birth, Rajasthan and Gujarat were the operational responsibility of WAC. No separate command was deemed necessary for this sector. WAC was responsible for covering the entire border from Ladakh to the Rann of Kutch. The south-western sector was accorded low priority with virtually no activity predicted to take place there. The Indian Government delegated some small police and paramilitary forces to deal with any Pakistani incursions. The actions fought in this sector were comparatively minor and the forces involved small. The desert offered a large space for manoeuvre and, even with many operational bases, the IAF would have been hard put to keep the area under surveillance.

There were only two airbases in the south-western sector in 1965: Jodhpur in Rajasthan and Jamnagar in Gujarat, both homes to training establishments. Jodhpur housed the Air Force Flying College, the cradle of would-be pilots, who trained on Harvards. Jamnagar housed the Armament Training Wing with a few Vampire fighters, a firing range to practice air-to-ground gunnery and a couple of Dakotas to tow drogue chutes as targets in air-to-air firing.

Eastern Air Command, a relatively young command formed in 1959 with its HQ at Calcutta, originally ran operations east of Delhi. As an extension of its operational activities, No. 1 Operations (Ops) group was raised at Tezpur in 1962. In June 1963 No. 1 Ops Group was shifted to Shillong and soon after redesignated as Eastern Air Command. The erstwhile EAC HQ at Rani Kutir in Calcutta was designated Central Air Command.

After 1962, air bases like Baghdogra, Hashimara, Chabua and Khumbhirgram were developed by the IAF. EAC had its share of modern aircraft with three squadrons of Hunters and one Canberra squadron, but Vampires and Ouragans were its mainstay, as its main focus of operations would be against the Chinese, who were considerably worse-off in terms of equipment and infrastructure. EAC suffered from poor radar coverage, a weakness that was supposed to be rectified by the establishment of observer posts along the border. Air Vice Marshall Rajaram led Eastern Air Command at Shillong till August 1963, when Air Vice-Marshal Minoo Merwan Engineer PVSM, DFC took over its command for a short while. In 1964, Air Vice Marshal Yeshwant Malse, another veteran of No. 1 Squadron from its first tour in Burma, took over EAC.

Central Air Command was raised in Calcutta under the command of Air Vice-Marshal Shivdev Singh, a veteran of Second World War, who had flown missions with the RAF Bomber Command over Europe. All operations along the Indo-China border in the central sector and the Indo-Nepal border were entrusted to the Central Air Command; its major airbases were Kalaikunda, Barrackpore, Agra, Bareilly, Bamrauli and Gorakhpur.

Following defeat in the China war, the Indian Government

speeded up the development of its armed forces. The army benefited the most from the infusion of funds. It raised six new divisions, increased its armoured forces and reequipped its troops with new infantry weapons.[1] The IAF received more transport aircraft and better radar facilities, but its fighting element remained virtually the same: De Havilland Vampires, Dassault Ouragans and Mysteres, Hawker Hunters, English Electric Canberras and Folland Gnats. All of these were either British or French in origin.

THE ANGLO-FRENCH CONNECTION: VAMPIRES,
OURAGANS, MYSTERES, HUNTERS, AND GNATS

Of the fighters, the Vampires and Ouragans were obsolete. The Vampire first flew in 1943 and had a top speed of 540 mph. The Ouragan did slightly better at 595 mph. Both aircraft suffered from significant performance degradation when fully laden with ordnance. While effective ground attack aircraft in the absence of air opposition, they had no business being in the skies when high-performance interceptors were present. The Vampires equipped six squadrons, of which two were

Plate 3: The IAF operated six squadrons of the obsolete
De Havilland FB52 Vampire

dedicated to photoreconnaissance (PR). 24 (*Hunting Hawks*), 101 PR (*Falcons*), 108 PR (*Hawkeyes*) and 221 (*Valiants*) squadrons were based in the east. Two squadrons, 45 (*Flying Daggers*) and 220 (*Desert Tigers*), were combined into a single unit and based in the west at Pune. Both 101 and 108 were reconnaissance squadrons and had a unit establishment of eight aircraft, half that of regular squadrons. The Vampire was no match for any aircraft in the PAF inventory. It could not even catch the B 57s in level flight and was useful only as a ground attack aircraft, when total air superiority was assured.

Plate 4: The Dassault Ouragan equipped three squadrons and was deployed entirely in the eastern sector

The same was the case with the Ouragans, 104 of which were acquired in 1954. Rechristened the *Toofani*, this straight-winged aircraft was a first generation fighter and, like the Vampire, could be used only in a ground attack role. Three squadrons, 4 (*Oorials*), 29 (*Scorpios*) and 47 (*Black Archers*) flew the Ouragan. All were stationed in the north-east, facing the Chinese.

When the PAF began induction of the Sabres in 1955, the IAF considered the Dassault Mystere IVA, which looked like a scaled-up version of the Ouragan. Indeed, the Mystere I was produced in 1951 by mating swept-wings (of 30 degrees), and a modified tail to an Ouragan fuselage. Mystere I prototypes led to Mystere

II prototypes and production versions. The Armee de l'Air ordered 150 Mystere IIs, with delivery starting in late 1954, but quick development of the Mystere IV made it available almost as soon as the Mystere II became operational.[2] Primarily an interceptor, it was inducted by the IAF in 1956, and enabled its pilots to go supersonic in dives (only). It was slightly faster but less manoeuvrable than the Sabre and was sluggish as an interceptor. A clean Mystere could perform creditably in air combat scenarios, but this capability was not discovered till after the 1965 war in the course of exercises with Gnat squadrons.[3] Unlike the Sabre and the Hunter, which were equipped with axial flow engines, the Mystere's engine, a Hispano-Suiza Verdon 350 turbojet producing 3,500 kg thrust, had a centrifugal flow compressor, which translated into a sluggish response if power was required at short notice. The Mystere was better suited for ground attack. Its armament stores included two 30 mm DEFA cannons, a full complement of rockets carried either as two underwing pods of 19 SNEB rockets each or an exposed set of twelve 60-lb rockets, and two 1,000-lb bombs, earning it the nickname 'Flying Armoury' and the admiration of its pilots. It would prove its worth as

Plate 5: In 1965, four IAF Squadrons were operating the Dassault Mystere IVA. A fifth squadron was being formed when war broke out.

an interdictor during its service with the IAF. Of the 110 aircraft originally bought, 80 flew with five squadrons, 1 (*Tigers*), 3 (*Cobras*), 8 (*Pursoots*), 31 (*Lions*) and 32 (*Thunderbirds*), all based in Western Air Command. 32 Squadron was still under conversion and did not take part in WAC operations during hostilities in 1965.

The air defense component consisted of two classic aircraft, the Hawker Hunter and the Folland Gnat. The Hunter, a descendant of the Hawker Seahawk, was the true equivalent of the Sabre. India would eventually employ the F 56 and F 56A fighter versions and the T 66, T 66D and T 66E trainer versions. The prototype was first flown on 20 July 1951, and the single-seat Hunter F1 entered service with the RAF in July 1954. It served the IAF with distinction for long, training generations of pilots in jet conversion, equipping ground attack squadrons and even an aerobatic unit. The Hunter flew its last sortie with the IAF on 8 October 2001, almost 45 years after its induction. With 16 T.10 rockets in addition to its devastating complement of four 30 mm Aden cannons, it doubled effectively in a ground attack role. Powered by one 10,150-lb thrust Rolls-Royce Avon

Plate 6: A line up of Hawker Hunter F56 fighters in England, prior to delivery to India.

Mk 207 turbojet, the F6 carried four underwing pylons for 500 or 1,000-lb bombs, twenty-four 76 mm rockets, or fuel tanks and had a maximum speed of 650 mph and a service ceiling of 51,000 ft.

A gentleman's aircraft and universally regarded as one of the most graceful jet designs ever, its pilots loved its handling and were confident about the Hunter's capability to take on the Sabres in air combat. It was highly manoeuvrable; a number of aerobatic teams were to operate the Hunter, including the IAF's 'Thunderbolts' in the 1980s and the RAF's famous 111 Squadron's 'Black Arrows'. The Black Arrows had already amazed the aviation world in 1958 by looping 22 Hunters in formation at Farnborough, a feat unlikely to be equaled.[4] Two Hunter-equipped IAF squadrons, 7 (*Battleaxes*) and 27 (*Flaming Arrows*)—both based at Halwara—would play a major role in the 1965 war. Another squadron with WAC was 20 (*Lightning*), based at Hindon, which sent detachments to the frontline in 1965 to augment the other two squadrons. 14 Squadron (*Bulls*) was based at Kalaikunda with Central Air Command (CAC); 37 (*Black Panthers*), was based at Jorhat; and, 17 (*Flying Arrows*) based at Chabua, served with Eastern Air Command (EAC).

THE MIDGET FIGHTER CONCEPT: THE FOLLAND GNAT

The IAF had been a pioneer in evolving the Light Fighter concept, an inclination continued by the Light Combat Aircraft project today. In pursuance of this, the IAF procured the Folland Gnat in the late 1950s. The Gnat, a British all-metal swept-wing interceptor, the first prototype of which first flew in 1955, was a compromise arrived at by the aircraft's designers to achieve the smallest possible size and high performance at a low price. Its specifications were impressive: close to supersonic speeds, a rate of climb of 10,000 ft per minute, a high roll rate, a favourable thrust-weight ratio and a service ceiling of 48,000 ft. It was powered by a Rolls-Royce Bristol Orpheus 101 non-afterburning turbo-jet engine, giving it a phenomenal rate of climb and acceleration. Its pilots could go to 45,000 ft from 'brakes off' in less than 4 minutes![5] In the words of Air Marshal

M.M. Singh, CO 15 Squadron in the 1971 war, and an Ouragan pilot during the 1965 war:[6]

The Gnat Mk 1, with a Bristol Orpheus turbo jet engine made under licence in India, was the most remarkable light fighter of its generation. In a clean configuration with 30 mm ammunition, it weighed 6,500 lbs. With the engine thrust of 5,000 lbs, its power-to-weight ratio was unmatched amongst its contemporary fighters, like the Hunter, Sabre and MiG 17.... The Gnat could outclass the Hunters at all altitudes and MiG 21 below 10,000 ft. Without reheat, however, the MiG 21 was no match for the Gnat. Moreover the Gnat could also out climb the MiG 21 with reheat up to 10,000 ft. The Hunter, with its manoeuvring flaps, could not out-turn the Gnat at low level. However, when it used the flaps, the Hunters bled its speed rapidly to 300 kts, while the Gnat could still maintain more than 400 kts at 5 g. The Gnats could always get behind the Hunters by superior manoeuvring in the vertical plane.

There's a fascinating tale behind the aircraft's induction in the IAF. In October 1954, an IAF team was sent to France and the United Kingdom to evaluate second-generation fighters like the Mystere and the Supermarine Swift. The team consisted of Air Commodore P.C. Lal, the Deputy Military Secretary, Group Captain H. Moolgavkar, OC Palam and Wing Commander Roshan Suri, a test pilot with HAL. The team broke the sound barrier while evaluating the Mystere in France on 15 October and then moved to UK to test fly the Supermarine Swift. The Swift turned out to be a disappointment, but about the time Lal was test-flying the Swift, he noticed a tiny aircraft doing manoeuvres close to Chilboten. On landing, Lal inquired about the aircraft and was told it was the Folland Midge, a prototype of the Gnat but on a slightly smaller scale. Lal made an appointment to meet the designer W.E.W. Petter, who was initially reluctant to sell the aircraft to India. In the course of the lunch meeting, Petter was slowly convinced that India was not the communist country he thought it was—apparently conversation about cricket was a critical factor in dispelling such an impression—and later invited Lal to check out the Midge.

The following month, the team went to Chilboten to test fly the Midge. Lal was the first to fly the aircraft and was impressed with its handling characteristics. Coming into land, he landed long in the centre of the runway, overshooting into the fence. The aircraft was slightly damaged with some dents in the nose but was repaired almost immediately. Moolgavkar, followed by Suri, took the aircraft up in the air again to evaluate it. Impressed with its handling characteristics, the team recommended that the aircraft be considered for the air defense component of the IAF.

A contract was signed in 1956 and in late 1957 the first Gnat (IE 1059) was airlifted in a C 119 Packet and flown to India. Twenty-two more Folland Gnats were sent to India, followed by 20 in knocked-down kits to be assembled by HAL. A Gnat handling flight, which was part of the Aircraft and Armament Testing Unit (AATU), was raised at Kanpur in 1958. Relinquishing its Vampires for six Gnats, 23 Squadron became

Plate 7: A Folland Gnat deploys its wheel bay doors as an airbrake during a test flight

the first squadron to equip with the Gnat in 1960 at Ambala. Further deliveries were made by HAL, which started producing the first Gnats with indigenous raw material from 1962 onwards.

By 1962, only two squadrons were equipped with the Gnat, 23 (*Panthers*) and 2 (*Winged Arrows*), the latter being less than six months old. In 1962, two squadrons were added to the list of Gnat squadrons: 9 (*Wolfpack*) Squadron re-equipped with them, while 15 (*Flying Lances*) was re-raised. In addition to these, 18 (*Flying Bullets*) was in the process of formation when the 1965 war broke out. The Gnat squadrons flying this midget fighter were untried and untested in action. No other air force flew this or any other aircraft coming close to the midget fighter concept; the Gnat flew in large numbers only in India. Elsewhere it had been employed in a trainer role.

The Gnat's size, 10 ft in height, 22 ft in length, with a wingspan of 28.5 ft was its main asset. Difficult to spot visually—as more than one pilot remarked after air combat exercises, 'you can only fight what you see'—and weighing half as much as its contemporaries, its agility and rate and tightness of turn were unmatchable. Its Bristol 'Orpheus' engine gave it a speed 50 miles greater than that of the F 86 Sabre at high altitude. This advantage was negated at lower altitudes, where most dogfights of the 1965 air war took place. The aircraft's designers employed several novel cost-effective methods of saving weight and minimizing size. The Gnat dispensed with an airbrake, using instead the main gear and nose wheel bay covers to act as airbrakes in flight, in a semi-retracted position. It did not have landing flaps. Instead, its ailerons would droop as flaps when the undercarriage locked down in the landing phase. Instead of having collectors for spent cannon shells, it used the ammunition container of the other gun to collect these shells. All this helped the Gnat keep its overall weight down, and helped it achieve its phenomenal thrust/weight ratio.

All this was achieved at a price. The controls were extremely sensitive, requiring its pilots to be always alert for any nasty surprises thrown at them. The aircraft would twitch with even slight pressure on the controls. Initial batches of Gnats were susceptible to problems with the failure of the hydraulic system and the Hobsons unit, which provided the longitudinal control to the tailplane. Some problems were encountered with the airbrake/landing gear bay covers extending during normal flight, while others had flame out problems. There were some pilot fatalities at both the RAF facility at Chilboten and the IAF's Aircraft and Armament Testing Unit at Kanpur. Both Hindustan Aeronautics Limited (HAL) and the IAF evolved methods to overcome and rectify these deficiencies. Squadron Leader Suranjan Das, an IAF test pilot, flew the Gnat during its developmental phase, from the 'Midge' with the Siddeley 'Viper' engine to the production version Gnat with the Bristol Orpheus Engine. The number of flame outs encountered by Das in his flights prompted him to remark, 'I got more hours on the Gnat gliding than I did with the engine running!'[7]

THE CANBERRA AND THE IAF

The English Electric Canberra was a common sight over the city of the Taj Mahal. The round and wide fuselage, the straight tapered wings, the dihedral tailplane and elevators, all contributed to a look of a Second World War twin-engined intruder bomber. But this was no piston-engined aircraft; it had two jet engines. Designed to succeed the famous Mosquito, and in service nearly four decades after its induction, it was the only modern jet design of British origin to be license-produced in the US till the advent of the Harrier. The Canberra was the first British post-war jet aircraft to be purposely designed for the bomber role.

First flown in 1949, it entered RAF service in 1951. In 1956, the IAF, looking for a replacement for the B 24 Liberators as the main component of its bomber strike force, chose the Canberra. The IAF's first order for sixty-five B(I) Mk 58 bomber-interdictors, seven T Mk 54s and eight PR Mk 57s (photo-recce)

Plate 8: The Canberra B(I)58 formed the mainstay of the IAF's bomber force, equipping three bomber squadrons.

was placed in 1957. Later, another six B(I) 58s (Bomber [Interdictor]), two T 54s (Trainer) and two PR 57s were acquired to take total acquisitions to ninety. The first unit to equip with the Canberra was 106 SPR Unit (*Lynx*), followed by 5 Squadron (*Tuskers*) with the B(I)58s at Agra. The T Mk 54s equipped the Jet Bomber Conversion Unit (JBCU). By Sept. 1958, 16 (*Black Cobras*) and 35 (*Rapiers*) Squadrons had re-equipped with the Canberra, taking to a total of five units that flew this aircraft.

Powered by two Rolls-Royce Avon engines, the Canberra presented a dramatic picture during engine start-up, spewing jet-black smoke from its intakes—as a result of its cartridge ignition—and misleading many a novice crewman into believing the aircraft was on fire. As it streaked across the sky at 580 mph, at 33,000 ft altitude, it was only marginally slower than the F 86 Sabre. Flying at a maximum altitude of 48,000 ft and carrying 3.5 tons of ordnance in its bomb bay, it satisfied the cardinal rule of bombers in the Second World War, 'Get in high with speed and get out fast'. The Canberra was extremely agile for its size and could even give a Starfighter a run for its money at altitudes less than 5,000 ft. The Canberra carried a crew of two, sometimes three, consisting of a pilot and navigator/bomb-aimer. It could carry a bomb-load of 8,000 lb, which gave it the capability to carry in one sortie what would take four Mysteres to deliver. Its intruder version with rockets and a four-gun external pack could step into a ground attack role, provided air superiority had been achieved.

At the IAF Academy, cadets were given the option of going in for 'advanced navigation for low level flying techniques', another description for navigation in Canberras. Both pilots and designated navigators were sent to the Jet Bomber Conversion Unit (JBCU) for training. Just as every pilot dreamed of entering the fighter stream, every navigator dreamed of being a Canberra navigator, the only avenue to train to fight against an enemy.

The Canberra could strike at high value enemy targets since it was equipped to fly interdiction missions by night, the only aircraft in the IAF to do so. Its induction meant an increase in the long-range strike potential of the IAF. Its design and operational doctrine envisaged it flying higher and faster than enemy interceptors for self-defence. This worked till 1950, as the Canberra was much faster than British frontline fighters like the Vampire and the Gloster Meteor. But the effect of radar and air-to-air missile armed interceptors like the Sabres and Starfighters was not anticipated. It was realized only belatedly that the Canberra would have to fly lower and lower and at night as an evasive tactic. The Canberra carried an 'Orange Putter' tail warning radar, which notified the pilot of interceptors vectoring it from the rear and enabled evasive action. A Canberra equipped with the Orange Putter reported being chased by a Mach 2 fighter before the liberation of Goa.[8] In war, this warned many a Canberra of approaching interceptors. Still, the aircraft's basic limitations remained and it was outdated by the time it saw service with the IAF. The Canberra would have fulfilled its role in the early 1950s, but not by 1965. Air Commodore Peter Wilson VrC, CO 16 Squadron during the 1965 war, opined thus on the Canberra:[9]

The Canberra was a strong, docile, easy to fly aircraft, but it was obsolete when the IAF bought them. It had been made obsolete by the transonic fighter aircraft, which had been introduced at the same time. She could not survive as a level bomber in the day and use at night against relatively small targets, such as airfield structures, required radar bombing and marking equipment, which the IAF did not have. It was effective against specialist targets during the day, but night use like the PAF B 57s were not possible because of the very poor light transmission of the windshield. Night shallow glide attacks on unlit ranges were an exercise in bravery, which brings me to the subject of IAF Canberra B 58 navigators. They were unique in the world as aircrew that flew on operations without a chance of getting out of the aircraft in an emergency. It was reprehensible that the British aerospace industry should sell such aircraft and that the Indian Government should buy them.

Wilson was referring to the fate of a Canberra navigator in emergencies, as only the pilot was equipped with an ejection seat. The navigator sat at a small table, buried deep in the fuselage, with his head at the knee level of the pilot. While the pilot could punch out in his ejection seat, it was a laborious routine for the navigator to go through the process of baling out. The navigator had to unbuckle himself from his position, move to the hatch and then pull the lever that opened the crew entry hatch. A windbreak then popped out of the hatch to protect the crew from the windblast. The navigator then jumped and released his parachute manually. This convoluted procedure assumed that there was sufficient altitude to jump out and deploy one's chute. If the Canberra was in take-off mode or landing finals, when there wasn't enough altitude, it meant certain death for the navigator. Many pilots refused to eject in an emergency; they tried to land their stricken aircraft rather than abandon their navigators and paid for it with their lives.[10]

Group Captain J.C. Sengupta will vouch for the fact that the Canberra had no business loitering around over hostile territory during daytime.[11] As a Squadron Leader commanding 106 Strategic Reconnaissance Unit since 1958, he was tasked with a clandestine reconnaissance mission over Pakistan on 10 April 1959. A mole in Indian Air HQ compromised the mission and PAF Sabres lay in waiting for the Canberra. Normally, the Sabres would have required sufficient warning to fly up to 45,000 ft in an attempt to intercept the aircraft; however, with advance information on the Canberra's flight path, the Sabres were already orbiting at 30,000 ft. The Canberra was clearly visible due to its contrails at that altitude. Sengupta and his navigator Flight Lieutenant S.N. Rampal had no idea of what lay in store till they heard and saw shots fired by a PAF F 86 Sabre. As the aircraft caught fire, Sengupta ordered Rampal to bale out. Rampal pulled the pop-up shield at the escape hatch and jumped out; Sengupta ejected moments later, fracturing both his legs as they hit the control column during the ejection. As with larger aircraft types, the Canberra had a steering wheel type control column that juts above the pilot's knees. An explosive collar and a spring force the control column to move away from the pilot and clear the path the pilot's legs would take during the ejection sequence. In this case, the control column failed to move out of the way of Sengupta's legs. The two aviators came down near the Pakistani town of Rewal. Sengupta landed in a gorge, suffering injuries that rendered him immobile, while Rampal descended on a village. Pakistan interned both Sengupta and Rampal only to repatriate them four days later.

It was not the first time an IAF aircraft had flown into Pakistani airspace. But it was the first time one side had used force to shoot down the other's aircraft, embarrassing the IAF a great deal. If the flight had been at night, a Starfighter would have replaced the Sabres. How a Sabre with a service ceiling of 48,000 ft had intercepted a Canberra flying at 50,000 ft was not clear. But it's possible that while making a turn to head for home, Sengupta may have inadvertently lost altitude, enabling the PAF pilot to shoot down the aircraft.

Later, the Canberra flew in the Congo and the Goa liberation actions. It was used with a heavy hand in the Goa conflict when waves were used to disable Dabolim airfield in view of expected air opposition. In the end, such fears were unfounded and the Canberras had a dry run. The Canberras faced more opposition in the Congo War. Several were damaged lightly by Katangan ground fire; a Canberra navigator was severely wounded on one occasion. But as described in the previous chapter, they managed to destroy all air opposition on ground. The Canberra earned the first gallantry awards for the IAF in over a decade, when the Tusker's CO Wing Commander A.I.K. Suares and his wounded navigator, Flight Lieutenant M.M. Takle, were both honoured with the Vir Chakra.

While the three bomber squadrons trained for the battle to come, the JBCU, led by a Squadron Leader, fulfilled a dual role. It trained pilots and navigators designated for induction into regular bomber squadrons and also contributed its nine TMk 66 bomber trainers to operational duty.

The Canberras were stood down in the Chinese conflict and saw no action besides photo-recce sorties. Before the 1965 war, two units were based at Agra with Central Air Command (CAC): 5 Squadron led by Wing Commander P.P. Singh; JBCU led by Squadron Leader P. Gautam; 106 SPR Squadron, with a unit establishment of eight aircraft, at Bareilly was led by Wing Commander M.R. Agtey. 16 Squadron led by Wing Commander Peter Wilson was based at Kalaikunda. At the outbreak of the war, the squadrons based at Agra carried out offensive operations with Western Air Command.

FROM RUSSIA WITH LOVE: THE MIG 21

The saga of the MiG 21 in the IAF, which continues to this day, began in 1962. It was the first true supersonic aircraft acquired by the IAF, indeed the first that could reach Mach 2. The Hunter, Mystere and the Gnat were capable of flying supersonic, albeit only in dives and not in level flight. Before the 1962 China war, India had looked for a supersonic fighter to counter the F 104 Starfighter inducted by the PAF. Three fighters were being considered, the French Mirage III, the American F 104, and the Russian MiG 21. The Indian Government's bottom line was clear: any purchase deal had to include license production of the aircraft. The initial choice of the IAF was the Mirage III, but its price tag and the reluctance of the French to include a manufacturing license scuppered the deal. The US refused to sell the F 104 without political strings attached.[12] This left the MiG 21. Its terms of payment and the license for local manufacture were appealing though, in the opinion of the IAF top brass, it was supposedly inferior in performance to both the Mirage and the Starfighter. Finally, the forceful intervention of the Defence Minister V.K. Krishna Menon ensured the choice of the MiG 21.[13] A deal was negotiated for the supply of one squadron and the setting up of factories at Nasik for the airframe, at Koraput for engines and at Hyderabad for avionics. The American ambassador then made a last ditch attempt to prevent the deal by a package offer of Northrop F 5s and heavy lift transports. The American offer was turned down.[14]

The MiG deal was signed in August 1962 and two months later, the first batch of seven Indian pilots, along with fifteen engineers to be trained as ground support staff, arrived in Russia. The pilots and engineers were led by Wing Commander Dilbagh Singh and posted at Lugovaya, a desolate air force base in Kazakhstan near Tashkent. The pilots included Squadron Leaders M.S.D. 'Mally' Wollen, S.K. 'Polly' Mehra, A.K. Mukherjee and Flight Lieutenant B.D. Jayal. The specially qualified pilots included a mix of Flying Instructors, Pilot Attack Instructors and Day Fighter Leaders, with plenty of flying hours between them. An unpleasant surprise awaited them.

The housing facilities for the pilots were appalling[15] and their Russian instructors lacked their pupil's experience. Indeed, most of the Indian pilots ranked them as 'below average'. The Russians rated all seven pilots 'excellent', a rating that did not surprise the Indians. They stayed in Russia for five months for their 'training', which included classroom instruction on the aircraft engines and systems. Flying training was scarce. Wollen recalls that the average training received during the five-month period was 'a shatteringly low four and half hours'.[16] MiG 21 pilots in the 1960s wore a cumbersome one-piece full-face spacesuit-type helmet with pressure suit, as opposed to today's more comfortable openface helmets. The pilots felt they were preparing for stratospheric flight rather than treetop height dogfighting.

On their return from Russia, these pilots formed the core group of fighter leaders of the new 28 Squadron, aptly named 'First Supersonics'. It was raised at Chandigarh and equipped with six MiG 21 F 13s (NATO Fishbed-C Type 74). The MiGs were shipped to Bombay, assembled and flown to Chandigarh. Dilbagh Singh had the honour of carrying out the first reheat assisted take-off on Indian soil, as he roared down the runway at Santa Cruz airport at Bombay. The next day he carried out the first official level supersonic flight over India.[17]

Preparations for operational status began in full earnest. A mere six aircraft for training was unhelpful, but the pilots made best use of what was available. The slim, sleek MiG 21F contrasts sharply with today's bulkier MiG 21bis. The MiG 21F, a basic design not yet developed into the potent fighter of later years, was a short-range interceptor with provision for two K-13 anti-aircraft missiles (AAMs). The Type 74 versions had a 30 mm integral cannon in the fuselage, but the latter Type 76 models had none. The aircraft's primary armament was the air-to-air missile. The 1965 war experience, with MiG 21s fitted only with missiles, led to a 23 mm cannon gunpack being designed and fitted on the MiG 21. Fitted externally to the centreline

Plate 9: Freshly inducted in 1963 were six MiG 21 F 13 fighters. The earlier version had the pitot tube fixed under the nose intake and had a single one-piece canopy and a slender spine. The F 13 was equipped with a 30 mm cannon. The version that saw combat in the war was the PF, which did not have any cannon. BC 821 (*on left*) was one of the first MiGs.

hard point, it meant a further reduction both in the aircraft's range, as it could not carry the centreline droptank, as well as its dogfighting agility.

IAF practice and training went well till 21 December 1963, when disaster struck at Adampur.[18] During a routine training mission, a miscalculation by Wollen and Mukherjee led to a collision between the two MiGs. Both pilots were able eject safely. They suffered spinal injuries as a result of the ejection but recovered later. The training regimen of the squadron suffered a severe setback and had to make do with four MiGs till mid-1965.

More pilots joined the squadron. One was Flight Lieutenant A.Y. Tipnis, who was annoyed at being posted out of his beloved Hunters to the MiGs. He arrived a day late, prompting Dilbagh Singh to tell Tipnis to return if he was not interested in the posting. By then Tipnis had seen the sleek aircraft and requested Singh to let him stay.

Singh left for a staff job in March 1965 and Wollen succeeded him as CO on 15 March 1965. During the same month, the Squadron received six MiG 21 PFs (Type 76). Owing to their 'roll-stabilization' system, these were more pleasant to fly than the MiG 21F. They were equipped with airborne intercept radar, the first such system in any IAF aircraft, and were useful for location and interception of targets within 20 km. The first Operational Readiness Platform (ORP) was mounted in April 1965. In order to gain proficiency in the usage of the airborne intercept radar, the pilots did their best to fly the most on the Type 76s. The Mach 2 capability of the MiG allowed it to match its nearest rival, the Starfighter. Wing Commander Kukke Suresh, a MiG pilot who flew Hunters with 20 Squadron during the 1965 war, describes the IAF's first true supersonic jet:

[The] MiG 21, although a high demand aircraft, is docile and has no aerodynamic vices. It has excellent handling characteristics and served to provide very valuable flying experience to a large number of IAF pilots. Many pilots, including some of the recent chiefs, swear by the aircraft. It is the docility of the aircraft that not only generates a good bit of confidence but also encourages forays into exceeding the limits of the stipulated flight envelope.

As war clouds brewed in August 1965, 28 Squadron was scheduled to move to Palam to implement night flying training, as Chandigarh did not possess a runway lighting system.

The MiG 21 did not make a significant contribution in the 1965 war, but nevertheless played an important role in building up the strike component of the IAF. Though initially termed a non-participant in the conflict, it has been clear since then that the MiG took part in the war in some minor actions, which laid the foundation on which this amazing aircraft was honed for the future.

THE PAKISTAN AIR FORCE

In 1965, the PAF was a powerful fighting machine. It had the resources to take on the numerically superior IAF and hold its own ground. A decade before, in 1955, it had not posed a threat to the IAF. Then its equipment had consisted of vintage Sea Fury fighters and Halifax bombers. Some Supermarine

Attackers formed the jet force; these were incapable of taking on even the Vampires or the Ouragans. This situation underwent a drastic change in the mid 1950s.

In 1954, Pakistan aligned itself with the US and joined the South-East Asian Treaty Organization (SEATO). Under it, as part of its Military Assistance Program, the US supplied the Pakistani Armed Forces with modern military hardware. The Pakistani Army was modernized with the supply of infantry weapons and tanks. The Armoured Corps received 400 M 48 Patton tanks and 200 M 24 Chafee medium tanks. In 1956, the PAF received 120 F 86 Sabre jets. At that time, the Sabre was the fastest and the most powerful aircraft in the subcontinent. It was the first in-production aircraft to break the sound barrier and had proved its worth in the Korean War against MiG 15s and MiG 17s. Twenty-four of these PAF Sabres were armed with the GAR-8 Sidewinder air-to-air missile at the time of the 1965 war. The Sidewinder itself had acquired a reputation by its performance with the Taiwanese Sabres against Red Chinese MiG 15s in 1958. The Sabres' front guns were potent. Its six guns helped it achieve a 'shot gun' effect over a large spread area, ensuring a higher probability of a hit. Though the calibre of the guns was small, the number of guns ensured that there

Plate 10: The PAF's mainstay was the North American F 86 Sabre. Two dozen in the PAF's fleet were equipped with the Sidewinder air-to-air missile as in this picture.

was still enough punch to be put in a small area.[19] The fact that one in five PAF Sabres was armed with the Sidewinder was enough to give its opponents food for thought.

The PAF also acquired thirty-two B 57 Martin Canberras, the American version of the British Canberra. The only modification was the redesigned cockpit, in which both the pilot and the navigator sat *in tandem* under a fighter style canopy; both were equipped with ejection seats, unlike the Indian version in which the navigator had to do without the ejection seat. Like its English counterpart, the B 57 was night capable.

Other potent additions to the PAF were a dozen F 104A Starfighter interceptors, acquired in 1961 from the US. The aircraft were drawn from Luftwaffe surplus. Unmatched by any aircraft in the IAF, it was dubbed 'The missile with a man in it' by the press when it first flew in 1956. It was a most apt description. Needle nosed and 'T' tailed with a pair of stubby wings, it looked revolutionary with performance unrivalled by any other fighter at the time. Its wings were exaggeratedly thin and some of the edges were so sharp that, to prevent injury to the air crew, they were covered with felt on the ground. The Starfighter could fly at twice the speed of sound, up to 1,320 miles per hour, and climb 50,000 ft in 60 seconds. It suffered from teething problems, with the F 104A claiming the lives of a few Luftwaffe pilots during training and induction flights. Later

Plate 11: The PAF's Mach 2-capable Lockheed F 104 Starfighter. 9 Squadron PAF had operated the F 104 since 1961.

versions, the 'G' and 'K' offered better performance. But like all high performance fighters of today, it lacked in manoeuvrability. It was a mistake for it to engage a Gnat in a turning dogfight because, at lower altitudes, the latter could fly rings around the Starfighter. It was a powerful opponent nevertheless, armed with a six-barrelled Gatling type Vulcan cannon and Sidewinder missiles. The PAF received two twin seat trainers in addition to the dozen single seaters, and in combat these could operate just as efficiently. Thus, with 120 F 86 Sabres, 32 B 57s and 14 F 104 Starfighters, the PAF could field a total of 166 front-line combat aircraft.

The PAF had inherited a network of airbases, situated forward and deep, from the pre-Independence British establishments. The most important and famous of these was the Sargodha airfield complex, 300 km from the Indian border, between the Jhelum and Chenab rivers and defended by extensive anti-aircraft batteries and radar warning systems. Other important bases included Peshawar, Kohat, Mauripur and Chak Jhumra, each equipped with similar defences. The PAF's presence in the south-western sector was concentrated at Mauripur, from where F 86s and B 57s operated. To support Mauripur, the PAF ran a Signals and Radar Unit at Badin.

Pakistan had an edge over India in terms of radar coverage. Two early warning and ground controlled interception (GCI) stations were established in Sakesar and Badin, each covering the northern and southern sectors of the country. Both were equipped with a FPS-20 Azimuth and an auxiliary FPS-6 height finding radar. With a detection range of over 300 miles, these units were the eyes and ears of the PAF and formed the backbone of the PAF's air defence network. However, unlike Indian radar, these units lacked mobility. With equipment housed in large domes, the units made for conspicuous targets. To counter this vulnerability, they were supplied with air defence support and were well protected with anti-aircraft guns. Auxiliary radar units were present at Rahwali and other locations. Pakistani coordination of fighters guided by ground radars was formidable, as demonstrated in the shooting down of Sengupta's Canberra.

In terms of overall capability, besides the PAF's acquisition of British airbases and acquisition of radar and signals assets, it also benefited from exposure to, and training in, NATO tactics. By virtue of Pakistan's membership in SEATO and CENTO, the PAF not only acquired hardware but also had access to training and operating procedures, including training in advanced air combat tactics rendered by the US. The USAF had begun the process of institutional absorption and re-validation of the tactics that the Sabre had used most successfully in Korea and over the Taiwan Straits. A great deal of this was passed on to the PAF, practically first-hand, straight from USAF aces that had served in Korea.

Air Vice Marshal Asghar Khan, the Air Chief under whose tenure it underwent its expansion, re-equipping, and training programmes, led the PAF. Khan had served with the pre-Independence RIAF and was the commander of 9 RIAF Squadron. He was known among officers of both sides as a man of integrity and honesty, and respected as a leader in the same league as Arjan Singh on the Indian side. He was the first non-British Air Chief of the PAF, and enjoyed a long tenure of over eight years starting in 1957.

NOTES

1. Major K.C. Praval, *Indian Army after Independence*, New Delhi: Lancer International, 1987, p. 326.
2. http://members.tripod.com/~BDaugherty/neam/mystere.html
3. Interview with J.F. Josephs: these exercises included 2-v-2 and 2-v-4 combat exercises. On one occasion, the Gnat CO Raghavendran recommended that the Mystere pilots conduct the debriefing since they seemed to have done much better in the exercise.
4. http://www.thunder-and lightnings.co.uk/hunter/index.html
5. The Sabre took in excess of five minutes to reach 45,000 ft.
6. Air Marshal M.M. Singh, 'Gnats Over Bangladesh', *Air Forces Monthly*, November 1991.
7. Group Captain Kapil Bhargava, 'Suranjan Das: The Man and the Professional', *Indian Aviation*, September 1999.
8. B.C. Chakravarty, ed., *Indian Armed Forces—Operation Vijay–Official History of the 1962 Goa Operations*, New Delhi: Government of India, 1974.
9. Air Commodore Peter Wilson, correspondence.

10. One recorded instance of this is an incident in the late 1980s, when trouble developed in a Canberra over Pune. The pilot and navigator decided to steer the aircraft away from Pune, but by that time they had lost altitude. The pilot, even though having the option to bale out, refused to do so.
11. *Link News Magazine*, Delhi, April 1957; *Asian Recorder*, 1957 p. 2635.
12. Major General Sukhwant Singh, *Defence of the Western Border*, New Delhi: Vikas Publishing House, 1981, p. 294.
13. Air Chief Marshal P.C. Lal, *My Years with the IAF*, New Delhi: Lancer International, 1986, pp. 112-113.
14. J.K. Galbraith, *An Ambassador's Journal*, Boston: Houghton Miffin, 1969.
15. Air Marshal M.S.D. Wollen, 'No. 28 Squadron—First Supersonics in 1965', *Indian Aviation*, Bombay, 1992.
16. Ibid.
17. 28 Squadron, unpublished history brochure.
18. Air Marshal M.S.D. Wollen, op. cit.
19. Interview with Air Vice-Marshal Janak Kapur.

CHAPTER 3

From the Kutch to Chamb: From Skirmishes to War

THE FIRST ENCOUNTERS

In the years following the 1962 conflict with China, the Indian Army was poised for defensive rather than offensive action, while the Pakistani Army, in preparation for a quick, limited offensive, deployed its forces close to the border. Such an aggressive deployment risked inducing clashes. The first took place in November 1964, when both sides fought fiercely in the Tithwal sector, and suffered heavy casualties[1]. In early 1965, an election was staged in Pakistan and the dictatorship of Brigadier Ayub Khan was legitimized as the elected Presidency. Khan took this as a mandate to escalate hostilities[2] with India. The historical and political background needed to elucidate this decision needs more attention than we can devote here.

Trouble finally arrived in the remote, dusty corner of Kutch, a region that had acceded to India at the time of Independence; its border with Pakistan was legally the international border. But Pakistan had laid claim to more than 3,500 square miles of territory north of the 24th parallel in the Rann of Kutch, disregarding the old border between Kutch and Sind.[3] The rich mineral deposits in the Kutch probably had some bearing on Pakistani actions. It was here that the Pakistani Army diverted Indian attention and began encroachments on Indian territory by setting up posts. Constant police patrolling on both the sides of the border led to clashes and mounting tension. To counter Pakistani offensives, an Indian Army Brigade Group was moved to Bhuj in March 1965. After more fighting took place on 8 April, it was joined by another.[4] Opposing them were one Pakistani Infantry division and two Armoured

Regiments. Matters came to a head in the early hours of 24 April.

On that day, an Indian post at Point 84 was attacked by Pakistani armour and mechanized infantry.[5] It was overrun by noon. Next in line was the company strong post at Biar Bet, attacked two days later by a strong Pakistani force of tanks and an infantry battalion. As battle raged, Indian Army HQ requested the IAF for a reconnaissance sortie to check out Pakistani deployment.

When the Kutch incursion took place, some Vampires were operated for recce purposes at the nearest IAF base, Jamnagar, on the Arabian Sea coast. One of these, a PR Vampire from 101 Squadron, piloted by Flying Officer Utpal Barbara, took off that morning.[6] Barbara, who had been briefed to look for tanks, flew into and across a desolate region which, thanks to its lack of landmarks, made navigation difficult. Nevertheless, he found the battle area where he spotted enemy armour, identified Pakistani M 48 Patton tanks on his second pass and recorded their presence photographically. He flew as low as 50 ft, risking the danger of being shot down by small arms or artillery fire from the ground forces. In spite of heavy machine-gun fire directed at him, he accomplished his task and flew home. The pictures taken by Barbara were useful in proving that Pakistan was using its American supplied weaponry against the Indian Army. India derived considerable political mileage from the pictures, though Pakistan alleged their fabrication. For his role in the Kutch operations, Barbara was awarded the VrC.

Barbara's flight alarmed the Pakistani Army, the lone Vampire seemed like a prelude to a massive air offensive by the IAF. There was much scrambling in asking for air cover, and to reassure Pakistani ground forces two PAF Starfighters were flown over the Kutch.[7] On another occasion, a pair of B 57s was scrambled to attack ground targets under the mistaken assumption that an IAF aircraft had strafed Pakistani troops.[8] These were recalled at the last moment. Pakistan's adventures in the Kutch should have alerted the IAF to the dangers of neglecting their offensive and support capabilities in this sector but even after the Kutch incursion, neither the

Plate 12: One of the PR photos brought back by Flying Officer Utpal Barbara in his Vampire shows two Pakistani M48 Patton tanks in the Kutch sands. The Indian Government made good use of these photographs to mobilize favourable International Opinion.

IAF nor the army planned for further operations in the southwestern sector.

At this stage, PAF Chief of Staff Air Marshal Asghar Khan contacted Air Marshal Arjan Singh with a 'suggestion' that the air forces not get involved in the ground clashes.[9] Singh pointed out to Khan that Pakistani Airborne Observation Post (AOP) aircraft were regularly seen in the area. While claiming that the army and not the PAF controlled AOP flights, Khan assured Singh that he would take care of the AOP flights. Singh made no commitments, although he did say that the IAF would support the ground troops logistically, and to this effect helicopters and transport aircraft would fly to army positions if needed. The discussion ended with an understanding that neither side would employ its air force in a combat role.[10]

Later, Khan claimed that he had threatened retaliation against IAF bases in the Punjab if IAF planes attacked Pakistani ground troops. Khan believed that the PAF was at a disadvantage in Kutch (it was not) and failed to consult either the Pakistani Army or Ayub Khan before communicating with Singh. Facing severe criticism for this omission, Khan defended himself by attributing the non-participation of the IAF in the clashes to his not-so-veiled threats to Arjan Singh.[11] But by 28 April, the Indian Government had decided to not let the clashes escalate into a full-fledged war. Singh has since then dismissed any suggestions that the IAF's non-participation was connected to Khan's threat and stated that in the Punjab, the IAF was prepared to take on the PAF. Singh pointed out that the IAF faced the same risk on 1 September and did not hesitate in using airpower.[12] Singh had already appraised the Defence Minister Y.B. Chavan and taken his consent to agree to this arrangement in principle. Khan's communication seems pointless; apart from the governments' decision to de-escalate the situation, it would not have deterred the IAF from joining the fighting if so directed. Indeed, as the events of September were to prove, the IAF got into the fighting fully aware of the escalatory potential of its participation. It is also puzzling that the PAF chief was ready to escalate the fighting on his own. Had airfields in the Punjab been attacked, full-fledged war would have come in April instead of September. Furthermore, Khan's communication with Singh, without contacting the Pakistani Army Chief General Musa or his President Ayub Khan, seems mysterious. Perhaps Khan anticipated a swift rejection of his 'plan' since Pakistan was not ready for total war at that stage. Interestingly, General Musa, the Pakistani Army Chief, and Nur Khan thought that Asghar's suggestion was 'nonsense'.[13] Others suggested that Asghar Khan's actions amounted to cowardice.[14] His counterpart, Arjan Singh, thought it prudent of Khan to want to avoid a flare-up. Whatever the reason, Khan did not remain the Air Chief for long; he retired in July and was succeeded by Air Vice-Marshal Nur Khan.

Immediately after the flight of the PR Vampires in the Kutch, Pakistan deployed its fighters in the sector. Two Starfighters were flown in from Sargodha to Mauripur before flying in the Kutch region.[15] On 24 June 1965, two months after the Kutch troubles and Barbara's flight, an Ouragan flown by Flight Lieutenant Rana Lal Chand Sikka took off from Jamnagar on a training sortie.[16] Sikka lost his way in poor visibility and strayed into Pakistan. The fighter was tracked from Badin and Sabres scrambled to intercept the fighter. Lost and low on fuel, Sikka forcelanded the Ouragan in a field near the village of Jangshahi. The rough landing tore away the undercarriage and the Ouragan came to a rest after a metal-wrenching landing. On getting out of the aircraft, Sikka saw PAF Sabres orbiting overhead and realized he had landed in Pakistan. He was interned; India protested and demanded the return of both the pilot and the aircraft. Sikka was repatriated on 14 August 1965, but the Ouragan[17] was never returned.

The decision to de-escalate hostilities on 28 April led both sides to the negotiating table. A ceasefire was agreed to on 1 May. By June, both sides agreed upon the de-induction of troops and the delineation of the border. The month of May saw some severe fighting in the Kargil region in Kashmir, and here too differences were resolved bilaterally. While Pakistan presented one face at the talks, the other was busy organizing the plan to 'liberate' Kashmir, through Operation Gibraltar.

GIBRALTAR: THE 'MASTER PLAN'

Operation Gibraltar, the brainchild of Major General Akhtar Hussain Malik, the GOC of 12 Infantry Division in Pakistan Occupied Kashmir (POK), seemed like a brilliant plan:[18] hundreds of trained 'Azad' (Free) Kashmiris would infiltrate into the Kashmir valley, recruit locals and incite them to rebel against India. Airports and radio stations would be seized and Kashmir would declare its 'independence'. Pakistan would bring Kashmir into its fold without resorting to major conflict. Accordingly, equipped with arms and explosives and organized to fight on the lines of Mujahid forces, hundreds of guerrillas infiltrated into Kashmir on 5 August. The failure of the plan needs a history of its own.[19] Suffice it to say that, much to the dismay of the plan's creators, local support from the Kashmiri people, which was a key component in the failure of the 'brilliant' plan, was not forthcoming.

As the plan ran aground, and the intruders ran out of supplies and hope, Pakistan made some last-ditch attempts to bolster their sagging morale. PAF transport aircraft violated Indian airspace at night to drop supplies by parachutes. Using terrain-napping radar, C130s flew these missions at low level between mountain ranges, often flying as deep as Srinagar to paradrop supplies at prearranged drop zones. The lack of air radar in the Srinagar valley as well as lack of IAF jet fighters stationed at Srinagar—in conformance with UN Resolutions—meant that these covert sorties went back unchallenged. However, even these supply drops failed to turn the balance in favour of the intruders.[20]

The role of the IAF in these counter-insurgency operations was limited to its transport and helicopter wings. Dakotas and Otters flew continuous supply sorties to forward airbases at Srinagar, Poonch, Jammu and Leh. There were two helicopter units in Jammu & Kashmir: 107 HU and 109 HU, both equipped with the Mi 4 helicopter. These provided support fire and transportation for troops. They were joined by 111 HU at the end of August. The pilots of the Mi 4 helicopters, which were fitted with rocket pods, flew 92 offensive sorties against the infiltrators. Both the material effect as well as the effect on the intruders' morale was devastating and these units were instrumental in helping to turn the tide of the guerrilla war. By the end of hostilities the helicopter units had flown hundreds of sorties. Several pilots were decorated with the Vayu Sena medal for their contribution.

The infiltrators received active help by the Pakistani Army artillery, which shelled known ingress points during infiltration attempts. Indian forward posts and installations were subject to heavy shelling; amongst the targets was an ammunition dump at Chamb, the attack on which caused extensive casualties, including the local Brigade Commander and several officers. Pakistani Artillery caused other damage: on 19 August, Poonch airstrip was shelled and an Otter aircraft of 41 LAS Squadron was damaged.[21] The airstrip was put of action for a short while.

Though the infiltrators failed to raise a revolt, they managed to create a great deal of disorder in Kashmir by acts of violence and arson. They blew up bridges, ambushed army convoys and murdered locals when was refused help. To stop infiltration, the Indian Army decided to block points of ingress and, in a series of moves against infiltrators, occupied posts in Tithwal sector and Kargil.[22] On 28 August, in the boldest counter-insurgency move the Indian Army had ever undertaken, it occupied the strategic Haji Pir pass[23] in the high Himalayas. Embarrassingly for Pakistan, a large chunk of territory in POK was taken over. Retaliation by Pakistan was inevitable and it chose to do so at the place that suited it the most: Chamb.

OPERATION GRANDSLAM (1 SEPTEMBER)

The town of Chamb is situated at the southern end of the 1948 ceasefire line (CFL), bounded by the Kalidhar Ranges in the north, the Manawar Tawi River in the east and the CFL to the west. The international boundary runs west, meeting the CFL to the south-west of Chamb. In accordance with the UN monitored ceasefire in 1948, both sides were limited to stationing a small number of troops in Kashmir; no jet fighters were to be stationed there. As the CFL was nearer to the international boundary in Pakistan than to the nearest state boundary in India, it was possible for Pakistan to deploy its army in a fraction of the time required by India. The nearest air base from which close support could be mounted for Indian troops at Chamb was Pathankot in the Punjab, 50 km away. While Pakistan could amass its troops and armour near the international border just kilometres short of Chamb, the nearest Indian reinforcements would be sitting hundreds of miles away in the Punjab. No wonder Pakistan chose Chamb for Operation Grandslam.

Pakistan employed 70 tanks and two infantry brigades for their offensive, the objective of which was to take the Akhnur Bridge some 20 miles away and cut-off the supply to south-west Kashmir, including the towns of Rajauri, Jhangar, Naushera and Poonch.[24] With luck, these towns would fall to the Pakistani Army before an Indian counter-offensive could be mounted. Like Gibraltar, it was assumed that India would not retaliate across the international border to the south, ignoring the assertions of the Indian Prime Minister Lal Bahadur Shastri that India reserved the right to retaliate across the entire border along Pakistan if an attack on Kashmir was carried out.

At the end of August, Pakistani forces began heavy shelling in the Chamb area. In one such shelling, the Indian Brigade Commander and his Grade 3 Staff Officer were both killed.[25] The shelling became a regular feature, and as dusk approached on 31 August, Indian soldiers had no clue of what lay ahead.

On 1 September, Pakistani artillery started shelling Indian forward positions at 0330 hours. The shelling was exceptionally heavy and continued till 0630 hours, at which time a Pakistani Army force of two Infantry Brigades and two Armoured Regiments attacked Indian positions.[26] 3rd Mahar was the forward-most battalion. It bore the brunt of the attack along, with a solitary squadron of AMX-13 tanks of the 20th Lancers. In spite of its determined resistance, the sheer strength of the Pakistani assault made its presence felt. With Pakistani shelling having put the Indian guns out of action, no artillery support was possible.

Faced with this critical situation, the Commander of the 191st Infantry Brigade asked for air support at 1100 hours, a request that reached Army HQ without delay. The Chief of Army Staff, General Chaudhuri met the Chief of Air Staff Arjan Singh in the latter's office and briefed him on the developments. The Chiefs agreed that air strikes against the Pakistani Army were the only way to prevent the Indian defences from being overrun completely. The authorization for air strikes, however, would have to come from the Defence Minister, Y.B. Chavan and the Emergency Coordination Committee (ECC) set up to tackle such emergencies. Both the CAS and the COAS went to Chavan's office at 1640 hours and briefed him on the situation. The Army Chief reiterated the need for air support and the criticality of the situation on the ground. Faced with a tough decision and with no time to consult the Prime Minister or the ECC, Chavan boldly gave the go-ahead for air support. At the same time, the Army Chief also took permission to mount a counter-attack, if needed, across the international border.

From the time that the request for air support was made by the forward commander at Chamb, to the time of the Defence Minister's approval, five hours had elapsed.[27] Within an hour of Arjan Singh walking out of the DM's office, the first fighters had taken to the air.

THE FIRST DAY AT PATHANKOT

The air base closest to the zone of conflict was Pathankot. Situated near the border between Jammu and Punjab, it was a mere minute's flying time from the border. The base commander was Group Captain Roshan Lal Suri VrC, a test pilot who, along with P.C. Lal and H. Moolgavkar was credited as the first Indian pilot to break the sound barrier while test-flying the Mystere in France.[28] Suri's assessment of the Mystere had played a significant role in the approval of its procurement. Prior to becoming a test pilot, Suri had flown operations in the Second World War as a Spitfire pilot with 10 Squadron, and earned a Vir Chakra for his sorties against the raiders in Kashmir during the 1947-8 war. Pathankot's officer-in-charge of operations was Wing Commander G.V. Kuriyan, another veteran of the 1948 Kashmir Operations and ex-Commander of 29 Squadron (*Toofanis*). Kuriyan had been posted to Pathankot, just before outbreak of hostilities, from his previous assignment at Agra. Pathankot had two squadrons of Mysteres: 3 Squadron led by Wing Commander Paul Roby, who was an experienced pilot on Toofanis as well, and 31 Squadron led by Wing Commander William Macdonald Goodman. The third squadron at Pathankot was the composite (45/220) Vampire squadron. There were no true air superiority fighters at Pathankot. 3 and 31 Squadrons had both just received a detachment of IAF Qualified Flight Instructors (QFI) from Fighter Training Wing (FTW), Hakimpet. The QFI pilots were all ex-Mystere pilots. They had arrived on 31 August and had been informed by Roby that, in anticipation of hostilities, time for operational conversion would be limited. And, it was possible that their first sortie would be an operational one. Roby did not know that his words would be so prophetic.

Based at Pune, 45 Squadron had been moved north in anticipation of hostilities just a couple of days before this. Led by Squadron Leader S.K. 'Marshal' Dahar, an enthusiastic and energetic Commanding Officer, its Vampires were ready, armed and sitting on the tarmac in anticipation of the CAS' orders.

Dahar briefed his flight commanders about the squadron's task.[29] Three missions would be flown: the first at 1719 hours, the second at 1730 hours and the third at 1740 hours. This would enable the last mission to arrive over the target at dusk, just as darkness set in, and to come back in fading light after executing its mission. Dahar would lead the first mission, the senior flight commander, Flight Lieutenant F.J. Mehta of 220 Squadron would lead the second mission, and Flight Lieutenant A.K. Bhagwagar would lead the last one. Bhagwagar was an experienced Vampire pilot and had been one of the IAF pilots sent to the UK to ferry back refurbished Vampires for the IAF in 1964. Amongst his companions on that long distance ferry had been Squadron Leader J.F. Josephs, one of the new arrivals from FTW on attachment to 3 Squadron.

Fate decreed a last minute shuffling. Just before the first take-offs, Bhagwagar approached Mehta for a change of plan. The last mission had special requirements: as the Vampires would return to Pathankot in the darkness of the night, they would require night-qualified pilots to lead the formation back. Mehta was one such pilot. Already weary from a long ferry flight from Jamnagar that morning, he agreed to the change. Bhagwagar was to be the leader of the second mission after Dahar's first.

One of 45 Squadron's flight commanders, Flight Lieutenant K.D. Mehra was scheduled to fly in the third wave. He was assigning pilots from 220 to the mission, when he faced an irked Flying Officer V.M. Joshi. Joshi was not night-qualified and Mehra had decided to put someone else in his place in the second wave. Joshi was adamant that he should fly in one of the flights. Mehra would have none of it. Failing to convince Mehra, Joshi went to see the Base Commander Roshan Suri who, seeing the youngster's eagerness, overruled Mehra's decision and allocated Joshi to the second flight.

The third wave consisted of senior night-qualified pilots. Mehra himself was assigned to the third mission, along with F.J. Mehta. The pilots kept flashlights in their cockpits, to help them read the poorly lit instruments.

TRAGEDY OVER CHAMB

Pathankot launched Dahar and his formation at 1719 hours, to be followed at 10-minute intervals by the second and third waves of the Vampires. As the Vampires were heading in a north-westerly direction towards Chamb, the sun was shining straight into the pilots' eyes; for many in the army and air force higher command, they represented the last hope of the Indian Army at Chamb.

The Vampire was the most obsolete aircraft in the IAF's inventory. Its first flight was during Second World War; at that time, even the propeller-driven Tempest had a higher rate of climb than the Vampire. In 1965, it was hopelessly out of place. The front portion of the fuselage of Mark 52 was constructed of wood and it lacked an ejection seat.[30]

The forward position of 3 Mahar in the Manawar Tawi area was at Alfa Batal. All eyes turned upwards at the sound of approaching aircraft. The arrival of the Vampires over the battlefield was greeted with relief that turned to horror as the aircraft made a strafing run on the 3 Mahar positions. Luckily, there were no casualities. The Vampires then turned their attention to the Pakistani tanks and carried out several attacking passes. The Pakistani Army defended itself; heavy ground fire hit and brought down the Vampire flown by Flight Lieutenant S.V. Pathak. The other members of the formation, Dahar and Flight Lieutenants Sahay and I.P. Ahuja, carried out another run and, having expended their ammunition, headed back to Pathankot.

The Pakistani Army called on the PAF for support. Soon, a pair of Sidewinder-armed F 86 Sabres, piloted by Squadron Leader Sarfraz Ahmed Rafique (5 Squadron PAF), and Flight Lieutenant Imtiaz Bhatti (15 Squadron PAF), flew into the battle area just as the second formation of Vampires led by Flight Lieutenant Bhagwagar came in for the attack. The jawans of 3 Mahar were mute spectators as the Sabres tore into the Vampires and shot down, one by one, three of them. In Bhatti's words:[31]

[C]lose to the area, we descended fast, looking all around and below us for the enemy aircraft. At about this time we also learnt that the C-in-C was flying around the area in an L 19. We did not see him; we later on discovered that he left well before we got there. Our search succeeded and I saw two enemy aircraft. They were crossing underneath us and I informed Rafique about it. He immediately acknowledged it, 'Contact'. Rafique said he was going for them. While covering his tail, I spotted two Canberras 9 o'clock from me at 5,000-

6,000 feet. Then I spotted another two Vampires trying to get behind Rafique. I instinctively broke off and positioned myself behind these two. In the meantime, Rafique had knocked down one of his two targets and was chasing the other. About now I had my sights on one of my own and was holding my fire. I was anxiously waiting for my leader to bring down his second and clear out of my way. When the Vampire I had targeted closed in on Rafique too dangerously, I called out to him break left. Within the next moment Rafique shot down his second, reacting to my call and broke left. Simultaneously, I pressed my trigger and hit one of them. Having disposed of one I shifted my sight on the other and fired at him. In the chase I had gone as low as 200 feet off the ground when I shot my second prey, he ducked and went into the trees. We had bagged four in our first engagement with the Indians. . . .

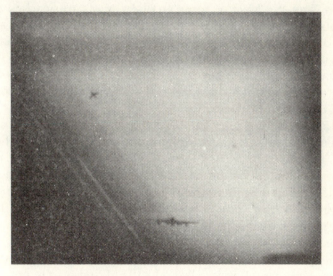

Plate 13: First contact: This amazing gun camera photograph from Flight Lieutenant Imtiaz Bhatti's F 86 Sabre shows two IAF Vampires trying to get on the tail of the Sabre flown by Squadron Leader Sarfaraz Rafique, which can be seen banking towards the top left.

Bhatti's account is notable in that he observed two Vampires try to get *behind* Rafique as he chased the first two Vampires. In their outdated aircraft, the gallant Indian pilots, had paid the price for turning into their attackers rather than making a run for it. However, Bhatti was mistaken in identifying Canberras in the vicinity as none were flying on the day. He also missed

Flight Lieutenant Sondhi's escape. Nevertheless, Rafique and Bhatti were credited with two kills each by the PAF.

As the Sabres exited, the third wave led by Flight Lieutenant F.J. Mehta came in to strike the Pakistani targets. Mehta had Flight Lieutenants K.D. Mehra and R. Verma and Flying Officer Manjit Singh as his wingmen. The last formation went about attacking ground targets, completely oblivious to what had happened to the second formation.

At Pathankot, an excited and apprehensive ground crew started their long vigil, awaiting the return of the Vampires. Three Vampires from Dahar's formation landed first, followed by a solitary Vampire from the second formation. Soon, another four Vampires landed. Some auxiliary pilots approached the pilots of the four Vampires, expecting to find Bhagwagar and his colleagues. They were shocked to find that the formation was the third, led by Mehta. Four Vampires were missing. The solitary Vampire that flew in after the first three was from the second formation. A shaken Sondhi described how the Sabres had destroyed his formation.

45/220 had lost four Vampires that day, one to AA fire and three to the Sabres. There was only one survivor: Flying Officer S.V. Pathak, from the first formation, had managed to bale out from his ill-fated Vampire. Flight Lieutenants A.K. Bhagwagar, V.M. Joshi and S. Bharadwaj, all from the second formation, were killed. Everyone at base felt the heavy loss of life. The Vampires had received a bad mauling from Pakistani air defence.

Mystere IVAs from 3 and 31 Squadrons followed in the wake of the Vampires. It is not clear why the Mysteres were not sent earlier instead of the Vampires. Even though the Mystere was no match for the Sabre, its superior speed gave it a fighting chance of extracting itself from mismatched dogfights. Perhaps it was assumed that the PAF would not intervene as war was not yet officially declared. Or, it may have been that the desperation of the ground situation required sending the first aircraft to be airborne, in this case the Vampires.[32] One reason cited was that, in view of their limited night-flying capacities, the Vampires needed to be sent first. But most pilots agree the

Vampires were sent because their CO, Squadron Leader Dahar, convinced the Base Commander and the OC Flying to send his squadron into action. While his desire to get into action was commendable, his decision to do so in obsolete Vampires still remains the subject of much heated debate.

The 12 sorties by the Vampires were followed by 16 sorties[33] by the Mysteres from Pathankot. 31 Squadron was the first, sending in 8 sorties. Led by the CO Wing Commander W.M. Goodman himself, the Mysteres in flights of four—caused plenty of damage on the ground, sometimes making as many as six runs over the battlefield.[34] To quote Wing Commander Goodman:[35] 'Our boys were in like a flash and in no time the whole place was ablaze with burning tanks and vehicles . . . the enemy will never forget the Mystere.'

Amongst others, Goodman's pilots included his flight commander Squadron Leader A.L. 'Tony' Mousinho, and Flying Officer Michael McMahon, a relative rookie in the squadron who had earlier flown USAF F 86 Sabres on deputation to the United States.

Plate 14: Wing Commander W.M. 'Jimmy' Goodman CO, 31 Squadron prepares for a mission during the war

It was a baptism by fire for the regular 3 Squadron pilots as well. Summoned from their billets and given a 'quick' briefing by the CO Paul Roby, the pilots had little time to grasp the details of the situation. The rudimentary details on the briefing were to fly to the target area and to attack any visible hostile targets. The first wave from 3 Squadron was led by Roby himself, with Squadron Leaders S.K. 'Pandit' Kaul, B.F. 'Kewal' Kewalramani and Flying Officer 'Dinky' Jatar.

The second wave, which was the final mission flown by 3 Squadron and by Pathankot-based jets that day, was led by Squadron Leader Ajay Sapru. Accompanying Sapru were Flight Lieutenants Tirlochan 'Tango' Singh, C.S. 'Doru' Doraiswami and Boman Rashid Irani. As the last formation arrived over the target area in fading light, it was difficult for the pilots to sight targets on the ground. Fortunately, the burning hulks of tanks and vehicles destroyed by the previous formations served as beacons. The pilots attacked camouflaged vehicle harbours. It was too dark to differentiate whether they were tanks or trucks or guns, but enough damage was done. As the last of the Mysteres pulled up and away, the anti-aircraft guns once again lit up the darkening sky. What was now significant was the complete absence of Sabres.[36] The sortie flown by Rafiqui and Bhatti was the only one mounted by the PAF all day.

On landing, the pilots found plenty of .50 calibre bullet holes in the Mysteres from ground fire. Sadly, this would be the last sortie flown by 3 Squadron's CO, Paul Roby, who was medically invalided by the squadron medical officer. Roby flew back with his cockpit seat soaked in blood, suffering terribly from an attack of haemorrhoids. In his absence, Squadron Leader S.K. 'Bhattu' Bhattacharya, an experienced Mystere pilot and on Station Staff as Flight Safety officer, took over 3 Squadron for the rest of the war as an Acting Wing Commander.[37] The last Mystere sortie was at 1905 hours. The day's operations by the Mysteres ended without loss. Pathankot had mounted 12 Vampire sorties and 16 Mystere sorties in a little less than two hours.

Pathankot's Station Commander, Group Captain Roshan Suri, was angered and saddened by the Vampire losses, as was the OC Flying, Wing Commander Kuriyan. Both called up

Wing Commander Krishna Dandapani, CO of the IAF Air Defence Centre (230 SU), which operated the Soviet-origin mobile Type P.35 Radar just outside Amritsar.[38] On being asked why Pathankot had not been warned about the presence of the Sabres, Dandapani replied that information on PAF fighters was passed on to the Sector Army Commander and had been routed through the correct official channels. He himself had no idea that Indian aircraft were operating in the Chamb area. The first indication of IAF operations came on observing Vampires on the unit radarscope, when they were heading for Chamb. The current system was clearly too bulky to speedily disseminate information to the correct end user, in this case, the IAF itself. Suri, Kuriyan and Dandapani agreed that future warnings would have to be communicated directly to the operations room at Pathankot.[39] But the damage was done; the Vampire losses had the immediate effect of imposing caution on all operations mounted by Pathankot.

The IAF claimed 13 tanks, 2 guns and 62 soft-skinned vehicles as destroyed. This assessment was released by the air force but was never confirmed by the army. Indian Army officers in the Chamb were to later claim that the IAF strafing and rocket attacks also destroyed three Indian AMX tanks, a dozen truckloads of artillery ammunition and one truck carrying tank ammunition.[40] The destruction of the latter resulted in shortage of tank ammo for the armoured squadron. Some Pakistani tanks destroyed by the army in ground battles were again attacked by the IAF and claimed as destroyed for the second time. The ambiguity over attacking Indian positions was probably due to lack of proper demarcation of the CFL and the terrible light conditions under which the Mystere and Vampire pilots had flown their missions. Intelligence briefing received by the squadrons, as well as any input from the Ground Liaison Officer with the forward troops had been negligible, leading to an incomplete assessment of battlefield positions and emplacements.

While considerable damage was inflicted on the Pakistani Army, far more significant was the effect on Pakistani Army planning. The presence of the IAF aircraft imposed a degree of caution on the Pakistanis, who did not expect the battle to escalate to the air, a miscalculation akin to the expectation that

India would not retaliate across the international border. Whatever regrets the Brigade and the Corps Commanders may have had that day in calling for air support, the IAF prevented a major Pakistani breakthrough.

A SABRE-SLAYER IS BORN: THE FIRST TRIUMPH

The next day, 2 September, was a quiet one. Battlefield damage assessment of the previous day's strikes in fading light had been insufficient and it was decided to fly a photo-recce sortie over the target area. As 31 Squadron had been originally tasked as a Fighter Recce squadron, Wing Commander Goodman was given the responsibility of carrying out a tactical recce over the battlefield. Goodman decided to fly the mission himself, with Flight Lieutenant C.N. Bal as No. 2. Since Pathankot did not have any air defence fighters to provide escort that morning, it was decided to send a heavy escort of four Mysteres from 3 Squadron in clean configuration. Squadron Leader Kewal Ramani would lead the escort formation.

As the Mysteres took off and flew towards Chamb, Remani noticed that his undercarriage light was still on, indicating an undercarriage bay door that had failed to close properly. He had to abort the mission. As Remani turned back to base, his No. 2 Boman Irani, unaware that Remani had a technical problem, followed his leader back to base. This left just the two Mysteres, being flown by Tirlochan Singh and Doraiswami as escort.

The formation flew in staggered line abreast formation, with Goodman and Bal flying abreast at low level and Singh and Doraiswami flying a km behind, and slightly more spaced out than the earlier two. Short of Akhnur, Tango noticed six Sabres circling ahead. Four of the aircraft were at a lower altitude while two kept top cover. Tango immediately called out a warning on the R/T. Though the Sabres had not yet picked up the Mysteres, it was clear that any fight at low level would be unequal and in favour of the PAF. Goodman decided to abort the sortie and turned back. The Mysteres put in a hard turn to port and made their way back to Pathankot. Tango and Doru followed suit, with the latter being the tail end Charlie in the formation, constantly weaving to keep his tail clear. Though the Sabres were at least 5 km away and had not noticed them, it would have been a close call had they decided to give chase.

A strike mission of Vampires, escorted by Mysteres, was planned keeping in view the disastrous losses suffered by the former on the first day. But the mission was soon called off. The IAF was convinced that ground support missions would need escorts to deal with PAF interceptors.[41] These missions would not proceed without escort by air defence fighters like the Hunter or the Gnat.

The IAF's sole MiG 21 outfit, 28 Squadron, was based at Chandigarh and Adampur and had carried out ORP sorties from both bases. The escalation of hostilities found the squadron in a strange position since Command HQ's Operations Instruction did not include a role for them. They had practised set piece NATO-style, high altitude bomber interception but not the close combat tactics that were to be required. Air Commodore K. Gocal, a Second World War veteran of Vengeance and Hurricane missions against the Japanese, and SASO at Western Air Command, had cleared the squadron for ORP duties (platform readiness for air defence) at a front-line base (Adampur).[42] 28 Squadron flew two sorties over Chamb on 2 September and another four sorties the next day; all the sorties were staged from Adampur. Orders to send MiGs to Pathankot were received on the evening of 3 September and two MiG 21 PFs (Type-76s) from Ambala—piloted by the CO, Wing Commander M.S.D. 'Mally' Wollen and his senior flight commander, Squadron Leader A.K. Mukherjee—were dispatched.[43] Air HQ also made arrangements to beef up fighter defense forces with Gnat fighters.

This last move fell on 23 Squadron based at Ambala. Led by Wing Commander S. Raghavendran, the squadron had trained intensively for air combat training for months and had evolved a fighter combat leader course.[44] After escalation of hostilities, a detachment of four Gnats led by Squadron Leader B.S. Sikand had been dispatched to Halwara. Now 23 Squadron received orders to move four fighters from Ambala to Pathankot and to also move the Halwara detachment to Pathankot. 23 Squadron would also send a detachment, led by Raghavendran, to Amritsar.

On a staff job at Ambala was a seasoned pilot, Squadron Leader Johnny William Greene. Prior to his posting in Ambala, Greene was a flight commander with No. 14 Squadron, flying the Hunter. One of the few IAF pilots to have done his Fighter Combat Leader course with the RAF, Greene, described as an 'old-timer', was a source of inspiration to the young Gnat pilots at Ambala.[45] Unsurprisingly, he was deputed as the detachment commander of the Pathankot-bound Gnats.

The assigned pilots received no information or briefing, just the order to take their aircraft and leave for Pathankot.[46] Their luggage was to follow later in transport aircraft. Accompanying

Plate 15: Leader and tactician: Squadron Leader Johnny Greene.

Greene were Squadron Leaders Trevor Keelor and Amarjit Singh Sandhu, and Flight Lieutenant M.R. 'Manna' Murdeshwar, all graduates of 23 Squadron's fighter combat leader course, designed in consultation with those that had completed the RAF version. The four pilots took off in fading light at 1745 hours and arrived at Pathankot during a drizzle at dusk. They flew the Gnats at very low level to avoid radar detection; consequently, the PAF was ignorant of their transfer to Pathankot. As the Gnats landed and taxied to their blast pens, the pilots observed the grim and sullen atmosphere on the base, a result of the burden of operations, as well as the losses suffered on the previous day. Murdeshwar, the youngest pilot, identified his academy course mates in the crowd that received the Gnats and happily waved. There were no waves back. The detachment from Halwara had already flown into Pathankot. Sikand's detachment consisted of Flight Lieutenants V.S. 'Pat' Pathania and 'Kicha' Krishnaswamy and Flying Officer P.S. Gill. Though Sikand was the seniormost of the eight pilots from the Gnat detachment, he let Greene take command in deference to his greater experience with fighter combat tactics.

After meeting with the newcomers, the Gnat pilots made their way to the overcrowded officers' mess. No rooms were available to rest. The pilots did not have their luggage for a change of clothes and went and lay down on some *charpais* (cots) in the open. After dinner they were called for the briefing by the operations-in-charge. His part of the briefing was curt and plain: 'We want you to shoot down the Sabres. How you do it is your problem, but the Sabres will have to be tackled.' Greene completed the briefing. The Gnats would take off at dawn, with a Mystere formation flying at medium altitude to lure out the Sabres. The Gnats would avoid radar detection by flying at low level. Once the Amritsar SU detected incoming PAF fighters, the Gnats would climb to engage the interceptors. It would be a classic baiting mission, it was designed to inflict losses on the PAF and to make the point that the IAF could engage in combat with the Sabres. The pilots dispersed at 2030 hours to doze off on the makeshift cots at the officers' mess.

3 September dawned with an air of excitement for the Gnat pilots. Woken up at 0300 hours for the meteorological briefing, the pilots had to walk all of 2 km to the briefing room. There were no preliminaries for the early rising, no tea, no breakfast. As one of the pilots remarked, 'Who gets up for us stupid pilots at 3 in the morning?'. They then walked to the dispersal area and checked their aircraft.

At 0700 hours, four Mysteres took off from Pathankot and set course for Chamb, flying at 1,500 ft. They flew north to the Akhnur Bridge and turned left to head for Chamb, avoiding flight over Pakistani airspace. Pakistani radar, which generated much activity, tracked the Mysteres, vectoring a roving combat air patrol (CAP) of Sabres and Starfighters to intercept them. Amritsar radar tracked six Sabres and two Starfighters coming into intercept the Mysteres. What the Pakistani radar failed to detect were the four Gnats in finger-four formation trailing the Mysteres, less than 300 ft from the ground. Johnny Greene was the flight leader, with Murdeshwar as his wingman. Sikand and Pathania made up the other section. Following Greene's lead section were the Gnats led by Trevor Keelor at 100 ft above ground level (AGL). Keelor had Krishnaswamy as his wingman, with Sandhu and Gill as the other members of the formation. Flying an eight-Gnat formation was a unique event. The pilots could hear Dandapani's calm voice on the R/T as he relayed 230 SU's information on incoming Pakistani aircraft.

As the battle area approached, the Mysteres turned hard right over the low hills to disappear from the scene even as the Gnats kept course at low level and high speed. Once the Mysteres had departed, Greene pulled up and led his section in a steep climb to 3,000 ft, with Keelor's section covering their flanks. Keelor first spotted a Sabre coming in from 5,000 ft above trying to latch onto Greene's section. Greene was leading his formation in a turn, and the Sabre followed suit trying to put itself behind Greene's wingman, Murdeshwar. Pathania called out a warning about the incoming Sabre to Murdeshwar. Greene called for a defensive break as the Gnat formation broke into a steep turn to port. But the No. 3 pilot, Sikand, broke in the opposite direction and separated from the main formation.

Keelor had meanwhile manoeuvred his formation behind the turning Sabre. He had to extend his airbrakes to lose speed, and pull a tighter turn to stay behind the Sabre. The Gnat lacked a separate airbrake and used its undercarriage bay doors as airbrakes extended in a semi-open position. As the turn was completed, Keelor found the Sabre was dead ahead, and he slammed the throttle to close in fast on the enemy aircraft, which was now sandwiched between Greene's section and Keelor's Gnat. Keelor opened fire with his twin 30 mm cannon from a distance of about 450 yds, closing in to 200 yds. In an instant, the Sabre's right wing appeared to disintegrate and it flicked over into an uncontrollable dive. The IAF had claimed its first kill. Trevor now circled back to join his wingman Krishnaswamy. Keelor became the first Indian pilot to claim a jet in air-to-air combat.[47] The Sabre was armed with Sidewinder missiles, making his feat even more remarkable. It was the first time that the previously untested in combat Gnat had fired its guns in anger.

But the fight was not over yet. While Keelor was dealing with the Sabre, Pathania spotted two more Sabres and engaged them even as a F 104 Starfighter was noticed above.[48] The Starfighter broke Pathania's attack on the Sabre and as the Indian pilots regrouped, engaged reheat to exit the area. His R/T being snagged, Murdeshwar had to go through the frustration of not

Plate 16: The Sabre Slayers, Flight Lieutenant V.S. Pathania (*left*) and Squadron Leader Trevor Keelor (*right*) just after their return from a low level escort mission from the frontline

being able to warn Pathania of the incoming Starfighter. While he could receive incoming transmissions, he could not transmit. At one point, Krishnaswamy found the Starfighter on his tail, which overshot him and presented a nice target. But as Krishnaswamy later admitted, he was so awestruck at the sight of the sleek and beautiful fighter that before he could gather his instincts to open fire, the target had slipped away.[49] The Gnats were now short on fuel, and they rendezvoused to fly back to base.

Back at base, amidst the celebrations, Sikand was missing and presumed lost in combat. Unknown to the Indian pilots, Sikand had lost contact with the formation as well as his bearings. Most aircraft at the time did not have radars or GPS systems. Pilots used their maps and aircraft compass to navigate back to base, using visible landmarks. After combat, IAF pilots would set east on their compass and head for that direction, with the hills from Pathankot towards Banihal running north-east being the first landmark. Once the hills were sighted, the pilots knew they were over Indian territory and would turn south-east and look for other features on the map. Another visible landmark was the river flowing out of Madhopur. Sikand's Gnat was low on fuel and over unfamiliar territory. Sikand found an airfield and landed, imagining himself to be in an abandoned airfield in Indian territory. He should have known better of course; such airfields were few and far in between. An unpleasant surprise awaited Sikand: he had landed at the Pakistani airfield of Pasrur. He was taken POW and the aircraft impounded.[50]

Sikand's disappearance forced Pathankot to launch two Vampires from 45 Squadron. Dahar and K.D. Mehra took to the air trying to locate Sikand's Gnat, believed to have crashed on its way back to base. Both flew at low level trying to trace the path of the returning Gnats, but failed to find any signs of Sikand or his Gnat.[51] No one could have guessed Sikand's Gnat had crossed over into Pakistani territory and landed at Pasrur.

After its capture, Flight Lieutenant Saad Hatmi of the PAF, who had previous experience on Gnats during a stint in UK, flew the Gnat to Peshawar.[52] Only after the war was the aircraft flight-tested thoroughly by the PAF. The PAF claimed that Sikand surrendered and landed at Pasrur after being intercepted by a Starfighter flown by Flight Lieutenant Hakimullah. The IAF maintained that Sikand landed the Gnat at Pasrur by mistake thinking it was Pathankot. While Hakimullah may have been in the same area as the Gnat, there is no evidence, other than PAF assertions to that effect, that he forced Sikand to land at Pasrur. Hakimullah himself had not seen the Gnat till he found the aircraft on the runway of Pasrur with its brake chute deployed.[53] An unwitting witness to Sikand straying off course was Wing Commander Dandapani at Amritsar, who watched as the lone blip got separated from the main formation, strayed off course and then finally disappeared off the scope. The radar unit personnel thought the aircraft had crashed; Dandapani insists that there were no other aircraft in the area as observed by them on the radar.[54]

Two days later, news that the PAF had captured Sikand's Gnat intact,[55] forced a grounding of all aircraft at Pathankot for some time to enable the change of radio crystals in them. It was feared that the PAF would be able to decipher and listen in on the frequencies of some IAF channels based on the crystals procured from Sikand's Gnat.[56]

The shooting down of the Sabre had the twin effect of destroying the Sabre's supposed invincibility and sending morale sky-high: the 'good news' was communicated by the CAS Arjan Singh to the Defence Minister that night. The next day Indian newspapers' headlines were plastered with the news of the Sabre being downed.

Plate 17: A pilot scrambles to Gnat IE1078 of 23 Squadron at Pathankot. The tent in the background is where pilots would wait for scramble calls.

23 SQUADRON'S SECOND KILL

On the next day, 4 September, 23 Squadron flew another mission at 1515 hours as an escort to Mysteres from Pathankot, with rendezvous over Chamb.[57] Greene led the formation while Squadron Leader Amarjit Singh Sandhu and Flight Lieutenants Pathania and Murdeshwar flew the other three Gnats. On arriving over Chamb, they did not find the Mysteres but found four Sabres attacking Indian positions.

The Sabres were flying a circuit as they attacked the Indian gun positions in turn. On Greene's signal, the Gnats plunged into the Sabres' circuit and within no time all four Gnats positioned themselves behind the Sabres as they broke out of the attack pattern. Greene latched onto the first Sabre, but found himself at a high angle of attack to the target's flight path and broke away.

Coming in behind Greene, Murdeshwar was in better position to attack his target and manoeuvred himself for a kill. He positioned the Sabre dead on between the diamonds of his gyro gunsight and pressed the firing button. The 30 mm guns rattled off a shell . . . and then fell silent. The Gnat was still suffering from teething developmental problems. One was the frequency with which its guns jammed. The Gnat had two 30 mm cannons placed on the inlet walls by the side. These were placed in such a pattern that the links that joined the bullets were deposited in the ammunition box of the gun on the opposite side. So instead of falling out into the sky, they travelled across a cross-feed before depositing themselves in the ammo box of the other gun. So when one gun refused to fire, the other gun also stopped firing, as the links had no place to go. Later the problem was solved, but on this occasion it resulted in the PAF escaping more damage.

Pathania drew blood in this battle. As one of the Sabres turned away and flew towards Akhnur, Pathania gave chase and fired three gun bursts. The Sabre started emitting smoke and crashed near Akhnur. Pathania reported that the pilot must have ejected, as he could see neither the pilot in the F 86 nor its cockpit canopy before it crashed. Later a Pakistani spokesman admitted that it lost one of its Sabres flown by Flight Lieutenant N.M.

Butt, who was picked up by a helicopter after ejecting safely and evading capture.[58]

The Gnats returned to base and in the officer's mess at Pathankot, there was no hiding the excitement amongst the pilots. 23 Squadron had taken on the PAF and made its mark. They had their first two kills and there was no stopping them. If it had not been due to gun stoppages, the Gnats would have claimed at least another two kills. Greene and Murdeshwar's gun camera footage shows Sabres smack in the centre of their gun sights. Some of the footage was used as a training film to be shown to other squadrons later in the war. Indeed, the Gnat pilots had established another measure of ascendancy. In the

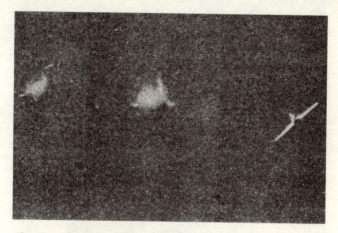

Plate 18: Flight Lieutenant V.S. Pathania's gun camera film shows the destruction of PAF Flight Lieutenant N.M. Butt's Sabre over the Akhnur sector. A PAF helicopter rescued Butt soon thereafter.

cases of outmanoeuvring their adversaries Murdeshwar, and perhaps even Krishnaswamy, in training exercises would probably have been awarded those additional kills.

As Pathania was shooting down the Sabre, the two MiG 21s from 28 Squadron were on an offensive CAP over the same area and were directed by Amritsar GCI to chase two Sabres. Wollen describes the encounter:[59]

On the afternoon of September 4, Squadron Leader Mukherjee and I flew a top cover mission to Mysteres attacking advanced columns of the Pakistani army. The Mysteres were intercepted by Sabres, probably from combat air patrol (CAP). Escorting Gnats tangled with the Sabres. The R/T natter was exhilarating, particularly the calls from a Gnat pilot (Flt. Lt. V.S. Pathania) reporting a Sabre destroyed. The aircraft engaged in combat were below us, but the GCI station, under whose direction we operated, had 'no pick-up' on their radar screen.

I decided to enter the 'arena' and dove earthwards. In a few seconds, we spotted some aircraft engaged in turning-combat, about 10,000 ft. below us. Coming down, I closed in on a pair of aircraft turning hard left. When the range decreased to around 1.5 km, we recognized the aircraft as our Mysteres. As we eased our turn, two Sabres, flying almost abreast of each other, crossed from left to right, below and in front of us. I wrenched my aircraft to the starboard (right) calling out to Mukherjee.

I picked up the Sabres heading north-west, very low and 1 o'clock to me. I went after the slightly lagging Sabre on the right. I later learnt that Mukherjee lost sight of me in the violent turn I had executed. The beastly pressure helmet/face piece is a bad thing to wear when 'dog-fighting'.

With a good overtake speed, in a slight dive, I released a missile at around 1,200 m, sighting through the 'fixed-ring and bead'; the radar cannot provide information so close to the ground. The missile sped towards the Sabre and exploded below it; perhaps ahead and on the

Plate 19: Wing Commander MSD Wollen, Commanding Officer of No. 28 Squadron with one of the early MiG-21 F-13 aircraft.

ground. In my excitement, I released the second missile when I was too close to the ground (90 m) and probably too close to the Sabre. For 0.6 seconds after release, the K-13 missile is unguided. During this time it headed downwards, started to flatten out and then struck the ground, not far ahead of me.

I engaged engine re-reheat, rapidly closed in on the Sabre, was tempted to brush against his fin and passed about 6 m over the aircraft. Naturally, the PAF pilot was surprised/shaken. I asked Mukherjee to engage the second Sabre, but got no response. We 'rendezvoused' over Jammu airfield (above AA-gun range) and returned to Pathankot.

Squadron Leader Muniruddin Ahmed,[60] the pilot of the Sabre, could pick out the details of the MiG's sleek lines as it passed by. Shaken by the closeness of the MiG, he called up GCI on the R/T and stammered, 'B-B-B-B-By G-G-G-G-God, he nearly hit me.'[61] Back on ground in the dispersal area, Flight Lieutenant F.J. Mehta met a seething Wollen, disgusted at the MiG 21FL. 'For a cannon, just for a cannon!' said Wollen. He seemed a far cry from the 'Little Lamb' moniker earned while Flight Commander of 3 Squadron in 1957. Mehta could do nothing but sympathize.[62] Ironically, had Wollen taken the older Type-74 aircraft to Pathankot, rather than the newer Type-76s, he might have bagged Muniruddin's Sabre with the Type-74s integral 30 mm cannon. But that was not to be.

This was the only significant mission flown by 28 Squadron in the early days of the war. The performance of the K 13s in their debut was disappointing. Even a marginally better performance would have resulted in the first kills by IAF MiGs, who would have to wait another six years before they would draw blood. It was also the last day for the composite 45/220 squadron at Pathankot, which received orders to move out to Ambala, where it spent the rest of the hostilities flying night CAPs and reconnaissance missions.

The kills in the air were apparently not the only gains for Indian forces on this day. The anti-aircraft guns of the Artillery Regiment claimed their first 'kill' as well. Havildar C. Potharaj of 127 (AD) Regiment, manning a 40 mm Bofors L-30 AA Gun at the Tawi Bridge near the town of Jammu, claimed to have shot down a Sabre as it flew near the bridge. Evidence suggests that this was the Sabre shot down by Pathania.

5 September passed off almost uneventfully, with both air forces flying CAP sorties but not encountering any air combat. Pursuing a bogie in the Lahore sector, a PAF Starfighter made a sonic double boom that was heard over Amritsar and interpreted as a rocket attack on the radar station. A subsequent press communiqué released by India mentions a rocket attack on an IAF unit by a PAF aircraft. MiGs and Gnats from Pathankot flew CAPs but no incidents took place.

NATH'S DAYLIGHT FORAYS INTO PAKISTAN

Till 5 September, the IAF had not committed any other aircraft beyond the Mysteres, Vampires and Gnats at Pathankot. Being based entirely at Halwara and Palam, the Hunters had not seen any action. The same was not true of the Canberras.

Unknown to the Pakistanis, and to even many on the Indian side, a lone Canberra PR 57 was being regularly flown by an intrepid pilot over key Pakistani locations in broad daylight for photographic information. The pilot was Squadron Leader Jag Mohan Nath, a veteran of the 1962 Ops. Nath already had a Mahavir Chakra under his belt for the daring photo-recce missions he carried out over Tibet at the height of the 1962 war with China; perhaps the only operations carried out by IAF aircraft not belonging to transport or helicopter units.

Nath's unit, No. 106 SPR Squadron was the air force equivalent of 'Army HQ Reserve'. They operated directly under the Chief of Air Staff, Arjan Singh and their level of briefing and mission objectives were always top secret—known only to the Chief and the pilots on the mission. To this end, Nath always had special access directly to the Chief's office. The squadron was commanded by Wing Commander M.R. Agtey and had a unit establishment of just eight aircraft (keeping in line with the U/E of PR Squadrons). However, during the 1965 operations, barely four Canberras were serviceable at any point of time.

Typical missions carried out before the operations broke out on 1 Sept were sorties over forward areas to photograph enemy army formations. Photo-recce sorties in a Canberra were not for the meek hearted. They had to be carried out in broad daylight at extremely low altitudes or, as Nath put it, at 'deck level':

All my missions were done at deck level during daytime. Tree top level. 30-40 ft off the ground. Because you did not want the radar to pick you up. So it was all low-level navigation based on timing. Flying at low level limits your area of vision, making navigation much more difficult. If you had been flying at a higher altitude, you have a greater field of vision allowing you to pinpoint your position much easier on a map. So while flying at low level, your mind always has to keep up with the calculations, how many seconds it takes, how long it takes all on large scale maps. And when I felt I was somewhere in the area that I wanted to photograph, I would accelerate the Canberra to its maximum speed possible and pull up steeply to gain height to 12,000 ft, where the cameras are switched on to take the photographs.

Why 12,000 ft? you may ask. 12,000 ft was the limiting factor because of the cameras, which were meant for the high altitude aerial photography. The cameras that we were using were the 20-inch and 36-inch used for high-resolution pictures. They used to give identical coverage and work as telephoto cameras. Whenever you plot it on the map, these smaller scale photographs would tally almost exactly with all the features on a similar scale map. For this camera the lowest altitude at which they would be effective is 12,000 ft.

So if you were lower than stipulated, there will be incremental movement due to the forward motion of the Canberra, which would result in blurring. So the definition in the photographs will not be up to the mark. Thus, it always required us to fly at a speed of 120-140 knots.

So my technique was to fly low-level, pick up speed in the last moments, and then climb on to 12,000 ft till such time the speed itself fell down closing to stall. The aircraft would almost be staggering.

So there was Nath, flying a huge aircraft like the Canberra at less than 50 ft altitude, climbing to 12,000 ft to take pictures and then diving down to the same low-level altitude on the way back home. It was a miracle that Nath came back unscathed.

5 September brought a new task for Nath: to take a Canberra to the Lahore sector in the Ichogil Canal area and to take photographs along it. No doubt this was in preparation for the impending Indian Army move across the international border.

The army would have needed information on not only the fortifications and bridges but also on the degree of preparedness of Pakistani Army formations.

Accordingly, Nath took off from Agra in his PR 57 and then proceeded over to Pathankot. After crossing over from Pathankot into Pakistan territory, he turned south-west to go over the Ichogil Canal area to start his filming. As was usual with his sorties, the timing and routing of the sortie were not disclosed to other Indian air bases.

As soon as the task at hand was accomplished, and as Nath turned back towards Indian territory, he noticed two PAF Sabres trying to get in a position to intercept him. As he was almost over Indian territory, or had already crossed over, Nath called out over the R/T for help from Indian fighters.

Meanwhile, Wing Commander Wollen was flying back in his MiG 21 to Pathankot after completing a regular 'show of force' sortie over the forward areas. Wollen was on landing approach when he heard Nath's call. Though low on fuel, Wollen elected to abandon his approach and go to Nath's aid. But his help was not needed. As Wollen approached the Canberra, the 'Sabres' chasing Nath turned out to be two IAF Mysteres. Since Nath's sortie was kept secret from all formations, No. 230 SU assumed Nath's returning Canberra was a PAF B 57 and scrambled two Mysteres. With the confusion sorted out, the aircraft returned to their respective bases without further excitement. But not before Wollen's MiG flamed out due to fuel starvation, as he completed his landing run and taxied back.

Nath was to carry out more daring 'raids' during the remaining days of the war, including a daylight mission to Quetta, right on the Pakistan-Afghanistan border and a photo-recce sortie on Badin. Unsurprisingly, at the end of the war, Nath became the first IAF officer to be awarded a Bar to the MVC, an achievement that makes him the highest decorated living IAF officer today.

At the end of the first five days of the war, the PAF had suffered less damage than the IAF though its losses were frontline fighters while those of the IAF were second line aircraft, with the exception of the Gnat flown by Sikand. The PAF had only been able to impose a small degree of caution on the IAF in employing its ground attack aircraft; it could not prevent close support missions. If anything, the air combat encounters instilled a newfound confidence amongst the Indian pilots: that the Sabre was not the invincible fighter it was made out to be and that the diminutive Gnat could take on the Sabre.

For shooting down the Sabres, both Keelor and Pathania were awarded the VrC, as was Greene for leading them into combat. Havildar Potharaj got a VrC for his 'kill' and Wing Commander W.M. Goodman, CO 31 Squadron was awarded the MVC for leading his Mysteres and blunting the Pakistan Army's offensive in Chamb. Both air forces had skirmished for five days. The stage was set for a greater battle to unfold.

NOTES

1. Government of India—Vir Chakra Citations for the year 1964.
2. Air Chief Marshal P.C. Lal, *My Years with the IAF*, New Delhi: Lancer International, 1986, pp. 121-2.
3. D.R. Mankekar, *Twenty-two Fateful Days*, Bombay: Manaktalas, 1966, p.17.
   Air Marshal Asghar Khan, *The First Round*, New Delhi: Vikas Publishing House, 1979.
4. Major K.C. Praval, *Indian Army after Independence*, New Delhi: Lancer International, 1987, pp. 336-9.
5. Ibid.
6. Utpal Barbara's Vir Chakra Citation.
7. Air Marshal Asghar Khan, op.cit.
8. John Fricker, *Battle for Pakistan*, Ian Allen, 1979, p. 42.
9. Ibid., p. 37.
10. B.C. Chakravarty, ed., 'Indian Armed Forces—Official History of the 1965 Indo-Pakistan War', New Delhi: Governmnet of India (unpublished).
11. Air Marshal Asghar Khan, op. cit., 1979.
12. Interview in *Times of India*, 28 April 1983; Gen Mohammad Musa, *Jawan to General*, New Delhi: ABC Publishing House, 1985.
13. Gen Mohammad Musa, op. cit.
14. Squadron Leader Shoib Alam Khan, 'The Fightergap', *Defence Journal Magazine*, April 1998.
15. Air Marshal Asghar Khan, 1979.
16. John Fricker, op. cit., 1979, p. 42; *Link News Magazine*, September 1965.

17. Sikka's Ouragan was IC 564.
18. Air Marshal Asghar Khan, op. cit.
19. For a detailed history of guerrilla activities, the unpublished Indian Armed Forces—Official History of the 1965 Indo-Pakistan War should be consulted. This document is not available in print but can be downloaded from http://www.bharat-rakshak.com/LAND-FORCES/Army/.
20. According to Fricker one of these transport sorties over Srinagar carried AVM Nur Khan as an observer; John Fricker, op. cit., p. 53.
21. An EME Naik Madan Prakash Kant received the COAS Commendation card for salvaging radio equipment from the damaged aircraft under fire.
22. Major K.C. Praval, op. cit., pp. 344-6.
23. Ibid.
24. Ibid.
25. Ibid.
26. Ibid.
27. Air Chief Marshal P.C. Lal, op. cit., p. 127.
28. Ibid.
29. Interviews with Wing Commander F.J. Mehta, Squadron Leader K.D. Mehra and Wing Commander G.V. Kuriyan.
30. The trainer TII and Mark 55 did have ejection seats.
31. Brigadier Gulzar Ahmed, *Pakistan Meets Indian Challenge*, Dehradun: Natraj Publishers, 1995.
32. This was certainly Air Chief Marshal Arjan Singh's view.
33. The actual number of sorties by Mysteres was 14. Two aircraft dropped out due to technical problems.
34. Pushpindar Singh, *Aircraft of the Indian Airforce 1933-1973*, New Delhi: New English Book Depot, 1973, p. 109.
35. Government of India Publication, *Harvest of Glory* has transcriptions of interviews with pilots including Wing Commander Goodman's statement that was broadcast on AIR in late October 1965.
36. Interview with Squadron Leader J.F. Josephs.
37. Bhattacharya had commanded 1 Squadron during the Goa Operations in 1961 and was awarded the VM.
38. Interview with Wing Commander K. Dandapani.
39. Interview with Wing Commanders K. Dandapani and G.V. Kuriyan.
40. Colonel Bhupinder Singh, *Role of Tanks in the 1965 War*, Patiala: B.C. Publishers, 1982, pp. 51-2.
41. Interview with Wing Commander G.V. Kurien; Pushpindar Singh, 'Laying the Sargodha Ghost to Rest', *Vayu Aerospace Review*, November 1985.

42. Air Marshal M.S.D. Wollen, 'No. 28 Squadron—First Supersonics in 1965', *Indian Aviation*, Bombay, 1992.
43. Ibid.
44. Interview with Group Captain M.R. Murdeshwar.
45. Ibid.
46. Ibid.
47. Confirmation from PAF records is however not available. According to John Fricker the Sabre hit by the Gnat was severely damaged by cannon shells, but was safely flown back to base by Flight Lieutenant Yusuf Khan. This makes Pathania's air combat kill the first to be confirmed by both sides. John Fricker, op. cit, p. 74.
48. Flown by Flying Officer G. Abassi PAF.
49. Interview with Wing Commander Kurien who debriefed all the pilots after return.
50. Sikand's Gnat (IE 1083) survives and is on display at the PAF Museum in Karachi.
51. Interview with Squadron Leader K.D. Mehra.
52. John Fricker, op. cit., p. 77.
53. www.pafcombat.com (Air Commodore Kaiser Tufail, 'Run . . . it's a 104').
54. Author's interview with Wing Commander Dandapani.
55. Sikand's aircraft photo was published in Pakistani newspapers, which was promptly reported in Delhi.
56. Interview with Group Captain M.N. Singh.
57. Pushpindar Singh, 'Laying the Sargodha Ghost to Rest', *Vayu Aerospace Journal*, November 1985; interview with M.R. Murdeshwar.
58. The *New York Times* quotes the Pakistani spokesman admitting the loss to IAF MiGs! Later on a claim was put forward that Butt's Sabre was probably hit by Pakistani own ground fire. The PAF's premier hagiographer, Fricker, 'admits' that it was quite possible that Pathania shot down Butt's Sabre. The *New York Times*, 5 September 1965; John Fricker, op. cit.
59. Air Marshal M.S.D. Wollen, op. cit.
60. Ahmed was later shot down and killed over Amritsar by AA fire.
61. John Fricker, op. cit., p. 139.
62. Interview with Wing Commander F.J. Mehta.

CHAPTER 4

The Challenge: Flare up on 6 September

THE GROUND SITUATION

On the ground, battle raged furiously in the Chamb sector. The Pakistani Army took Chamb and advanced to the west bank of the Manawar Tawi. With the attack's momentum lost due to stiff resistance by the Indian Army, the Pakistani Army briefly halted to regroup and resumed its advance on 3 September. This halt cost them the chance to take Akhnur. The Pakistani Army then attacked Jaurian on 3 September, took it the next day, and by 5 September, was 6 miles from Akhnur. At this critical stage, to relieve pressure on Akhnur, and in a dramatic escalation of hostilities, the Indian Army opened a new front in Punjab.

On 6 September, the Indian Army crossed the international border in the Lahore-Kasur sector.[1] XI Corps led by Lieutenant General Joginder Singh Dhillon attacked on three prongs, each in the form of one infantry division supported by armour and artillery. The 15th Infantry Division led by Major General Niranjan Prasad made the northernmost attack, along the Grand Trunk road to Lahore. The 7th Infantry Division, led by Major General H.K. Sibal attacked on the Khalra-Burki axis, while the 4th Mountain Division led by Major General Gurbaksh Singh made the southernmost attack along the Khemkaran-Kasur axis. The Lahore-Kasur sector saw fierce fighting throughout the day. By nightfall, 15th Infantry Division had reached the outskirts of Lahore, while the 7 Infantry Division had captured Burki. After same initial success, the 4th Mountain Division had to retreat to its starting point in the face of a heavy Pakistani artillery barrage.

THE CHALLENGE: FLARE UP ON 6 SEPTEMBER

No account of the 1965 war is complete without mention of the Ichogil Canal between the Indian border and Lahore. It runs north-south, approximately parallel to the international border for about 70 miles from the river Ravi to the river Sutlej. It is a protective moat, 140 ft wide and 15 ft deep, with steep cement concrete sidewalls and strong fortifications along its embankments in the form of pillboxes and gun emplacements. Ostensibly an irrigation facility, its primary aim was to be an obstacle to protect Lahore; it was a formidable one for the Indian Army and a *de facto* bombline for the IAF throughout the war.

However, on 6 September, not one sortie was flown in support of the army. It is not entirely clear whether the IAF was in the loop regarding the army's plans to cross the international border. The only briefing that the air force received in relation to the ground offensive was to hit 'targets of opportunity'.[2] Random targets, like army formation HQs and radar stations, were assigned. The intelligence provided was poor, occasionally, targets were not found after reaching the designated area. Why did the IAF not attack Pakistani airfields as the army launched its offensive? It failed to fully exploit its advantages of surprise, a time of its choice and the initiative. Many pilots from Pathankot recollect their standing instructions, 'No attack on Pakistani airfields unless attacked ourselves'. Some recollect the Station Commander, Group Captain Suri indicate the instructions as issuing from Command Headquarters.[3] A Squadron Commander from Adampur remembers the same instructions being given by the Senior Staff Officer from Command HQ.[4] Whatever the reason behind the inaction, the IAF lost out on a critical opportunity to hit hard at the PAF's offensive air capability, with little risk of attrition and to influence the outcome of the war. It seems plausible that there was a political dimension to the decision. It is not known whether it was made by Air Headquarters, in conformance with political guidelines, or was explicitly imposed on the IAF by the civilian political establishment. Whatever the details of that particular decision, it had its effect on ground realities very soon.

THE TIGERS TAKE TO THE AIR

One of the surprised officers who received a briefing to attack a 'target of opportunity' was Wing Commander Om Prakash 'Omi' Taneja, CO of 1 Squadron (*Tigers*) based at Adampur. 1 Squadron's unit strength was approximately fifteen Mystere IVAs and seventeen pilots. Half its pilots had been attached to the squadron just before hostilities broke out. Some were sent to join the squadron as late as 3 August. Since most of these pilots were sent directly from instructional duties at training establishments, they were put through a rigorous flying programme to be declared fully operational in a span of two to three days of their arrival.[5] Among the new arrivals were Squadron Leader D.E. 'Denny' Satur (Flight Instructors School, Tambaram) and Squadron Leader A.B. 'Tubby' Devayya (from Fighter Training Wing, Hakimpet). Similarly, the other Mystere squadron 8 Squadron (*Pursoot*) received some new arrivals from Training Command: Squadron Leader Godfrey Salins, Flight Lieutenants B.I. Singh and Lal Sadrangani amongst others.

Air Commodore K. Gocal, the Senior Air Staff Officer (SASO) of WAC, briefed Taneja on a visit to Adampur and assigned a Pakistani Army Formation HQ in the Gujranwala-Wazirabad sector as a target. When Taneja asked why efforts could not be focussed on hitting PAF bases, he received the stock reply that the decision came '. . . from above'.[6]

As dawn broke on 6 September, four Mysteres of 1 Squadron roared down Adampur's runway on the first mission to be flown by the base.[7] Taneja led the formation, with Flight Lieutenant D.S. Brar as his No. 2. The second pair of Mysteres was led by one of the senior Flight Commanders of the Tigers, Squadron Leader P.R. 'Paddy' Earle with Flying Officer S.S. Dange as his wingman. The Mysteres were equipped with rocket pods and external fuel tanks for extended range.

Arriving at the designated target area, the pilots found no sign of the supposed 'Formation HQ'. Not wanting to abort the mission, Taneja decided to look for other targets. Flying near Rahwali, the formation noticed a train pulling into the railway station at Ghakker. On observing fuel tankers on the train, Taneja called for the formation to attack. While three of

THE CHALLENGE: FLARE UP ON 6 SEPTEMBER

Plate 20: Personnel of 1 Squadron, *The Tigers*, arm a Mystere IVa cannon in preparation for a ground attack sortie.

the formation's Mysteres were able to dispense their ordnance, Earle's rocket pods got jettisoned as soon as he armed his rockets to fire.[8]

The formation destroyed the train and the railway track. As the Mysteres were busy attacking, a frantic call for help was sent to the PAF air defence centre. The Sakesar GCI directed two F 104 Starfighters of 9 Squadron on a dawn patrol to look for the Mysteres. Flight Lieutenant Aftab Alam Khan led the formation; Flight Lieutenant Amjad Hussain Khan was his No. 2. Both Starfighters had been on CAP at 15,000 ft. Khan instructed Hussain to maintain the same altitude and act as a radio relay, while he dove his Starfighter below to look for the Mysteres. As he came to a lower altitude he spotted Taneja's formation and jockeyed himself to manoeuvre behind them.[9]

Earle was the first to spot the Starfighter and call out a warning. The Mysteres promptly exited, at tree-top height, back towards base. Tree-top flight at 450 knots, a standard escape procedure for Mysteres, ensured difficulty for interceptors in visual sighting and attack. If coming from a higher altitude, an attacking fighter ran the risk of 'mushing' into the ground if it misjudged its altitude. At tree-top heights, the attacking fighter's main weapons, cannon or homing missiles, were blunted. Heat seeking missiles of that era tended to lose the IR signature of the jet engine in the backdrop of heat emanating from the ground. Even attacking with cannon fire was a daunting task, requiring the attacking pilot to have a high degree of concentration. A single mistake entailed a 'controlled flight into terrain'. 1 Squadron had practised low-level flight extensively, starting with its tenure at Kalaikunda where they had graduated from deck level runs at 200 knots to those reaching 350 knots, a speed felt adequate to render chase difficult for an interceptor.

Khan followed the Mysteres down in pursuit, lost sight of one section but then found Earle's section in the rear. Selectively using his afterburner to get into position, he found a Mystere in his sight and, on hearing the lock-on confirmation tone, launched one of his Sidewinders. Khan made the mistake of looking out of the cockpit, at his wings, to see if the missile had fired and was blinded by the flash as the Sidewinder left the rails. Instinctively he pulled back on the stick and the Starfighter zoomed upwards. Khan did not get a visual on the Sidewinder's impact, but a Pakistani Army unit called to confirm that one of the Mysteres had been shot down and had crashed near Rahwali air base.

On seeing the Starfighter behind him, Earle had jettisoned his fuel tanks. It was this that the Pakistani Army formation had seen exploding on the ground. The fuel tanks had caught fire, with whatever vapour was left in them, as they hit the ground. Short of fuel, Earle landed his Mystere at Pathankot, while the remaining Mysteres led by Taneja landed back safely at Adampur.

When Earle got back to Adampur, Taneja gave him a 'rocket' for jettisoning the drop tanks, a valuable commodity. If lost every time enemy aircraft were spotted, the squadron would be grounded for lack of droptanks before the war was over. Taneja issued orders to 1 Squadron that pilots were not to jettison external tanks except when they were in a position to kill or about to be killed by an enemy fighter. The Mysteres would ensure their operational safety by hugging the ground as they did that morning. From that moment onwards the Tigers were the only squadron that zealously guarded its external drop tanks throughout the war, while their sister squadron at the same base, No. 8 reached a critical level where it almost ran out of its tanks.

THE BATTLEAXES

The Tigers were not the only squadron attacking targets across the international border that morning. Hawker Hunters from Air Force Station Halwara, located south-west of Ludhiana city in Punjab, got into the action as well. Group Captain G.K. John commanded Halwara. The base's complement included two squadrons of Hawker Hunters: 7 Squadron (*Battleaxes*) led by Wing Commander A.T.R.H. 'Zach' Zachariah, and 27 Squadron (*Flaming Arrows*) led by Wing Commander G.D. 'Nobby' Clarke VrC, a veteran of the 1947-8 Kashmir war.

Plate 21: Officers from 7 Squadron (*Battleaxes*) at their Hunters' dispersal at Halwara AFS. *From left to right*: Flying Officer C.G. Pandiya (*Technical Officer*), 'Doc', Pilot Officer Kondaiah (*Technical Officer*), Squadron Leader M.M. 'Rusty' Sinha, Squadron Leader Sube Singh 'Chacha' Malik, Wing Commander Toric Zachariah, unidentified, Squadron Leader G.G. Daniels, unidentified, Squadron Leader Ajit Singh Lamba, unidentified.

Since there had been some indication all year of the proverbial balloon going up, John had started war preparations at Halwara, including placement of camouflage nets and co-ordination of AA guns. The AA guns were controlled by both the army and IAF (separately). Clarke's flight commanders were Squadron Leaders Jog, Balchandani and Donald Conquest.

The first to be equipped with jets in the IAF, the 7 Squadron had been based at Palam since the early 1960s and been led by Wing Commander L.M. Katre. Zachariah took over the command of the squadron in August 1964. On alert since 23 August, many pilots felt they would be left out of the action. Pathankot was the only base launching sorties against the PAF for the first five days of September, and it was widely believed that the international border would remain sacrosanct. Pilots looked for transfer to those units that they believed would see action in the days to come. Unsurprisingly, Squadron Leader A.S. Lamba jumped at the opportunity to transfer to a Gnat unit at Ambala, even though he had barely six hours on the type. However, he accepted two missions with 7 Squadron on 6 September before leaving. Lamba never transferred and stayed on with 7 Squadron.[10]

On the night of 5 September, instructions arrived at Halwara too regarding the possibility of action erupting in the Punjab Sector the next day.[11] Zachariah's briefing was almost identical to that received by Taneja; he duly spread the word on the anticipated action to other senior pilots. 7 Squadron's technical officers were Flying Officer C.G. Pandiya and Pilot Officer R. Kondaiah, both senior officers with 3-4 years of service[12] and entrusted with the power plant and airframe maintenance for the squadron's Hunters. Zachariah briefed them on the operations to follow, including details on the weapons load. The Hunters were to be equipped with T-10 rockets in addition to drop tanks.

The T-10 rockets came in two variations, a high explosive version and a hollow charge version for anti-armour and bunker busting activities. Since it wasn't clear what sorts of 'targets of opportunity' would be encountered, Zachariah ordered that the Hunters be armed with both types so that on firing, one rocket of each type from under each wing is released; it was an imperfect compromise, but the only one available. The ground personnel and crew worked through the night on the painfully slow, laborious process of arming, refueling and fitting rocket rails on the Hunters.

On the morning of 6 September, the *Battleaxes* flew their first strike mission across the international border. Zach led the first mission with senior Flight Commanders, Squadron Leaders S.S. 'Chacha' Malik, M.M. 'Rusty' Sinha and A.S. Lamba. As the Hunters taxied from the dispersal to the runway, the squadron's airmen lined up near the take-off point, where the Hunters turned onto the runway, to wave off the pilots. This was their war as well; they fought through the pilots.

The first mission was to attack Pakistani military targets in the Lahore Kasur area. When no movement was detected at the Kasur railway station, the formation vented their frustration, i.e. their weapon stores, in an area where only a solitary horse carriage (*tonga*) stood. Appropriately, the *Battleaxes* refer to the first strike sortie as the 'Tonga Strike'. It was not immediately possible to assess the damage to the railway station's facilities.

An armed recce mission by Flight Lieutenant D.K. 'Dice' Dhiman and Flying Officer P.S. 'Pingo' Pingale revealed little. After their return to Halwara at 1600 hours, Pilot Officer Kondaiah and his team of aircraft fitters were busy organizing the recovery and rearming of the returning Hunters on the ground, when the loud roar of a jet engine made them look up. The airmen and officers caught their first glimpse of an enemy aircraft as a PAF F 104 Starfighter made a low-level, high-speed pass over the airfield. Though it was the first glimpse of the adversary, there was no fear among the ground crew, only excitement. A six-ship formation to the Lahore area, led by Squadron Leader Malik, saw the Starfighter at 1,000 ft with full afterburner coming back from Halwara. The Hunter pilots could only catch a glimpse of the sleek fighter as it flashed by.

Unknown to the Indian pilots, the Starfighter was on a recce mission to gather information for planned PAF raids on Indian bases that evening. Starfighters flew similar missions to Adampur and Pathankot that afternoon, but remained undetected by even the radar unit, 230 SU, at Amritsar.

PLANNING THE PAF AIR RAIDS

In Pakistan the immediate reaction to the Indian Army offensive across the IB, and the subsequent IAF raid, was one of panic. President Ayub Khan was visibly shaken[13] at the sudden escalation of hostilities. In a meeting with military staff, the Chief of Air Staff of the PAF Nur Khan proposed implementing their operational plans, i.e. a full-scale raid on IAF airbases and targets. Ayub Khan gave the go ahead to Nur Khan. With that, the initiative of attacking the air bases of the rival air force slipped from the IAF's hands to the PAF's.

Even as the PAF planned its strategic move to hit IAF bases, one of its squadrons flew missions supporting the Pakistani Army against Indian formations, which were advancing along the Lahore-GT Road axis. 19 Squadron from Peshawar, led by Squadron Leader S.S. 'Nosey' Haider, flew a six aircraft strike mission at 0930 hours against the leading elements of the Indian Army's thrust towards Lahore.[14] The leading battalion of the division, 3 Jat, led by Lieutenant Colonel Desmond Hayde, had its columns strafed and rocketed by PAF Sabres. The unit lost all its RCL guns in the attack. A troop of Sherman tanks sent to support Hayde's battalion was attacked from the air and incapacitated. The Sabres returned in the afternoon and the attack saw the first usage of napalm bombs against Indian troops.[15] 3 Jat became the first Indian Battalion to cross the Ichogil canal but had to withdraw following a strong counter-attack by Pakistani armour. In the absence of Indian armour and the loss of all its RCL guns, thanks to the PAF, the unit could not face the attack. The withdrawal of 3 Jat was a serious setback. Throughout the day the PAF conducted almost continuous raids on Indian troops. Ideally, Indian fighters should have been flying combat air patrols, cab-rank style, over the frontline.

Meanwhile, preparations were on in earnest at Sargodha. At 1530 hours, two Starfighters were sent to reconnoitre Adampur and Halwara. Returning from their third strike, 7 Squadron encountered the one flown by Flight Lieutenant Hakimullah. The original PAF plan called for 59 sorties to hit multiple targets simultaneously at airfields at Jammu, Pathankot, Adampur,

Halwara, Jamnagar and radar units at Amritsar and Ferozepur. PAF logistics, however, appear to not have planned for this eventuality, and chaos and confusion reigned at the staging airbases at Sargodha and Peshawar.[16] These problems ensured that only one attack was carried out with a full complement of aircraft, this was an almost complete breakdown of PAF plans.

PAF 19 Squadron was chosen for the Pathankot raid, as it was the only airfield besides Srinagar within range of the Sabres from Peshawar. Squadron Leader S.S. Haider led the raid with eight Sabres,[17] equipped with armour piercing ammunition for their front guns. Two Sabres with Sidewinder missiles would fly top cover. The stage was set for the worst air raid ever suffered by the IAF.

PAF RAID ON PATHANKOT

At Pathankot, the station commander, Group Captain Roshan Suri had just returned from a meeting of WAC station commanders. He briefed the squadron commanders of the impending army move to cross the international border and also told his eager subordinates that, though missions against opportunity targets were authorized, operational orders prevented counter air missions against PAF bases. Several officers raised objections at the announcement, and for most it did not go down too well. Pathankot had launched several sorties by 3 and 31 Squadrons that day. Sorties were flown against Dera Baba Nanak outside the Jammu and Kashmir area as well as the regular targets in the Chamb-Jaurian area.

Evening was approaching Pathankot as Wing Commander Dandapani made a phone call to Pathankot air base from Amritsar's 230 SU. Dandapani asked for Suri, and on being told that he was not available was put through to Wing Commander Kuriyan, the OC Flying. Dandapani told Kuriyan that they had painted several Sabres, coming from the vicinity of Sargodha and going 'off the scope', as they went below the radar horizon. But he could see one lone aircraft coming in at an altitude of 19,000 ft. This lone aircraft was probably scouting the way ahead for the main formation. This had all the tell-tale signs of an incoming raid. Dandapani suggested that Kuriyan scramble Pathankot's air defence fighters. Here, things get confusing. Dandapani insists that Kuriyan refused to scramble the air patrol and pooh-poohed his fears of the incoming raid. Kuriyan claims to have immediately informed Suri about the incoming raid and asked for permission to scramble the CAP but was refused by Suri who, in turn, ordered Kuriyan off the shift.[18] A senior pilot on the scene suggested that a couple of Gnats be scrambled but the request was turned down.[19] Squadron Leader J.F. Josephs, duty pilot that day in the ATC, could overhear the radio conversation between Kuriyan and Dandapani. As one ATC officer turned to him and asked, 'What the hell is going on?' Josephs replied 'Don't ask, just watch the west'. Even as frantic attempts were made to get Base Ops on the phone, all eyes in the ATC turned west.

Meanwhile, Flight Lieutenant Tirlochan 'Tango' Singh of 3 Squadron was leading his four Mystere formation on a strike mission against ground targets at Chamb.[20] The strike had been planned on receipt of information from an earlier mission that Pakistani forces—trucks and tanks—were being withdrawn by road from Chamb to reinforce defences elsewhere. Flying Officers M.R. Murdeshwar and Janak Kapur of 23 Squadron were flying top cover in two Gnats. The endurance of this mission was limited only by the flight endurance of the Gnat escort. Once the Gnat reached its limit and had to return, the Mysteres would have to as well, or be devoid of air cover.

After the attack, Murdeshwar informed Tango that he was low on fuel and would have to turn back. Tango replied, 'Manna, one more round, lets finish them off.' Murdeshwar agreed and the Mysteres went in for another run. At this point Kapur called over the R/T, 'Backbay Leader, Bingo!'. Bingo was the code to indicate that there was only enough fuel for immediate recovery and nothing else. Murdeshwar called out to the Mystere formation to finish their run and make for base.

The attack run over, the Mysteres turned for home, cruising along at 500 knots. Soon they outpaced the Gnats by a considerable distance as the Gnat cruised at a much slower optimum speed of around 400 knots. But the number three in the Mystere formation started straggling. Flying Officer D.S. 'Dinky' Jatar had observed his undercarriage lights come on and could not fly at more than 250 knots. Murdeshwar decided to slow down to escort the straggler and instructed Kapur to carry on as the latter was low on fuel and could not afford to fly at lower speeds.

Soon the Mystere formation and Kapur's Gnat were out of sight, leaving behind Murdeshwar's Gnat and Jatar's straggling Mystere. Jatar called Murdeshwar on the R/T to inform him that the slow airspeed was burning up his fuel and that he would require a direct approach to Pathankot. Murdeshwar still had some reserve left and let Jatar make a direct approach to the runway.

With his engine burning the last vapours of fuel reserves, Jatar landed the Mystere while Murdeshwar flew on to make a teardrop turn to try and land in the opposite direction. Jatar took the Mystere to the end of the runway and had started taxiing back on the parallel taxi track when, starved of fuel, his engine flamed out. The Mystere rolled to a halt. Murdeshwar was now coming into land in the opposite direction and could see out of the corner of his eyes Jatar's Mystere slowing down on the taxi track, when his attention was drawn to the sudden spurt of R/T transmissions as the ATC frantically announced 'Incoming raid, incoming raid!' Murdeshwar cursed his fuel state. With enough fuel, he could have attempted a brave intercept of the incoming aircraft. By this time he had landed and was taxiing into a blast pen.

Kuriyan was driving into his garage at home as he heard ack-ack guns open up. He looked towards the airfield to see eight Sabres come over the horizon. Four bore down at low level firing their machine guns, while the other four peeled off and kept high altitude cover. As the four Sabres pulled out, another four bore in strafing buildings, installations and aircraft. The AA guns had opened up and the sound of the eight Sabre's Browning machine guns strafing the airfield joined them in an ear shattering crescendo. Josephs dove to the floor of the ATC but not before noticing—a sight that stays with him to this day—that 4 Sabres had drop tanks and four did not.[21] There was chaos on the ground as aircraft were taxiing to a halt and others were parked out on the ORP.

As Janak Kapur steered his Gnat into a blast pen and climbed out, a junior officer yelled, 'Sir, look up, they are attacking!' Kapur looked up to see the Sabres pulling up. The Sabres noticed Murdeshwar's Gnat on its way to the blast pen. A volley of bullets straddled the Gnat just as Murdeshwar jumped out of the aircraft and out of the blast pen. Within seconds, the bullets destroyed the Gnat.[22]

The fate of 3 Squadron's Mysteres that had just landed back from the mission was no better. Flight Lieutenant Tirlochan Singh had taxied his Mystere to the dispersal and was alighting from the jet as a Sabre made a strafing run on his aircraft. By the time it came back for a second pass, Tango was out of the aircraft and into the trench in a jiffy. His No. 2 Flying Officer Russell Montes was still strapped in his seat when a Sabre's gun burst kicked up chips off the wall of the blast pen. The airmen, who were just putting the chocks under the wheels, shot an accusing glance at Montes for firing off his guns inside the pen. Luckily, realization dawned as the Sabre pulled out of the dive and screamed overhead, guns still blazing. Montes had a quick struggle with his harness and unstrapped himself. About to get out of the cockpit, he noticed that the airmen had not yet bought the ladder to dismount. There was no hesitation as he took the 6 ft drop from the cockpit ledge to *terra firma* and made a quick dash to the trenches. There he had to face more dust in his face from the Sabre's bullets during its second pass and the exploding ammunition from his burning Mystere.

Assuming it was a decoy, the Sabres left alone Jatar's Mystere on the taxi track. Instead, they attacked the row of MiGs and Mysteres along the blast pens in the airfield. The CAP was not scrambled. The Gnats on ORP too escaped damage. However, the two MiGs, which were being refuelled after returning from an earlier flight, went up in flames. Unfortunately, at the time, there was an engineering order in force that pilots were not to start or switch aircraft off inside blast pens.[23] This also applied to refuelling of aircraft. These revetments were properly camouflaged and built specially to protect the aircraft. Their positioning was such that a strafing aircraft would not have been able to align his sights on multiple aircraft in a single dive. The pilot would have had to make more than one attack, leaving himself open to anti-aircraft fire. The order meant that aircraft had to be manhandled in the pens after refuelling and were left out in the open, vulnerable to air attack.

Pathankot's Air Traffic Control (ATC) tower at that time was newly built. It did not house the ATC staff as yet; the actual ATC was located in a trench covered by a tent on the opposite side of the tarmac, where ATC controllers operated using portable R/T sets. Wing Commander M.S.D. Wollen was one of the pilots scheduled to take-off that particular evening. He had earlier flown a CAP with Mukherjee and his MiGs were being fuelled and serviced. When the attack began, Wollen dove into the ATC trench and watched the raid from there.[24] The only Indian aircraft in the air was a Mystere on CAP piloted by Flying Officer Michael McMahon from 31 Squadron, with hardly fifty hours on the type to his credit. Luckily, Wollen recognized the danger of McMahon getting caught in an unequal combat and instructed him to head south and return later.[25] McMahon eventually landed after the raid was over. After this experience two-aircraft CAPs became the norm. The CAPs were typically flown by the pilots on detachment from FIS, pending assignment to attack sorties.

Plate 22: Ground crew of 31 Squadron along with the Officers—Wing Commander Goodman, CO, Squadron Leader A.L. 'Tony' Mousinho, whose Mystere was destroyed on the ground during the Pathankot Raid, and Flying Officer Michael MacMahon, who was doing the lone Combat Air Patrol over Pathankot when the Sabres came in.

As the Sabres left, 10 plumes of smoke rose in the air. The raid had been highly successful, resulting in the destruction of ten IAF aircraft: six Mysteres (four from 3 Squadron,[26] two from 31 Squadron), one Gnat, one Packet and two MiG 21s.[27] Three other aircraft were damaged. Luckily, there had been no loss of life on the ground. The Packet had flown in earlier from Bareilly. Though the aircraft was a write off, much of its fuselage was intact. Ground crew personnel stripped the aircraft wreck of all useable spares. The hulk that remained was later to receive a direct hit from a B 57 night raid. This marked the second occasion that the MiGs had encountered the Sabres: a rather one-sided affair. 28 Squadron had the ignominy of being caught napping on the ground. Its pilots had a grandstand view of two of their MiGs, which were undergoing refuelling and parked outside their blast pens, being destroyed in the attack. As Josephs recollects ruefully, 'They [the Sabres] had a field day.'[28] Mysteriously, even though there were no Indian aircraft in the air, the airfield's AA guns failed to score. The Sabre pilots slipped away unscathed; the airfield defenses were caught napping. The PAF pilots were later to report the destruction of all ten MiGs, a claim faithfully echoed on Pakistani radio later that day and heard with incredulity by the Pathankot pilots. For the PAF this raid was a cakewalk, but the next ones were not going to be.

ABORTED STRIKES AND CLASSIC AIR BATTLES:
PAF RAIDS ON ADAMPUR AND HALWARA

Two more strikes—on Adampur and Halwara—were planned by the PAF. Both were to be eight aircraft missions, but poor Sabre serviceability ensured that both raids were flown at less than half their planned strength. A three-Sabre strike on Adampur consisted of Squadron Leaders M.M. Alam and Allauddin Ahmed and Flight Lieutenant Saad Hatmi. There was a delay of 50 minutes between the take-off timings of the first PAF strike mission to Pathankot and the strike on Adampur.[29] The PAF expected fighter opposition.

About the time of the attack on Pathankot, 7 Squadron flew its fourth strike mission of the day with four Hunters in the

Taran Taran area. The squadron's CO Wing Commander Zachariah led the formation, codenamed 'Grey'. Its members were Squadron Leaders A.K. 'Peter' Rawlley and M.M. Sinha and Flight Lieutenant S.K. Sharma. The pilots had just reached Taran Taran when Sinha spotted the three Sabres coming in at low level.

As the Sabres spotted the Hunters, they shed their drop tanks and climbed as the Hunters went vertical and followed. In the dangerous low-level fight that followed, Rawlley found a Sabre on his tail and while trying to execute a defensive break, flew into the ground after completing 270 degrees of the turn. Rawlley probably misjudged his altitude during the turn, not surprising as the combat was taking place barely 200 ft above ground level. Both Sinha and Zachariah took high deflection shots at the Sabres and missed. Alam, the Sabre pilot that had tangled with Rawlley, called to abort the strike and extricated his aircraft from the fight. Alam claimed two Hunters in this combat and was awarded the kills by the PAF, even though only Rawlley can be attributed as a loss on the Indian side.

As Alam's formation exited the area, it crossed a formation of three Sabres led by Squadron Leader S.A. Rafiqui on a strike to Halwara. Alam warned Rafiqui about the presence of 7's Hunters. Rafiqui had earlier shot down two Vampires from 45 Squadron over Chamb on the first day of the war. In spite of Alam's warning, Rafiqui carried on with his strike mission.

Meanwhile, the low-on-fuel Hunters left the Sabres and started recovery. Zachariah reported Rawlley's loss in action to the base to alert them. As Zachariah and the other two Hunters landed back at Halwara and were taxiing back to their dispersal, the three PAF Sabres pulled up over Halwara for a gun attack.[30] On the ground, technical personnel were engaged in maintenance, while some others milled about the tarmac in anticipation of returning Hunters. Suddenly they noticed the Sabres bear in and open fire with their front guns. The airraid siren sounded immediately as the ack-ack guns opened up, lacing the sky with tracer. The ground crew and personnel dove headlong into the trenches. They need not have worried: the Sabres were not attacking them, but two Hunters that were on a CAP over the airfield.

Two 7 Squadron pilots—Flying Officers P.S. 'Pingo' Pingale and A.R. 'Adi' Ghandhi—were on CAP, this being the IAF policy when missions were being launched or recovered. Both were in the air as Toric's formation landed, and as they went into a left-hand orbit, just crossing the southern perimeter of the airfield, the Sabres bounced the Hunters.

The first thing Pingale noticed was the sound of machinegun fire, which was quite unusual. It is difficult to hear gunfire or any assorted noise when wearing the pilot's helmet inside a Hunter cockpit, unless the source of the sound is very near. A quick glance to his left made his heart jump. He could see that his wingman Ghandhi, who was 200 yds away, was still in his station, Rafiqui's Sabre, which was between Ghandhi and himself, had sneaked in with all the six Brownings blazing away at his Hunter. Pingale broke into the attack, even as the Sabre whizzed past him. But his controls were sluggish and his cockpit was already filled with smoke. He levelled the Hunter and pulled the overhead ejection handle. After a brief momentary pause, which seemed like a lifetime, the ejection cartridge fired and Pingale was thrown into the air clear of the Hunter, a mere 100 ft above ground level. He landed after a short descent by parachute outside the airfield.

Ghandhi's aircraft was also simultaneously hit and badly damaged by the second Sabre, flown by Rafiqui's No. 3 Flight Lieutenant Cecil Chaudhary. As Ghandhi rapidly took stock of the situation, he could see Rafiqui's aircraft firing at Pingale, who ejected soon afterwards. Even though his Hunter was badly damaged, Ghandhi manoeuvred behind the Sabre and opened fire at point blank range. Though fired without precise aim, the 54-ft spread of the Hunter's four 30 mm cannon hit the Sabre. Ghandhi could see the Sabre was damaged, streaming smoke at 150 ft and losing altitude.

Meanwhile, the Sabre on Ghandhi's tail scored more hits on his target. As the Hunter lazily rolled to the right at 150 ft, Ghandhi ejected and landed on the outskirts of Halwara airfield. In the process he broke his ankle and was invalided to the Military Hospital in Delhi.

This seesaw battle was not over yet. The Sabres were

continuing their strafing as 27 Squadron came to the rescue. Flight Lieutenant D.N. Rathore and Flying Officer V.K. Neb, who were on another Hunter CAP north of the airfield, were directed towards the Sabres. Arriving over the airfield, they saw two Sabres on a strafing run. Rathore, the flight leader, latched onto one of the Sabres as it went into a strafing run and hit it with cannon fire at a range of 500 yds. The stricken Sabre started banking to the left, and then dove into the ground in a sheet of flame some 6 miles from the field.

The other Sabre abandoned its attack and pulled up steeply to gain height. Rathore's No. 2, Neb, who had not done any air-to-air firing before and was still under operational training, closed into less than 100 yds and fired at almost point blank range. The fusillade from the four 30 mm cannons was devastating. A puff of smoke came from the Sabre, which turned into a 'sheet of flame' as it blew up.

Plate 23: This montage of photos from Flying Officer V.K. Neb's gun camera film (*1.5 seconds in all*) shows the destruction of Yunus Hussain's Sabre.

Even as the Sabres' debris was falling to the ground, both Hunters reformed and flew back to base. The Hunter pilots claimed three Sabres shot down. This was a great morale booster for the rest of the pilots at Halwara. It was believed that the defending Hunters had shot down all three attackers. Though two Hunters were lost, the Indian pilots who ejected were safe. Two Sabre wrecks were recovered, and the bodies of the PAF pilots Squadron Leader Rafiqui and Flight Lieutenant Yunus were given a decent burial after personal effects like identity cards and documents were collected. Rafiqui's body was found intact quite close to the wreckage, probably thrown out on impact.

While Neb certainly shot down Yunus, it is not clear who shot down Rafiqui: Ghandhi or Rathore. As Rathore had claimed shooting a Sabre some 6 miles from the airfield, exactly where Rafiqui's Sabre was discovered, near Heren village, Ludhiana, it is very likely that Rathore shot him down. The only discrepancy was that there were two Sabres in the air when Rathore and Neb arrived and not three. The third, flown by Flight Lieutenant Cecil Chaudhary made it back to base at Sargodha, with minimum fuel in its tanks and the engine almost flaming out on landing. Rafiqui, Pakistan's most vaunted pilot after his spectacular success over Chamb—till Squadron Leader M.M. Alam's unbelievable claims—was awarded Pakistan's

Plate 24: Rafiqui's Sabre wreckage (*52-5248*) lies in a field outside the village of Heren, 6 miles from Halwara. Rafiqui was most probably downed by Flight Lieutenant Rathore.

highest leadership award, the Hilal-e-Juraat. His citation states that his guns jammed and he lost his life while trying to save his companions. Later the PAF Shorkot Road airfield was named after him.[31]

For the personnel of 7 Squadron, it had been a hectic 24 hours. It had started with arming and preparing the Hunters in the morning, recovering returning aircraft and launching them again, seeing the Starfighter in the afternoon, and the air-battle later in the evening, hearing about the death of Peter Rawlley who was missed much,[32] and finally experiencing a B-57 raid and the paratroopers' raid. As one officer remarked, 'We were in a state of numbness and shock—but the work went on. It never stopped.'

The Halwara and Adampur raids were the last daytime raids against Indian airfields in Punjab in the war. Since neither of the two raids was successful, Pakistan discontinued similar dusk

Plate 25: IAF Chief of Staff chats with Flight Lieutenant Rathore (*on Singh's left*) and Flying Officer Neb during a visit to Halwara after the war.

raids and limited itself to night raids by B 57s. Never again was a daylight raid attempted on Halwara, Pathankot or Adampur.[33]

Besides the airbases in Punjab, the only other target that was attacked was the Amritsar radar centre.[34] The PAF planned to use an ELINT RB 57 to home in on the transmission of the radar of 230 SU and for the Sabres accompanying the RB 57 to do the rest. The first RB 57 had problems with its equipment, and when the second RB 57 was used, the anti-aircraft fire put up by guns at the radar site was so intense that it knocked out one of the engines of the RB 57. As the accompanying Sabres were unable to locate the radar station, the raid was aborted. Similarly, two T 33 trainers sent to attack the auxiliary low-powered radar at Ferozepur failed to locate the target. Another pair of T 33s strafed a deserted airfield at Bhuj.

THE B 57 NIGHT RAIDS

The last raids of the day were by PAF B 57s from Peshawar and Mauripur on the Punjab airfields and Jamnagar. B 57s from Peshawar attacked Pathankot, Adampur and Halwara with 4,000-lb bombs.[35]

Adampur was preparing to launch two MiG 21s on the Operational Readiness Platform (ORP) when the B 57 came over. Squadron Leader S.K. 'Polly' Mehra and Flight Lieutenant 'Pushy' Dass were scheduled to take-off. As both pilots were walking to the aircraft dispersal, the PAF B 57 came roaring overhead. The runway lights were on in anticipation of the launch of the MiGs. There could not have been a better moment for the B 57 pilot to begin his bombing run.

As the bombs fell, both Mehra and Dass were caught in the open and prudently made a run for better cover. Noticing a static water tank nearby both pilots ran towards it in their cumbersome pressure suits. Mehra made a headlong dive into the water and with a smooth splash started swimming away. Dass, who was on the heels of Mehra, remembered that he could not swim and didn't jump. However, sheer force of circumstance made him gingerly step into the water tank while holding on to some vegetation on the banks! The B 57 succeeded in hitting the two MiGs on the ORP. One of the Type 76s was destroyed and the other MiG was damaged in the raid. This was the third and last MiG lost by the squadron during the war. Though this was a small raid by a solitary aircraft, the destruction of the MiG was notable. The B 57 pilot earned admiration and a nickname, '8-Pass Charlie', from the Adampur Mystere pilots.[36]

Mauripur was the PAF's bomber base. Earlier, a part of its B 57 force was moved to Peshawar, with the rest to follow. These were about to take-off when they were hurriedly called back and briefed for the mission to Jamnagar. Finally, a force of six bombers left for Jamnagar, arriving in the middle of a dark and cloudy night. The B 57s used the lighthouse at Mandvi as a landmark to navigate to Jamnagar airfield, which was four minutes flying time away. The B 57s dropped their loads, fired their rockets and flew back to Mauripur to carry out two more raids that night. At least four Vampires near the ORP were damaged in these attacks that night.[37] There were several Naval Seahawks and Air Force Otters dispersed in the open around the airfield, but no damage was done to them. Not all the attackers got away unscathed.

The standard practice of the B 57s was to operate in pairs. One aircraft would launch target locator flares over the airfield while the other attacked. However, something was clearly amiss with the B 57 that carried out the fourth raid of the day. It's not clear whether there was a second B 57 in the area but, in any case, the flares over the airfield while the B 57 came over were too close for comfort. The crew was probably blinded by the flares, which lit up the aircraft as a target for the ack-ack gunners. The B 57 flew through the AA barrage but crashed outside Jamnagar. The bodies of the pilot Squadron Leader Shabbir Alam Siddique and his navigator Squadron Leader Aslam Qureshi were recovered from the wreckage. Siddique's logbook/diary was recovered. It revealed that the PAF had been on alert since March and had carried out practice missions on IAF targets since April.

By the end of the day on 6 September, the PAF could claim to have done well. It had attacked Indian ground forces effectively and raided the IAF's airfields. Though the failure of the raids on Halwara and Adampur and the loss of three of its aircraft on these raids was a setback, it had managed to destroy eleven aircraft on the ground and three in the air. Initially, more than twenty aircraft were claimed as destroyed on the ground across all airfields and another seven shot down in the air, including the destruction of seven MiG 21s at Pathankot. These claims were exaggerated, but thanks to the fiasco at Pathankot, the actual losses the IAF suffered were considerable. Due to losses suffered on the ground at these forward airfields, the MiGs were withdrawn to Ambala and deployed from there.

The happenings of the day were not too encouraging for the IAF. That night, when Air Marshal Arjan Singh informed the Defence Minister of the 'mishap' at Pathankot, Chavan urged him to move on, 'Forget about the past, we will think only about the future'. Clearly, the Defence Minister, unlike his predecessor, understood the mechanics of war, an encouraging factor for both the Army and the Air Force Chiefs.

CONFUSION ON THE GROUND:
THE PAKISTANI PARATROOPERS

As night fell, both sides began planning for the next day's operations. IAF Canberras and PAF B 57s were already in the air on counter strikes. The Pakistanis had not played all their cards. That night, they planned to drop more than bombs on Indian airfields.

A little after the B 57s crossed the Indian border, three C 130 Hercules transport aircraft took off for the same targets.[38] They carried some 60 paratroopers, each of the elite Special Services Group (SSG). After Independence, Pakistan had chosen to form special compact commando forces trained in sabotage and disruptive activities behind enemy lines. The time had come to put this force to the test. The C 130s were to drop the paratroopers near Indian airbases. They would then regroup, capture the airfields and destroy aircraft, disrupting the Indian air effort and return to base, following the numerous rivulets and streams that flow from Punjab into Pakistan. The plan was bold and imaginative on paper, but when put into practice, went haywire.

Pathankot, Halwara and Adampur were the chosen targets. Each of the Hercules dropped its load of paratroopers on or around the designated airfield. Right from the moment the Pakistanis landed at Pathankot, under the command of Major Khalid Butt, things went wrong. It was about 0200 hours and in the pitch dark of the night the paratroopers failed to rendezvous quickly. The criss-crossing network of irrigation canals, streams and boggy fields hampered their movement. By daybreak the paratroopers were still a confused lot. By then a villager had informed the Pathankot subarea HQ and a force of about 200 men was mustered and inducted into the rounding-up operations. Most of the Pakistanis, including Butt, were prisoners within the next two days.

At Halwara, a B 57 had raided the airfield and left when the Hercules came over and dropped its stick of commandos. The descending parachutes were clearly visible even in the dark sky. The airfield security officer equipped all the technical airmen and officers with rifles and pistols and instructed them to fire in the general direction of the grass just inside the perimeter, to deter any paratroopers trying to infiltrate the airfield. Some paratroopers landed inside the airfield perimeter in the residential area. Before they could recover from the shock of the landing, they found themselves prisoners of war. They were captured by the local police, reinforced by the Muleteers of an Army Supply Corp Animal Transport Company in the area. The remaining paratroopers were rounded up soon after. However the detachment commander Major Hazur Hasnain and one of his men captured a jeep and escaped to Pakistani lines.[39] Squadron Leader Krishna Singh, a Ground Duty Officer at Halwara in the Accounts branch was instrumental in organizing round up parties and personally captured the commander of one of the paratroop detachments. Singh became the only officer from a non-combatant wing to be decorated with the VrC in the 1965 and 1971 wars.

The Adampur detachment too suffered the same fate as the one at Pathankot. Dropped too far from the airfield and unable to assemble, they took refuge in the cornfields at daybreak. The only Indian forces available were some elements of the Punjab Armed Police. Reinforced by two armoured cars from the local NCC Squadron, and a company of infantry from the

XI Corps HQ, they formed hunting groups and rounded them up. Enraged Punjabi villagers killed some of the paratroopers. The detachment commander Captain Durrani was captured soon after.

The Pakistani plan to neutralize air bases through unconventional methods failed. Of the 180 commandos dropped, 136 were taken prisoner and 22 killed in encounters with the army, police or civilians. Approximately 20 managed to escape to Pakistan. Most of them were from the detachment dropped near Pathankot, only 10 miles from the border. Some of the paratroopers managed to evade capture and hid in the tall *sarkanda* grass for periods up to ten days.

For the mission to succeed, the paratroopers had to be dropped close to their targets with good knowledge of the terrain at the drop-zone and they had to rendezvous quickly. Sixty men was too large a group to do so quickly without detection, and too small to hold out for themselves if cornered. The objective of the raid was similar to that carried out by the British on Pebble Island during the Falklands war, where 45 men dropped by helicopters inside the airfields succeeded in destroying many Argentinean Pucara aircraft before the defenders were alerted. The Pakistanis learnt their lessons the hard way. Though the Indians mounted no such operations, they did learn from Pakistan's mistakes and put it to good use later in the 1971 war. From the IAF point of view, it seemed a stupid and pointless exercise. As Air Chief Marshal Lal put it, 'What this operation aimed to achieve is difficult to understand.'[40] While its aims were ambitious, the execution of the plan was remarkably poor. Its most noticeable effect was to stir up Punjabi civilians to form mobs that went about cutting crops to hunt down Pakistani paratroopers and beating many a poor beggar on suspicion of being a disguised raider.

SHADOWS IN THE NIGHT

The Pakistani paratrooping adventure did induce undue sensitivity among planners of both sides. In Pakistan, almost all raids by Canberras, in which the lead aircraft would drop para flares, were taken as a paratroop attack on the airfields. Rumours floated, causing much confusion. On one occasion, reacting to reports of an invasion of the Sargodha air base, a C 130 loaded with commandos was dispatched to Sargodha from Air HQ. The C 130 landed in the dark at Sargodha, and as the commandos deplaned from the aircraft, they were mistaken for Indian paratroopers by an alert sentry and an exchange of fire took place for three hours.[41] No information on casualties is available.[42]

The paratroop scare was not limited to the Pakistani side. Similar comical incidents, indicative of confusion and strained nerves, also occurred on the Indian side with some regularity. Ground protection was stepped up and carried out by personnel of the IAF squadrons. The pilots and commanding officers slept in the crew room, fully armed with pistols and other weapons. One night at Adampur, due to a false alarm the ground crew of 1 Squadron started a firefight with the ground Motor Transport section of 8 Wing.[43] The exchange of fire by both sides went on for 10-15 minutes in which they blazed away with rifles and pistols from the safety of their trenches. No casualties occurred, prompting one pilot to quip, 'Fortunately our firing skill on the ground was not up to our standards in the air.'[44]

Another incident occurred when a duty officer, who had dozed off, suddenly awoke from his nightmares with a blood-curdling scream and started yelling, 'Enemy fire, fire'. Since it was a black-out, and since it was pitch dark inside the crew rooms, no one knew who was shouting and where the screams were coming from. The duty officer kept tumbling around in the dark, shouting and screaming at the same time, which gave the impression that an entire enemy platoon had invaded the crew room. More officers woke up in the dark and added to the bedlam and confusion. Pistols were drawn for what they thought to be the 'ultimate close quarter battle', but before the shooting match could start, the CO, restored order by giving orders not to take out arms.[45] Much hilarity ensued at the duty officer's expense.

Nothing illustrates better the adage that a small firearm is a dangerous thing in a pilot's hand (or that the safest place for a pilot is the cockpit) than the comical 'Sten training' incident at Pathankot. 23 Squadron's pilots had been issued 9 mm Sten carbines to counter the paratrooper 'menace'. The Sten had a hair-trigger at the best of the times and was a dangerous thing to handle roughly. Flight Lieutenant Pathania was issued one but was unable to operate it. Flight Lieutenant Tushar Sen happened to see Pathania's predicament and offered his 'help'. Sen commenced his demonstration. He loaded the magazine and was cocking the handle even as he explained, 'You pull the handle like this to the cocked position, and your finger should be resting on the trigger here. . . .' Apparently, Sen himself had not experienced the sensitive hair trigger on the Sten. As he pulled back the cocking handle, his finger slipped on the trigger. The Sten let loose a burst of 9 mm rounds, which flew just inches above the heads of the pilots relaxing on the sleeping cots. Flying Officer M.R. Murdeshwar recalls his eyes and 'a thousand others' turned on the perpetrator of that moment.[46] Verbal comments, if any, have not been recorded.

Similar confusion occurred elsewhere, and on one occasion, as will be narrated later, the CO of the only supersonic fighter squadron was pulled up on suspicion of being a paratrooper himself. Lieutenant General Harbaksh Singh, in his autobiography, *A Soldier Recalls: In the Line of Duty* recollects an emergency call from Group Captain D.E. Bouche, the station commander of Ambala, on the night of 8 September. Bouche told Harbaksh that Ambala was under the attack by paratroopers and that he had seen parachutes descend with his own eyes. Though troops were mobilized and search parties combed the area, it became quite obvious that Ambala was neither attacked by paratroopers nor bombed by the PAF B57 Canberras, thus leaving the source of Bouche's initial report a mystery to this day.[47]

NOTES

1. The Army operations and events are gathered from various publications on the conflict including Major K.C. Praval, *Indian Army after Independence*, New Delhi: Lancer International, 1987;

THE CHALLENGE: FLARE UP ON 6 SEPTEMBER

Colonel Bhupinder Singh, *Role of Tanks in the 1965 War*, Patiala: B.C. Publishers, 1982, and B.C. Cakravarty, ed., 'Indian Armed Forces—Official History of the 1965 Indo-Pakistan War', New Delhi: Government of India (unpublished).
2. Interview with various pilots, Group Captain Capt O.P. Taneja, AVM A.S. Lamba.
3. Interview with Wing Commander G.V. Kuriyan.
4. Interview with O.P. Taneja.
5. There were rough edges sometimes left over after conversion, sorted out eventually as the war went over. Jimmy Bhatia recalls: 'Once I remember... we were doing a search and strike over the Lahore axis. In fact, I was flying with 3 QFIs. I was the only regular pilot flying with them. On one of the moves, one pilot made a blunder—while crossing over, he went between number 1 and 2. The AC was 30 ft away—I was so scared. I made a cross control move just to avoid him, I went under him, I was at 200-300 ft, I could see trees so close, it was a hair-raising experience. That was the pitfall with non-ops pilots, they had had long breaks. They were all good pilots though, no doubt about that. By the end of the war, everyone was doing well.'
6. Interview with O.P. Taneja.
7. 1 Squadron's War Diaries, '1965 Operations'.
8. Earle was to comment on this particular operational mishap later: 'On Toofanis and Mysteres the underwing weapons could be triggered by static electricity. Hence, a mandatory static check after start up. Was the test done properly? In peacetime these were done with a pilot in the cockpit—I'm not sure whether this was so during ops—it could also have been sabotage'.
9. John Fricker, *Battle for Pakistan*, London: Ian Allen, 1979, p. 87.
10. Lamba eventually earned a VrC, and the distinction of flying 7 Squadron's first and last missions of the war.
11. Interview with AVM A.S. Lamba, VrC.
12. Officers of the Technical stream usually got their rank late compared to those in the flying stream. Thus, an officer with three years of service would still be a Pilot Officer, whereas someone from the flying stream could become a Flying Officer within a year of commissioned service.
13. John Fricker, *Battle for Pakistan*, op. cit., p. 85.
14. PAF version is from John Fricker's book; Indian version is from K.C. Praval's book. John Fricker, op. cit., pp. 82-9, Major K.C. Praval, *Indian Army after Independence*, op. cit., 1987.
15. John Fricker admits usage of napalm. John Fricker, op. cit., p. 89.
16. Ibid., pp. 91-2.
17. The PAF Pilots who flew on this mission were S/L Sajjad Haider, F/L Jamshed Akbar, F/L Ghani Akbar, F/L Mazhar Abbas, F/L

Khalid Latif, F/L Dilawar Hussain, F/O Arshad Choudhry and F/O Abbas Khattak.
18. Interviews with Wing Commander Dandapani and Group Captain Kuriyan.
19. Interview with Squadron Leader J.F. Josephs.
20. Interview with Group Captain M.R. Murdeshwar and Group Captain Kuriyan.
21. Interview with Squadron Leader J.F. Josephs.
22. Murdeshwar's destroyed Gnat Serial Number was IE 1112 (from logbook records).
23. Personal correspondence: Squadron Leader Tony Mousinho.
24. Air Marshal M.S.D. Wollen's interview by Dr. Shiv Shankar Shastry.
25. Interview with Group Captain M.R. Murdeshwar and Group Captain Kuriyan.
26. Correspondence with Squadron Leader Tony Mousinho VrC. One of the aircraft destroyed in the attack was IA 1007, which Squadron Leader Mousinho had flown just before the attack.
27. B.C. Chakravarty, op. cit., n. 1.
28. Author's interview with Squadron Leader J.F. Josephs.
29. John Fricker, op. cit., p. 92.
30. Government of India's press releases; Air Marshal Ghandhi's interview in *Probe* Magazine, 1992.
31. When AM Arjan Singh visited Pakistan in February 1966, he carried Rafiqui's identity card with him, which was passed on to Rafiqui's brother by the PAF.
32. Handsome, extremely popular and considered one of the best pilots on the Hunter, Peter Rawlley was well known in the Hunter pilot's circle in the 1960s. News of his death on the first day of hostilities was greeted with disbelief among other squadrons, like no. 20 at Hindon.
33. Later in the war, close to ceasefire time, four PAF Sabres approached Pathankot at mid day, made a half-hearted pull-up and then turned back. It's not known what the purpose of this particular mission was. The air raid warning was initiated and all IAF personnel had made their way to the trenches before the all-clear was sounded.
34. John Fricker, op. cit., p. 100.
35. Ibid.
36. Interview with Group Captain Taneja; 1 Squadron War Diary.
37. B.C. Chakravarty, op. cit, n. 1.
38. John Fricker, op. cit.; Air Chief Marshal P.C. Lal, *My Years with the IAF*, New Delhi: Lancer International, 1986; D.R. Mankekar, *Twenty-two Fateful Days*, Bombay: Manaktalas, 1966.
39. Brigadier Zahir Alam Khan, *The Way it was*, Karachi: Ahbab Publishers, 1998.

40. Air Chief Marshal P.C. Lal, op. cit., p. 138.
41. John Fricker, op. cit., p. 108.
42. Air Commodore Mansoor Shah, *The Gold Bird: Pakistan and its Air Force*, Karachi: Oxford University Press, 2002, pp. 182-4.
43. No. 1 Squadron unpublished history brochure.
44. Ibid.
45. Ibid.
46. Interview with Group Captain M.R. Murdeshwar.
47. Lieutenant General Harbaksh Singh, *In the Line of duty—A Soldier Remembers*, New Delhi: Lancer International, 2000, pp. 357-8.

CHAPTER 5

The Sargodha Raids and the Air Battles of 7 September

Of the PAF attacks planned on 6 September, only the Pathankot raid was carried out without glitches; the Adampur raid was aborted and the one on Halwara ran into two Hunter combat air patrols, resulting in the loss of two Sabres. PAF war plans were ambitious but, thanks to poor logistical support on the ground and faulty timing, their execution was only partially successful. The PAF destroyed aircraft on the ground and in the air but did not deal the crippling deathblow envisaged by the PAF. The raids ensured that a riposte by the IAF was headed the PAF's way.

THE PURSOOT IN ACTION

8 Squadron (*Pursoot*) had been in preparation for the war for some time. It had practised regular combat air patrol, and point defense from dawn to dusk. It had also done strike and close air support training. Another skill to be emphasized was airfield strike practice. Radar deficiencies played a part in 8 Squadron's training, its pilots practised rat-and-terrier tactics. A pair of Mysteres would get airborne, do a split and then, with mental dead reckoning, carry out an intercept after a brief separation.

The *Pursoot* finally found itself in action on the night of 6 September. On that evening, a panic call was made by the Indian Army to Adampur—Pakistani tanks and troops were pouring across the Dera Baba Nanak Bridge. The squadron's senior Flight Commander Madhukar 'Mickey' Jatar was assigned the strike mission. A tall man from a military family, and 'a giant in more ways than one',[1] Jatar was known for his sense of humour and bonhomie. He had selected three pilots for the strike. His 'Black' formation included Flight Lieutenants Pramod 'Chopi' Chopra (Black 3), Vinod 'Pat' Patney (Black 4) and Vinod 'Jimmy' Bhatia (Black 2). Bhatia would fly wingman to Jatar and Patney would fly wingman to Chopra. Chopra, a keen pilot and outdoorsman, earned a private pilot's license at Delhi's Flying Club before signing up with the IAF. Later, he proceeded to show off by doing unscheduled aerobatics over his hometown during a cross-country flight.[2] Bhatia, the youngest fully operational pilot in the squadron, had been part of a group of IAF pilots trained on the Sabre[3] with the USAF in 1963 and had already acquired a reputation as a keen pilot and flying 'hog'. Like Chopra, Bhatia's family was from the former unpartitioned Punjab: Chopra's from the small village of Dilawar in Wazirabad district; Bhatia's from the North-Western Frontier Province.[4] Patney had already shown off his flying skills in the IAF academy by winning the cadet's flying trophy.

Bhatia recounts the story of that night, which would see the first of many missions flown by the Black formation during the war:

On the 6th we got a panic call from the army that Pakistani tanks had broken through, and that CN was under threat. It was the evening and dusk was approaching—we had little time. All the aircraft were quickly loaded with SNEB and we were given a quick briefing by the GLO. The Black formation was assigned the target. It was getting late. We made a motherless charge to the aircraft, no RT check nothing. Normally to prevent FOD, the air intake guards were removed at the tyre checkpoint. We were so delayed, so in a hurry that as Pat came on to the runway, and the checker forgot to remove the guards. I saw the guards were in and kept pointing at him; finally the checker came and removed the guards. We rolled, retracted undercarriage, and got airborne. Mickey's fire warning light almost immediately came on. He called out 'Chopi, take over' and had to break off. Chopi slotted in, became #1, Pat slotted in to him, and I dropped back to #3. As we approached the international border, I had a bit of a scare. These SNEBS had these reinforced plastic covers—they were stressed to 450 knots. At 410 knots I heard a bang, and the aircraft yawed violently to the right, so now I had a flat plate facing forward, decelerated, recovered, and then heard another bang, and the left one was gone.

It was like flying with two airbrakes on. I could see Chopi and Pat at full throttle ahead. I followed though and made it to the target area.

As the three jets arrived, they were greeted by the sight of a mass of Pakistani tanks kicking up a fearsome amount of dust in the bulge, threatening Pathankot. The light in the late evening was extremely poor but Chopra, Bhatia and Patney pressed home their attacks with rockets and guns, accounting for 4 tanks and an unknown number of troops. Jatar's 'Black' formation would go on to commendable work in the war,

Plate 26: Flight Lieutenant Pramod 'Chopi' Chopra of 8 Squadron gets ready for a sortie in his Mystere.

resulting in all its members—Jatar, Chopra, Patney and Bhatia receiving the Vir Chakra for this and other subsequent strikes in support of the army. More attacks by the IAF lay ahead.

The first of these came in the form of a dozen Canberra sorties flown on the night of 6 September against Sargodha. These were flown by the Agra-based 5 Squadron, with B(I) 58s led by Wing Commander Prem Pal Singh and the Jet Bomber Conversion Unit led by Squadron Leader Padmanabha 'Bob' Gautam VM (a veteran of operations against the Katangan forces in the Congo).[5] Unable to find their target in the poor light, the Canberras dropped their bombs by blind reckoning in the approximate vicinity of Sargodha. The PAF scrambled Starfighters to intercept the bombers, but thanks to the tail warning radars of the Canberras, none of the Starfighters came within shooting distance.

A Canberra strike mission was also directed at Mauripur, the only strike launched against this target during the war. This was undertaken by 35 Squadron, then based at Pune.[6] However, the mission was aborted *en route*. The Canberras could not find the target and jettisoned their payloads off the coast. The PAF scrambled Sabres to intercept this mission and, in the process, suffered their first casualty of the day. Flying Officer Sikander Azam, who had taken off from Mauripur, crashed near Karachi. The cause of the crash was never ascertained.

THE TIGERS RAID SARGODHA

Orders from IAF Command Headquarters went out late on the night of 6 September to Adampur and Halwara, for the Mystere and Hunter squadrons to plan strikes against PAF airbases. Aircraft from Pathankot would continue their support to the army. The responsibility of carrying out the first strike on the Sargodha complex fell on 1 Squadron at Adampur. Wing Commander Taneja received instructions from WAC staff officers on the night of 6 September, as the first reports of the raid on Pathankot arrived. Taneja, who had led the squadron's first strike, an attack on a supply train at Gujranwala the

Plate 27: The Adampur Tigers—1 Squadron after the war. *Standing left to right*: J.P. Singh, A.J. Singh, V.K. 'Frisky' Verma, A. Sridharan, DMS Kahai, P.R. Earle, O.P. Taneja, unknown, Sudarshan Handa, D.S. Brar, P. Rajkumar. *Sitting Left to Right*: K.K. Bakshi, unknown, unknown, De, Brahmawar, Raje.

previous day, would lead the first retaliatory raid at the break of dawn.[7] While 1 Squadron would attack Sargodha, 8 Squadron would simultaneously raid a satellite airfield in the vicinity.

The time over target given to Taneja was 0555 hours, Indian Standard Time. Expecting poor light conditions further west, Taneja asked for the time over target to be delayed by 15 minutes to 0610 hours. But as Hunter squadrons from Halwara were already tasked with strikes for that time, the time over target was not changed. As 1 Squadron's pilots gathered for a briefing by Taneja at 0415 hours, the air raid warning came on and all lights were switched off. Taneja carried out the briefing by torchlight.

The Sargodha complex consisted of four airfields: Sargodha (Main), with Chota Sargodha to the west, Wagowal to the north and Bhagtanwala to the east. The network was situated across the river Chenab, with the Kirana hills rising 1,500 ft to the south-east. 1 Squadron was given Sargodha (Main) as its target, with estimated time over target set at 0555 hours, on 7 September. Since Sargodha was over 300 km from the border, with a flight time of 30 minutes from Adampur, the return was estimated at an hour. Being on the outer limits of the Mystere's range, no tactical routing was possible. They would limit themselves to a single attack run over the targets.

1 Squadron planned to send 12 aircraft for the first attack. Euipped with rockets, Taneja would lead the first wave of four aircraft in the 'Red' section, followed by the second wave in the 'Pink' section led by Squadron Leader D.E. Satur, again equipped with rockets. The last wave of four aircraft in the 'White' section was to be led by Squadron Leader S. Handa; these aircraft were equipped with 1,000 lb bombs. Two reserve pilots were on standby, in case aircraft in the first waves encountered problems. In the face of air opposition, the Mystere, heavily laden with ordnance and flying at the extreme range of its fuel capacity, would be dead meat against the far more manoeuverable Sabre.

The pilots assembled at their aircraft at 0510 hours, at which point the air raid warning went off again. The aircraft technicians and armourers preparing the aircraft took cover in

THE SARGODHA RAIDS AND THE AIR BATTLES

trenches, as a PAF B 57 swooped down and dropped its bomb load without hitting anything significant. Work resumed as soon as the raid ended.

The mission ran into glitches right away. When Taneja reached his Mystere he found his parachute missing. Unlike other aircraft, where parachutes are integrated with the seat, the Mystere pilots had to carry theirs and fit them into the seat before buckling in. All pilots carried their parachutes with the exception of the CO, who had the privilege of having his parachute carried by an airman. A brief search found the parachute in a nearby ditch. Apparently, the airman carrying out the CO's chute had dumped it there as the raid warning went off.[8]

After some delays in aircraft starting up, Taneja finally took off in the dark with Adampur's runway lights still switched off. Flight Lieutenant 'Frisky' Verma followed, also taking off in the dark. The runway lights then came on and the remaining pilots took off. However, Nos. 3 and 4 of the first wave encountered problems on getting airborne. *En route*, Squadron Leader Earle found that his drop tanks were not feeding into the main lines and returned to Adampur, but not before buzzing Chander airfield, which was found abandoned. No. 4, Squadron Leader Sridharan, lost his way and later formed up with the aircraft of the last formation led by Squadron Leader Handa.

The second formation, 'Pink', led by Squadron Leader D.E. Satur took off without any hitches. His formation consisted of Flight Lieutenants A.K. Brahmawar and J.P. Singh and Flying Officer S.S. Dange. On hearing that some of the allocated aircraft could not complete the mission to Sargodha, the standby aircraft was ordered to take-off. Squadron Leader A.B. Devayya, the reserve pilot, took off in a Mystere requisitioned from 32 Squadron, which was still in the process of conversion and did not take active part in the war. As 1 Squadron could muster only twelve serviceable aircraft that morning, two aircraft had been requisitioned from 32 and kept on reserve. The second standby pilot was Flight Lieutenant B.S. Raje, who was not called upon to fly that day.

The last formation, 'White', ran into problems soon after

take off. Squadron Leader Handa and his wingman Flight Lieutenant D.S. Brar were separated from their subsection consisting of Flight Lieutenant D.M.S. Kahai and Flying Officer Rajkumar. Having lost sight of the earlier formations in poor light, both subsections could not hit the initial waypoint. They aborted the mission and landed back at Adampur with their ordnance. The lone Mystere that lost its way from the first wave (Sridharan) joined this formation and returned as well.

Meanwhile, Taneja led his aircraft at tree-top height for maximum terrain masking. Navigation was by instruments and dead reckoning. Five minutes before time over target, the seven Mysteres were detected by PAF radar; Sargodha and its fighters on combat air patrol went on alert.

The Mysteres came roaring over even as the defending AA guns started firing erratically. IAF Canberras had already attacked Sargodha the previous night; more raids were expected. The time then was 0558 hours, about 3 minutes later than the planned time over target, but the light conditions were as bad as expected. Taneja pulled up short of Sargodha and led the first dive with Verma onto the airfield. Identifying a large four-engined transport on the tarmac, he attacked and destroyed it with his rockets. Pulling out of the dive, he noticed a Starfighter and three Sabres on the operational readiness platform and immediately broke radio silence to inform the second formation to attack them. However, light conditions were too bad for Satur to see the aircraft indicated by Taneja and they attacked other targets in the technical area, including hangers and circular aircraft pens with aircraft in them. One Starfighter on the ground was observed burning furiously and was claimed destroyed but no conclusive evidence was obtained.

GALLANTRY OVER SARGODHA:
DEVAYYA'S STARFIGHTER

As Taneja pulled out of the single pass and turned back for base, Squadron Leader Devayya, the reserve pilot, joined him. Devayya had tagged along in between the first two aircraft and the second formation of four, and on pulling out joined up with Taneja, whose wingman 'Frisky' Verma lost sight of his leader during the pull-out due to the poor light. He joined up with Satur's formation on his exit from Sargodha. The Mysteres then hit the deck to head for home.

One of the first PAF fighters on the scene was a F 104 Starfighter flown by Flight Lieutenant Amjad Hussain Khan of 9 Squadron. Armed with two Sidewinders, he was looking for easy pickings. Khan had missed action the previous day, when his leader Aftab Alam Khan had attacked the Mysteres at Rahwali. Now flying against the same squadron, the first targets he spotted were two Mysteres flying in a south-easterly direction, about 6-8 miles from Sargodha. The Mysteres were at around 200 ft, skimming over the treetops. He chose the last aircraft in the formation, Devayya's, and followed it down.

The action was short but seemingly decisive, Hussain got behind the Mystere and let loose his Sidewinders. Both missed Devayya's Mystere and flew straight into the ground. Hussain then closed in on the Mystere, using his afterburner and let loose with his six barrelled Vulcan cannon and was delighted to see the shells hit the Mystere. Convinced that the stricken aircraft was doomed, Hussain broke off to search for the second Mystere in the vicinity.

Plate 28: Squadron Leader A.B. Devayya of 1 Squadron created history on 7 September, when he shot down a F 104 Starfighter during a mismatched, brave and ultimately fatal encounter.

But Devayya had survived the attack and his aircraft was still flyable. He could either fly back home or eject if things worsened with the aircraft. A third option was to fight it out. But Sargodha was at the extreme range of the Mysteres and no allowance was available for air combat manoeuvres. Even simple evasive manoeuvres would guzzle up valuable fuel. Even on the raid, there had been no tactical routing to avoid hotspots. This lack of fuel had limited the attackers to just one single pass over the airfield. Devayya was faced with an unenviable choice. He could face the Starfighter head on and fight it out, in which case, even if he survived, he would have no fuel to fly back across the border. Or, he could just fly on hoping to evade the pursuing Starfighter. But Devayya, 'an unusual type of character, one of those Second World War types', unsurprisingly chose to stand and fight.

Seeing Devayya's Mystere coming to take on his F 104, Hussain turned around to take it out. He used his superior climb and acceleration to outrun the aircraft and then turned to come back. However, Devayya still stuck with the Starfighter and Hussain reduced his speed in an attempt to out-turn the Mystere. Although it possessed the speed to out-fly anything in the subcontinent, the Starfighter had the behavioural characteristics of a brick when dogfighting. Seeing his chance, Devayya closed in and opened fire with his DEFA cannon. The

Plate 29: Flight Lieutenant Amjad Hussain Khan PAF with a F 104 Starfighter before the war.

Starfighter was in a steep turn, just a couple of hundred feet above ground level, as the turning Mystere shot away its controls. Hussain, who found his controls frozen and his aircraft still turning into the ground, lost no time in pulling the ejection handle and punching out of the stricken Starfighter. The parachute deployed just before he hit the ground; later, he safely made his way back to Sargodha.[9] There was however, no sign of Devayya after the engagement.

Hussain never knew the pilot who shot him down. Devayya is believed to have perished when either his Mystere went out of control and crashed or during an unsuccessful ejection at low level. The SNCASO ejection seat of the Mystere did not possess the zero-zero capability of the Hunter's Martin Baker seat; and, at a low level, the seat's chute would have failed to deploy. Some mystery remains though. If Devayya was conscious enough to shoot down Hussain, why he did not survive? Was he wounded, or did the damaged Mystere lose control so fast that he could not react adequately? Hussain claimed one Mystere destroyed and reported being shot down in combat by a second Mystere, the version for years to come.[10]

The remaining Mysteres, oblivious of the dogfight that had taken place, flew back to Adampur. Taneja expected Devayya to return at any moment and headed for debriefing. The squadron thought Devayya had gone to 32 Squadron to hand over their aircraft and were blissfully unaware of the action that had taken place. Only later did it occur to Taneja that Devayya was missing. He only knew that he had a Mystere on his tail as they exited out of Sargodha. And, 'there was this flash, like the sun reflecting off water, which could have been a missile hitting the ground', as he lost contact after an undecipherable radio call about an aircraft in the vicinity. Devayya was listed missing in action even as hope persisted that he had baled out and been taken prisoner of war. Devayya's exceptional act of gallantry would remain unknown to the world for years to come.

As 1 Squadron was attacking Sargodha, 8 Squadron attacked Bhagtanwala airfield (in equally bad light) with eight aircraft.[11] 'Jimmy' Bhatia takes up the tale:

On the 7th we launched the first counter-air-strike. The RAF had had this policy of clustering airfields and that was the case at Sargodha. As per intel, the aircraft were dispersed all over the fields. So we were to launch an 8 AC [aircraft] strike at Bhagtanwala two formations of 4 AC each, launch at early AM, regroup and then carry on. The route took us close to Amritsar. Salins led the second formation. We flew so close to Amritsar that we got fired on by our own AA. We saw the shells coming up around us. It was almost dark when we took off, in the predawn period. Anyway, as the black puffs appeared around us, one pilot in the formation thought it was a Sabre and called out a Bogey! In fact, as more shells exploded, he called out multiple bogies. Mickey called out on the RT 'Shut up and get down'. Actually, we used to frequently get fired on by Adampur AA! A Sabre then crossed us on top at higher level, and we reported it. It was a sitting duck had we decided to take it out. He didn't sight us though. He was more visible—we were at 300 ft, but we did not want to break off our strike. We found some AC on the field when we got there and made 2 attacks but I don't know what the status was, whether they were decoys or not.

Squadron Leader M.S. 'Mickey' Jatar led the raid with his 'Black' formation. Squadron Leader Godfrey Salins led the second formation. Bhagtanwala was not a regular staging airbase of the PAF but an emergency airfield. Intelligence reports had indicated that that morning, two Sabres, short of fuel after returning from combat air patrol had landed at Bhagtanwala. Jatar noticed Sabres being readied on the operational readiness platform and led his section to attack them, strafing and firing rockets at his targets. One of the Sabres was destroyed, while another was claimed damaged.[12] However, it is not clear whether the targets attacked were decoys. No damage assessment was available. The rest of the formation also carried out rocket runs and strafing on the airstrip. The Mysteres made their exit as usual, flying at 100 to 200 ft on the return trip.

THE SECOND WAVE: FLAMING ARROWS
AND BATTLEAXES

The next raid on Sargodha was originally planned for 0615 hours. The PAF records the raid occurring at 0547 hours local time, about 10 minutes after the Mysteres departed. The

THE SARGODHA RAIDS AND THE AIR BATTLES

Hunters on this raid were from Halwara. 27 Squadron was assigned the task of attacking Chota Sargodha, 20 minutes after the first raid by the Mysteres.[13]

Even as preparations were underway for the attack, a B 57 came over Halwara at 0430 hours for a bombing run; little damage was done to either the runway or the dispersal area. This raid by the B 57 did cause a slight delay in the time over target of the planned raids by both the Hunter squadrons at Halwara. Since air defense fighters would have been alerted by the first raid, it was decided to send four Hunters armed with rockets and bombs in ground attack configuration, escorted by two Hunters armed with front gun ammunition and carrying extra drop tanks for additional endurance. But as the formations prepared for take-off, a Hunter from the escort detail failed to start-up. As it was too late to detail another aircraft, only one Hunter, piloted by Flight Lieutenant D.N. Rathore, fresh from a Sabre kill the previous day, took off in the fighter role. Squadron Leader D.S. Jog led the ground attack aircraft, with Squadron Leader O.N. 'Piloo' Kacker, Flight Lieutenant T.K. Chaudhuri and Flying Officer P.S. Parihar as his wingmen.

Pulling up at their target, the formation found no aircraft on the tarmac. They flew on to find another airfield, this time with Sabres parked on the runway. Rathore dove into the first attack and opened up with his guns. His high-speed approach[14] caused him to overshoot the airfield; the result of the attack was not clear, as light conditions were still poor. Rathore cursed profusely as he hauled his Hunter in a steep turn back towards the airfield, where he found the others attacking a factory-like installation. The AA was already alerted and opened up on the attackers. Then, 'all hell broke loose'. A couple of Sabres on combat air patrol pounced on the Hunters.

A Sabre dove from above and around Rathore's starboard side, opening fire on Chaudhuri's Hunter. Rathore turned towards the Sabre, which broke off the attack and turned into Rathore's path. Both aircraft crossed each other's path, narrowly avoiding a collision in mid air. Another Sabre got on to Rathore's tail and was shaken off. Jog's Hunter received hits from another Sabre. As suddenly as the air battle started, it ended. The Sabres disappeared, and the Hunters found themselves alone in the sky.

Jog was relieved to find all four Hunters still present. Rathore joined them after shaking off his pursuer and noticed Kacker losing speed. The other aircraft reduced their speed to maintain formation with Kacker. Sabres or AA fire had hit Kacker's fuel tanks, resulting in severe loss of fuel. It could also have been a notorious problem with the Hunter's fuel transfer system. A glance at the fuel indicators told Kacker that there was no chance of making it over the border. Then the fuel ran out, turning on the warning lights. As the fuel starved engine flamed out, Kacker knew he had to eject. As the Hunter's nose dropped, Kacker pulled the ejection handle and floated down on his parachute, but not before the R/T was thick with the choicest Punjabi expletives being thrown around by Kacker about his fate and that of his aircraft!

Kacker came down near the now-abandoned village of Burjlal, by the bank of Chenab River, about 25 miles southeast of Sargodha. Gathering his wits, he quickly got rid of his map, his log card and the badges on his flying coveralls. As local villagers rushed towards him, Kacker, thanks to a childhood spent in the Punjab and the Frontier Provinces, introduced himself as a PAF pilot in fluent, rustic Punjabi. The village folk, who had never seen a fighter pilot for real, were deceived. An instant hero, Kacker became the centre of adulation and cleverly demanded arrangements for a horse-ride to the highway so that he could flag a bus for his 'home base', Sargodha. Kacker almost made a getaway but for the arrival of a villager, Midas Hussain Shah, who had seen him bale out. As Kacker continued to captivate the villagers, Shah ended the party by accusing him of being an IAF pilot and having him tied up. A few hours later a search party from Lalian Police Station saved Kacker from an angry crowd. Kacker spent the next five months as a prisoner of war.[15]

The four remaining aircraft of the formation flew off, but were jolted when five Hunters passed them at great velocity, proceeding towards Sargodha. Jog was alarmed.[16] The Hunters were not from his squadron and would fly straight into the prowling Sabres. Jog could not warn them as their R/T was on a different frequency. The four Hunters landed back at base with very little fuel left. Chaudhuri had had a narrow escape as his drop tanks were holed severely. Jog's questions about the five Hunters, which had passed them on the way out, were answered when he saw three of them come into land.

The three Hunters were from the mission by 7 Squadron, which had followed right on the heels of 27 Squadron's strike. The CO, Wing Commander 'Toric' Zachariah led the strike. Initially the formation had Squadron Leader A.S. Lamba as No. 2 for Zachariah. Another sub-section consisted of Squadron Leader M.M. Sinha and Flight Lieutenant S.K. Sharma as the strike component, with escort provided by Squadron Leader S.B. Bhagwat and Flying Officer J.S. Brar. All the strike aircraft were equipped with two 100-gallon drop tanks and T-10 rockets. Zachariah had been shown a 1958 vintage photo of Sargodha Main to acquaint him with target environs, but had found the picture of limited intelligence value.

This strike too had had a delayed take-off due to the PAF B 57 coming over Halwara and dropping some thousand-pound bombs just before the morning briefing. The ground crew was working on arming the aircraft in pitch dark, aided only by the light from Pilot Officer Kondaiah's Vespa scooter. The loading of the aircraft was carried out before the all-clear was sounded. As soon as the arming was done, Kondaiah had called on the assigned pilots before he retired to the mess for sleep. As he knocked on Squadron Leader Bhagwat's door, Kondiah expected a groggy, underslept pilot to respond, but to his surprise, Bhagwat promptly opened the door in full flying gear. 'I am ready,' said Bhagwat. The anticipation of the potentially dangerous strike had made early risers out of the pilots.

The aircraft took off on schedule: four aircraft in ground attack configuration, with Bhagwat and Brar carrying drop tanks but no rockets. When the formation took off, S.K. Sharma fell back when the elevators on his aircraft went into manual. Zachariah proceeded with five Hunters.

Halfway through the flight across Pakistani territory, Lamba observed three fighters at 11 o'clock, above at 4,000 ft altitude. Lamba alerted Zach over the R/T about the jets, now identified as Sabres. As standing orders were not to engage fighters when laden with ordnance, Zachariah put the formation into a hard turn to port. As Lamba followed Zachariah in his turn, he could see Bhagwat and Brar on his left too go into the turn, as did 'Rusty' Sinha to his right. Halfway through the turn, Zachariah fired his rockets into the grounds and punched his drop tanks, followed by Lamba and the rest of the formation. One of Lamba's drop tanks refused to jettison. In spite of the asymmetric handling he followed Zachariah down to ground level. Lamba called out to Zach to find out whether they were headed for home, but received no response over the R/T.

As Zachariah and Lamba completed the 180 degree turn to head for Indian airspace, Lamba was horrified to see Bhagwat and Brar continuing their turn beyond 180 degrees, straight back into Pakistani airspace. Lamba called out on the R/T: 'Straighten out, we are heading home!' but received no acknowledgement. When he saw them last, both Hunters were continuing with the turn that would have led them to engage the Sabres head-on. Both Zach and Lamba lost sight of Sinha, who was also in the turn at the beginning. Zachariah now led Lamba's Hunter back to base, skimming over Pakistani territory at low-level. On the return they flew over Chak Jhumra airfield,

Plate 30: Squadron Leader S.B. Bhagwat went missing with his wingman Flying Officer J.S. 'Lil Ben' Brar on the morning of 7 September, near Sargodha.

and noticed several aircraft on the ground but low on fuel, with no drop tanks and Sabres in pursuit, they carried on. When both reached Halwara, Sinha had landed ahead of them. However there was no sign of either Bhagwat or Brar.[17]

Bhagwat and Brar had engaged the Sabres and were shot down near Sangli Hill. PAF Squadron Leader M.M. Alam was credited with shooting down both the Hunters. This ended the disappointing raids by the Hunters; in ten sorties, they had lost three Hunters to AA and prowling Sabres. The anticipated success of the first raid seems to have played a part in the unwise decision to send the second mission so soon on its heels. Indeed, 27 Squadron seems to have attacked the wrong target. They hit Wagowal instead of Chota Sargodha, a fact confirmed by Rathore's photo-recce pictures. Zachariah reported on aircraft observed at Chak Jhumra to command HQ, so that a raid could be planned to hit them. However nothing was done to follow up on this valuable piece of information.

THE THIRD WAVE: THE TIGERS RETURN

Back at the Mysteres base at Adampur, Taneja was miffed on learning that the last formation of the morning raid, led by Squadron Leader S. Handa, had returned after failing to hit the initial waypoint. A testy Taneja was mystified by the navigational failure of Handa's formation, when the reserve pilot Devayya could take-off after them and still push through to complete the mission. Taneja gave an unprecedented order. Since the 'White' formation had returned with their ordnance stores intact, he ordered them to refuel and carry out the attack on Sargodha in *broad daylight*. Without flinching, Handa accepted this order with gusto. A daylight raid went against the existing doctrine of carrying out only dawn or dusk raids. Since the PAF did not expect a daylight attack, it worked out in favour of the daylight raiders.

The outer belt of PAF ground observers first reported four Mysteres flying at low level at about 1010 hours. The PAF scrambled several Sabres and a Starfighter and held them in a circuit east of Sargodha, in an attempt to intercept the incoming formation. Much to the surprise of the Pakistanis, the four Mysteres slipped through the patrolling fighters undetected and arrived over the air base, firing their cannons. The Mysteres were loaded with two thousand-pound bombs and front gun ammunition. Handa dropped his bombs on a bulk petroleum installation and, noticing three Sabres on the operational readiness platform, pulled up to strafe them. He succeeded in destroying one of them with cannon fire and damaged the other two. His wingman Flight Lieutenant D.S. Brar aimed for a Starfighter on the operational readiness platform, but his bombs refused to detach from the hard points. Cursing, he jettisoned them over some aircraft hangers.

The second subsection leader Flight Lieutenant D.M.S. Kahai didn't suffer from Brar's gremlins. His bombs found their mark on a bulk petroleum installation, near a couple of Sabres, on the operational readiness platform. In the same run, Kahai noticed two other Sabres and an F 104 on the tarmac. Having expended all his bombs, he readied himself to let loose a strafing salvo with his cannon, but hesitated when he saw ground crew milling around the aircraft. Kahai muttered, 'Run, you bastards run', before firing off his salvo on the three aircraft. Fortunately for them, the PAF airmen did scamper for cover. His wingman, Flying Officer Philip Rajkumar, attacked other aircraft on operational readiness platform and an ATC building. By the time Sabres on combat air patrol were vectored to intercept the Mysteres, all four aircraft had exited at low-level. Handa called to find out if all the members were okay, which was confirmed by the tail-end Charlie, Rajkumar. The Mysteres flew on at full engine power and barely outran the chasing Sabres, landing on their last fuel reserves at Adampur.[18]

This raid was the most successful of the day and was estimated to have destroyed or damaged over seven PAF aircraft. Handa received the VrC five days later for this successful attack. Kahai was awarded the VrC after the war.

After the success of the daylight raid, the Tigers tried a repeat by conducting another, the last, on Sargodha at 1520 hours. Four Mysteres comprising the 'White' formation were tasked for the raid. However, the leader's aircraft developed fuel transfer problems and he returned to base along with his No. 2. The remaining two, Flight Lieutenant J.P. Singh (as leader), on his second raid of the day over Sargodha, and Flight Lieutenant U.B. 'Babul' Guha carried on to complete the strike.[19]

The formation proceeded without any tactical routing for its target. As Singh was pulling up for the attack, Guha reported 'Bogeys' and called for 'Buster'. Singh completed his attack on an enemy missile dump, then jettisoned his rocket pods and hit the deck for the return leg home. Singh noticed that Guha had done the same but was trailing by nearly 800 yds. Further back at 1,500 yds, he saw two F 86 Sabres on chase.

Flight Lieutenant A.H. Malik and Flying Officer Khalid Iqbal were flying the Sabres. Earlier in the morning, Malik had had a narrow escape from being caught in the strafing done by Handa's formation and had been a witness to his Sabre going

Plate 31: Squadron Leader Sudarshan Handa, in full combat flight gear poses with his Mystere IVa. Handa led the most successful raid on PAF base Sargodha on 7 September.

up in flames on the operational readiness platform. Malik targeted Guha's Mystere, obtained lock-on, and shot it down with a Sidewinder missile. A second missile was fired at the Mystere leader, but Singh escaped without damage. Singh never saw Guha's aircraft go down, but he knew something was wrong as soon as he lost radio contact with him. No ejection was reported. Guha's was the first aircraft lost to an air-to-air missile in the 1965 air war and was the first and only Mystere to be lost in spite of the low-level tactics adopted by the squadron.

This brought the IAF offensive on Sargodha to a close. 31 sorties were flown from dawn to dusk, with a loss of five aircraft and five pilots: an attrition rate of almost 20 per cent. The counter air offensive sorties had been very expensive in terms of men and machines. The unsuitability of the machines for the mission was due to their small range, which precluded tactical routing. All the aircraft fell in air combat, not to ground fire, which suggested the constraints the aircraft suffered in an attacking role. The IAF claimed 15 aircraft destroyed or damaged on the ground. Claims for 3 F 104s, 2 C 130s and half a dozen Sabres were made. The PAF admits the loss of the Starfighter in the air and one Sabre on the ground. A conservative estimate would be that it lost about six aircraft in the air and on the ground. Despite the bravery of the strike pilots, the results of the raids did not justify their cost. Subsequently, most IAF claims were scaled down. 1 Squadron was credited with one Sabre and one C 130 confirmed destroyed on the ground, and 6-8 other aircraft probably destroyed on the ground. Since almost all the raids involved a single pass over the airfield, the results could not be clearly observed or confirmed by other pilots.[20] The fuel constraints forced many anxious moments for the 'Tail-End Charlies'—the 10 minute fuel warning light often lit up with them still some distance away from base.

The PAF claims four Indian losses in the first strike. However, there were two strikes, from two different squadrons, Nos. 1 and 8, which the PAF thought were one. The PAF also thought that the two raids by Hunters of 7 and 27 were one raid. In this mission, the PAF claims five IAF Hunters, all supposedly shot down by Squadron Leader M.M. Alam. This was an incredible claim, which was comprehensively debunked later. In the fourth strike, the PAF and IAF agree that none of the attacking aircraft were downed. In the fifth and final strike, the PAF and the IAF agree on the fact that one Mystere was lost, shot down by Flight Lieutenant Malik.

RAID ON CHANDER AND RAHWALI

It was not just the Mysteres from Adampur that saw action on 7 September. Mysteres from Pathankot also participated in retaliatory strikes against PAF airfields.

That morning, shortly after he had completed a morning combat air patrol, Flight Lieutenant C.S. 'Doru' Doraiswami of 3 Squadron was called into the briefing room. The other pilots of 3 Squadron had already assembled. The Station Commander, Group Captain Roshan Suri, came in to brief them on Pathankot's reply to the previous day's air raids.

The targets to be attacked were airfields at Chander and Rahwali (near Gujranwala). A four-aircraft formation was detailed, to be led by Squadron Leader Jasbeer 'Jessie' Singh and including Flight Lieutenants B.R. 'Boman' Irani, Tirlochan 'Tango' Singh and Doraiswami. The Mysteres would carry drop tanks and two rocket pods with thirty-eight 57 mm SNEB rockets. Their task was to attack targets at Chander airfield, using SNEBs, and to then continue to Rahwali airfield to strafe aircraft or other targets, such as ammo dumps, suitable for 30 mm DEFA cannon. The pilots were surprised that two airfields were to be targeted by a single formation. The Mysteres would have been operating at their extreme range and would have no fuel reserves left. There would be no allowance for air combat, as fuel would be just about sufficient to carry out the attack on the two airfields. There was also the possibility that once the first target Chander was attacked, Rahwali would be alerted, with Sabres lying in wait, an unappetizing prospect. Intelligence reports on these airfields turned out to be poor.

Since the Gnats did not have the range to provide escort to the Mysteres over the two airfields, 'Tango' suggested that two Gnat aircraft be sent to establish a combat air patrol over the second target, to coincide with the time over target of the Mysteres over Rahwali. This suggestion was ruled out as it was felt that the Gnats would show up on Pakistani air defense radar and invite participation from the Sabres. Doraiswami suggested that two more Mysteres, configured in air defense mode with only drop tanks and guns, accompany the formation. The escorting Mysteres would trail in broad frontage formation, about a kilometer behind the attack formation, and pull up before the main formation to set up a combat air patrol over the airfield while the rest of the formation carried out the attacks. The escorts would join up with the strike Mysteres as they moved on to the next target, where a similar procedure would be carried out. Suri ruled this out as well.

The briefing over, the strike formation of four Mysteres took off with Squadron Leader Jasbeer 'Jessie' Singh leading the strike. A keen senior pilot and QFI, Jasbeer was respected for his character, demeanour[21] and that ineffable quality so beloved of all warriors, *josh* (gusto). Flying as his No. 2 was Flight Lieutenant Boman Irani who, earlier in his career, had had the unique experience of successfully landing a Vampire 2-seater solo, after his instructor had ejected out in an uncontrollable spin. Apparently, the force of the ejection had steadied the aircraft out of its spin and Irani, then a young pilot officer, was able to land the Vampire without its canopy and the right side pilot's seat, much to the chagrin of the instructor.

The formation's No. 3 'Tango' Singh had to drop out soon after getting airborne, as his aircraft's undercarriage did not fully retract. Doraiswami now moved up to take the No. 3 position. He informed Jasbeer that he would be busy keeping a watch on the tail of the formation and would not be able to help with map reading, normally the No. 3's task.

The three Mysteres flew in line abreast formation over a broad frontage of 1.2 km, with Singh slightly ahead. As the Mysteres crossed a canal that was to mark the pull-up point near the first target, the aircraft pulled up to 4,500 ft and spotted Chander airfield. Much to their surprise, instead of the hustle and bustle of a busy airfield, they could see no activity at all. The airbase was not operational and was completely deserted. After doing one orbit over the airfield, Jasbeer called on the others to follow him to the second target—Rahwali airfield.

The Indian pilots followed the railway line from Chander to Rahwali and pulled up over the outskirts of Gujranwala town. They then followed the road to Rahwali and, on arriving over the airfield, faced the same dismal sight that greeted them at the earlier target. Rahwali was also a non-operational airstrip and there was no activity at all on the airfield. As the aircraft orbited over Rahwali, Singh noticed the tell-tale sign of a rotating antenna at the far end of a runway at Rahwali. It was the same radar unit that was witness to the previous day's early morning encounter between Aftab Alam Khan's Starfighter and Paddy Earle's Mystere.

Singh signalled his attack on the radar unit over the R/T. Though Irani and 'Doru' could not see the radar, they followed. Singh's rockets were on target. The radar disappeared in a cloud of dust and debris. Irani, who also placed his rockets accurately on the target, immediately followed him. As he pulled up, he could clearly see the radar vehicle with its antenna in the early warning station. Doraiswami put his Mystere in a dive, picking up the target amidst a cloud of dust and smoke from the previous aircraft's rockets. The salvo of SNEB rockets hit the target right on the radar vehicle, as Doraiswami pulled out from the dive and made a 180-degree turn back to base. He could see that the target area was now engulfed in fire and smoke and no sign of the radar antenna could be picked up.

At some stage before the attack on the radar had commenced, Jasbeer Singh had called out 'Bogey'. Both Doraiswami and Irani scanned the skies, found no sign of Sabres and replied on the R/T that their tail was clear. After pulling out from the raid and heading towards Pathankot, the Mysteres jettisoned their empty drop tanks and began forming up. The Mysteres were now flying at low level at around 570 knots. As they were forming up for the homeward bound trip, Singh again called out a 'bogey' on his tail.

Doraiswami was almost abreast of Jasbeer Singh, at about 1.2 to 1.5 km, and Boman Irani had got into position about 250 m behind Singh. Responding to his call on the bogey, Doraiswami radioed back that his tail was clear—a call that was reconfirmed by Irani. The Mysteres were flying at tree-top level, around 50 ft above ground level. Singh was flying even lower at around 30 ft off the ground. Still concerned about enemy aircraft that might be chasing their formation, Singh was banking and weaving once in a while and checking his tail. Weaving at such a low altitude and constantly checking one's tail was a dangerous exercise. Three minutes into the return flight, as Singh banked left to check his tail, his left wing touched the ground and the Mystere cartwheeled into the ground and exploded in a huge fireball. Doru and Boman were stunned. A quick check behind each other's aircraft confirmed that there were no Sabres in the vicinity. Both pilots pulled up to a safe height on crossing the border and landed back at Pathankot.

It was at the mission debriefing that they realized that Singh had probably mistaken one of the Mysteres as an enemy aircraft before the attack. Preoccupied with keeping his tail clear, he mistook one of the Mysteres for a PAF aircraft. Jasbeer Singh's absence was felt deeply in 3 Squadron. As Squadron Leader J.F. Josephs put it, 'He was a nice solid guy, good to have around at any time'; Doru's praise was simpler, 'he was a brave pilot'.

THE PAF RAIDS

The PAF too flew offensive raids on 7 September, mainly attacking targets in eastern and northern India. Attacking the main airbases at Halwara, Ambala, and Adampur was too risky. It attacked Amritsar, the base for the IAF 230 Signals Unit, for the first time. Codenamed 'Fish Oil' by the PAF, this unit was showered with considerable attention throughout the war (details of which will be provided in a later chapter).

Another target picked by the PAF was Srinagar, a transit base for flights to Leh. According to the UN ceasefire treaty of 1948, India was not allowed to station jet fighters in this part of Kashmir. Though a Gnat had carried out some trials in Leh the previous year, no jet fighters were based in Kashmir. Air defense of the Srinagar field was entrusted to ack-ack guns and there was little early warning available. No radar coverage was available, which even if provided would have been of limited use in the mountainous terrain. The airfield lay bare for attack.

Squadron Leader S.S. Haider led the PAF raid at 1600 hours.[22] After his earlier successful raid on Pathankot, Haider chose Srinagar, as it was the only airfield within range of his Sabres from Peshawar. As usual, no warning was available to the defenses until the Sabres were almost overhead. Haider

THE SARGODHA RAIDS AND THE AIR BATTLES 147

and his wingman attacked two Dakotas parked near the ATC. Both aircraft had to be written off. The other two Sabres strafed and thoroughly shot up a Caribou parked on the apron ahead of the terminal. A Sabre hit and damaged by the AA was trailing flames as all four Sabres disappeared over the mountains, heading back for home. It seemed unlikely that the damaged Sabre would make it back to the air in the near future.

The raid netted the Pakistanis three aircraft destroyed on the ground, one of which belonged to the IAF. One of the Dakotas belonged to the civilian Indian Airlines Corporation. The Caribou belonged to the Royal Canadian Air Force contingent of the United Nations Military Observer Group in India and Pakistan (UNMOGIP). Its chief, Lieutenant General R.H. Nimmo, an Australian, who had flown into Srinagar in the Caribou in August, was now stranded in Kashmir for the rest of the war.

Despite these attacks, no fighters were moved to Srinagar for the rest of the war. In 1948, the airfield had been the only operational supply line through the year, as the Banihal pass is blocked during the winter. But in 1965, the Jawahar Tunnel was already open and a dependable road line was available even if the airfield was knocked out. No air support was given to the army in this sector; Srinagar received further attacks later in the war. In spite of the provocation, no jets were moved to the airfield for protection duties.

Meanwhile on the ground, 1st Corps, whose offensive in the Sialkot sector was supposed to start on 8 September, was building up in the Samba area. Armoured units and tanks were transported along the Grant Trunk Road and soon attracted the attention of the PAF. The PAF vainly attacked Beas Bridge hoping that its destruction would delay the buildup of Indian forces. No damage was done.

7 Squadron's Hunters, flown by Lamba and Dandass, flew further close support missions in the Kasur area.[23] The flight commander Squadron Leader S.S. Malik carried out a successful strike against the Suleimanke headworks in a four-aircraft strike. On another lone mission to locate some missing IAF Dakotas near Batala, Flight Lieutenant 'Dice' Dhiman

stumbled into a PAF formation of four Sabres and a Starfighter. After some anxious moments and evasive manoeuvres, Dhiman managed to fly back to Halwara and land back on fumes.

The IAF had lost seven aircraft in the air, all but one in the attack on Sargodha, plus another aircraft in the raid on Srinagar. The IAF could not have sustained this rate of attrition. However, it could draw consolation from the fact that, of the four raids on Sargodha Main, it had achieved complete surprise twice without its aircraft being intercepted. Much needed to be done in terms of making the raids truly effective. The Mystere was definitely not the aircraft to carry out long-range strikes, as its endurance limited it to a solitary pass over the target. The effort of flying to the target and achieving complete surprise was wasted as the attacking aircraft could not loiter around over the target long enough to clearly identify targets and hit them.

Thus ended the IAF strikes for 7 September. Six strikes were launched, during which five aircraft were lost. The PAF claims ten aircraft shot down, which is reason enough to celebrate 7 September as PAF Day. But claiming five aircraft over the course of six raids, on a heavily defended airfield, is hardly reason for celebration on part of the defenders. The PAF did not deal a crippling blow to the IAF, as the Israelis did to the Arab Air Forces in 1967. The damage done was miniscule compared to the size of the IAF. Indian losses over Sargodha were perhaps magnified and blown out of proportion, to justify the claim that the PAF was saving Pakistan itself.

7 September marked the end of the doctrine of daylight, dusk and dawn raids on airfields by the IAF and the PAF. Neither airforce could sustain the attrition they had suffered. Thereafter, no raid took place in the western sector against the airfields of the opposing side. The eastern sector saw plenty of air combat on this day, including a classic airbattle that makes a strong case for the IAF calling 7 September IAF day as well; that story is covered in another chapter. In the south-western sector, there was air action on 7 September, preceded by a skirmish or two of a slightly different nature, involving the Naval Air Arm as well.

THE ANTONOV 12 EXPERIMENT

Unknown to most scholars of the 1965 air war was IAF's innovative attempt to try and use Antonov (An) 12s, the star acquisition for the IAF's transport fleet in the 1960s, as bombers. The An 12 was the Russian equivalent of the C 130 Hercules. Powered with four turboprop engines, the An 12s made it possible for the IAF to maintain a continuous lifeline to Ladakh and the Kashmir Valley. Depending on the airfield and terrain, their cargo payloads ranged from 9 to 20 tons.

Inducted in 1963, the An 12s equipped two squadrons, 25 and 44, both based at Chandigarh, a major transport base and staging ground for all supply runs to the northern sector and Ladakh. Chandigarh's station commander was Group Captain T.N. Ghadiok VrC, ex-CO of 44 Squadron during the 1962 war.

Plate 32: The Antonov 12 over the Himalayas.

On the evening of 4 September, Wing Commander R.A. 'Reggie' Rufus KC, CO of 25 Squadron was at his residential quarters in Sector 8 (Chandigarh city), when he received a phone call from Wing Commander P.S. Michael. He informed Rufus that full-scale hostilities had erupted and advised him to return to his airfield as quickly as possible. Rufus returned by jeep and met Ghadiok, who informed him that all An 12s at Chandigarh had to be moved out of harms way. Ghadiok gave orders to both 25 and 44 Squadron to refuel and fly to other bases, out of reach of the PAF.

The first squadron to move out was No. 44, led by Wing Commander T.L. Anderson VrC, SC. By that time, Air Commodore Gocal had decided that the An 12s should move to Kanpur. The weather had started to close in on central India and it would be too late if the move was delayed. As No. 44's aircraft were taxiing out, Ghadiok told Rufus to stay back. He needed Rufus' help in airtesting six of the An 12s that were being returned to serviceable status. While Rufus stayed back, the remaining An 12s from 25 Squadron flew to Kanpur. Early next morning, 25 Squadron's An 12s, led by Squadron Leader Sen, took off and made their way to the IAF base at Nagpur, then commanded by Air Commodore Moolgavkar. Joining them were two An 12s that flew direct from Chandigarh, flown by two pilots with no instrument rating. The two pilots flew under cloud cover to make the hazardous flight, in spite of the protestations by Group Captain Purushottam, the ops in-charge, to call them back to Chandigarh.

On 5 September, Rufus flew a sortie to Poona to pick up some artillery guns and flew them back to Chandigarh. As he landed and taxied to the apron, he sensed something was afoot. Group Captain Ghadiok's station wagon was waiting for him. Ghadiok greeted him and dropped a bombshell. Rufus had been selected for a 'special mission': to lead a formation of five An 12s in a bombing raid into Pakistan. This was unheard of in An 12 circles. Rufus agreed, suggesting that the other four pilots be split between 25 and 44 Squadrons.

Sure enough, soon two pilots from 25 Squadron, Squadron Leaders Bal Krishna Desoares KC, and B.K. Singha joined him. Squadron Leaders P.K. Datta and Douglas Augier arrived from 44 Squadron. All the pilots were experienced multi-engine pilots. Rufus was a Kirti Chakra awardee, well known for his single engine landing of an Il 14 carrying the then Prime Minister Nehru a few years ago; Desoares had been awarded his KC for rescuing a comrade after his Dakota crashed at 18,000 ft altitude at Rhimkhim. Singha had been a Dakota pilot earlier; Naga insurgents had shot down his aircraft during a supply drop at Purr. He spent about a year as a prisoner of the Nagas before being released. Datta was the pilot chosen to fly the Dalai Lama to Delhi after he crossed over to India. 'Dinky'

THE SARGODHA RAIDS AND THE AIR BATTLES

Augier had started as a Liberator pilot and had flown the radar equipped 'Nosey' Dakota with no. 10 Squadron, before moving on to the Antonovs.

Unknown to Rufus, although almost all the pilots had no prior experience in dropping bombs in the An 12, Augier had carried out secret trials earlier in the year where An 12s dropped bombs at the Tilpat range. Secrecy at that time of the trials was so tight that even Rufus was left in the dark about them.

Squadron Leader Augier narrates the events leading up to the trials and the formation of the 'elite' transport bombers:

The use of the An 12 in the bombing role was conceived by Group Captain Surinder Singh (affectionately known as Susu), Director of Operations in the then Western Air Command. In May 1965 he asked for a pilot from 44 Squadron, with bombing experience to do some trials at Tilpat.

Although there were pilots who had done bombing on Liberators, they all found reasons not to go and sent me, who had not done a single bomb drop. I flew to Palam on the 14th May and did a familiarization fly over Tilpat range. On the 20th May, I did 2 drops of 8 x 500 lbs. bombs. The bombs were put on cast iron cradles, specifically made to fit the four moving transporter rails on which loads were normally carried for supply drops. For normal supply drops, the axle, which connected the four transporter rails to ensure that they moved together, was removed, as it was found the axle slowed down the release of the load.

However, for the first bombing trial they replaced axle on the transporters to ensure stability and the pin, which defused the bomb, was linked by a thin rope to wires, which ran along the insides of the aircraft loading bay. The first briefing we were asked to do the drop from about 1 km but our drops were usually carried out much lower. Group Captain Surinder Singh agreed to the lower drop.

On the first drop the axle on the transporters were holding up the bombs and I thought the bombs would overshoot the target. There was no way in which to abort the drop once it had commenced, so I pulled up hard and the bombs fell out. I did a tight turn and looked down and there was a huge cloud of dust and I thought I had bombed Tilpat village. One can imagine the thoughts that raced through my mind at the time. I called up Surinder and asked him if everything was all right and he replied that we would talk about it at the debriefing. At the debriefing he said the many of the bombs had overshot the target.

We decided to stop using the axle on the transporters and let the bombs roll out by gravity for the next drop, which was uneventful. As dropping at Tilpat seemed to be dangerous, I recommended that we do further drops in a more suitable range.

In September 1965 the political situation had turned tense and all crews were asked to remain on 24 hours standby. I flew in ammunition and troops to Pathankot on the 1st and 3rd of September from Kanpur and Nagpur. I was surprised to see a few families watching the take-offs and landings from flying control the operations as a number of sorties were being flown to the sensitive areas on the border. I was anxious; I had an 8-ton load of ammunition, which was being unloaded and had there been a strike it would have been disastrous. After unloading we were then sent to Hindon and on the way the low fuel lights came on and we landed just as a heavy shower of rain came in from the opposite direction. As Hindon was short of fuel, or rather they wanted to preserve what they had, they gave us the minimum we needed to get back to Chandigarh.

On the evening 4th of September, all An 12 aircraft based in Chandigarh were ordered to go south. I was sent ahead to report on the weather conditions as a weather front was over Central India. It was dark when we took off and I remember the excessive R/T natter between Pakistan Airlines aircraft and Palam flying control and here we were broadcasting to the world that a large number of aircraft were heading south. I flew through the weather front and for the first and only time saw St. Elmo's fire dashing around the cockpit windshield. Group Captain Molokai who seemed to want to take over operations met us at the airfield. The next morning we were sent to Poona and took more troops to Pathankot via Chandigarh. We then flew to Pathankot again and back to Chandigarh.

On landing back at Chandigarh I was told that five crews had been selected to carry out a 'special operation' and I and my 'bombing crew' were one of them. We were to assemble in Kanpur and flew there that night. Before going I asked that the pilot's seats in the aircraft be refitted with the armour plating that was removed during day-to-day operations, to increase the payload. I cannot remember the exact weight but they were extremely heavy. The captains selected for the 'special task' were Wing Commander Reggie Rufus, Squadron Leader Singha (who along with Flt. Lt. Dicky Raphael now a dentist in Perth, was a guest of the Nagas for a number of years) Squadron Leader P.K. Datta and one whose name I cannot remember (possibly Squadron Leader Desoares) I got the impression that the captains and crew selected were not exactly blue-eyed boys in the scheme of things.

I could feel the unspoken tension among the crews that were assembled in Kanpur. I was the only person who had ever dropped bombs and knew the drill and so had to hastily brief the rest of the crews.

The crews had had less than a day's familiarization with the task on hand when, on the evening of 6 September, Rufus was ordered to take the five An 12s to Palam. Their mission to bomb targets in Pakistan was now very much 'on' and they would need to fly down to Palam to load up with bombs. But the take-off from Kanpur was delayed. By mistake two An 12s taxied to the opposite end of the runways and since they could neither take-off nor reverse, airmen had to push one of the aircraft out of the way. It was 2000 hours and valuable time had elapsed before airmen were rounded up for the onerous task of pushing the giant transports out of the way.

Before the An 12s could take-off, a MiG 21 landed at Chakeri. Out of the cockpit stepped Group Captain Dilbagh Singh, who had borrowed it from No. 28 Squadron at Ambala for a sortie to Palam. But because of the Pakistani raids on Pathankot, Halwara and Adampur, there was a red alert over Palam and the MiG was diverted to fly to Kanpur. Rufus came to know about the devastating Pathankot raid and subsequent attacks on Halwara and Adampur in conversation with Dilbagh Singh.

After some time, the 'Red Alert' was called off and two An 12s took off, one piloted by Rufus. However, both were told to return to Chakeri for some more time. Finally Rufus and his pilots moved their aircraft to Palam late in the night. At Palam, the loading bombs into the Antonovs was going to take time and Rufus was summoned for a meeting at Western Command Headquarters.

Rufus arrived at WAC's briefing room to find the AOC-in-C Rajaram, Gocal and Group Captain Purushottam huddled over a map, planning the attack by the An 12s. The target given to the transports was none other than the Sargodha complex. Though originally the entire mission was to be carried out in the darkness of night, the delayed arrival at Palam and the subsequent take-off would mean the Antonovs would be caught in emerging daylight during the return leg. Moreover, none of the five pilots had practised formation flying on these large aircraft during daylight, let alone fly them together during night. The debate continued for some time, before saner counsel prevailed. It was decided to cancel the sortie for that night and to do it later in the war.

As the discussions went on, Rufus had a conversation with 'Bomber Harris', Group Captain Surinder Singh himself. Singh, an enthusiastic proponent of using An 12s in a bombing role, asked Rufus about his opinion on the mission. Rufus had no qualms in suggesting that this was a 'suicide mission'. None of his team had practised formation flying by day; here they were being asked to do it at low level at night, in a hostile environment covered by AA guns and radar-equipped night fighters. To this, the Group Captain replied, 'Come on Reg! All this is a supply drop sortie'. Rufus declined to reply.

Finally, the AOC-in-C and his team decided to call off the strike, and to move the An 12 'bombers' out of harms way. Rufus suggested that the crew billet themselves under the aircraft wings and take-off in the morning. Gocal shot down the idea as he expected another 'Red Alert' over Palam the next morning. After much haggling, the WAC team decided to let Rufus decide on his destination. Rufus thought about it and then picked Hakimpet, near Hyderabad as his port of destination. Not only was Hakimpet well out of range of Pakistani bombers, but Rufus was on good terms with Group Captain P.V.S. Ram, the station commander. Rufus returned to his team and told them the news, which was greeted with much relief. Reggie Rufus candidly admits, 'We had made our peace with our maker. That's how scared I was.' Dinky Augier was to comment, 'I will admit it was an anxious time for me and one I would not like to go through again.'

The Antonovs then took off from Palam to head for Hakimpet in the dark. Dinky Augier continues:

As we set off for Hakimpet I decided that we would go low level for practice but after flying for about 10 minutes my navigator told me he was 'uncertain of his position'. I am quoting the words written on the navigation room of No. 1 Air Force Academy in Begumpet. 'Man is never lost, he is only uncertain of his position.'

THE SARGODHA RAIDS AND THE AIR BATTLES 155

We climbed and landed at Hakimpet in the early hours of the morning. The day after we landed in Hakimpet, Reggie Rufus flew back to Palam for a briefing. He was briefed that we should start training immediately and standby to be called up. Security was tight in Hakimpet. We got off the air crew bus and were heading for the aircraft when a sentry shouted, 'Halt who goes there? Password'. My reply was not exactly polite. Probably '"Surinder Singh" off'.

During our training we called in the local artillery and asked them about the radar controlled anti-aircraft L24s that Pakistan used. The officer replied that an An 12 shows up on the radar as a Squadron of Hunters. It was evident then that the tactical method would be to go in low and at night.

My logbook records that every night we did a low level cross country not above 500 ft for the next 7 nights and one day sortie of fighter affiliation. The first night we tried to go in formation at night!!! I will not forget that as we reached the first turning point I was almost looking inside Reggie Rufus' cockpit. At the debriefing after landing his navigator, whose name I remember but shall remain nameless, said that he had changed course a bit so that he would be on the correct heading for the next leg. I resisted the urge to strangle him on the spot. We stopped training about the 17th September, which must have been about the time that a ceasefire came into force.

During this time, the Antonovs carried out several sorties, some during the night, with the navigation lights turned off. Enough missions were flown that the local newspaper Deccan Chronicle termed them 'Pakistani bombers', sparking off a scare amongst the populace of Hyderabad and Secunderabad!

Thus ended the idea of using the Antonov 12s as bombers. Though no operational mission was flown during the war, the IAF's experience led to their highly successful use in that role during the 1971 war.[24]

THE 'WHITE TIGERS'

In spite of the events of August 1965, no measures had been undertaken to reinforce or establish better interception facilities in the southern sector. As war clouds gathered in August, the only fighters worth their name in Jamnagar were eight Sea Hawk fighters and a Vampire trainer of the Indian Navy's 300 'White Tigers' Squadron. Normally the Sea Hawks were either based at Dabolim (Goa) or onboard the INS *Vikrant*, the aircraft carrier. But as the *Vikrant* was undergoing her periodic maintenance refitting at the dock, the Sea Hawks were moved to Jamnagar for their armament training. The other squadron on board the *Vikrant*, 310 Squadron flying Alizes, was based at Santa Cruz, Bombay.

When hostilities broke out in September, the Sea Hawks were placed directly under the of Western Air Command. The Air OC Rajasthan had already chalked out plans to employ the Sea Hawks in a strike against Badin on the morning of 7 September. But before the strike could be executed, the planes were recalled to Santa Cruz, to provide air defense coverage for Bombay.[25] This proved to be a mistake.

The first PAF raids in this area came on 6 September. Mauripur was initially the bomber base of the PAF. Earlier, part of its B 57 force was moved to Peshawar, with more about to be sent. These were about to take-off when they were hurriedly called back and briefed for strike on Jamnagar on 6 September. Finally, a force of six bombers left for Jamnagar, coming in at very low level in the fading light and clouds at 1920 hours. The bombers used the lighthouse at Mandvi as a landmark to navigate to the Jamnagar airfield, four minutes flying time away.[26] The B 57s dropped their loads, fired their rockets and flew back to Mauripur. Some ground installations and the ATC tower and a couple of aircraft were damaged in the raid. Two more raids followed that night. At least four Vampires near the ORP were damaged in these attacks. Several Naval Seahawks and Air Force Otters in the open, around the airfield, escaped damage due to their good dispersal. Another target was Porbandar, which was suspected to house a radar station. This strike was called off.

On 7 September, the Sea Hawks moved to Santa Cruz at Bombay, using the undamaged western part of the Jamnagar runway. The day passed off uneventfully. At night, Pakistani Navy (PN) ships struck, sneaking up around midnight to the coast of Dwarka, about 100 km from Jamnagar, and shelling the harbour, port and coastal installations.[27] The task force included the cruiser PNS *Babur*. The Pakistanis mistakenly believed that Dwarka housed an AEW Radar with Huff/Duff[28] beacons to guide Indian bombers.

The only Indian Navy ship in the vicinity was the INS *Talwar*, anchored off Okha under the command of Commander Dharweshwar. The *Talwar* intercepted wireless at around 2200 hours, assumed it was the target and sounded action stations. However, the Pakistani fleet seemed to move on to other targets. At 0015 hours on the night of 7/8 September, the PN taskforce opened fire and some fifty 6" shells landed in Dwarka over a period of 30 minutes. Most of the shells did not explode, and, to accompany the din of the main armament, the Pakistanis erroneously identified aircraft in the air and fired their anti-aircraft guns. An aircraft was claimed shot down, though how it was identified is not clear. The Indian Navy was caught unawares by the shelling of Dwarka and the Pakistani Navy taskforce steamed back to Karachi before it could give chase. The failure of INS *Talwar* to sail forth and engage the Pakistani Navy had a telling effect on the ship's captain, who brooded for a long time on the missed opportunity.[29]

The Dwarka shelling infuriated many navy officers and their pride was affected for some days to come. Had Sea Hawks from Jamnagar carried out regular recce sorties over the ocean, they would have deterred the Pakistani Navy even though PAF Sabres would have outmatched them. At dawn on 8 September, an Alize from Bombay carried out a recce sortie, but failed to sight the PN taskforce.[30] The Sea Hawks carried out dawn-to-dusk combat air patrol sorties from Santa Cruz and were also prepared to launch anti-ship strike sorties. On 11 September, an Alize of 310 Naval Squadron operating from Bombay finally observed a group of PN ships off Okha. The Alize's radio signal reporting the ships never reached base. It was only after repeated signals that Sea Hawks were sent from Santa Cruz.

The Sea Hawks were ordered to move to Jamnagar on the night of 11/12 September. However, no contact was made with any PN ships when the Sea Hawks flew recce sorties. Towards the end of the day, all but one of the Sea Hawks flew back to Bombay. The lone aircraft was left behind due to a technical snag.

It was when the last Sea Hawk was flown back to Bombay after repairs, that the first 'air raid' occurred over Bombay. Lieutenant P.D. Sharma, the naval pilot flying the Sea Hawk found his radio not working and unable to identify himself to Santa Cruz Control, decided to approach the airfield at low level. On his approach, he was mistaken for an enemy aircraft and the airfield defenses opened up, lighting up the sky over Bombay. This was the first time that Bombay had sounded an air raid alert. Luckily Sharma landed safely at Santa Cruz.[31]

The squadron carried out 106 sorties during the war. There was only one casualty: Sub Lieutenant K.P. Verma was killed after he took off for a dawn combat air patrol (as No. 2) from Santa Cruz and crashed into the sea shortly thereafter, on 18 September. The leader lost contact with Verma's Sea Hawk IN 185 soon after take-off.

This account of naval air operations is not complete without the mention of the lone Indian Navy Alize, which was deployed with Western Air Command for electronic surveillance duties on the Western border. It was clearly the most advanced aircraft in terms of electronic surveillance equipment and far surpassed any aircraft that the IAF could have fielded in those days. The Alize started flying low-level sorties in Indian territory from the Kashmir region. These covered picking up radar transmissions, getting fixes on Pakistani radar locations and passing the information on to the IAF. The peripatetic Alize's sorties took it over the Punjab and Rajasthan sectors and by war's end it was based at Jodhpur. A Dakota followed it from base to base with support and service crew. At the best of times, it presented a strange silhouette that defied recognition by Air Force crew as well as the Army AA gunners and earned it the occasional hostility of both. There were many occasions on which the Alize was intercepted by the IAF's Hunters or was fired at by the AA gunners.[32]

NOTES

1. Air Marshal Vinod Patney.
2. Before 8 Squadron, Chopra had served with 1 Squadron, where he had earned the nickname Green Babu in 1964, a moniker

awarded by Philip Rajkumar and Frisky Verma on seeing Chopra burst into the crew room shouting 'Green Babu, Green' after he had passed the test for a Green instrument rating for the first time. It was a nickname that stayed with him as long as he was in 1 Squadron. Chopra was a senior Flight Lieutenant and Rajkumar and Verma were junior Flying Officers but as Rajkumar testifies, he never seemed to mind.

3. A long running joke amongst IAF pilots who had trained on the Sabre was that if they were ever shot down behind enemy lines, they would simply fly the Sabre back.
4. Bhatia's father had served in the police force and along with Brigadier Ayub Khan enforced security for Peshawar airport at the time of the Partition of the subcontinent, when BOAC was flying in those fortunate refugees who were able to afford the airfare.
5. During his stint with UN forces, Gautam destroyed several Katangan aircraft including a Fouga Magister at Kolwezi airfield. He received the VM for his efforts.
6. Pune's Station Commander was Group Captain R.M. Engineer, DFC.
7. Details on the raids by the Tigers at Sargodha are based on interviews with Group Captain Taneja and the Tigers War Diaries.
8. It was after this incident about the missing parachute that rumours floated around in the squadron that the CO was brave enough to fly a mission without carrying his parachute. Taneja however dismisses the story!
9. John Fricker, *Battle for Pakistan*, London: Ian Allen, 1979, p. 112.
10. The first announcement by the PAF was that Amjad Hussain accidentally flew through the debris of a Mystere that he had just destroyed. However (Fricker, 1979), a *de facto* PAF official publication, admitted that Hussain was in fact lost in aircombat with a Mystere over Sargodha. No Mystere pilot reported air-combat with PAF aircraft that morning. In a recent article Air Commodore Kaiser Tufail, PAF (Mystery of the Downed Mystere) has claimed that Hussain's Starfighter collided with the Mystere. The definitive answer for this mystery rests with Hussain obviously and we welcome clarification.
11. Pushpinder Singh and Ravi Rikhye, *Fiza'ya: The Psyche of the PAF*, New Delhi: Society for Aerospace Studies, 1991.
12. Pakistani and Indian sources alike have both claimed that only decoys were based at Bhagtanwala.
13. Air Chief Marshal P.C. Lal, *My Years with the IAF*, New Delhi: Lancer International, 1986, pp. 135-7.
14. Ibid.
15. *The Dawn*, Pakistan Day Special, 6 September 2003; Air Commodore Kaiser Tufail, 'Speed shooting classic'.

16. Air Chief Marshal P.C. Lal, op. cit., pp. 135-7.
17. Interview with AVM A.S. Lamba.
18. Interview with Air Marshal Philip Rajkumar in *Times of India*, 7 September 2001. *http://timesofindia.indiatimes.com articleshow.asp?artid = 2002174516&sType=1*
19. Taneja was annoyed that the raid went in at half strength. Ideally, he would have aborted the raid when two aircraft fell out of the attack. But by the time he received the information, J.P. Singh and Guha were on their way to the target.
20. The frustrating lack of damage assessment in the war was noted in the Tigers' war diary.
21. Though this was an operational accident, it had an interesting sequel. To bolster the claims of the AA gunners as well as the F 104 pilots keeping combat air patrol over Sargodha, Singh was claimed shot down over Sargodha in (Fricker, 1979). John Fricker, op. cit., 1979, p. 112.
22. All Pakistani versions are from Fricker, 1979. John Fricker, op. cit., pp. 112-16.
23. Pushpindar Singh, *The Battle Axes—1942-92*, New Delhi: Society for Aerospace Studies, 1992, p. 92.
24. Squadron Leader Augier participated in bombing trials after the war in May 1966. A joint exercise was planned with the Canberras and the An 12s were successful in blowing out the target on the range—leaving no target for the Canberras to attack! By that time, the pilots had refined their technique. Experience had taught them that if they lined up a set of rivets on the nose of the aircraft with the target as they ran into the dropping zone the aircraft would do a good drop—whether it was supplies or bombs.
25. B.C. Chakravarty, ed., 'Indian Armed Forces—Official History of the 1965 Indo-Pakistan War', New Delhi: Government of India (unpublished).
26. John Fricker, op. cit., p. 101.
27. Rear Admiral Satyinder Singh, *Blueprint to Blue Water: The Indian Navy 1951-65*, Lancer International, 1992.
28. Huff Duff is slang for HF/DF—High Frequency Direction Finding.
29. Rear Admiral Satyinder Singh, *Blueprint to Blue Water: The Indian Navy 1951-65*, Lancer International, 1992.
30. Ibid.
31. B.C. Chakravarty, op. cit., n. 25.
32. Vice Admiral Hiranandani, *Transition to Triumph: The Indian Navy 1965-72*, New Delhi: Lancer International, 1999.

CHAPTER 6

Missed Opportunity: The War in the Eastern Sector

Prior to 1971, Pakistan was subject to a unique geographic and demographic division. Its eastern wing, home to Bengali and Bihari Muslims—more than half of Pakistan's population—and separated by a 2,000-km long stretch of Indian territory from the western wing, was a nation by itself. In 1965, the East Pakistani was as patriotic as the West Pakistani. This patriotism had not been repaid in kind. West Pakistan never accorded the defence of East Pakistan any importance: a central military doctrine of the Pakistani Armed Forces was the geographically challenged 'the defense of the east lies in the west'. Pakistani ground forces in the east consisted of a division of troops led by Major General Fazal Muqeem Khan. Air defence was provided by a PAF squadron (No. 14) of 12 Sabres based at Tejgaon. The Pakistani Navy patrolled the coastal approaches with a few patrol boats and gunships. The thinness of this arrangement needs little commentary.

The Indian Army's Eastern Command, led by Lieutenant General Sam Manekshaw, MC, bore operational responsibility for its eastern sector. Two Corps and six Divisions faced the Chinese threat from the north. One Mountain Division was embroiled in the Nagaland insurgency. A possible explanation for the Indian Army undertaking no offensive operations in 1965 in the eastern sector was that doctrinally, the invasion and occupation of East Pakistan was never a viable option for India. Faced with a hostile population of 150 million patriotic East Pakistanis, and with little familiarity with ground topography, an invasion would have been foolhardy, while simultaneously exposing India's northern flank to the Chinese.

Air Force operations in the eastern sector fell under the purview of two Air Commands. Eastern Air Command (EAC) covered the north-eastern states east of West Bengal, including the China border along NEFA (now Arunachal Pradesh) and the Burma border. All operations over Uttar Pradesh, Bihar and West Bengal, which had a direct border with East Pakistan, were under the purview of Central Air Command.

Central Air Command (CAC) faced the lone PAF squadron. Led by Air Vice-Marshal Shivdev Singh, it operated out of Rani Kutir, Regent Park in Calcutta's Tollygunj. CAC oversaw a strong network of airfields, a legacy of the Second World War: Agra, Ranchi, Baghdogra, Barrackpore and Kalaikunda. Its central airfield was Kalaikunda, 7 km from Kharagpur—the home of the Indian Institute of Technology, in Midnapore district of West Bengal—and 180 km (20 minutes flying time) from the East Pakistani border. No. 16 Squadron (Canberras) led by Wing Commander Peter Maynard Wilson, and based at Kalaikunda, provided the offensive component of the Command. Half its aircraft were later ordered to move out to Gorakhpur, out of range of any attacks from East Pakistan. A squadron of Vampires (No. 24—Vampire FB 52s) and only one Hunter Squadron (No. 14) was available to meet the Chinese threat. 14 Squadron (*Bulls*), led by Wing

Plate 33: Chief of Staff Arjan Singh with 14 Squadron personnel after the war.

Commander Denis Anthony La Fontaine, was based at Kalaikunda; two other Hunter Squadrons were with EAC airbases at Jorhat and Chabua. 24 Squadron (*Hawks*) led by Squadron Leader Madhabendra Banerji was based at Kalaikunda.

Indian Army deployment in the north-east required extensive logistical support from transport aircraft such as the Dakotas and C 119 Packets. A few Dakotas were leased from Kalinga Airways, the civilian outfit that flew in the NEFA sector. No. 2 Air Defence Area Headquarters, based at Jaffarpore, 3-4 km from Barrackpore, provided air defense support for the entire sector. Radar coverage in the eastern sector was poor: 411 SU at Rampur Hat provided some rudimentary GCI capability, while 55 SU, a Second World War vintage radar, provided some early warning capability for Kalaikunda.

Operational deployment plans for the Hunter squadrons in the Eastern Sector only envisaged a Chinese threat; no offensive role against East Pakistani targets was conceived or planned. The only role planned in case of hostilities against Pakistan was air defense for Indian installations. In mid-1965, CAC intelligence reports indicated that PAF Sabres based in East Pakistan could break for the west by a long night flight. This was not as far-fetched as it sounded, given the meager radar coverage in east and central India. A Sabre would have just enough fuel to make a ferry flight to the west—presumably, under cover of the night. However, it would have to fly at altitudes that could lead to its detection by radars based in the east—and there would be absolutely no allowance for the Sabre to engage in air combat. What was to be done once the Sabres were detected? To test the possibility of using day fighters like the Hunter for night interception, CAC decided on a practice run.

The task of testing the viability of the Hunter for night interception was assigned to senior pilots at Kalaikunda. Wing Commander Peter Wilson would fly a Canberra at medium altitude at night so that radar could track him and vector a Hunter for interception. In 1965, IAF radar was just efficient enough to put air defence fighters in the proximity of an intruder. The air defence fighter still needed either airborne radar or visual aids to locate the intruder and effect the interception.

Wilson took off on a dark, moonless night, and soon afterwards a Hunter T66 two-seater trainer, piloted by Wing Commander La Fontaine, CO 14 Squadron and his senior flight commander, Squadron Leader O.N. Kacker, followed. The Air Defence Controller vectored the Hunter onto the Canberra. Coming astern of the aircraft, La Fontaine and Kacker were delighted to spot the orange glow emanating from the Canberra's engines. If they could spot the Canberra at night, they could spot Sabres making a run from the east. The Hunter had found itself a new role.

Wilson then throttled back the engine RPM to a very low but sustainable level. La Fontaine and Kacker watched in disbelief as the glow from the jet pipe died out leaving them to face the pitch-black night. The pair convinced themselves that they could make out the silhouette of the Canberra about 500 yards in front of them, and called Wilson on the R/T asking him to switch on his landing lights. Wilson did so and a shock awaited the Hunter pilots: the Canberra was just abreast of them, a considerable distance from their imagined placing. A collision in the dark had been a distinct possibility. The three pilots returned to base, convinced of the impracticality of night interceptions by Hunters. La Fontaine ruefully remarked, 'Our ego was in our boots.' Later Kacker left 14 Squadron and joined 27 Squadron to fly operations in the western front—his tale has been recounted elsewhere. He left behind an important legacy: his training of younger pilots in 14 Squadron. It would pay rich dividends for the IAF.

PLANNING FOR THE RAIDS

IAF formations and bases had made 'Operational Plans' for three contingencies: hostilities with China, hostilities with Pakistan and hostilities with both countries simultaneously. However, the 'plans' only detailed potential targets for attack. It was left to the Command Headquarters to work out the methods and means to achieve these objectives. CAC's primary task was the destruction of the PAF Sabres based in East Pakistan, along with targets in southern East Pakistan including shipping ports.

Initially, Indian military plans did not involve ground, air or naval forces in the eastern sector. Nevertheless, on the evening of 6 September, immediately after the Indian Army attacked across the international border in Punjab, the code-word signifying hostilities against Pakistan was flashed from Air HQ to Central and Eastern Air Command. Accordingly, Chittagong and Jessore were earmarked for an early morning offensive the next day. Surprisingly, Tejgaon airfield at Dacca was left out.

Group Captain M.B. Naik, Station Commander Kalaikunda, received a visitor from IAF top brass on the evening of 6 September. Air Vice-Marshal Shivdev Singh, the AOC-in-C of CAC arrived for a meeting with Naik and squadron commanders to discuss offensive operations in the eastern sector. Singh, formerly a Stirling bomber pilot with the RAF Bomber Command over Germany in Second World War, planned to knock out the Sabres in East Pakistan. As in the western sector, the number of aircraft chosen for the task was small, and the intelligence given to the pilots poor. Singh had made up his mind about launching offensive operations. It was only a question of who would carry them out and when. Both the senior officers conferred in Wing Commander R.D. 'Dicky' Law's office, the OC Flying of the base. Strangely Law himself was evicted, as matters were deemed too sensitive for his ears.

Wing Commander Peter Wilson was the first squadron commander to be briefed. His task was a two-aircraft mission to Chittagong to report the presence of, and destruction of, any PAF aircraft based there. It was late 2300 hours—at the time of Wilson's briefing. A night raid, using moonlight for navigation, would have been ideal, but time to prepare and arm the aircraft was at a premium. It was decided to launch the Canberras just before dawn to make use of first light.

Wing Commander La Fontaine, unaware of the content of Wilson's briefing, was next. Intelligence reports indicated that some Sabres were located at Comilla; some of these were thought to have been flown to Jessore. These conflicting reports failed to confirm their exact location. Several strategies for tackling the Sabres were discussed: either a direct attack on the base itself or a sweep to lure the Sabres up to contrail height. Through the night Singh, Naik and La Fontaine could not make up their minds on what role to, commit to, i.e. to strike Tejgaon or to conduct a sweep. Several times during the night, aircraft ground crew were told to equip four Hunters with four drop-tanks and rocket rails and then to remove them and leave them with two droptanks and a gunpack for an air combat role for the sweep. The ground crew got little or no sleep (and neither did La Fontaine!). In the end, a compromise was worked out. To draw the Sabres out and up, La Fontaine would fly a high level sweep over the Tejgaon/Jessore area, where Indian radar would plot both the Hunters and any intercepting Sabres. Another intelligence report falsely indicated that the Sabres were equipped with Sidewinders. La Fontaine indicated the possibility of losses occurring if the Sidewinder-equipped Sabres jumped the Hunters. To plan for such an exigency, a formation of six aircraft, with four in front and two following, was to be flown, taking off at 0430 hours and returning at 0630 hours to Dum Dum Airport in Calcutta. The Hunters would then be rearmed with rockets and additional fuel for a strike on Tejgaon. A C119 Packet would transport rockets, ammunition and ground personnel from Kalaikunda to Dum Dum. Four Vampires from 221 Squadron, led by Flight Lieutenant Goriya were briefed to carry out the second raid on Tejgaon. The raid never happened. Flight Lieutenants Alfred Tyrone Cooke and S.C. Mamgain would fly the Hunter pair behind La Fontaine's formation. Their first task: provide top cover for 221 Squadron's Vampires. Their secondary task: to provide backup for La Fontaine's formation in their sweep between Tejgaon and Jessore.

Before we go into the details of Kalaikunda's offensive operations, a look at offensive operations flown by other airbases is revealing. Two other squadrons, 37 and 4, were assigned targets in the east.

EASTERN AIR COMMAND OPERATIONS: RAID ON KURMITOLA

The second Command Headquarters in the East to receive the code word for hostilities against Pakistan was EAC HQ at Shillong. It had several airfields capable of transport operations, including Chabua, Tezpur, Jorhat, Gauhati, Hashimara and Walong. Its operations focused on providing logistical support to Indian Army formations in the north-east, facing the Chinese threat. The offensive component of EAC consisted of two Hunter squadrons (already mentioned), and another three squadrons—4, 47 and 29—of Ouragans. These were the last in the IAF still flying the Ouragan. On the notification of the outbreak of full-scale hostilities from Air HQ, EAC ordered a strike on Kurmitola airfield, which was coming up near Dacca as its international airport.

37 Squadron (Hunters) was assigned the raid on Kurmitola. The squadron was part of 14 Wing based at Chabua, a station commanded by Group Captain E.J. Dhatigara KC. Dhatigara was a transport pilot who had earned his laurels in the 1950s, flying supply operations to beleaguered Indian Army posts engaged in operations against Naga rebels, and who enjoyed a good working relationship with the squadron's CO, Wing Commander McNeil. At the outset of war, under the instructions of the SASO EAC Air Commodore Pandit, a detachment of four Hunters was sent to Gauhati, headlong into a conflict between the detachment leader Squadron Leader Mian Niranjan 'M.N.' Singh and the Gauhati Station Commander. Singh, an experienced Hunter pilot, had joined 37 Squadron after an earlier stint with 27 Squadron and disagreed with the station commander on the operational deployment of the Hunters.

Gauhati was primarily a civilian airport, hurriedly equipped to fight a war. Air Force installations were located inconveniently, at a distance from the main airfield. A 10-ft high barbed wire fence that separated access from the pilot's debriefing hut, surrounded the airfield. The pilots devised ingenious methods to circumvent this problem. Instead of moving from the hut to the aircraft during a scramble, pilots on ORP waited underneath the aircraft. When the ATC needed to scramble the pilots on the ORP, they would fire a Very flare cartridge. In typical IAF style, it was a makeshift arrangement that worked.

Just after midnight on 6 September, Singh awoke to a telephone call from the station commander, who excitedly mentioned the 'green light' given to mount strikes against East Pakistan and called Singh and the Army Ground Liaison Officer (GLO) for a meeting in his office at 0200 hours on 7 September. Singh arrived to find the Army GLO absent and the station commander closing the door and windows. The station commander then proceeded to take out an old photograph from his desk drawer and laid it out on the table. The 4ft x 2ft black and white photograph dated 1946, supposedly of Kurmitola and its surrounds, showed a 1,500-yds runway and some sandbag pens. The station commander said, 'I want you to look at this'. Singh's demeanour, that of paying no attention and looking elsewhere, irked the station commander who angrily burst out, 'This is a top secret photograph and you can't even be bothered to look at it?' Singh replied, 'What for? This thing is more than 15 years old. You think the place still looks the same?'

At this point the Army GLO arrived and tempers cooled. The station commander pointed out to Singh his objectives, the principal one being to attack the newly constructed airport at Kurmitola and destroy its runway, ATC and Signals Unit, thus preventing its small PAF detachment from being deployed. Singh pressed for permission to attack Tejgaon, home of the PAF Sabres. The station commander refused, with specific instructions to 'avoid flying over Dacca under any circumstances' as Tejgaon—mysteriously—was considered a civilian airport and under operational constraints active at the time, considered off-limits.

Time over target was fixed at 0530 hours and 37 Squadron's entire detachment of four Hunters, armed with cannons and rockets, was assigned to the raid. As the jets lined up for take-off, Singh's Hunter failed to start. Singh immediately pulled out a very disappointed No. 4 from the formation and took over his aircraft. The remaining three Hunters roared down the runway.

The Hunters flew at low altitude through the Shillong hills; the flight to Kurmitola, approximately 300 miles from Gauhati, took about 40 minutes. On the last 80 miles of the run, rain over East Pakistan came bucketing down in sheets. Visibility rapidly worsened; the ground beneath them appeared flooded and landmarks were scarce. Moreover, the Hunters were tactically routed to prevent flying over areas where they would be detected. They flew due south and then west. The heavy rains and poor visibility prompted the No. 3, Flying Officer Janak Kumar, to decide to abandon the strike. He attempted to contact Singh on the radio, calling out 'Leader?' Strict radio silence was being maintained and though Kumar was using the leader's call sign, he was unwilling to give an official call to abandon the strike. Singh refused to acknowledge the radio calls for fear of being located.

Finally, the formation arrived over Kurmitola where the pilots located and identified its airfield; some construction work was underway. The mission's original plan called for two Hunters to attack the runway and two to attack the Signal Unit. Since the formation had been reduced to three Hunters, Singh decided to lead all the aircraft against the runway. The Hunters strafed and rocketed the runway before turning north for the journey back home. The effectiveness of the strike was doubtful in view of the airfield's operational status. During the return leg, Singh saw a PAF Sabre zoom past him from west to east, about a thousand yards in front of the formation. Singh was on the edge of his seat. The Hunters were in a very vulnerable position, with no fuel reserves to spare for air combat. But poor visibility aided the Hunters as the Sabre failed to notice them.

Visibility and rains so adversely affected flying conditions that the PAF lost a Sabre sent up to intercept the raiders. On news of Kurmitola and other targets being attacked, a section of Sabres was sent up with the GCI vectoring the fighters towards the raiders. Flying Officer A.T.M. Aziz (No. 14 Squadron) announced visual contact with the raiders on R/T and reported chasing them. Aziz was at low altitude; moments later his Sabre spun into the ground and exploded.[1] The Hunters reported no engagements with Sabres.

On return, the Hunter formation pulled up to 10,000 ft altitude. Kumar had lost contact with the formation. Singh noticed and called out to Kumar, breaking radio silence. No response was heard. Singh suspected the worst: that Kumar had fallen victim to an interceptor or AA fire. Despondently mulling over this loss, he tried the missing Hunter again. Kumar came on the air, confirming his safety and temporary loss of direction, and homing onto the formation, using the Green Satin navigational aid, reached base with the rest.

Back at base, the pilots headed for a debriefing with the station commander and the Army Liaison officer. The intelligence officer Flight Lieutenant Handa joined them. The station commander was fuming; shaken by the news of the ineffectiveness of the raid, he summarily ticked off the pilots and threatened to courtmartial Singh for not adhering to his 'personal orders to attack Dacca'. Singh was taken aback. Permission had been refused for a golden opportunity to catch the Sabres on the ground and now he was being blamed for not attacking Tejgaon.

The Army Liaison officer intervened. He had heard Singh ask, and be refused by the station commander, for permission to attack Tejgaon. The Intelligence Officer intervened as well. He had advised the station commander, via a forwarded report, that the PAF Sabre squadron was based at Tejgaon. Handa insisted that the station commander had acknowledged the report by signing it. The station commander denied having seen Handa's report. Undeterred, Handa produced the intelligence report, signed by the station commander. The station commander had chosen to ignore it.

It was then that news of the PAF's retaliatory strikes on Kalaikunda reached them: Sabres had attacked, achieving full surprise and inflicted real damage. Singh's frustration was understandable. Had his request to attack Tejgaon been approved, his formation could have destroyed the Sabres as they prepared for the raid on Kalaikunda.

An infuriated Singh complained to McNeil and CAC HQ. The detachment of Hunters reverted to the command of Chabua; the SASO Air Commodore Pandit took over operations at Gauhati. 37 Squadron stayed out of operations. A few days later some of its Hunters were sent to the western front to Hindon, possibly to relieve Hunter squadrons at Halwara, but arrived too late to be effectively deployed.

THE OORIALS STRIKE LAL MUNIR HAT

On 7 September, a Pakistani Army jeep convoy near the East Pakistani village of Lal Munir Hat was surprised to observe some straight-winged jets buzz them at low level. The jets then pulled up in a turn to make an attacking run, and let loose with their cannon and rockets. Starfed and rocketed, the Pakistanis defiantly answered with a token volley of small arms fire. After their run, the jets headed for home. 4 Squadron (*Fighting Oorials*), based at Hashimara, executed this raid on Lal Munir Hat, a four-Ouragan strike led by Squadron Leader M.M. Singh. The Ouragans claimed the destruction of several jeeps and vehicles. The destruction of the convoy marked the only occasion that Ouragans of the IAF saw combat in a full-fledged war. Ouragans had flown against the Portuguese in Goa in 1961, and in minor counterinsurgency operations against the Naga rebels in the early 1960s. They did not fly in combat again and were retired in 1967.

We now return to operations in and around Kalaikunda.

RAID ON CHITTAGONG

Kalaikunda's first strike into East Pakistan was on the Chittagong airfield, as air intelligence had mistakenly reported the deployment of Sabres of 14 PAF Squadron. Two Canberras of 16 Squadron were armed with two 1000-lb bombs and ammunition for the 20 mm cannon pack. Wing Commander Wilson flew the lead aircraft, with Squadron Leader Shankaran as his navigator. Squadron Leader Karve, with Flying Officer Rajwar as his navigator, flew the second aircraft. Both aircraft left Kalaikunda in the early hours of 7 September, they first flew from Kalaikunda to the lighthouse south of Calcutta. From there, in the darkness, the aircraft flew over the Bay of Bengal to approach the Chittagong lighthouse from the sea. The monsoon rains made their job even more difficult in navigating to the initial waypoint. Opposition in terms of interception by Sabres was a possibility, so the plan was to attack the airfield individually, with a time lag of 10 minutes before the time over target of each aircraft. Karve would keep orbiting the Chittagong lighthouse, while Wilson would go in to bomb the airfield. In case they encountered Sabres, Karve would be informed by radio; he would abort the mission at that stage.

Chittagong airfield was identified and Wilson made his run in to attack the intersection of the runways. Both the bombs were dropped on the intersection after making three runs on the airfield. Much to the consternation of the crew, the bombs failed to explode. Their unreliability can perhaps be traced to their vintage, that of the Second World War. This problem would be repeated in the Bangladesh war six years later, when Hunters had to make a second pass on targets firing cannons in the vain hope of igniting the bombs.

The second Canberra, flown by Karve, was called in and did a good job in placing the bombs on the runways. Fortunately, the bombs exploded. Both Canberras returned safely, but not before 14 Squadron's Hunters intercepted them and nearly shot them down. Strangely, 14 Squadron had not been informed of the raids and possessed no information on the incoming aircraft. La Fontaine's squadron had started off on its mission to sweep over Jessore. The two Hunters configured for air defence, flown by Flight Lieutenant Alfred Cooke and Flying Officer S.C. Mamgain, had just taken off and were heading towards the border when they sighted Wilson's Canberras returning from the raid. Assuming that the Canberras were PAF B 57s, the Hunters started the attack run on the Canberras before realizing their identity and breaking off. Thankfully, Cooke remembered the difference between the American (tandem cockpit) and British models of the Canberra.

Wilson noted down the description of the raid with one word, 'FIASCO!' Despite Karve's bombs exploding on the runway, no strategic value was gained from the attack. On receipt of news of Chittagong and other targets in East Pakistan being attacked, several Sabres were scrambled, but failed to intercept the attackers.

24 SQN AT BARRACKPORE: THE 'RAIDS' ON JESSORE

Parallel to the Canberra raid, 24 Squadron's Vampires launched their first mission against Jessore. Squadron Leader M. Banerji led the four Vampires from Barrackpore. Banerji had had a typical IAF adventure since being posted in as OC of 24 Squadron on the day war had broken out:

I took over as OC 24 Sqn. on 1st September. I was posted in—my papers came with rank and posting. I had been at 45 Sqn. in Pune and before that, flying Mysteres with 31 Sqn. at Pathankot. Then in '64 November, I moved from Pathankot to Pune. I thought I was going to stay there, but they moved me. CAC and EAC were new to me. In April, they had called me back from Pune to Pathankot. Anyway, I showed up there, and on the 1st I had a briefing at the Ops room, which was in the ATC building. But really, there was no real briefing on the role for us. The station commander, Naik was there. I was still trying to figure out the squadron, the pilots. I read the intelligence, which was poor. If you believed everything they said about Pakistani Air Defence, you would think a fly wouldn't get through! I was told when I got to KKD that I'm supposed to go to Barrackpore as the operating base. I said, 'What is in Barrackpore?' They said everything. Now from 24 Sqn. I had A.N. Sanyal as my flight commander and I only knew one pilot, N.M. Suri. I knew no one else. Anyway, I didn't know the pilots, I didn't know the planes. You know the little quirks in each aircraft that pilots know. I did not know the sectors or flying area. I was told that on the 5th evening that I should push off to Barrackpore. I went on 6th morning and the station commander of Barrackpore, S. Mukherjee, said, 'What are you doing here?!' So I had 8-10 planes, Vampires, they were all serviceable. And 8 or so pilots. Subir Dey was there amongst them. I said to the SC, 'What is my briefing?' He said, 'you haven't been told?'

Banerji and his men settled in and dispersed. At 1500 hours Banerji was called to the station commander's office. The C-in-C Shivdev Singh was present, speaking of strikes across the border. Banerji was still in his flying overalls. After finishing, Singh asked, 'Any questions?' Both the station commander and Banerji replied in the negative. After he left, Banerji turned to the station commander and innocently inquired, 'What was he talking about?' The station commander was equally in the dark. At 1900 hours the station commander dropped by the guest house. Meanwhile, a Dakota had brought over the personal effects for the pilots. The station commander then said, 'You're going in tomorrow'. Unsurprisingly, Banerji's response was, 'Where?' only to be told to be patient. The station commander came back later and at 1000 hours Banerji had confirmation that his squadron was to attack Jessore with 4 Vampires loaded with rockets and guns.

Banerji was facing a tough task. He didn't know where the pilots were on the base. It was pitch-dark, and the base was covered with ponds from intermittent rainfall. Walking around this watery obstacle course in the darkness was an unappealing prospect. Nevertheless, he located some officers including the engineering officer, whom he instructed to load up the aircraft. More problems awaited and it needed the technical crew to come to the fore:

Now, we had some plans worked out, some maps made for the strike on Jessore. At this stage, I probably made a mistake. I didn't know whether I should tell the pilots now about the fact that we were going in on the morning or wait. They were tired, they hadn't had much sleep. Should I put them through this? Why not brief them in the morning? Now our rockets had not arrived, actually, the carriers for moving the rockets to the jets had not arrived. So I spoke to the senior NCOs at night. They were reluctant to carry live rockets to the jets. I talked to the chief sergeant. I said this is an emergency, we have to cut-off the hand to save the person. He said to me, sir, if you want, we will carry the rockets on our shoulders. I said you do that. And that's what they did. The boys carried the live rockets to the jets and loaded them. It was against all norms. Only our men will do this. No matter what you might think, that the men are not smart, that they are not educated, that they are *dhila-dhala*, when the time comes they will do anything and everything that is required. I learned this as a pilot officer. All the system's lapses are made good by our men time and time again.

As morning broke, Banerji summoned his pilots and told them of the planned raid. The initial reaction was one of surprise, with Sanyal in particular suggesting that they should have been told earlier, prompting Banerji to question his decision of not having told them earlier. As Banerji's formation took off, the weather was 'dodgy'; there was low cloud, some showers. To make things worse, in the poor visibility the pilots were naturally apprehensive about the jute mill chimneys around Barrackpore. The poor visibility continued: 'So we took off and we were turning left and right to avoid the clouds. My god, we were dog-tired. We reached the target area and I couldn't see anything. I called out on the RT, "Can anyone see anything?" No one answered. Now, I wasn't going to loiter around and risk getting clobbered, so we came back without firing a round.'

The Vampires had flown over the Kishenganj area, where elements of 8 Mountain Division of the Indian Army were stationed. Army personnel including officers were outside early in the morning, shaving and starting their daily routines. As the Vampires flew overhead at low level, some of the army officers looked up and instinctively ducked their heads, prompting one to remark, 'If those chaps don't turn pretty quickly they'll be in Pakistani territory.' Apparently, even the Indian Army had no clue about the missions the IAF had planned. An aggravating surprise awaited Banerji on his return from Jessore: 'After landing, we talked about not being able to spot the runway. But one of the boys said, "I saw the runway." But I hadn't heard him on the RT. Then, I was told, that the Vampire I was flying had a problem. When it was in a turn, it couldn't transmit or receive on the RT. This is what happens when you are not familiar with the aircraft.'

Banerji asked for permission to repeat the strike and was granted it. The Vampires now had a rough idea of their target's location. As they arrived over the target area, 'Sunny Boy' [Sanyal] called out a sighting. The Vampire pilots saw one hangar and one runway. Nothing else. Banerji called off the strike but not before Sanyal went in and fired his entire rocket load at the runway. Sanyal was flying at 100 ft rather than the designated height of 500 ft for that kind of attack, and as he went in that low, the ricochet from the explosions damaged his aircraft. Nevertheless, all aircraft recovered and flew back to Kalaikunda. No more strikes were to be launched from Barrackpore:

Anyway, we went back for a 3rd strike to Jessore. As we were getting airborne, two Hunters flew overhead and the AA immediately opened up. It was chaos. One hour later the same thing happened. Senapati, who had come back by that time, just blew up. He said, 'What the hell is going on? There is a raid on, you are trying to start a sortie, where is the station commander, where is the OC flying? Why are you trying to launch? What are the AA gunners doing? Trying to shoot our Hunters down?' The Air 1 Mazi Khanna also said, 'What is going on here?' I cleared myself, clarified as many details as I could and said, 'Let us know what to do.' But we didn't launch that third strike.

There were no further attacks. 24 Squadron stayed on in Barrackpore for another 3 days or so, and were then ordered to move to Gorakhpur. All aircraft from 221 Squadron were sent to Gorakhpur as well. A.N. Sanyal was sent off to WAC Pathankot on detachment, to fly Mysteres. When Banerji left he had 13 Flight Lieutenants with him. 24 Squadron vegetated at Gorakhpur. Two aircraft were left behind at Barrackpore, only to meet an unfortunate end in a PAF raid. Thus ended 24 Squadron's role in the war; Gorakhpur also became the home of other squadrons, sent there for recuperation in anticipation of a long war.

THE HIGH LEVEL SWEEP TO JESSORE

The last major raid mounted by Kalaikunda before the Pakistani riposte was the high-level sweep carried out by 14 Squadron's Hunters over Jessore. The first formation of four Hunters took off to patrol and draw out the Sabres. La Fontaine's formation climbed to its favoured altitude of 20,000 ft. They flew around for an hour, but encountered no opposition. La Fontaine learned later that Indian radar lost the Hunters soon after take-off and tracked them only on finals. The radar could not have located Pakistani Sabres taking off, or warned La Fontaine's formation. The PAF did track the Hunters near Jessore heading in the general direction of Dacca. Several Sabres were scrambled, but failed to make contact with the Hunters.

Meanwhile, Cooke and Mamgain had a similarly frustrating experience. After reporting to the squadron at 0430 hours, Cooke briefed Mamgain on their role: air defence for La

Fontaine and air defence cover for Vampires at Jessore. Cooke and Mamgain started up and taxied out even as La Fontaine's formation took off. As the pair taxied out, they noticed four Vampires loaded up with rockets and droptanks. Mamgain called out to Cooke on the R/T, pointing out that the Vampires had not started up. As the two formations needed to be over Jessore at the same time, the Vampires, which flew at lower speeds, should have taken off earlier. Cooke acknowledged this but told Mamgain that they should still take-off on time and orbit over Jessore till the Vampires arrived. They should then go to Dum Dum to give air cover for La Fontaine's four-aircraft formation, landing after their high-level sweep over the Dacca/Jessore area. The sweep was supposed to be at 40,000 ft—contrail height—so that, should the PAF Sabres come up to intercept, they (i.e. La Fontaine's formation) would have visual contact by the contrails. Cooke and Mamgain (Red 1 and Red 2) took off in near darkness at approximately 0500 hours, just before dawn. Weather conditions were low cloud at about 500 ft as rain fell in light drizzle patches. After take-off, the pair turned east towards Jessore, approximately 100-110 miles away. Shortly after take-off Cooke had his run-in with Wilson's Canberra. The pair proceeded on to Jessore while trying to make R/T contact with the Vampires. There was no reply. At Jessore, as per the briefing they orbited at 3,000-4,000 ft for 15-20 minutes. Cooke could see the runway at Jessore as well as its ATC building but could not see any aircraft on the ground. Their orders were to not attack anything at Jessore, that being the Vampires' task, but only to provide them air cover in case they were attacked by PAF Sabres. The pair left and, after covering La Fontaine's landing, landed at Dum Dum to refuel.

La Fontaine's Hunters had landed at Dum Dum at 0600 hours. Security seemed disquietingly lax. The civilian ATC neither questioned the Hunters credentials when asked for clearance nor made any effort to identify them or check with IAF officials based at Dum Dum. The Hunters were supposed to be refuelled with four drop tanks and fitted with rockets for the mission to Tejgaon, but Group Captain George Jolly informed La Fontaine that the C 119 Packet from Kalaikunda had not yet arrived.

La Fontaine called CAC headquarters. The Senior Air Staff Officer there, Air Commodore Murat Singh answered. Since civilians, including Burmah Shell Petroleum Company personnel, were present, La Fontaine did not wish to explain his problem openly lest information regarding the timings of the raid be overheard. La Fontaine spoke in 'code', 'Sir, we have landed in Dum Dum. This is in preparation for the party that we were supposed to attend. But the presents that we were supposed to carry and which were to come from Kalaikunda haven't arrived. So without the presents, how are we supposed to go to the party? If there is any delay in the presents, I will need a new time for the party.' La Fontaine was pretty pleased for having conveyed the message effectively in code. The response was earth shaking. There was an explosion at the other end of the line. 'LA FONTAINE!' expostulated Singh in his distinctive Punjabi accent. 'What cock are you talking?'

Apparently the SASO was not aware of war plans. But he was prudent enough to guess at the significance of La Fontaine's presence in Dum Dum. Singh asked La Fontaine to wait while he called the AOC-in-C at Kalaikunda about his 'party' and 'presents'. La Fontaine heard back from Singh within minutes. The SASO spoke to M.B. Naik, the station commander, who told him Kalaikunda was under attack by the PAF. Naik also told the SASO that they had received orders from the Prime Minister's office,[2] prohibiting any offensive sorties against targets in Eastern Air Command. 14 Squadron was to be relegated to the air defence role with immediate effect. The Hunters were already fitted with four drop tanks each for the long haul to Tejgaon. The ground crew struggled to remove the outer tanks to bring the Hunters back to air defence configuration, in which the Hunters would carry only the inboard tanks.

THE PAF ATTACK ON KALAIKUNDA

Squadron Leader Shabbir Syed led the small detachment of twelve Sabres of 14 PAF Squadron at PAF Tejgaon. The station commander was Group Captain Ghulam Haider, who had been informed in advance that he was on his own once the conflict started. On hearing about hostilities, Haider had planned a

MISSED OPPORTUNITY: WAR IN EASTERN SECTOR 179

strike on Kalaikunda to destroy CAC's Canberras and Hunters. He had received an alert and instructions for dispersal as early as 2 September, he nearly succeeded in his objectives. The Pakistani response to the Indian attacks struck the IAF hard.

At 0640 hours on 7 September, Kalaikunda's personnel were just emerging for the day's activities. Everything seemed peaceful. At the time air battles were being fought over Sargodha. The calm belied the shape of things to come for, at the same time, five Sabres were pulling up over Kharagpur to come in for an attack on Kalaikunda. CAC was short of radar coverage, and no warning was received about the attack as the Sabres kept low. Squadron Leader Shabbir Syed led the Sabres from the direction of the Bay of Bengal, over uninhabited territory, where no observation post could relay their approach.

Flight Lieutenants Haleem, Basheer, Tariq Khan and Afzal Khan accompanied Syed. After take-off at 0600 hours, the formation carried out a 300-km flight over sea. Because of the necessity of low-level flight all the way, the Sabres carried a full load of external fuel in two 120 and two 200-gallon drop tanks, leaving only their 0.5-inch machine-guns as weaponry. Kalaikunda was jolted out of its routine by the clatter of machine guns as the Sabres bore in to attack. There could have been no worse time for the base to be caught unawares.

Only three ack-ack guns were in position to defend the airfield. The rest of the guns had arrived only the day before and had not yet been positioned and dug in for deployment. As the Sabres streaked over the airfield, the ack-ack opened up erratically as there was no time to reorganize their fire. Three guns would hardly make any difference to the AA potential of the airfield.

Wilson and Karve's Canberras, which had just returned from the Chittagong raid, were parked in blast pens on one side of the runways. Both Wilson and Karve, along with their navigators, were attending the debriefing meeting with the base commander when the attack occurred. The massive Canberras, already refuelled and being re-armed when the raid started, did not escape the notice of the Pakistani pilots. Both went up in flames. Four Vampires of 24 Squadron were lined up on the other side of the runway, armed and fuelled for the attack on Jessore. The Sabres made short work of these too.

The Sabres recovered safely to Tejgaon at 0744 hours PST, some one and a half hours after they had taken off. The Pakistanis claimed 14 Canberras destroyed, 6 others damaged and 4 Hunters damaged. Had the claim been true, 16 Squadron would have been eliminated. But the PAF pilots mistook Vampires for Canberras and missed out on the Hunters as targets. Haider had submitted his strike plan before hostilities. It was approved with the clause that it would be put into action immediately if hostilities were to break out in the west. After the war he was decorated with a well-deserved medal; the raid was certainly one of the most successful of the war.

The PAF pilots rejoiced but got carried away and made the same mistake the IAF made over Sargodha. They sent a second mission to attack Kalaikunda, now in a full state of readiness. Little did the PAF pilots realize that they were headed for aircombat.

ALFRED COOKE'S EPIC BATTLE

At around 1030 hours, the pall of gloom at Kalaikunda was swept aside as an alarm was raised, warning of incoming Sabres. The four Sabres came roaring in low, led by Flight Lieutenant Haleem. Squadron Leader 'Mama' Sahni, the radar officer at 55 SU in Kalaikunda, briefly picked up a blip on his scope near Port Canning. He immediately alerted Wing Commander Dicky Law, the OC Flying and informed him of the possibility of multiple aircraft coming in for another raid. Law looked up his roster; two Hunters were flying a CAP to the north of Kalaikunda, taking care of Dum Dum and Barrackpore. Law told Sahni to call this section back to Kalaikunda, to intercept the incoming raid immediately.

Flight Lieutenant Alfred Cooke and Flying Officer S.C. Mamgain were on CAP, 60 miles north of the airfield at 20,000 feet. Cooke, a lanky 6' 3" youngster, universally regarded as the squadron's top air defense pilot, had grown up dreaming of being a fighter pilot as he watched Hurricanes, Spitfires, P 51 Mustangs and P 38 Lightnings tangling in practice air

MISSED OPPORTUNITY: WAR IN EASTERN SECTOR

combat near his childhood home of Agra. Now, with 600 hours of Hunter flying under his belt, including grueling practice in low-level air combat with 'Piloo' Kacker, the moment of truth for Cooke had arrived. 'Piloo' had constantly defied IAF regulations on low-level combat training to put Cooke through his paces. It would stand Cooke in good stead for what lay ahead. Even as his mentor and dear friend 'Piloo' was baling out over Sargodha, Cooke was getting ready to put his training at the hands of Kacker to good use. The stage was set for one of the greatest air battles in the history of air combat in the subcontinent.

Earlier in the day, while having breakfast at Dum Dum in

Plate 34: 'I was taught the right way by Piloo—learn by the book, and then when you are done, throw the book away'—Cooke with his beloved Hunter (BA 339). His steed during his epic air battle would be BA 250.

their tent, the pair had received a scramble order and took off. They were under the control of 411 SU at Rampur Hat, approximately 130 nautical miles away from Dum Dum. Cooke and Mamgain were vectored to an area about 80 miles north of Dum Dum, at 25,000 ft. 411 SU informed the pair that there were two bogeys at 25,000 ft just east of the India/Pakistan border, and that they were only to engage in case the bogies crossed the border and entered Indian airspace. Cooke and Mamgain orbited on their side, and presumably the PAF Sabres did the same, about 15 km away. No visual contact was made. As the bogeys left, Cooke and Mamgain returned to Dum Dum at approximately 0900 hours.

The excitement for the day, so far a case of simple false alarms, began with the next call from 411 SU. Cooke and Mamgain were given another scramble order and vectored north of Dum Dum to approximately the same area covered by the previous sortie. Two PAF bogeys were reported flying at 25,000 ft, on the Pakistani side of the border. The IAF pair was told to orbit at 25,000 ft on the Indian side of the border and to only engage the bogeys if they crossed over into Indian airspace. The pair complied but, as before, made no visual contact with any PAF Sabres.

After about 15 minutes of orbiting, the 411 SU controller informed Cooke that Kalaikunda was under attack again and asked if they had enough fuel to go there and intercept. Cooke checked his fuel and asked Mamgain about his fuel status. Both had enough to go to Kalaikunda to carry out the interception. Cooke informed the Controller at 411 SU and immediately asked for 'pigeons back to base'. They were told that they were approximately 120 nautical miles away and given a heading for Kalaikunda. The Hunters headed back at approximately .9 Mach (500 knots). During the flight to Kalaikunda, Mamgain was falling back at one stage; Cooke lost visual contact with him and kept calling out on R/T 'Keep up, keep up', and even throttled back a bit to assist him. As Mamgain was still lagging, and as Cooke needed him level, Cooke told him to catch up and get into position. Or else, he would ask the Controller to vector him onto Mamgain. These stern words from a man Mamgain respected, clearly broke through his apprehension. Remarkably, Mamgain caught up, and informed Cooke that he was scared. With candour, Cooke admitted he was scared as well. This was the first time that anyone of them would be facing hostile aircraft. In a moment of solemnity, Cooke informed Mamgain of their duty to defend their base and their squadron.[3] Cooke continued to talk to Mamgain, urging him to use all his skills in the dogfight that lay ahead. Cooke led both Hunters in a shallow dive at .9 Mach towards Kalaikunda, calculating his speed and rate of descent so as to arrive 10 km short of Kalaikunda at 500 ft, aiming to keep any and all Sabres in front and above. As planned, about 10 km from Kalaikunda, the IAF pair was now down to about 500 ft and flying at about 500 knots. Once below 10, 000 ft, they had lost R/T contact with 411 SU and had tried contact with Kalaikunda but to no avail.

On arriving at Kalaikunda, as Cooke made visual contact with the Sabres, the IAF pilots were treated to a chilling sight: three PAF Sabres were employing a classic front gun racecourse pattern of attack, as another kept top cover. Three Sabres were making the attack run on the western side of the airbase, i.e. the runway, while the other kept top cover on the eastern/ATC hangar side of the runway. Cooke's response was immediate, a classic piece of bravado, as he called out to Mamgain, 'Look at those bastards! Let's get them. I'm taking these three this side— you break and take on the ones on the other side. Good luck!' As Cooke was to note later, this was not in accordance with tactics, as normally the wingman would have stayed glued to the leader's tail. But Cooke, seeing the three Sabres on the western end had thought there were three on the eastern side as well. Under the circumstances, he decided the best thing to do was to take a chance, split up and take on three Sabres each: a remarkable decision.

Flight Lieutenant Haleem was leading the Sabre formation, with Flight Lieutenant Basheer as his wingman. Flight Lieutenants Tariq Habeeb Khan and Afzal Khan formed the second pair in the formation. It is not clear which of the pilots were in the attacking three. One Sabre was in its strafing run, as Cooke and Mamgain pounced. Though the Sabres were operating on the extreme range of their endurance, they outnumbered the Hunters two to one.

Cooke got behind one Sabre, fired at it and chased it so low that one can see the trees in his gun camera film. In the confusion that ensued, Cooke got behind Afzal Khan's Sabre in what became a classic dogfight, employing scissor man- oeuvres. Both the Sabre and the Hunter did their best to cut speed, fall back, turn and get behind each other or to break out by accelerating when their speed fell too sharply. Cooke seized the initiative on one such occasion. As Khan tried to straighten out of the turning dogfight and break out, Cooke used his better acceleration to catch up and open fire with his 30 mm cannon, hitting the Sabre, which broke up in the air. Flight Lieutenant Afzal Khan, the pilot, was killed.

Those are the bare bones of the story. The details as recounted by Cooke make for exhilarating reading—an account notable for the range of emotions expressed—from the moment of engagement to the kill:

I went straight for the Sabre who was in a dive for front gun attack. There was another one, just turning to dive for his attack. This guy warned the Sabre in the dive that I was coming for him and he abandoned his front gun attack and pulled out of the dive and did a hard right turn. I was closing in very fast. Got my gunsight on him momentarily and fired a short burst (1/4 sec) as he pulled away from me and I overshot his line of flight. I lost sight momentarily and when I made visual contact again I got behind the Sabre. He jettisoned his drop tanks and I did the same. I was terrified when I saw how easily he could out-turn me. They employed the classic scissors movement-Turn-Reverse-Turn. The wider turning aircraft would land up in front. I did notice that that his speed would drop off very quickly and that he had to dive towards the ground to build up speed again. At this stage of the dogfight I made sure that I was always above him and tried to stay behind him. I made use of the better thrust/weight ratio of the Hunter to achieve this. I noticed that his leading edge slats would open when turning and this would increase his rate of turn but he would sacrifice his speed in so doing. When I saw this, my mind went back to the classroom when I was a cadet learning about the Principles of Flight—how slats increase the stalling angle and give you more lift. However, with it comes increased drag and unless you have increased power to overcome the drag, speed will drop off. I knew then that these guys were going exactly as per the Book and I knew verse + chapter what they were doing. When his speed dropped off he would dive down to build up speed and then start fighting again—pulling out of the dive at tree height (50 ft or less) with me following, hoping that I would 'mush' into the ground. I got my gunsight on him when we very low and took a shot at him. I started firing at a range of 600 yds and I could see that he was below tree-line height. I did not realize that I was that low and that my wing tip was actually hitting the scrub. I stopped firing to get away from the ground and saw his aircraft explode into a ball of flame and I could not avoid flying through the fireball and debris.

Cooke's baptism by fire had just begun but Piloo's training had already paid off.

Plate 35: This gun camera shot from Cooke's Hunter shows the last moments of Flight Lieutenant Afzal Khan's Sabre as it skimmed the tree tops (*circled in white*). Moments later the Sabre would run into a volley of 30-mm cannon shells from Cooke's Hunter, which would destroy it and kill its pilot.

The citizens of Kharagpur had a grandstand view of the roaring air battle from the top of their homes. The IIT students cheered loudly every time the Sabres—or the Hunters, it didn't seem to matter—seemed to be on the receiving end. During the scissors, Cooke could see Khan's face clearly and still remembers him wearing a white helmet like his own, with the name stenciled on the back. Khan's Sabre crashed near the IIT campus on a farmer's hut, killing two civilians.

Meanwhile, Mamgain went after the two Sabres trying to sneak in on attacking the ground targets. The Sabres had already finished one attacking run when Mamgain arrived on the scene. The two Sabres immediately turned and engaged Mamgain. In the dogfight that followed, Mamgain hit one of the Sabres and claimed it shot down.

Cooke then immediately latched onto the tail of a second Sabre, which had attempted to get behind him, and fired at it, damaging it severely. Large bits of the Sabre's wings were torn off as Cooke's bullets repeatedly found their mark. We return to Cooke's own words as he chased his second opponent:

On recovering from this (Afzal Khan's kill) a quick look around and I saw another Sabre behind me. I took violent evasive manoeuvres and during the criss-cross scissors we would cross very close to each other. I got into an advantageous position behind him and started firing while he was trying to get away from me by diving and turning towards the ground. (All this action took place between ground level and about 4,000 ft.) While firing at him I noticed that he steepened his bank and dive even more and something at the back of my mind warned me that that he was being warned by another Sabre who could be behind me. I kept on firing and closing in rapidly on him and I could see pieces of his aircraft disintegrating. I stopped firing, as I was so close (100 yds) that if I did not break away I would collide with him.

Plate 36: Cooke's second target was a Sabre with a drop tank hang up. Almost certainly the Sabre flown by Flight Lieutenant Tariq Habib Khan, this Sabre's fate is described as 'written off due to lack of spares' in PAF accounts.
In the photos on left, the PAF roundels on the wing can just be made out as well as the forward slats of the Sabre, which have opened up. What is significant in Cooke's gun camera photos is the amount of terrain detail captured. Most air combats typically happened at higher altitude that does not show any such detail in film.

The Sabre damaged by Cooke disengaged to escape and head back to base. Other Sabres were around, including the one that Cooke had suspected of being on his tail:

On recovering from this I immediately pull upward to the right and saw another Sabre behind me. I out-manoeuvred him and got behind as he pulled up in a vertical climb and then winged over to go into a vertical dive with me, following and firing at him all the time. In the vertical dive, I kept firing at him as he pulled out of the dive and moved away from me. I was mesmerized and so full of adrenaline that it took me some time to realize that I would be flying into the ground unless I pulled out of the dive myself. I pulled back on the joystick with my finger on the trigger and got out of the dive with guns still firing until I had expended my ammunition.

One down, two chased off. But another Sabre lurked and in fact, Cooke's No. 2, Mamgain, was in danger of getting shot down by that Sabre before Cooke intervened: 'I was very shaken at this stage and I turned back towards the airfield to get my bearings and equilibrium back. It was then that I noticed my No. 2 Mamgain over the airfield doing a leisurely turn at about 1,500 ft with a Sabre about 1,500 yds. behind him and closing in fast. I warned him and gave him a 'break port' order and then came up to take on this Sabre also.'

Cooke would have been justified in escaping at that point himself, as he had no ammunition left. But Cooke chased this Sabre anyway, armed with little more than film in his gun camera. He stuck to the Sabre's tail as the PAF pilot made some desperate moves in an effort to try and get away from Cooke:

This guy tried to shake me off by doing loops and barrel rolls right over the airfield. I got behind him to firing range and tried to take a shot but there was no ammo. I closed in even closer and tried another shot, but again, no luck—no ammo. While I was behind him during this aerobatic display I called up No. 2 to come and take over and shoot this bastard down—I got no answer and thought the worst—that Mamgain may have been shot down. I called up again on R/T,

Plate 37: Sabre No. 3 in Cooke's guns shows an aircraft in a steep dive with a starboard drop tank hang up. Cooke expended his ammunition as he chased this Sabre in a steep dive.

pleading with any other Hunter who could be airborne to come and take over and shoot this bastard out of the sky. It was at this stage that I noticed grey puffs of smoke appearing in front of me and all around me and I realized that the AA was firing at me as well.

Wing Commander Law commented on the amusement evoked by the PAF pilot's aerobatics display as he was chased by Cooke. Rarely can have a pilot gone through such desperate, evasive manoeuvres while not realizing that his adversary was out of ammunition. The unnerved Pakistani pilot finally disengaged, started climbing and headed towards East Pakistan. Cooke followed about 2,000 yds behind. The chase took Cooke all the way to the border, whereupon he finally gave up and decided to head for Dum Dum. But his adventures had not yet ended. Once Cooke was away from the not-so-friendly AA fire he looked around and noticed that he had sustained some damage to his

Plate 38: Sabre No. 4, after being chased off Mamgain's tail, does aerobatics over Kalaikunda as Cooke chases him with no ammunition in his guns.

portside wingtip and saw the pitot tube bent up about 70 degrees. Gun film would reveal that this had probably happened on one of his close approaches to the ground, most probably as he took his shot at Afzal Khan's Sabre. This meant that Cooke had no air speed indicator (ASI).

By this stage, Cooke was up to about 10,000 ft and had made R/T contact with 411 SU. Cooke reported the dogfight and told 411 SU that he was very low on fuel, had no ASI and asked to get Hunters airborne from Dum Dum to shepherd him in and cover his landing. 411 SU had no joy trying to contact the 14 Squadron detachment at Dum Dum. In the meantime, Cooke was over Calcutta and changed to Dum Dum Airport's civil frequency and told them that he was coming to land in emergency. The ATC informed Cooke that there was a Pan American Boeing 707 on long finals. This failed to impress Cooke; he insisted that he was very low on fuel and cut in ahead in front of the Boeing 707, to put his Hunter onto the runway at what felt like excessive speed. Cooke deployed the tail chute and, using heavy braking, was able to safely bring the aircraft under control and turned on to the taxi track. While taxing back to the Bull's dispersal area, his engine cut out about 600 yds from the parking area. The Hunter was out of fuel. A day of action, quite unlike any other for pilots in this war, had come to an end.

The ground crew ran over and Corporal Bhasin asked Cooke to jump out of the cockpit, as there was no ladder with them. Cooke jumped and the burly Bhasin caught him like a baby. Cooke slumped, his overalls soaked in sweat. The airmen were perturbed to find that Cooke had no drop tanks and that his gun ports were blackened. The stern Flight Sergeant was even more concerned because Cooke had damage to his left wingtip and there were branches and leaves stuck there. He said, 'Sir, I'll have to tell the CO that you have been flying low!'

La Fontaine spoke to Cooke after he landed; the adrenaline of combat had momentarily wiped out Cooke's recollection of any details of the fight. Later in the evening, after the remaining pilots had seen the gun film a startled La Fontaine was moved to say: 'It was frightening, bits and pieces of the Sabre were flying off and the trees were scraping the wing tips.' In conversation with Cooke, La Fontaine said, 'Alfred, you fired at four different Sabres!' 'I don't know sir!' replied Cooke. 'I just can't remember!' Cooke returned to Kalaikunda later that night, spent and exhausted. He would be able to reconstruct the battle with amazing detail once he had recovered from the intense adrenaline rush. The dogfight had felt like a blur, not just of emotions but of visual impressions as well: Cooke went into a turn, there was a Sabre in front of him, he fired and broke away 'to avoid the trees', another Sabre came up in front of him, and, 'I fired again'. More trees; break away, fire at the Sabre again and so on. It had been fought at frighteningly low-level and often at dangerously close range. It had seen one pilot, Cooke, take on four different Sabres and fight them in contrasting styles. His mastery of the Hunter and his knowledge of how to best exploit its strengths against a formidable adversary like the Sabre, had seen him emerge triumphant.

Amazingly, Cooke had tangled with all four Sabres. His gun camera film shows that he fired at four different Sabres and hit three. The first obviously got hit and broke up. A second Sabre, hit repeatedly, is seen with a tank hung under its left wing. The third Sabre had a tank hung on the starboard wing. This is followed by another Sabre, which Cooke remembers as being clean, with no underwing tanks. However, a closer look at the film reveals the fourth Sabre as carrying a starboard drop tank as well. But it seems clear that this was the fourth Sabre, as the second (Tariq Habib Khan's) had already disengaged and the third had escaped after making a steep dive.

There are conflicting reports about the actual number of Sabres shot down. Dicky Law, the OC Flying, who watched the entire air combat, reported seeing two Sabres go down: one in the immediate vicinity of the airfield and another that flew some distance away from the town. The Sabres had, in fact, circled the Dhudkundi range before coming into attack Kalaikunda. This, coupled with the fact that they had to exit out of Kalaikunda at high speed with Hunters in the chase, burned up the meagre fuel reserves of the Sabres. This is corroborated by reports, from a police station near the border, of a lone jet aircraft coming in low, trailing smoke and the pilot ejecting just across the border. Radio intercepts also reported ejections due to the low fuel situations of the Sabres. Mamgain's gun camera evidence was inconclusive but, keeping in mind Dicky Law's report of two Sabres being downed, was given the credit for a Sabre kill. The PAF only admitted the loss of one Sabre, that of Afzal Khan's. Years later, the PAF was to admit the loss of another Sabre, which returned too badly damaged to be recovered, apparently written off after returning from this raid due to 'lack of spares'. The extent of the spares required is not known. Flight Lieutenant Tariq Habib Khan, who suffered a drop tank hang up just before the combat, was flying this Sabre, the one recorded in Cooke's film. If the report is to be believed, Cooke had two kills that day.

Unfortunately for Cooke, the Hunter he flew that day (BA 250) was loaded with ball ammo rather than HE ammo. Tariq Habib Khan's Sabre would have met a more spectacular end than just being 'written off due to lack of spares' had that been the case. The ball ammo probably saved the third Sabre from going down, since it was the recipient of only a short burst or two. In the annals of air combat, Cooke's battle ranks as a classic.

Later, in its official history, the PAF would claim that nine Hunters took on the attacking Sabres. The PAF versions are a backhanded compliment to the Indian pilots, as Cooke would comment years later, on finding this particular story: 'I thought, wow, what a compliment, thanks very much—did it feel like there were nine Hunters in the sky?'

Plate 39: IAF Chief of Staff Arjan Singh talks to Cooke and Mamgain during a visit to Kalaikunda after the war. Cooke was not shy in extolling the virtues of the Hunter over the Sabre. Mamgain would buy Cooke a Gurkha *khukri* after the war as a token of appreciation.

The Pakistani gamble to capitalize on their earlier success failed, as Kalaikunda remained operational for the rest of the war. The second raid destroyed two more Canberras, taking to eight the total number of IAF aircraft destroyed on ground at Kalaikunda that day. The next day, the local police recovered the grisly remains of Flight Lieutenant Afzal Khan, badly mutilated and charred; civic authorities gave him a proper burial at the Muslim cemetery in Kalaikunda.

THE CASE OF THE MISSING SABRE

Wing Commander La Fontaine supplied a morbid sequel to the air combat. After Afzal Khan's body was sent to the mortuary, a doctor in charge removed the blood stained 'bone dome' (flying helmet) and sent it to La Fontaine 'to keep as a war trophy'. Better sense prevailed. Not fancying a blood stained helmet as a war trophy, La Fontaine called Flight Lieutenant P.S. Puri, instructed him to go with crew men to the wreckage to tear out a piece with markings like the PAF Star and Crescent, which would make a good display trophy. La Fontaine forgot about it and after a couple of days, on seeing Puri asked him about it. The laconic Puri responded, 'Its not there'. La Fontaine responded, 'If it's not there, at least get the panels with the roundels . . . or some serial number, anything.' Puri left, to be cornered after another couple of days by La Fontaine about the same topic. Puri answered 'Sir, it's not there.' La Fontaine was perplexed. 'You mean to say the PAF sent in unmarked aircraft?' 'No sir,' replied Puri. 'The wreckage itself is not there. We did not find it. This is all we could find,' and he held up a burnt rubber gasket.

The wreckage of the Sabre was never found. Even though Khan's body was recovered, the aircraft was never recovered except for the burnt rubber gasket, which was identified as an engine fitting. Three months after the war, the local police called in Wing Commander Dicky Law to identify aircraft parts recovered from a scrap merchant. The aircraft parts were clearly identified as non-Indian, and were presumed to have been from the Sabre.[4]

Afzal Khan's Sabre crashed south of Kalaikunda, within a

MISSED OPPORTUNITY: WAR IN EASTERN SECTOR

few kilometres of the Indian Institute of Technology. IIT students had pounced on the crash site and made away with whatever pieces they could find of the aircraft. Communication equipment, Browning machine guns were hacked from the wreckage and whisked away into the student's hostels and secret hiding places. The IAF Military Police had to raid the student hostel rooms in the days to follow, to recover the wreckage.

The shooting down of the Sabre and the possible destruction of another two were small consolation for the havoc wrought in the first raid. But it did point out to the PAF that the IAF was still standing on its feet and was trading blows. The PAF was not deterred by its losses, for in the next few days they attacked IAF fields like Barrackpore, Baghdogra, Gauhati and unused airstrips like Agartala. Many IAF officers praised the way the lone PAF Squadron flew in the east. Wing Commander Wilson, the CO of the Canberras at Kalaikunda viewed the PAF in the east as 'highly motivated, well led and well trained'.

Plate 40: 14 Squadron PAF before the war. Squadron Leader Syed Shabbir Hussain (*standing second from left*) was the CO—on his left is the Station Commander Dacca. Kneeling on the ground, second from left is Flight Lieutenant ATM Aziz whose Sabre crashed while chasing Hunters over Dacca; kneeling extreme right is Flying Officer Afzal Khan, shot down by Alfred Cooke over Kalaikunda.

Kalaikunda was not raided thereafter, but the first two raids damaged the airfield as well as morale. Kalaikunda did not plan any strikes after this. The raid put the spotlight on the practice of dispersal of aircraft in airfields in terms of war.

PANIC AT BARRACKPORE, CHAOS IN JORHAT

Meanwhile at Dum Dum, 14 Squadron's Hunters were on ORP. La Fontaine had informed the air defence centre in Barrackpore of the availability of Hunters on ORP, with the first two pilots being himself and Flight Lieutenant J.S. Virk, the squadron adjutant. Soon, as both the pilots were on ORP, the order came from Dum Dum ATC to scramble and head for Barrackpore, which was under attack. Virk's Hunter failed to start up, and on the clearance from the ATC La Fontaine scrambled into the air alone. He looked for a safe place to drop his fuel tanks and did so in a paddy field.

Short of Barrackpore, a Packet came in for finals. The Barrackpore ATC informed the Packet that the airfield was under attack and told it to hold its present position. The pilot, Wing Commander Kamat, CO of the Packet squadron radioed back, 'Is this an exercise or what?' The ATC replied, 'No this is the real thing. We are under attack! Orbit your present position.' 'This is Red One!' La Fontaine responded on the R/T. 'Tell me where are the Sabres, I will be over there in 30 seconds, keep my tail clear.' There was silence from the ATC. La Fontaine came over Barrackpore, and frantically flew circles and tight turns trying to spot the Sabres while calling the ATC. 'Red One to tower!' La Fontaine radioed again, 'Tell me where are the Sabres, where are the Sabres?' More silence.

On the ground, Wing Commander Senapati looked up to see ack-ack guns open up on a single jet fighter, which to his horror, he identified as a Hunter. With no radio or telephone access, Senapati could only pray for the Hunter. La Fontaine was unaware of the AA fire as he jinked around, trying to spot the attacking Sabres. It was a false alarm. There were no attacking Sabres. La Fontaine never found out why the Barrackpore ATC gave its panicky call about the air attack.

MISSED OPPORTUNITY: WAR IN EASTERN SECTOR

The Packet then thundered into land, and at the end of the runway, all the crew ran out of the aircraft and jumped into the slit trenches headfirst!

A month or so after this incident, Wing Commander Senapati happened to run into La Fontaine. As conversation turned to recent events and the incidents in eastern sector, La Fontaine happened to mention that he flew the sortie in a Hunter to Barrackpore on that fateful day. Senapati asked La Fontaine, 'You must have been furious at the ack-ack gunners for firing at you that day.' La Fontaine replied, 'No I wasn't, I didn't know they even fired at me.' Sengupta was incredulous, 'You mean to say that you didn't see those black balls of smoke?' La Fontaine replied, 'No I didn't see a damn thing.' Senapati replied in amazement, 'What kind of scan were you keeping man! You couldn't see the ack-ack explosions? They were all over your Hunter! This is incredible!'

Clearly, chaos prevailed in the air defence establishment in the Eastern Sector. Enemy air raids and parachute drops were dreamt up and Air Defence Controllers lived under constant pressure to separate the genuine from the false alarms. An incident at Jorhat illustrates this point as well.

On that day, the Air Traffic Controller identified a Dakota flying low over the airfield, circling lazily. In peacetime, it could have been one of the numerous visitors, coming in for a transit stop. But the advent of the war and the devastating raid on Kalaikunda were keeping the controller on the edge of his seat. When the Dakota failed to fire the colours of the day, the worst seemed to have come true. It was probably a Pakistani attempt to drop paratroopers onto the airfield. Immediately, two Hunters from an airborne CAP were directed to attack the Dakota.

Flight Lieutenant H.M.P.S. Pannu, an instructor at the Transport Training Wing, Begumpet, was flying the IAF Dakota laden with Avon engines and cannon ammunition for 17 and 37 Squadrons. As he heard the controller yell on the R/T about the parachutists and saw Hunters approach him in a menacing fashion, he raised his undercarriage and flew away from the airfield. The lead Hunter had already switched on his guns and had the Dakota in the 'bead'. As Pannu shouted on the R/T about mistaken identity, one of the Hunter pilots recognized Pannu's voice as his instructor's from his days as a cadet at the Air Force Academy. Flying Officer Bains immediately warned the lead Hunter not to fire. The Dakota landed safely at Jorhat. Pannu had to be restrained from firing his service revolver in the general direction of the Air Traffic Control Tower.

After the losses suffered in the two raids by the PAF, and the receipt of orders to stop offensive action in the east, the Canberras were moved to Gorakhpur. The Vampires were sent to Panagarh to provide CAP cover in West Bengal.

GALLANTRY AT BAGHDOGRA

The Eastern Sector was relatively quiet after the Kalaikunda raids on 7 September. Other airbases within the range of the Sabres at Tejgaon were Barrackpore (Dum Dum), Baghdogra, Guwahati and Tezpur. Baghdogra was a relatively new air base situated in the Siliguri corridor, where a 30 km salient of Indian territory separated Nepal and East Pakistan. With its proximity to the border, it was vulnerable to sneak raids by commandos. Several Vampires of 101 Squadron including a two-seater trainer version were based at Baghdogra, which also served as a transit stop for aircraft ferrying supplies to NEFA.

On 10 September, the Vampire detachment was briefed for missions across the border. The time was 1630 hours; crews relaxed in the anterooms. A C 119 Packet had landed an hour ago and was being prepared for dispersal by laying camouflage nets on it. Two Vampires were readied for the planned recce sortie. Squadron Leader M.J. Marston, who had joined the squadron in the middle of operations from Eastern Air Command Staff Headquarters, was deputed to fly as co-pilot to one of the senior flight commanders, Squadron Leader V.B. Sarwardekar. The second Vampire was a single seater to be flown by Flying Officer J.K. Mohla. Both aircraft were armed with front gun ammunition and equipped with additional drop tanks. Sarwardekar started his Vampire and taxied the aircraft out to the end of the runway, where he lined up and waited for

Mohla, who had had problems starting his engine, to catch up. An impatient Sarwardekar called up Mohla on the R/T, who replied that his engine had started and that he was on his way. Sawardekar switched off, asking Mohla to quickly catch up.

Then, suddenly, the R/T crackled, this time it was the ATC tower. 'We are under attack! No. 2 do not move!' Four Sabres had pulled up from a high-speed pass and climbed around to start their first attacking run. Mohla, whose aircraft was still in the pen, switched off his aircraft and stayed put. However Marston and Sarwardekar, positioned for take-off at the end of the runway, made a prominent target on the gleaming concrete surface.

The airmen were running for cover when the first Sabre opened up. The exploding shells of the ack-ack guns soon joined the clattering sound of the machine guns of the Sabres. The four attacking Sabres employed a classic attack pattern of two sections. One section went for the Vampire at the end of the runway and strafed it. Pieces and panels flew off the aircraft as the bullets hit the Vampire and the tarmac surrounding it. The drop tanks carried by the Vampire were riddled and the aviation spirit that gushed out almost immediately ignited into a blaze. Oily black smoke enveloped the aircraft. The ground crew had already given up the pilots as dead. Then the canopy opened and a figure struggled out of the seat harness. It was Sawardekar. He jumped onto a dry patch just near the cockpit, and looked back to see Marston jump down on the other side of the aircraft. Marston lost his balance and fell in the burning fuel. Sarwardekar went back to pull Marston out and extinguished his burning overalls. A fire tender and a crash wagon reached the aircraft, now burning furiously and surrounded by exploding ammunition. Marston was severely burnt and was evacuated to a hospital. But for his dud engine, or the ATC's warning, Mohla would have met the fate of his seniors. Had the Sabres been some 5 seconds late on their TOT, Mohla too would have been caught in the open.

Meanwhile, the other two Sabres went for the C 119 Packet. The bullet-riddled Packet, while not catching fire, had to be written off due to the damage it suffered. The raid lasted a little over 2 minutes. AA fire hit one Sabre and it flew away, trailing smoke, to an unknown fate. It might have failed to make the 200-mile flight back to Tejgaon. All flying at Baghdogra was cancelled till the damage was repaired. Even as the aircrews were retiring to bed, rumours floated in about paratroopers being dropped near the border; these proved baseless. Once again, the lack of early warning was made painfully apparent to Eastern Air Command. The approach of the Sabres—flying at long range from their homebase—went undetected, with no measures undertaken to intercept them. Marston succumbed to his injuries on 14 September at the Military Hospital. In February 1966, Sawardekar received a well-deserved Kirti Chakra—the equivalent of the MVC for gallantry not in the face of the enemy.

CAPs CAPs AND MORE CAPs

On the heels of the Indian Government's edict that no offensive operations were to be carried out against the Pakistani forces in the eastern sector, the aircraft of Central and Eastern Command found themselves saddled with a drastically reduced workload. 14 Squadron at Kalaikunda resorted to flying standing combat air patrols from dawn to dusk over the Kalaikunda-Dum Dum-Barrackpore circuit. Since no other operational activity was called for, and since the threat of PAF raids was still felt, 14 Squadron's Hunters kept an unending vigil over the skies over Calcutta. Its pilots averaged three to four CAPs daily.

The monotonous CAP flying affected both the pilots and the aircraft. To sustain the sortie rate, the Hunters were turned around rapidly on the ground, leaving little time for the engines or the brakes to cool down before the next pilot took the aircraft to the air. Braking on landing had another unforeseen effect. Since the brake pads were already heated up, there were a number of overshoots on landing. One Hunter had to engage the crash barrier at the end of the runway.

One of the pilots who overshot on landing was Squadron Leader Mohinder Singh 'Minhi' Bawa, CO of EFTI Patiala at the outbreak of hostilities. An ex-20 Squadron pilot with significant hours on the Hunter, Bawa was on detachment to 14 Squadron. His experience with the overheating brake pads was similar to that of other pilots. Returning from a routine CAP, he was directed to land on the downwind, along the sloping runway at Kalaikunda. Aided by the tail wind and the downward gradient, the Hunter continued to roll even as it was running out of runway space. Braking did not help. The aircraft overshot and came to a stop off the runway, at which point the over heated brake pads were overcome by a minor conflagration. Fortunately, the ground crew was able to put out the fire before serious damage could result.[5]

To the credit of the ground crew again, engineering officers and airmen burned the proverbial midnight oil to get the damaged and stranded aircraft back to flying trim, part of the effort that saw 14 Squadron put in nearly 800 hours of CAP flying in that period.

The effect of the routine on the pilots was a bit more insidious. Its monotony meant that the only break that the pilots could expect was 'detachment' to Dum Dum International airport, where they engaged in a spot of game hunting—in this case small birds—with their personal weapons. More than a few mystified looks from passengers using the airport were directed at the sight of (amongst others) Squadron Leader Virk, Flight Lieutenant Cooke and Flying Officer Sawhney trudging around in the high grass, wearing G-suits and high boots. Virk cut a dashing figure as he twirled his Smith and Wesson pistol around his index finger. Detachment to Dum Dum also meant an opportunity to check out Calcutta nightlife. Already recognized as heroes, the 14 Squadron pilots were mobbed wherever they went.

THE PAF RAIDS ON BARRACKPORE AND AGARTALA

This raid on Baghdogra was not the last the PAF carried out in the eastern sector. On the morning of 14 September, it was announced on All India Radio that a mock air raid alarm would be sounded at 0815 hours and that all citizens should take part in the drill by taking cover appropriately. This air raid drill was to be carried out in important cities and installations.

That morning, Corporal G.C. Chakraborty, an airman working for No. 2 AD Area HQ at Barrackpore, was getting ready for the day's duty. As he stepped outside his quarters located near the southern end of the runway, he heard jets scream across at low level. Since the noise of the jets was not that of the familiar Goblins of the Vampires or the Avons of the Hunters, Chakraborty looked up and saw two jets bearing down in his direction. There were tiny flashes in front of the aircraft. Chakraborty recognized the Star and Crescent emblems on the tails of the aircraft, as they streaked over his quarters. Chakraborty stood paralysed. There were no trenches dug at the quarters. Remembering a small pond nearby, he ran and dove for cover into the pond, still wearing just a towel on him. Safe in the water, he watched the entire attack.

The Sabres pulled up over the Ishapore Rifle factory and made their attack run over the airfield. The first section of the Sabres strafed transport aircraft in the dispersal area. An airman of 48 Squadron, A.C. Nisar Ahmed, was sitting on the wing, refuelling a C 119 Packet and was caught in a hail of bullets from the lead Sabre. Ahmed was killed instantly. Sergeant Dushyant Singh, who was standing below the aircraft on the tarmac, was injured in the face by shot-up gravel. The aircraft wing was burnt out.

A second C 119, parked near the Palta gate, was undergoing engine replacement. Both engines had been removed for maintenance to HAL Barrackpore. The aircraft was peppered by bullets and was damaged beyond repair. A third aircraft was also hit, this one a Dakota of 11 Squadron, being readied for the regular 'Carnic Courier'—the supply run to the Car Nicobar Islands. This Dakota was fully loaded with fuel and supplies and went up in flames, as the high-octane fuel caught fire instantly. Luckily no air crew were in the aircraft.

Meanwhile, the second section of the Sabres strafed the Zoola Hangar and as they completed the first pass, the first section started their second pass on the ATC building. The stores section was set on fire as kerosene lamps, used to light up the runway, caught fire. The second section of the Sabres made their second and last run on the airfield. They noticed Vampires of an auxiliary squadron parked on the northern end of the runway, but failed to hit any as the Vampires were better dispersed, and the AA fire was well coordinated to foil the attack run of the Sabres. One of the Sabres was hit and was streaming smoke as it exited out towards the general direction of East Pakistan. Apparently, this Sabre landed at Jessore, not far away.

Two Hunters, flown by Squadron Leaders P.K. 'Banjo' Banerji and Minhi Bawa were on combat air patrol in the vicinity. 55 SU informed them of the raid but the call for intercept arrived too late. The Sabres' two attacking passes had ended rapidly; the skies were empty over Barrackpore by the time the Hunters arrived. To add potentially dangerous injury to insult, Banjo and Bawa arrived over Barrackpore to be greeted by anti-aircraft fire. Yet again, fortune favoured 14 Squadron and saved its Hunters from friendly fire.

The PAF claimed the destruction of four aircraft: one C 119, one Canberra and two Dakotas. No Canberras were based at Barrackpore at that time. While the engineless C 119 was written off, and the Dakota was burnt out, the C 119 with the burnt wing was recovered after the war.

When the air raid siren was sounded in Barrackpore, people thought it was a drill, but their impressions of a mock air raid were quickly corrected by the strafing. The PAF used the opportunity of the practice air raid siren to plan and execute an actual attack. The Sabres had flown down from Tejgaon equipped, with four drop tanks for extended range, and had only their front guns to carry out the attack. Barrackpore did not receive any further raids even though the air raid alarm was sounded frequently.

The second raid of the day was on Agartala airfield, suspected of housing some transport aircraft. The Sabres did not find any aircraft and instead strafed the ATC building. An unfortunate civilian ATC officer present in the tower was killed but no damage was done to the airfield.

Tejgaon's Sabres did not fly strike missions again after 14 September. The PAF claims it lost three Sabres in the eastern sector. One (Aziz) chasing targets over Kurmitola, the other (Afzal Khan) shot down over Kalaikunda, and the last (Tariq

Habib) rendered unserviceable due to battle damage. Before hostilities had flared up the PAF lost a Sabre, which suffered a bird-hit and crashed north of Sylhet, killing the pilot Flight Lieutenant Hasan Akhtar. To their credit, even with an officially acknowledged strength of only eight aircraft, the PAF squadron carried out attacks on Baghdogra and Barrackpore. After 14 September, the detachment was given instructions to conserve its strength, thus rendering credible Indian claims that the detachment suffered more than four losses.

In the eastern sector, the IAF lost thirteen planes on the ground; none were lost in aircombat in the east. The PAF' detachment showed considerably more daring and initiative than the IAF. The Indian pilots did not lack the enthusiasm to take on the Sabres but were not given a free hand to do so. This became apparent when Air Marshal Arjan Singh paid a visit to Dum Dum after the war and told La Fontaine that he should have made the attack on Tejgaon on 7 September with guns, without waiting for rockets. La Fontaine pointed out that the SASO had informed him of the decision to curtail operations in the east, much before his planned TOT of 0930 hours over Tejgaon. Arjan Singh's disappointment suggests he was not party to the order—a political decision that he disagreed with—to hold back.

Had CAC's and EAC's Hunters been given a free hand, it would have been a matter of days before the depleted Sabre squadron was either knocked out or grounded by strikes on airfields. A hint at what was possible was provided by the subjugation of the same PAF squadron in the 1971 war, when it lost five Sabres in combat, and an equal number on the ground, before MiG 21s from Gauhati rendered the runways unserviceable to ground the surviving aircraft.

This still remains one of the big 'what ifs' of the war.

NOTES

1. It was never found out why Aziz's Sabre crashed, though (John Fricker) suggests that the Aziz distracted by an IFF frequency change, pushed his stick down while at low altitude. John Fricker, *Battle for Pakistan*, London: Ian Allen, 1979, p. 117.

2. The 'Indian Armed Forces—Official History of the 1965 Indo-Pakistan War' confirms this. P.V.R. Rao, the then Defence Secretary personally gave orders to the IAF to stop all offensive action in the east, for reasons best known to the government. The PAF did not have any such con-straints put on them.
3. Interestingly, Cooke chose to emphasize loyalty to the squadron first: a classic pilot's reaction, one similar to the motivational tactics used in the army, where it was found that the Regimental affiliation and unit *izzat* was a greater motivator than fighting for the country.
4. The disappearance of the Sabre's wreckage is not as incredible as it sounds. Air Chief Marshal La Fontaine recollects another incident in the 1960s, when a Canberra that crashed near the Dhudkundi range was left unguarded. When the IAF went to recover the wreckage, the recovery party found that local scrap merchants and villagers had stolen the entire wreckage.
5. Correspondence with author.

CHAPTER 7

The Second Week of the Air War

8 SEPTEMBER

The Ground War

8 September marked the beginning of a shift away from the previous week's strategy of confrontation by the IAF. Losses suffered in counter air sorties versus the damage inflicted by them had not added up to a favourable equation since their immediate effect on the ground situation had been negligible. The IAF's change of strategy was based on its assessment that a long conflict of attrition lay ahead, requiring staying power on its part to contribute to the Indian Army's dogged campaign into Pakistani territory.

The fighting on the ground continued, with no let up in its ferocity. The Indian Army's IXth Corps' offensive in the Lahore sector was bogged down. The 15th Infantry Division led by Major General Niranjan Prasad which had reached the west bank of the Ichogil canal by 6 September was thrown back and by nightfall on 8 September, was desperately fighting a Pakistani counter-attack. Prasad, the only Indian Army General to wear IAF pilot's wings—earned on a Second World War deputation, flying Vultee Vengeance missions in the Arakan—was ambushed by a Pakistani Army patrol and abandoned his attaché-case in his jeep, both of which fell into Pakistani hands. Prasad's attaché-case contained documents with several uncomplimentary remarks directed at his superiors. The reading of these over Pakistani radio proved an embarrassment for the Indian government. Coupled with the ambush, these reverses led to Prasad being relieved of his command; Major General Mohinder Singh took over his post.

The second prong of the Indian attack on Burki took the 9th Infantry Division to the Ichogil canal, where it sat and fought it out with the Pakistani Army on the other bank for the rest of the war. This advance to Burki brought Indian artillery guns within range of Lahore International Airport, close enough for the US to request a temporary ceasefire when time came to evacuate its citizens from Lahore. On both divisional fronts, the IAF could do little to influence the ground war.

Further south, the IAF was sorely missed as well. As the 4th Mountain Division—the famous 'Red Eagles' under Major General Gurbaksh Singh.[1] advanced towards Kasur, a Pakistani counter-offensive at the Ichogil Canal threw them back to their starting point. The Division almost broke up under the counter-attack—almost. The Pakistani Army used an armoured division, supported by an infantry division, against the 4th Division. By the evening of 6 September, the 4th Division was forced to retreat. The Pakistani Army sat idle on 7 September and resumed its offensive the next day. The story of the battle that followed over the next two days has been recounted many times.[2] In spite of losing Khem Karan, the truncated 4th Division, supported by an Independent Armoured Brigade, regrouped and destroyed the Pakistani armoured offensive in the battle of Assal Uttar ('The True North' not 'The Right Answer').

At a crucial moment on 8 September, when it looked like the 4th Division would crumble under the Pakistani offensive, the IAF was called for help. There was plenty of armour to hit on the GT Road and in the Kasur sector. The Pakistani supply lines were busy supporting their army units. The IAF attacked these but missed out on having significant influence on the tactical ground battle. In the end, it was 4th Division alone that fought with the Pakistanis in a fierce battle, with no quarter asked for or given. If Khem Karan was the only battle that was being fought by the army, the IAF might have been able to concentrate its efforts, but it was not.

Far north of the GT Road, a little south of Jammu on the Pakistani side was the city of Sialkot, selected as the objective of an offensive by the Indian Army's strike element: 1st Corps. Commanded by Lieutenant General P.O. Dunn, 1st Corps included three Infantry/Mountain Divisions and the army's premier formation, the 1st Armoured Division, led by Major General Rajinder Singh. With the 6th Mountain Division led by Major General S.K. Korla, 14th Infantry Division led by Major General R.K.R. Singh and 26th Infantry Division led by Major General M.L. Thapan, the Corps launched its offensive on the night of 7/8 September. It planned to advance south and, after capturing the towns of Phillora and Chawinda, turn west and cut-off the Sialkot-Gujranwala road and hence Sialkot from Lahore. The 26th Infantry Division advanced the furthest; the Pakistani Army countered with its 6th Armoured Division. Between 8 and 16 September, some of the fiercest tank battles since Second World War were fought in this sector. Villages, towns, hills, all changed hands frequently. Both sides slugged it out, achieved little, sacrificed much and imposed great strains on their supporting infrastructure. With battle raging on the ground, there were plenty of targets to choose on both sides; the PAF did its part too.

What was the IAF's part in the ground war? After two days of expensive counter-air operations, it switched over to ground interdiction. Ground attack fighters were sent to harass Pakistani supply lines, the railway system and armoured formations. As the IAF settled down in the course of operations, it consolidated its forces. Administratively, aircraft of the same lineage were kept in a common pool: all Hunters were concentrated at Halwara, while Gnats were pooled at Ambala. Mysteres were based at both Adampur and Pathankot. Squadrons flew less as an atomic entity and more as part of a larger pool. As a result, formations with members from mixed units were common. A four-aircraft Gnat air defense patrol could consist of two Gnats from 2 Squadron and 9 Squadron; a Hunter strike from Halwara could be drawn from 7, 20 and 27 Squadrons. Though the effectiveness of this arrangement was questioned, it proved useful for combat air patrols.

Common pooling enabled the availability of aircraft round the clock—and also that one unit was not crippled due to shortage of aircraft or spares, while another hogged the flying.

Lightnings to the Front

By the afternoon of 7 September, Halwara had lost six Hunters in the air, and two had been damaged on the ground by B 57 attacks. Only two of the three Hunter Squadrons in the western sector had seen action, while the third, 20 Squadron was still based at Hindon, without seeing a shot fired in anger.

Late afternoon on 7 September, Wing Commander Amrit Lal Bajaj, CO 20 Squadron received orders to move one flight of Hunters to Halwara. The aircraft and pilots would augment the existing squadrons there and cover for the losses suffered till then. Bajaj deputed one of his Flight Commanders, Squadron Leader Bhupendra Kumar 'Bhup' Bishnoi, and five other pilots to fly the Hunters over by the day's end. Bajaj announced to the gathered pilots that only senior pilots had been deputed, much to the disappointment of the junior Flying Officers whose hopes of seeing action were dashed.

When the time came for the first detachment to take-off the No. 2, an instructor from Training Command, attached to the squadron, was not found. He had apparently gone to collect his identity card and papers and been held up. An anxious WAC HQ bombarded Hindon with calls querying the delay. Bajaj could wait no longer. He noticed Flying Officer Dilip Kumar Parulkar, innocently loitering in the squadron crew room. He called him into his office and asked if there was anyone fully operational on the Hunters who could accompany Bishnoi. Unknown to Bajaj, Parulkar had placed himself in the crew room for precisely such an opportunity. With just two years of commissioned service and a brand new fully-ops certification on the Hunters under his belt, a crack at frontline duty had seemed unlikely. Parulkar immediately announced his ops status (earned ten days previously) and volunteered to accompany Bishnoi's detachment. Bajaj grudgingly agreed. Parulkar was off, running out of the office and into the crew room, pre-empting any second thoughts on the part of his CO.

The first section of two Hunters was ready. Parulkar grabbed his helmet and joined Bishnoi on the tarmac. The two took-off and after a flight of 40 minutes, arrived at Halwara. The duty pilot at the Halwara ATC, Squadron Leader Paranjpe of 27 Squadron, called out to the Hunter pilots to authenticate themselves. The Hunter pilots sheepishly realized that in their urgency to get to Halwara, they had forgotten to collect their authentication tables, which contained the code of the hour for Paranjpe's authentication request. When this was communicated to the ATC, Paranjpe, a Maharashtrian, asked Parulkar if he was one, and getting an affirmative response, asked him to speak fluently in Marathi as authentication. Given that most PAF pilots probably spoke Punjabi, an Indian ATC officer that spoke Punjabi would not have tried this method of authentication.

Within hours, 20 Squadron's second detachment arrived. Squadron Leader N.C. 'Nimmi' Suri, attached to No. 20 from the Aircrew Examination Board, led this four-Hunter formation. Accompanying him were Flight Lieutenants C.K.K. Menon, Amarjit Singh Khullar and D.S. Negi. 7 Squadron assumed administrative command of both detachments.

Raiwind Rail Attack

On 8 September, the IAF attacked tanks, convoys, artillery emplacements and targets of opportunity, like trains, bridges and ammunition dumps. Raiwind, situated north of Lahore and north-east of Kasur, was the only link on the railway line to Kasur; supplies and reinforcements coming in by rail to the Lahore front were routed through its station. Unsurprisingly, Raiwind was showered with special attention by the IAF throughout the war. It was easy to locate by air. IAF pilots simply crossed the Ichogil Canal and flew on to the railway line, which they followed to the Raiwind railway junction. The high priority the Pakistanis gave the Khem Karan offensive saw daily reinforcements and supplies come in great numbers by rail. The Kasur sector bristled with targets. One of the first raids on Raiwind was carried out by 20 Squadron on the evening of 8 September.

On 8 September, the newly arrived pilots of the Lightnings got the chance to fly their first mission of the war: a ground attack sortie. Flight Lieutenant C.K.K. Menon was tasked as the leader and briefed to carry out an offensive sweep in the Kasur area; any Sabres that they encountered were to be engaged. Menon's formation members were Khullar, Negi and Bishnoi. Four Hunters were loaded with rockets and cannon ammunition; fully fuelled and armed with 16 T.10 rockets apiece, the first Hunter took to the air at 1800 hours.

Flying at 100 AGL and 580 knots, the four Hunters crossed the border. Shortly after crossing the Ichogil Canal at Burki, the formation turned 30 degrees left to head south-west, to approach Raiwind from the north. As they passed over its railway station, a goods train pulled into the marshalling yard. Noticing that the train was carrying military stores, Menon signalled his intention to attack. The section flew well past the railway station, throwing a fake to the AA gunners, it appeared that the Hunters had failed to sight the train. The Hunters went into a wide turn and on emerging, Menon pulled up to start his attacking run, followed by Khullar, Bishnoi and Negi.

The Hunters were now abreast of the train, with their positioning calculated so as to put the section facing the broadside of the train. Menon put his Hunter in a shallow dive. The anti-aircraft defenses were alerted and ready. Flying through a fusillade of AA fire, Menon got the locomotive in his sights. He fired his cannons to check his aim and fired a salvo of T.10 rockets. Menon could not see his rockets hit the target as he pulled out of the dive, a bare 100 ft over the train.

The rockets ran true and exploded on target, lifting the 100-ton locomotive off the rails along with three of the wagons. Only yards behind, Khullar fired his rockets into more wagons. As the Hunters pulled up, the train wagons, loaded with ammunition, blew apart explosively. Meanwhile, Bishnoi started his attacking run and along with Negi, used his rockets to finish off the untouched rear end of the train. The unrelenting AA fire stayed heavy throughout. The wagons exploded in sequence, ripping apart both the train as well as the railway track. Bishnoi called up Menon on the R/T to confirm the effectiveness of the attack. The railway yard was engulfed in roiling thick smoke, shrouding the devastation on the ground.

The action wasn't over for the day. The four Hunters reformed and headed south-east towards Kasur. They still had plenty of front gun ammunition; Menon and Khullar even had a few rockets left. The formation noticed an armoured column near Kasur and attacked. Menon and Khullar took out a few tanks with their rockets; Bishnoi and Negi, having expended their rockets on the train, used their cannon on other soft-skinned vehicles. The Hunters also stumbled upon two Pakistani Army convoys and strafed them. More than 30 light vehicles were destroyed or damaged in this pair of attacks.

The only damage to the Hunters was small holes in their fuel tanks by shrapnel. Menon had his air speed indicator (ASI) knocked out by one AA hit. All four pilots landed safely; Menon had to be shepherded in the finals. The pilots were credited with the destruction of an ammunition train carrying shells for Pakistani tanks at Kasur-Khem Karan. As deduced from R/T intercepts, its destruction left Pakistani tanks in the sector with less than 30 shells each: another factor in blunting the Pakistani Army offensive.

Meanwhile, Mysteres from 8 Squadron attacked armoured formations, transport facilities and communications infrastructure in the Pasrur, Sialkot and Chamb Sectors. During the strike on Chamb, Flight Lieutenant Vinod 'Jimmy' Bhatia distinguished himself. As the 'Black Formation' came under heavy fire, using rockets and cannons, Jimmy pressed home with repeated passes to account for two tanks. His Vir Chakra citation after the war would mention this strike in glowing terms.

Most of the IAF effort on 8 September was in support of the ground forces or in interdiction. Perhaps in view of the heavy losses suffered the day before no sorties were planned directly against air bases. The PAF took this as a sign of their air supremacy, an ambitious claim that failed to take cognizance of the fact that both the IAF and PAF shied away from attacking each other's air bases directly. Neither could stop the other from flying interdiction missions nor plan counter air sorties to take out the other's assets. Surprisingly, given that IAF was in the thick of action providing support to the 1st Corp's offensive in the Sialkot sector, no aircraft were lost on this day on either side nor did the IAF encounter the PAF, which flew 22 combat air patrol sorties.

8 Squadron notched up a first on 8 September. Though most Pakistani paratroopers had been captured or killed within a day or two of their drop on the night of 6 September, a handful had evaded capture and were still in the area neighbouring the airfields. Some of them had entered the perimeter of the airfield and taking refuge in the tall *sarkanda* grass, took potshots at aircraft and officers moving about in the airfield. Officers were ordered to remove their rank insignia while going about their duties. When the sniping became too much of a nuisance to ignore, a rather drastic solution was thought of. Flight Lieutenant Pramod 'Chopi' Chopra took off in a Mystere and strafed the area behind the bomb dump at 8 Squadron's dispersal area. Chopra thus became the first IAF pilot to strafe his own airfield. Squadron Leader Handa followed suit a couple of days later—again at Adampur—by strafing grassy areas next to the runways. No bodies were recovered or infiltrators claimed killed, but after these strafings the potshots stopped, the infiltrators presumably got the message and abandoned the airfield perimeter.

Later that same evening, 8 Squadron sent seven of its aircraft to Palam in anticipation of B 57 raids. These night flights were not without their share of excitement for the pilots, as Jimmy Bhatia explains:

Another funny one was when we used to do night flights to Palam for dispersion. We used to do individual take-offs because the runway was damaged. Chopi, Pat and I were going to go. Chopi was #1, and I followed. Pat was going to follow and he hadn't joined up. He kept asking, where are you? Finally he said contact, and said that he could see our tail lights. We carried on to Panipat. Pat said, yeah, I can see your tail lights. When we landed he asked what altitude we were flying at. We said about 10,000 ft. He had been at 25K, chasing a star all the way! I almost got thrashed on that same trip. I went to meet my parents who were in Patel Nagar. I was still wearing my G-suit, got on a scooter and was stopped by some local volunteers. They saw Jimmy on my overall and became very suspicious. I had to coax them to let me go and said come to my parents place; I'll show you where I live.

In 1964, India had acquired the VK-750 Surface to Air Missiles

(NATO SA-2 Guideline); a battery of these was deployed at Delhi. The Guideline was huge, almost the size of a medium aircraft. Its effectiveness at high and medium altitudes had been demonstrated in shooting down the CIA U-2 flown by Francis Gary Powers over the Soviet Union. The missiles first saw action on 8 September, when a contrail was observed high over Delhi. As no Indian aircraft were supposed to be over Delhi then, the SAM battery launched a SA-2. Though the explosion of the missile suggested a direct or proximity hit, no wreckage was found. No confirmation of Pakistani activity over Delhi on that day has been forthcoming; the incident remains one of the few mysteries of the war. No PAF aircraft were lost in the vicinity of Delhi. The only loss of the day was Flt. Lt. Sadruddin's Sabre, which was shot down by anti-aircraft fire as he crossed over to Pakistani territory after finishing an interdiction mission in the Lahore sector. He ejected safely and landed in Pakistani Army lines.

9 SEPTEMBER

Flying on a Wing and a Prayer

By the morning of 9 September, the battle at Khem Karan had started. One of the first missions of the day was a four-Hunter strike led by Wing Commander Zachariah of 7 Squadron over Kasur. While attacking ground targets, Zachariah lost sight of the second subsection, consisting of Squadron Leader Lele and Flying Officer M.V. Singh. During the ground attack dive, his Hunter was subjected to severe ground fire. One hit knocked out the electricals of the aircraft, jamming its controls. Reverting to manual, Zachariah pulled out at the last moment, barely skimming the ground. The return leg was done at a mere 260 knots. After landing at Halwara, the damage to Zach's aircraft became evident. Inspection by ground crew showed that the Hunter had actually struck the ground, damaging the jet pipe and tearing off the airbrake. Zachariah had had a brush with Mother Earth.[3]

The No. 4, M.V. Singh, of 27 Squadron was hit by AA fire and had to eject over Kasur. A badly injured Singh landed in

Pakistani army lines and—was shifted to a Military Hospital for treatment. Singh was well taken care of—Pakistani Army doctors went as far as to prevent Pakistani Intelligence from questioning him till he had recovered[4] —and spent the rest of the war as a POW.

A mixed formation of 7 and 27 Squadron Hunters, led by Squadron Leader Bishnoi, was then detailed for close support and interdiction. Bishnoi's No. 2 was Flight Lieutenant Gurbux Singh Ahuja, who had transferred from Air Force Storage Depot (AFSD) Sulur at the beginning of the war to 27 Squadron. The second section consisted of Flight Lieutenant S.K. Sharma of 7 Squadron and Flying Officer D.K. Parulkar.

The Hunters flew at 100 ft above ground level; Bishnoi led the formation with Ahuja on his left. Sharma and Parulkar followed about 500 yds away, to Bishnoi's right. The four Hunters arrived at Kasur at low level. Noticing dust raised by the movement of a heavy armoured column, Bishnoi alerted the formation and the Hunters switched on their electricals to arm their rockets. As they reached their target, the anti-aircraft fire from the heavy .50 inch machine guns on the tanks greeted them.

Bishnoi led the first attack. He pulled up to 300 ft and rolled into a dive onto a cluster of three tanks. His salvo of eight rockets had immediate effect. As he pulled away from the target, three tanks could be seen burning. Ahuja and Sharma followed, with rocket attacks on tank targets. They accounted for several tanks and armoured personnel carriers as well as soft-skinned vehicles. The Hunters made repeated passes, flying through the wall of flak, till they had expended all their rockets and front gun ammunition.

The last to dive into the attack was the No. 4, Parulkar. His Hunter faced the concentrated fire of the AA machine guns of the tanks, which had by then found time to correct and coordinate their fire. Just into the dive, Parulkar's Hunter was hit. The first thing Parulkar noticed was the explosive decompression as a bullet pierced the pressurized cockpit. The bullet pierced the floor of the cockpit, travelled up and through Parulkar's right arm, through the seat's headrest and finally made a hole in the Plexiglas canopy. Parulkar was lucky. He was crouching to the front to peer thru the gunsight when the bullet went through his headrest, otherwise his head would have been in the path of the bullet. The resultant depressurization misted the cockpit, obscuring visibility. Since there was a hole in the canopy, the airstream cleared the condensation on the windscreen. Parulkar continued the attack and fired off his rocket salvo at the tanks.

As he pulled out of the attack, Parulkar felt sharp pain in his arm and felt his flying suit being soaked with blood. He decided not to report it to Bishnoi, sensing the attack might be aborted if he mentioned that he was wounded. Bishnoi by then had expended his second salvo of rockets on other tanks and commenced gun attacks on soft-skinned vehicles. At the end of his fourth pass, Bishnoi called for the formation to assemble for the flight back.

On exiting the target area, Parulkar radioed Bishnoi and informed him that he had been hit in his right arm by ground fire and was bleeding profusely. The rest of the formation was concerned. Although Parulkar could fly back with one arm, he would need both to land. Bishnoi suggested that Parulkar eject as soon as they were over Indian territory. Parulkar refused, assuring Bishnoi that he would be able to land safely. The formation decided that Parulkar would land last so as to not block the runway if his landing failed. Parulkar's Hunter was not the only aircraft to be hit by ground fire. Sharma's Hunter had borne the brunt of the AA fire and he found that his aircraft was losing fuel fast, prompting much concern and careful monitoring through the return flight.

Bishnoi used to bring his formations back at high speed and low level before peeling off to land, a method that often caused problems for the base's AA gunners. As the Hunters would suddenly pull up over the horizon, the gunners had little time to effect an accurate recognition. On this occasion, as the Hunters peeled off prior to spacing out for landing, Sharma pulled up prematurely underneath Ahuja's aircraft; the rocket rails under Ahuja's starboard wing were picked up by Sharma's port air intake; the outer starboard wing control surfaces were ripped from the wing. Parulkar watched the mid-air collision in horror as Ahuja's Hunter, which seemed to come clear of the collision, rolled slightly from one side to the other and back. Ahuja was desperately trying to get the aircraft under control. The Hunter turned over on its back and plunged to the ground just outside the airfield perimeter in a huge fireball. Ahuja never had a chance to eject.

Bishnoi landed first. Sharma managed to land his damaged Hunter immediately after. The ground crew was amazed at the damage to Sharma's Hunter. The rocket rails had cut cleanly through the upper lip of Sharma's port air intake and had been embedded there. The Avon engine ingested a large amount of debris, but its power was adequate to carry out the forced landing. After this incident, Bishnoi was ordered to change his landing tactics.

Moments later, Parulkar made his approach. Dizzy due to the loss of blood, he carried out an overshoot and came around. He was able to land successfully during the second attempt.[5] Ambulances and crash tenders approached his aircraft, but ignoring them, Parulkar taxied his Hunter to dispersal. The bullet wound in his right upper arm had left the bone exposed. Parulkar's overalls were drenched in blood. Still in extreme pain, he was rushed to the base hospital to have his wound stitched up by the Station Medical Officer, Squadron Leader Prudvi. Parulkar was back on his feet again and in the squadron mess by the evening, narrating the day's operations to his squadron mates.

An inspection of Parulkar's Hunter revealed how lucky he had been. After striking Parulkar in the arm, the bullet had gone through his headrest and through the top of the ejection seat. In the process, it had severely frayed the static line that connects the drogue parachute with the main parachute of the seat. Had Parulkar managed to use his badly injured hand to fire the seat, the main chute would not have deployed, as the static line would have severed with the force of the opening impact of the drogue chute. The seat would have dropped to the ground without the main chute deploying. Parulkar was ignorant of this damage,[6] making his decision to attempt the landing even more commendable.

Those Damned Gnat Guns

Meanwhile, Flight Lieutenant Viney Kapila who had arrived with the Gnat detachment of 9 Squadron was on ORP at Halwara, along with Squadron Leader H.P.S. Harry Chatwal, when they were scrambled. Once airborne, both Gnats were vectored to the border area where four Sabres were loitering. The Fighter controller Flight Lieutenant K.Y. Singh positioned both Gnats perfectly behind the Sabres. Kapila and Chatwal closed in and observed two sections of Sabres, one flying at a much higher altitude than the other.

At this stage, the Gnat pilots did something unusual. The pilots split up, with Chatwal going after the lower pair of Sabres and Kapila going for the Sabre pair at higher altitude. It was tactically unsound to split the formation, as by staying together the Gnats would have covered each other's tail. However, in the heat of the battle, the pilots split up and went for separate sections.

As Chatwal closed in on his pair of Sabres, he was noticed and the Sabres put in a defensive turn. Chatwal chased the pair and soon lost R/T contact with Kapila. The Sabres engaged in hard turns and breaks, till Chatwal finally lost contact and flew back to base.

Kapila did slightly better. About the same time that Chatwal's targets broke off, Kapila's Sabres did the same. However, in the break, Kapila was able to keep the trailing Sabre within sight and latched onto it. In spite of the Sabre's attempt to break off, Kapila closed in to 175-200 yds. With the Sabre squarely in his sight, Kapila fired his cannon, which immediately jammed after firing 3-4 shells. A disgusted Kapila broke off and headed back to Halwara. The gun camera film that showed the Sabre nicely in his sights, was like salt in his wounds.

Pathankot's Mysteres were active against Pakistani Army targets on the ground. Wing Commander Goodman led his Mysteres on an attack on Raiwind that promptly made a shambles of a tank transporting train. An estimated 26 tanks were either destroyed or damaged. 3 Squadron's Mysteres saw action in the Sialkot sector, where Flight Lieutenant Tirlochan 'Tango' Singh—a leader in perfecting 3 Squadron's ground attack tactics, using 4-aircraft formations during and after the war—distinguished himself by leading a very successful mission that destroyed 8 tanks. 23 Squadron's Gnat detachment provided top cover on all Mystere strikes launched from Pathankot.

Further south in the desert, the Indian Army's Southern Command launched its ground offensive. The 11th Infantry Division, led by Major General N.C. Rawlley, advanced in the Gadra Bulge and captured the town of Gadra in the face of light opposition by Pakistani Rangers. This move attracted numerous PAF attacks. On 9 September, Sabres carried out a total of nine raids on Gadra Road, homebase for the Indian offensive. A pumping station and a goods train were hit, killing 10 railway employees and injuring 17 more. The same day, four B 57s from Mauripur carried out a relatively ineffective morning raid on Jodhpur airfield. Though little damage was done to Air Force installations, the constant raids throughout the war disturbed the Air Force Flying College's training syllabus and prompted the shifting of training establishments further south a few years later.

PAF B 57s then attacked Adampur between 2055 hours and 2155 hours. A direct hit near a trench killed five airmen from No. 3 AOP Flight. LAC Abdul Rahman Moochikkal, Cpl. Joginder Singh, AC 2 Chakravorty, AC 1 Rajinder Singh and AC 1 Ram Bhajan were the first NCO and other ranks to be killed in the war.

The Search for Fish Oil

'Fish Oil' was the code name given by the PAF to the lone radar operated by the IAF's 230 Signal Unit, based near Amritsar. The radar set was a P 36, supplied by the Soviet Union in 1964. Wing Commander Krishna Dandapani, a fighter pilot and flying instructor who had flown Tempests and Vampires, led the unit and had the unenviable task of making it operational. When hostilities were imminent, it became his responsibility to see that the IAF's only eyes were operational throughout the war. Amritsar's proximity to the border gave little lead-time in arranging the defenses and PAF Sabres and Starfighters attacked often. The anti-aircraft defenses for the site consisted of the reasonably effective L 60 AA guns.

Other than the unit in Amritsar, there was no significant Air Defence Control (ADC) Centre in the western sector. Ferozepur had a small radar, lacking in ADC capabilities, to cover the south-western sector. It fell upon the Amritsar radar to observe potential incoming raids and inform the respective air bases. The method of reporting intruders was long winded. It required Dandapani to inform the ADC Officer in Adampur, who in turn would inform Ambala, which then coordinated the scrambling of fighters to intercept the incoming raids. As most of the IAF's offensive air bases were close to the border and reaction time was minimal, a system slowly evolved whereby Dandapani would also inform the air base where an incoming raid was expected.

Radar protection was a huge task. Since 230 SU was the sole GCI radar of the IAF in Punjab, it was high on the PAF's priority list of targets. Designated 'Target Alpha', its strategic control over Indian fighter and bomber operations was not under-estimated. Unlike Pakistani GCI radars at Sakesar and Badin, 230 SU possessed the advantage of being completely mobile; its location was easily changed if so needed. Since there were no permanent fixtures, identifying its location precisely was a problem for the PAF during its numerous, futile raids.

The first raid on 230 SU took place on 6 September, when the PAF used a RB 57 to home in onto the radar's transmission. As it neared its target, heavy fire from Amritsar's AA guns damaged the RB 57, forcing it to limp back on one engine. Having failed to locate 230 SU, the accompanying Sabres abandoned the strike.

The next day, the PAF flew a T 33 mission over Amritsar and believed that they had enough evidence to pinpoint the radar's location. This was followed by an attack on the evening of 9 September, when four Sabres armed with napalm bombs were launched from Sargodha. The PAF raid fell apart due to the effective camouflaging of the radar site and its AA defense. Harried by intense AA fire, the Sabres, despite being in 230 SU's vicinity were unable to obtain a precise fix on its location.

Forced to abort the attack, the Sabres dropped their napalm bombs in the countryside. Some of these fell on residential areas, killing civilians. Dandapani assumed at the time that the PAF pilots had jettisoned their external drop tanks, not realizing that napalm had been dropped.

Ironically, the original Russian advisers for the operational deployment of the radar had suggested that the main radar antenna be placed on a specially constructed platform. Dandapani had protested vociferously at the time. Doing so would make the unit's position obvious from the air. He had his way, as the radar unit was never put in such a conspicuous position. The unit was well protected by a bevy of the L 60 AA guns. One of the guns was placed on the platform on which the radar equipment was supposed to have been placed. The equipment itself was at ground level, further away from the platform. The AA gunners on the platform earned Dandapani's admiration, the thought of facing a marauding Sabre with its front guns firing was a daunting one.

PAF Sabres attacked on 10 September, with 14 sorties flown in two missions. The first saw the Sabres employ 2.75-inch FFARs (Folding Fin Aerial Rockets). Once again, the Sabres did not find the radar equipment. The rockets fired in the unit area were ineffective; some Sabres jettisoned their rockets without arming or firing them. Dandapani recovered one of the rockets and kept it as a souvenir. It is displayed in his front room to this day. Other souvenirs were the drop tanks jettisoned by the Sabres. The empty tanks made excellent luggage carriers, and the officers of 230 SU fabricated trunk cases out of the Sabres' drop tanks as a reminder of those dangerous days. Dandapani vouches for the 'excellent imported material' of his luggage carriers. The second raid of the day damaged one of the IFF aerials but did not prevent the unit from carrying out its usual duties.

The next day the Sabres came close to striking their actual target, when four came attacking with their front guns. Amritsar's AA guns drew their first blood, shooting down a Sabre that was engulfed in flames as it exited the target area and crashed on the outskirts of the town. The body of Squadron

Leader Muniruddin Ahmed of the PAF was recovered from the crash site. After his providential escape at Wollen's hands in the opening air battles of the war, Ahmed's fortunes had taken a turn for the worse.

Over the next few days, more attacks followed but none managed to put the radar unit out of action, thanks to the tenacity of the AA gunners and the clever camouflaging of the equipment. On an inspection flight to Amritsar during the war, Air Vice-Marshal P.C. Lal was unable to locate the site from his Vampire. Landing at Amritsar airfield, Lal made his way to 230 SU and saw the camouflaged equipment. The equipment and installations were festooned not only with camouflage nets but also with branches of trees, leaves and other greenery and shrubbery. Dandapani had sent a few detachments in trucks to adjoining areas to cut branches and trees as camouflage for the equipment and buildings. Impressed at the arrangements, Lal queried Dandapani on the source of his inspiration. Dandapani replied, 'Oh, it was not my idea, it was Shakespeare's'. Lal laughed, recalling *Hamlet* in which the prophecy to the king said, 'Unless the forest moved, the king was not defeated.'

The radar unit attracted a number of high profile visitors during the war. The Chief Minister of the southern state of Tamil Nadu made a visit to the unit, as did Mrs. Indira Gandhi, the future prime minister of India. The stories of its gallant AA gunners, ably led by Major Kapur, soon became familiar in the coverage of the war by the press.

Further PAF attacks on subsequent days failed to disrupt the site's activities. Amritsar radar was also indirectly responsible for the PAF losing one of its specialized RB 57 aircraft. While simulating a planned raid on the radar, a Pakistani B 57, making a run over radar at Rahwali, was shot down by Pakistani AA gunners on 11 September. Both crew members were killed. Throughout the attacks by the PAF, Dandapani's unit escaped any loss of life. The last attack was on 21 September, the last day of the war. The AA guns spoiled the incoming raid's aim, and the Sabres dropped their stores, including napalm, on the village of Chertta, causing extensive civilian casualties. By the end of the war, the AA gunners had notched up an impressive tally of Pakistani aircraft shot down. Dandapani was awarded a richly deserved VSM Class II in recognition of his leadership during hostilities.

10 SEPTEMBER: THE MYSTERES AT THE BATTLE OF KHEM KARAN

10 September marked the fighting of one of the most crucial battles in Indian military history, the Battle of Assal Uttar in the Khem Karan sector. After two days of dithering, the Pakistani Armoured Division pressed forward for its final breakthrough. The overconfident Pakistani Army mistook 4th Division's tactical withdrawal for a rout and attacked, rushing headlong into an ambush. The spearheads of two Patton Regiments were lured into two sickle shaped formations of Centurion tanks, which closed the trap and severe fighting commenced owing to the tenacity shown by Indian defenders. Obscure places like Mahmudpura, Bhikiwind, Patti, and Assal Uttar attained nationwide fame in the next few days. The 1965 war's first Param Vir Chakra, India's highest military honour, went to Company Quarter Master Havildar Abdul Hamid for sacrificing his life in the fighting. Notably, the Pakistani Divisional Commander was ambushed and wounded while his artillery commander Brigadier Shammi was killed. By the end of the day, half the Pakistani tanks were in Indian hands. The bold Pakistani strategy of capturing Beas Bridge and strolling down the GT Road to Delhi had failed.

At commencement of the fighting, both sides were so placed and movements so complex that it had become difficult to distinguish friend from foe. No bombline could be drawn. Even under these difficult circumstances, the IAF gave a helping hand as Hunters from 27 Squadron flew close support missions. Due to the B 57 attacks at night, the IAF withdrew its aircraft to rear airbases like Palam and Hindon to prevent damage. 1 Squadron's Mysteres, which were withdrawn to Palam on the night of 9 September, were directly flown into action from there. After completing their close support mission, they landed at Adampur.

At 1500 hours, Wing Commander Taneja led a mission of four Mysteres on a close support attack in the Lahore sector. As they exited the target area, two Sabres pounced on them. Low on fuel, Taneja forbade the Mysteres from taking on the Sabres and adopted the low-level return home. As they hugged ground back to base, the Sabres gave up the chase, confirming the effectiveness of this particular method of escaping air attack.

Another strike at 1730 hours, led by Squadron Leader P.R. Earle, went to the Kasur sector to take out enemy armour and ran into a hot reception. 'Paddy' takes over the story:

The formation consisted of self (P.R. Earle); S.S. Dange; S. Handa; and Frisky Verma. We took off in the evening. We observed tanks galore at Khem Karan. I was hit on my first pass by ground fire. The fire warning light came on, and the JPT was off the clock. My No. 2, Lofty confirmed that my aircraft was on fire.

At that moment, Handa asked me to give him cover for second attack, which I did. Later he told me in the bar that night that he had seen an enemy flag car—hence his request for cover for another attack. During this second pass, Frisky was also hit and he had to rely solely on the emergency hydraulic system. The Mystere, unlike the Hunter and Gnat, could not revert to manual control in the event of hydraulic control problems. In a Mystere if the emergency failed, you had better be in level flight and an adequate height (300 ft +) to eject.

After I saw them pull out of the attack, Handu acknowledged he had me in sight. We headed for home at a reasonable altitude so that Frisky or I could, if necessary, eject safely. I was blissfully unaware of the extent of my damage, as the cables to my instruments had burnt out! Though I could see smoke in my rear view mirror, Lofty was my fire warning light! He was to radio me if the fire got worse.

Because of Frisky's damage he had to use the minimum of control to preserve emergency hydraulics. Consequently, we were sitting ducks limping back at a few thousand feet, with two of us out of the action should we be intercepted.

As I headed for base I asked 230 SU for pigeons (direct course) to base and got a bum steer from a Pakistani station that gave me a westerly heading! I then asked for Wg. Cdr. Dandapani by name (we started using use names a lot. Dandu (Dandapani) was a F/O in 8 when I joined in '51). He rustled up some Hunters who were returning to Halwara to provide an escort for part of the way.

Verma handled his damaged aircraft with skill and, in spite

of the auxiliary systems failing, made it safely back to base. The ground crew turned around Verma and Earle's aircraft rapidly, in readiness for the next planned sortie by the squadron, a feat that earned them the pilots' unstinting praise.

Mysteres and Canberras were used for the first time in the tactical role of attacking armoured forces on the move. Further north, on the Lahore-Amritsar Road, 31 Squadron's Mysteres made a concentrated attack on Pakistani formations.

35 Squadron, which had earlier carried out the aborted raid on Mauripur near Karachi, was tasked with carrying out sorties in the Kasur sector. The squadron had last seen action in the Goa operations, when eight of its Canberras had disabled the runway at Dabolim airport. Then, no Portuguese air opposition or anti-aircraft fire was present. Now, targets like Mianwali, Sargodha and Chaklala presented a different picture. The squadron managed to fly for only four days, from 7-10 September, before a mishap on the ground forced the squadron to see only limited action for the rest of the war.

Four Canberras from Agra, to be joined by Hunters of 7 Squadron from Halwara, were to attack targets at Kasur. Once finished, the first four were to be replaced by another four that would rendezvous over Ferozepur, escorted by Gnats. The first pair of bombers arrived over Halwara as the Hunters taxied to the runways for take-off. The second aircraft in the formation suffered a bird hit, which broke the Plexiglas shield at the bomb-aimers station, blinding the navigator. He tried to jettison the bombs and, in panic, released them with the bomb bay doors still closed. The pilot then made a hurried approach to land at Halwara. After a high-speed landing on the wrong runway, the Canberra's tyres burst and the aircraft broke through the runway crash barrier and came to a standstill. The pilot tried to retract the undercarriage during the landing, a dangerous move in an aircraft fully loaded with bombs. But luckily he did not have to resort to that.

With the runway blocked the Hunters were unable to take-off. Only the second section of bombers completed the mission with Gnats as escort. The damaged Canberra had stopped quite close to 7 Squadron's hangar and stayed there for a few days, inducing much nervousness in all officers and technicians passing by. The aircraft was fully loaded with a 4,000 lb bomb load and was a juicy target to PAF fighters or bombers. A direct hit would have had disastrous consequences. As an 'erk' wryly commented, 'We used to pray as we passed that aircraft.'

Chinoy's Long Walk Back Home

The day belonged to Flying Officer D.P. Chinoy, part of a four-Mystere interdiction mission from 31 Squadron that attacked ground targets of opportunity, like convoys and tanks, in the Phillora sector. East of Phillora, Chinoy's formation attacked a Pakistani Army camp.

The Mysteres let loose with their rockets and Chinoy was elated at his target disappearing in a blaze of debris and smoke. But his elation was short-lived. As he pulled out of his attacking dive, his aircraft was hit repeatedly by AA fire. As Chinoy left AA range, he went flat out for the border. He was already separated from his wingman. The Mystere was badly damaged but still flyable and Chinoy nursed it towards the border. Two minutes from the border, the cockpit caught fire. Chinoy knew he would not last the two minutes; he pulled the lever that jettisoned his canopy and ejected. The air blast knocked him out for a second or two and he found himself hanging from the silken canopy, with the afternoon sun above and the cornfields of the Western Punjab below. The stricken Mystere had already crashed. It didn't take much time to deduce he was still in enemy territory. From the sounds of the battle, he judged the frontline as being 20 miles away. Then, suddenly, he came under rifle fire from unknown locations and could only pray that none of the bullets carried his number on it. As he hit the ground, he detached his chute, threw away his flight helmet, and gathering his wits, quickly surveyed the situation.

There was nothing to suggest that anybody was looking for him or that the Pakistani Army had sent search parties. There were no signs of troops. Chinoy quickly ran for cover, hid in a grass patch and started crawling north-west and running when there was no cover. Soon he was exhausted and disoriented.

THE SECOND WEEK OF THE AIR WAR

His 1:1,00,000 scale map was useless. After a quick breather and after ripping off excess flying clothing, mainly the G-suit fittings and straps, Chinoy continued his scrambling from bush to bush. At 1600 hours he nearly stumbled onto a local villager and dove into the nearby grass. Luckily, the villager did not see Chinoy, who decided to wait till dark to resume his trek. Chinoy hid till 1845 hours and emerged at sundown, to start walking in the general direction of the border. On reaching a road, he walked along some distance from it. He marched for about five hours, by which time his throat was parched and his legs severely tired. His back ached from the shock of the ejection. Both thirst and lack of sleep were taking their toll. Then like an oasis, a well appeared in front of him. The tired pilot doubled over and drank water by the bucketful. The water revived him and resurrected his urge to make it back home. Soon he noticed a convoy of vehicles approaching. Chinoy was on alert, but identified the leader in the vehicle as a Sikh: it was an Indian Army convoy. He walked over and identified himself. Within hours he was back at Pathankot.

PAF B 57s attacked Halwara at night, which took the brunt of 31,000 lb bombs dropped during the raid. Some buildings, and five Hunters in the repair and salvage hangar, were damaged (these were repaired quickly over the next couple of days). The most severe damage was to airmen's cycles parked outside the hangars. Meanwhile, in anticipation of launching strikes from Pathankot on the following day, several Mysteres

Plate 41: Flying Officer D.P. Chinoy, in flying suit, back on operations after his long walk home.

from 8 Squadron were flown there from Adampur. The first to leave were Flight Lieutenants Pramod Chopra and Vinod Patney. Another 4 Mysteres carried out an armed patrol before landing at Pathankot. Later that night, Squadron Leader Jatar and Flight Lieutenant Bhatia went to Pathankot on an Otter.

11 SEPTEMBER

Gallantry Awards

11 September opened to a buoyant mood for the country. News of a big Pakistani offensive smashed at Khem Karan trickled down to the papers and to the aircrew. The day before, All India Radio had announced the first lot of gallantry awards. Of the total of 6 Maha Vir Chakras (MVC) and 16 Vir Chakras (VrC), nearly half were awarded to the IAF. MVCs were awarded to Wing Commanders W.M. Goodman and P.P. Singh. 8 VrCs were also awarded to the IAF. Besides the pilots who scored kills in the air (Ghandhi, Neb, Rathore, Cooke, Mamgain), Squadron Leaders Handa and Jatar, who led the missions on Sargodha on 7 September, along with Flight Lieutenant Tirlochan Singh, were awarded the VrC. This brought the IAF's gallantry medal count to 10 VrCs, including the awards to Keelor and Pathania which were announced earlier on 6 September.

THE ABCs OF CLOSE AIR SUPPORT AND
ARMY-AIR FORCE COOPERATION

A feature of the war was that the IAF flew few close air support missions. There were plenty of reasons for this. The IAF had divided its functions between two separate organizations. Air Defence operations were the responsibility of Air Defence Area, Western Air Command, while Advance HQ, Western Air Command, controlled offensive operations. Because of the hectic pace of air operations against the PAF in the initial days of the war, two-thirds of all IAF sorties were devoted to combat air patrols and strikes against PAF airfields. All requests for close air support that came from army formations, were routed to Advance HQ, WAC. However, since most ground attack fighters were blocked in the sorties being allocated by Air Defence Centre, the requests piled up with Air Force HQ.

Advance HQ had allocated Tactical Air Centres (TAC) for each army Corps. Any request from a forward Army unit was sent through the hierarchy, i.e. through the battalion, brigade and divisional commanders, till it finally reached the Corps commander. At the end of the day, the Corps Commander would, in consultation with the TAC Commander (with rank of Wing Commander), prioritize the requests for close air support. The TAC Commander then would communicate the requests to the station commanders, with whom they had radio contact. The station commanders themselves were under pressure to carry out the demands of other establishments: air defence requests from Air Defence Control, WAC, and missions directed to them by both WAC HQ and Air HQ. After these were taken care of, at the earliest, close support missions were flown the next morning, hardly a speedy response.

Further problems arose. When aircraft arrived over their target areas, the forward air controllers with the army formation could not guide them. An inability to communicate with low flying aircraft, and faulty radio sets, resulted in improper communication between the ground troops and the pilots. On one occasion, a forward air controller could not communicate with the aircraft that had arrived overhead because his radio had been rendered unserviceable by the jolts it had received when being transported in a jeep. Unsurprisingly, the army took a dim view of the effectiveness of these sorties.

The IAF was so caught up in its interdictory role that battlefield support to the army was given lesser priority. It was not always the fault of the IAF. An incident at Adampur is illustrative of the confusion and comedy prevalent in those days. Wing Commander 'Omi' Taneja, the Tigers CO, remembers an army formation complaining about the lack of close support sorties. Taneja was surprised; his squadron was waiting for a call from the army for close support and had wondered why it had not done so. Apparently, the Ground Liaison Officer had locked up some of his codes in a cupboard and forgotten about them. As a result, he was unable to decipher messages regarding close support at the Corps HQ.

A primary disadvantage was that all the squadrons were made responsible for all the TAC centres. This resulted in pilots providing close air support across the whole front, rather than concentrating in a particular area where they could have gained knowledge of the terrain. This would have been the case had a particular squadron been made responsible for only one TAC, but requests for sorties were routed to all the three airfields: Pathankot, Adampur and Halwara.

Back to the Action

At 1100 hrs on 11 September, 1 Squadron launched a four aircraft formation to attack a railway bridge at Kasur. Led by Squadron Leader D.E. Satur, the formation flew at 100 ft AGL and encountered heavy ack-ack fire over the target. While attacking the target, the fourth aircraft in the formation, flown by Squadron Leader R.K. 'Uppi' Uppal, was hit by anti-aircraft guns and caught fire. Uppal's last transmission indicated his aircraft was out of control as the servo pressure was reading zero. The No. 3 in the formation, Flight Lieutenant J.P. Singh saw the aircraft crash two miles south-east of Kasur. No ejection was seen: Uppal, an experienced QFI, would be sorely missed.

Plate 42: Squadron Leader R.K. Uppal was killed when his Mystere was hit by AA fire on an interdiction mission in the Lahore-Kasur sector on 11 September.

In this raid, both Satur and his No. 2, Flight Lieutenant A.K. Brahmawar suffered malfunctions, as their rockets did not fire. Back at base, the fault was traced to a malfunction of the armament leads, something that seemed to be occurring with suspicious frequency. A watch was kept and soon the malfunction was traced to sabotage by two airmen, who had tampered with the microswitches on the aircraft. The airmen were arrested and taken away by Air Intelligence personnel.

Taneja then led a strike mission with Flight Lieutenant D.M.S. Kahai to attack some artillery bunkers near Lahore. Identifying targets south-east of Lahore, they dropped 4,000 lb bombs. They were dropped so low that Kahai saw one of the bombs dropped by Taneja bounce back 500 ft into the air. Taneja's Mystere was hit by small arms fire but both pilots got back to base safely.

Halwara's Hunters mounted some sorties in the Lahore-Kasur sector. An armed recce by two Hunters of 7 Squadron reported heavy traffic moving on the Kasur Road. A four-aircraft strike, led by Squadron Leader M.M. Sinha, with Pritam Singh, D.K. Dhiman and K.C. Cariappa (on attachment from No. 20) was launched. The mission was highly successful, resulting in the destruction of many small vehicles.

On another mission mounted by 7 Squadron that day, Squadron Leaders S.S. Malik and N.C. Suri flew a strike against the Lahore-Kasur Road Bridge, over the Upper Bari Canal. The bridge was destroyed successfully. On the return leg, Malik and Suri sighted two F 104 Starfighters, but did not engage. Flight Lieutenant Hakimullah was flying an F 104 in the same area and reported seeing two Gnats. While trying to engage, he noticed what he believed to have been two MiG 21s. Seeing the odds stacked against him, Hakimullah decided to exit the scene at Mach 1.1 at tree-top height, something the MiG 21s would have been unable to match. Hakimullah landed at the satellite airstrip at Risalawala, almost running out of fuel in the process. However, Indian records do not mention any encounter between MiG 21s and the F 104. Hakimullah might have confused Hunters with MiGs and panicked.

Returning from a strike, two of 27 Squadron's Hunters reported aircraft milling around at the Chak Jhumra airfield.

7 and 27 Squadrons planned a joint strike, which was cancelled in view of the calls for close air support from army formations.

8 Squadron launched a total of five strikes on 11 September. To kick things off, Squadron Leader Godfrey Salins led a two-aircraft strike that accounted for a tank and an unarmoured vehicle. Then the squadron's 'Black Formation' saw plenty of action, as Squadron Leader 'Mickey' Jatar and Flight Lieutenants Pramod Chopra, Vinod Patney and 'Jimmy' Bhatia flew two strikes. The first (8 Squadron's third of the day) was launched from Pathankot and was directed at Pasrur. After finishing the strike, the formation returned to Adampur. The second (8 Squadron's fifth of the day) was in close support to the battle at Khem Karan. On this sortie, Chopra's determination in making repeated attacks through heavy ground fire earned him a VrC after the war. His rocket and cannon attack accounted for 2 tanks, in addition to several gun emplacements and unarmoured vehicles.

The Black formation would earn more laurels in the war. The formation flew well together, a fact attested to by its junior members, Vinod Patney and 'Jimmy' Bhatia respectively:

Mickey put the Black formation together; basically he took the most experienced pilots and put us together. We flew well together and flew the most missions out of all the pilots in the squadron.

Mickey formed the Black formation. Black was Mickey's call sign. So we became Black 1 (Mickey), Black 2 (myself), Black 3 (Chopi) and Black 4 (Pat). I flew wingman for Mickey and Pat was wingman to Chopi. People only gave us the name after the war. All four of us got awards. The Black formation had great understanding. Often on the RT we didn't have to speak. We had trained so much together and at that level, things become easy. So many times in the briefing room, between Mickey and Chopi, one of the two would just stand up and say SOP, and we would walk out to the aircraft. 1-2-3-4 like that. We reached a stage, where we knew this is the mission, this is what we have to do, and the rest is SOP. When you reach that level, things become easy.

Though no daytime sorties were flown, the MiG 21s were cleared for night operations on 11 September. Since the MiG 21 pilots had no experience in using the airborne interception radar at night, they were not effective in countering the B 57s. On subsequent days, a steady daily rate of four to six sorties was managed with the seven remaining aircraft. During the last days of the war, Halwara was cleared for MiG 21 operations and a couple of sorties were flown on 21 September. The last sorties of the war by the MiGs were flown on 22 September, when the squadron flew two forward sweeps and four air combat patrols.

Lumbering Giants as Bombers

One of the PAF's innovations in the war was their aggressive usage of the C 130 heavy transport aircraft in multiple roles. As early as March 1963, Pakistan had received four C 130 Hercules transport aircraft. This was the initial component of the total package of five C 130s supplied to Pakistan under the US Military Assistance Program. The PAF had employed the C 130 in supply dropping missions to support Operation Gibraltar in August. On 23 August, a lone C 130 flown by the CO of 6 Transport Squadron, Wing Commander Zahid Butt, had flown across the ceasefire line into Indian territory over Kashmir and tried dropping supplies to the beleaguered 'mujahid' fighters. Lack of radar coverage and the mountainous terrain made it impossible to detect this night drop of supplies. After the outbreak of full-scale hostilities, C 130s carried out the paradrop of the SSG Commandos near Indian airfields under cover of darkness.

An enterprising initiative taken by the C 130 squadron involved the conversion of these transports into bombers. Seeing the relative success of dropping supplies accurately in very small drop zones, the Station Commander of Chaklala, Group Captain Eric Hall thought of such a conversion. The C 130s would drop its bomb load out of the cargo bay from the rear ramp entrance. The vulnerability of such a large aircraft would limit its usage to nighttime drops against soft targets. One problem the C 130 crew faced was the restriction on flying with the rear ramp open, which would limit the airspeed to about 150 knots. Flying the C 130s without the rear ramp doors, which increased the speed to about 280 knots, solved this problem.

The C 130s' first mission was on the night of 11/12 September, against Kathua Bridge 16 km east of Pathankot and about 30 km from the border. The target chosen was ideal. The short distance from the border would give Indian interceptors very little time, even if they got airborne in the night. The CO, Wing Commander Zahid Butt flew the mission. He carried along a VIP: Eric Hall, the Station Commander of Chaklala. They reached the target safely. During the bombing run Butt reported interception by an Indian fighter and took evasive action after the bombs had been released. On successful return to the base, they discovered a 1-cm bullet hole in the port wing tip. However, no Indian fighters reported interceptions in the night.

B 57s and Night Interceptions

Adampur and Halwara were again attacked that night by B 57s but no damage was done. The B 57 that attacked Adampur, dropped its load two miles from the airfield in open fields. While these raids were not always successful in causing material damage, they did make insomniacs out of the IAF pilots. Another effect of the night raids was to prompt another try at night interception. It didn't end well, as Squadron Leader Don Conquest confirmed:

The scariest thing that happened to me was almost getting shot down by our own ack-ack. Since we had no night interception capability, we couldn't do anything about the B 57s. So G.K. John, the station commander decided that two Hunters would take-off at dusk and orbit the airfield (even though we had radar gunsights, it was useless at night and we would need ground control), but perhaps we could orbit, they would pick us up on their radar and we could perhaps deter them from showing up.

So Dhiman and I took off. We had been told that if we got a positive ID on something, we should shoot. Well, we saw nothing and so after 90 minutes we came back. The runway lights were still off. Dhiman came back, and landed safely. I came in and suddenly the whole sky opened up around me. I was buffeted violently. I was praying to get out alive. I opened the throttle and scooted through and went away from the field.

Clarke came on the R/T and asked, 'Don how are you?' as did John, to ask me if I was OK. I said I was OK, but I wasn't sure about the aircraft. John asked me if I could land and if I couldn't I should eject. I said I would come back, though I was bit apprehensive at getting anywhere near to those guns.

I said 'Ask them to take it easy'. So I came back, landed, and then and met John in the dugout. The problem with those AA guys was that if one fired, they all fired, putting a lot of metal in the air. Anyway, they were poor in their aim; they didn't hit me.

Not all aircraft in the IAF inventory were suitable for night flying. Though theoretically almost every type had the instrumentation to fly at night, operational problems often prevented effective deployment. For example, the Gnat's instruments were so well lit that their images reflected off the bubble canopy. Peering at the stars and potential intruders was a difficult task indeed. Night landings were touch and go, highly risky and to be done only by experienced pilots.

12 SEPTEMBER

As dawn broke on 12 September at 0630 hours, four Mysteres of 1 Squadron, led by Squadron, Leader Handa took off to bomb Pasrur. Two carried 1,000 lb bombs, the others T.10 rockets. The mission had little luck. Handa's bomb dropped just short of the runway and skipped a thousand yards to explode in the adjoining village of Sikandrapur. Fortunately the village was deserted due to the fighting and no civilian causalities occurred. The No. 2 aircraft in the formation, Flight Lieutenant D.S. Brar's, had a malfunction and its bombs did not release. This left the other two aircraft equipped with rockets. Flight Lieutenants D.S. Kahai and V.K. Verma rocketed the runway, cratering it. However, the damage caused by rockets was easily repairable when compared to the damage caused by bombs. It was not known if the PAF repaired the runway or not. The Mysteres recovered to base safely.

Squadron Leader Paddy Earle and Flight Lieutenant J.P. Singh then flew a two-aircraft sortie, with the objective of destroying a bridge over the Ichogil Canal headworks. But when they reached the designated target area, they could not find the bridge. Both pilots came back to base with their weapons load intact. The zeal with which the Mystere pilots flew low is illustrated by the fact that Singh's Mystere came back with telephone wires wrapped around its pylons. Needless to say, no disciplinary action was taken against him.

3 Squadron from Pathankot planned a four-aircraft strike mission for the Chawinda area. The strike was to be led by 'Pandit' Kaul, but when he dropped out due to technical snags, Flight Lieutenant Doraiswami took over the lead. Over the target, anti-aircraft fire hit the port wing of Flying Officer Potnis' Mystere, probably holing the fuel tanks as it began to streak a white plume. Potnis' rocket pods refused to fire and when he decided to jettison his external stores, only one of his external drop tanks fell off! Flying back in the asymmetrical configuration, Potnis noted his ASI showing 160 knots even though he was flying at more than 300 knots. On approaching the airfield, having no indication of his top speed, he gingerly lowered his undercarriage. The Mystere was still at a speed above the threshold for lowering the wheels and its undercarriage bay doors promptly buckled under the airflow. The drama finally came to an end as 23 Squadron's Wing Commander Raghavendran shepherded Potnis through the finals.

The previous day had seen the renewal of the Indian offensive to take Phillora in the Sialkot sector. In spite of PAF attacks, Indian Army formations occupied Phillora by the afternoon of 12 September, a move that created concern in the Pakistani High Command. Later in the day, tanks belonging to C Squadron of the 17 Horse (Poona) observed a Pakistani helicopter, a Bell OH-1, landing south of Phillora. One of the tanks fired a high explosive shell and knocked down the helicopter; a rare case of a tank using its primary armament to down an aircraft. The helicopter carried a distinguished passenger. The GOC of Pakistani 15th Infantry Division, accompanied by his staff, had come to carry out a first-hand assessment of the ground situation. The GOC was killed and the helicopter recovered in its damaged condition by No. 1 Armoured Division.

THE SECOND WEEK OF THE AIR WAR

Moves to take Khem Karan back by the Indian 4th Division ran into obstacles. First, one of the battalions (4th Sikh) ran into an ambush and 129 of its men were taken POW. Another battalion (2nd Mahar) was sent forward to relieve the 4th Sikh; it ran into an ambush from the air. At around 12 noon, as the troops were marching to the battle zone—strung out in the open—the Sabres struck, strafing the formation. 40 of the gallant Mahars died that day, along with another eight men of the 4 Grenadiers who were accompanying the Mahars; an equal number were wounded. Air attacks also slowed down one of the battalions of JAK Rifles. A troop of Sherman tanks of the Deccan Horse, which managed to reach Khem Karan, was strafed from the air. The Pakistani Army subsequently captured the tanks, which got bogged down during evasive manoeuvres. All these attacks from the air helped frustrate attempts to recapture Khem Karan. By the end of this planned raid, 200 men were killed and captured and about eleven tanks were lost. When Major General Sukhwant Singh wrote, 'There were occasions when the PAF single-handedly repulsed attacks by the army,' he probably meant this day. 4 Grenadiers lost a further 10 men to air attacks later in the war. There was no support from the IAF, leaving some Khem Karan veterans bitter about the IAF's failure in close support.

B 57s attacked Jamnagar, Jodhpur, Adampur and Pathankot at night. In the four raids on Jamnagar, a Hunter trainer and a Dakota were damaged at the repair and salvage hangar. Jamnagar's Armament Training Wing received a visit from PAF B 57s and F 86s on the night of 12 September till the early hours of 13 September, during the course of which some 23 bombs fell in the military quarters area. Another attack on the following night caused real damage as two Vampires, a Dakota and a Hunter were destroyed on 14 September. Jodhpur airfield was also attacked four times by the B 57s but only the taxi track was damaged. Jodhpur was raided frequently and futilely for the IAF did not have enough aircraft to mount attacks from there. In Adampur one of the bombs hit the fuel dump, which burned for quite some time. Fortunately no attacks on Adampur followed, as it would have been easy for attacking bombers to pinpoint the airfield in the night using the blaze from the fuel dumps. A Mystere was destroyed at Pathankot along with a fuel bowser.

13 SEPTEMBER

The next day, each air force carried out sporadic raids. PAF Sabres attacked a diesel oil train at Gurdaspur on the morning of 13 September. Anti-aircraft fire hit and damaged a Sabre whose pilot ejected near the border. Although Squadron Leader A.U. Ahmed baled out, he was possibly injured severely by AA fire and was dead by the time his chute landed. Meanwhile, the train at Gurdaspur railway station had three of its wagons set on fire, endangering the entire train. Chaman Lal, a fireman at the railway station, uncoupled the burning wagons from the train and saved the rest of the wagons. The three wagons were detached and separated but Chaman Lal died of burns. A grateful nation awarded him its highest civilian gallantry award, the Ashoka Chakra.

Adampur and Pathankot's Mysteres were active again. 8 Squadron attacked ground targets in the Lahore area. As usual, ground fire was heavy. Flight Lieutenant L. Sadarangani, whose first sortie for the day, a CAP flown with Flight Lieutenant Chopra (his coursemate) had been more sedate, was shot down. Sadrangani ejected and was taken prisoner of war. Flight Lieutenant Vinod Patney had a better time and describes the day's events in understated fashion:

On 13 September, we attacked targets in the Kasur/Khem Karan area. The second sortie of the day was the one for which I got my VrC. Nobby was #1, #2 was Lal, and I was #3. We had 20 T.10 rockets, 4 in each salvo. Lloyd was briefing us, but the GLO changed the briefing. There was a clear division on the ground between the Indian and Pakistani targets. Four Gnats were given to us as air cover, but they had to go back early as their fuel ran out. We stayed. We lost Lal on the first or second attack run. I saw him eject and go down. I made five passes over the target area. I changed the settings on the rockets to reduce the number of rockets per salvo. That's why I was able to make five passes. It was possibly quite reckless to have done this.

Patney was awarded the VrC for this effort. Squadron Leader 'Mickey' Jatar and Flight Lieutenant 'Jimmy' Bhatia flew a strike against Pakistani Army targets, around the 'incredibly elusive' Ichogil Canal. As Bhatia describes it, finding the canal was one thing, having the army believe it was difficult to locate was another:

I did a 2 aircraft mission with Mickey to locate the barrage along the Ravi. The army wanted to cross along that point, the Pakistanis wanted to flood it. So we had to destroy the barrage and we found nothing. The GLO swore there was one and the sortie came to us. We went there and there was no barrage. We came back to Dera Baba Nanak, and then followed along from there to Lahore. Still no barrage. Strange! We went back and said we would follow the Ichogil Canal from the South Bank. The canal would start at the north bank—it was actually a siphon system. The canal ran under the riverbed—we saw the headworks on the north side. We dropped bombs on that. When we came back the army refused to believe us.

Later in the day, Squadron Leaders 'Gags' Dhawan and Ravi Badhwar flew a strike against targets of opportunity in the Lahore and Kasur sectors. They spotted bridges and attacked with T.10 rockets. Damage from this strike could not be confirmed.

31 Squadron launched a four aircraft mission in the Sialkot sector led by Squadron Leader Shekaran. The formation was equipped with T10 rockets and carried out an offensive recce in the Pasrur-Satrah-Daska area. They first came across a Pakistan Army convoy, moving on the Mundeke-Sialkot road and made short work of it. Shekaran then led the formation towards Pasrur, where he noticed another convoy on the outskirts of the town. He decided to carry out an attack on this convoy as well.

As Shekaran and his No. 2 Flight Lieutenant C.N. Bal, finished their first attack and pulled out, the second section led by Squadron Leader I.S. Sandhu with Flight Lieutenant T.S. Sethi as the No. 4, rolled in for the attack. As Sandhu banked his Mystere in a left orbit, he took a quick glance towards his right to confirm Sethi was in his position and to check for 'bogeys'. To his surprise, Sandhu saw that Sethi was not in his position. About the same time, Sandhu saw another aircraft turning steeply to his right, further away at about 1,000 yds. It was too far away to be recognizable. Assuming it to be a hostile,

Sandhu radioed Shekaran who called off the strike. As the three aircraft went into full throttle, putting in a hard turn to the right, Sandhu felt his aircraft rocked by a hit. No damage however was evident and he was able to make it safely back to the base after jettisoning his rocket pods en route. There was no sign of Sethi's aircraft. Attempts to raise him on R/T were futile. Sethi, a popular man who had good-humouredly bore the many jokes directed at him by his squadron mates, was shot down and killed by AA near Pasrur. It was probably the same AA fire that Sandhu felt hitting his aircraft.

Led by Denny Satur, 1 Squadron then launched a highly effective raid on a tank concentration, south-west of Ichogil

Plate 43: No. 2 Squadron at Ambala before the 1965 war.
Standing left to right: 'Kooki' Kapur, 'Hitler' Shankaran (*Technical Officer*), 'Pondy' Jayakumar, Doc Mishra, N.K. Malik (*RIP 1965 Ops*), 'Jit' Dhawan, 'Boss' Bharat, 'Prince' Raina,' Cee Pee' Sharma, Nair, 'Naughty' Nautiyal, 'Ben' Brar. Kneeling left to right: Ashley Rodrigues, 'Kakles' Kale, Ashok Joshi, 'Kamli/Henry' Khanna, 'Mazi' Mazumdar, G.S. Ghuman, 'SAAB' Naidu, John Bhatti, 'Dopy' Rao.

Canal. The Mysteres used their front gun ammunition and rockets to destroy at least three tanks and numerous 'B' vehicles. Later in the day, Wing Commander Taneja and Flight Lieutenant Brar attacked a mango grove, which was being used as a tank shelter, south-west, of the Ichogil canal.

Baptism of the Flying Arrows

The second squadron to be equipped with the Gnat in the IAF was 2 Squadron (*The Flying Arrows*). It had flown the Toofani till 1960, when it received the Gnat. In 1964, following the upgradation of the ranks of the commanding officers in a squadron to Wing Commander, a group of new officers was posted to the squadron. Wing Commander Bharat Singh, an experienced pilot on the Hunters was posted to command 2 Squadron. Two pilots joined from 14 Squadron in the east. One was Squadron Leader Johnny Greene, who was commanding the Bulls before the rank upgradation took place. The other was Squadron Leader Ranjit 'Jit' Dhawan, Greene's flight commander with the Bulls. Later Greene was posted out on his staff assignment in Ambala.

By 29 August, all pilots and personnel of the squadron had been recalled from leave, with the aircraft split in two detachments based at Agra and Ambala. Squadron Leader Dhawan and Flight Lieutenants A.K. Mazumdar and A.N. Kale went to Agra. The rest, led by Bharat Singh, were based at Ambala. Later Dhawan handed over air defence of Agra to the Gnats of 15 Squadron, under Wing Commander M.J. Dhotiwala, and moved his detachment to Ambala. Dhawan takes up the tale:

I was posted to No. 2 Squadron at Ambala, sometime in 1964. We were under the command of Wg. Cdr. Bharat Singh who had taken over the squadron at about the same time. In the April of 1965 we moved to Bareilly along with 15 Squadron, which was recently re-raised on the Gnats. This was to activate Bareilly as a station. In September we were back in Ambala with detachments in Adampur and Halwara, escorting Hunters and hanging around in our own battles. When the hostilities broke out, we were doing duties in Agra. So from Agra itself, I flew to Ambala taking the detachment that was there. We had eight aircraft and a very capable chap by the name of A.K. 'Mazzi' Mazumdar. He's also a decorated chap, very very fine chap.

We were sitting in Agra, then we were order to move to Ambala. This was done in general storm weather and we reached Ambala after flying in some heavy thunderstorms, that evening. There were a few of us who were night-qualified, like Bharat Singh, Mazumdar, P.P. Sharma and self, who had some night flying experience on the Gnat. Then there was Reggie Upot who also did some night flying, but then he always did night flying!

The daily routine would be do some night flying before dawn early morning, take a bath and get some rest. Then we used to be on the ORP, looking out for the colours to be fired from the ATC. We used to have a detachment at Halwara. Most of the action was at Halwara, which was attacked by the PAF in the night quite often. So these B 57s used to come and he (the Pak pilot) used to follow the good old Halwara canal, and did his damn circuit and give us hell every night! Five minutes to eight and the ack-ack would open up on him!

At Ambala, at one point of time, there were nearly 52 Gnats (including eight Gnats sent from 15 Squadron to augment the other three squadrons) to manage from three different squadrons, 2, 9, and 23. We had a wonderful engineer officer by the name I.G. Krishna, very fine man, phenomenal head; he used to remember tail aircraft numbers, unserviceability, no. of hours done; what needs to be done like his head was totally computerized. We formed a great team. We knew exactly what the mission was and he knew exactly what his support was and between us we managed to arrange all the support required between Bareilly, Ambala, Halwara, and Pathankot for the Gnat.

2 Squadron saw action for the first time on 13 September. At 1000 hours, two Gnats flown by Squadron Leader N.K. Malik and Flight Lieutenant Kale—both experienced pilots—were scrambled to intercept the Sabres heading towards Amritsar. Arriving over Amritsar, Kale spotted two Sabres and went into a turn to bring the Gnats behind them. Lined up for a clear shot, he found his aircraft was a victim of the gremlin that plagued most Gnats during the war. His cannons refused to fire.

Suddenly, two more Sabres appeared behind the Gnats. One took a shot at Kale who broke off the attack and went into a series of dives and turns in a vain attempt to shake off his pursuer, in the course of which the aircraft descended from 20,000 to 3,000 ft. When the Gnat's engine flamed out due to the damage caused by the Sabre's guns, Kale ejected and came down near Ferozepur. The successful Pakistani pilot was Flight Lieutenant Yusuf Ali Khan. Meanwhile, Flight Lieutenant Bhatti chased the second Gnat pilot, Squadron Leader N.K.

Malik. As Bhatti closed in onto the Gnat and was about to fire, Malik went into a downward barrel roll and escaped.

The Gnats saw further action when Squadron Leader 'Prince' Raina, who had replaced Johnny Greene as the Flight Commander, tangled with Sabres in the same sector. The Sabre scored some hits on Raina's aircraft, which had a few bullet holes in the rear fuselage near the jet pipe. But Raina disengaged and successfully recovered back to Halwara even though his brake parachute was damaged and could not be used. Meanwhile, Dhawan's aircraft suffered a brake failure while landing and ran into the crash barrier at the end of the runway.

The hectic day served as a baptism in battle for the 2 Squadron pilots. Flight Lieutenant Kale was admitted to a hospital in Ferozepur, as he recovered from his ejection injuries. Some pilots visited him and returned to report that he was in good spirits: heartening news for the rest of the squadron.

On the same day, Sabres attacked Srinagar airfield again and dropped 18 bombs. The UN Caribou, parked on the airfield in its damaged state since the raid on 7 September, was hit again. Three Mi 4 helicopters were hit and damaged. Four Sabres attacked Jammu airfield in the wee hours of the day; an unserviceable Dakota was destroyed. The operations room and ATC stores room were also hit. No fighters were based at Jammu, which was host to transport and light aircraft exclusively. This situation persisted till 1971, when Jammu was used only as an emergency base to recover returning fighters.

8-Pass Charlie

When night fell, Adampur faced its worst air raid of the war. B 57 bombers flew three raids. The first raid was at 2200 hours, by a lone B 57. Adampur's pilots had admiringly referred to a very effective B 57 pilot, executor of the first raid on 6 September, which destroyed one of the MiGs on the ORP, as '8-Pass Charlie'. On this night, '8-Pass Charlie'[7] is believed to have showed up again.

The name '8-Pass Charlie' was derived from the number of passes the B 57 would make in each raid. Normally it would come up over the target and dump its load of 8 bombs at one go, without giving time for the defenses to react. The typical load that was carried was about 4,000 lbs, 8 bombs of 500 lbs each. But '8-Pass Charlie' would make eight different runs and drop just one bomb each on select targets. The pilot would try to pick out individual targets on the ground in the moon-light, and try to carry out an effective attack each time. Whether in reality it was one aircraft making eight passes, or four aircraft making two passes, is not known, but for the Indian pilots on the ground who admired the style of attack, '8-Pass Charlie' was always an individual pilot!

This time, the B 57's bombs found their marks on the fuel dump. The worst damage occurred in 32 Squadron's hangars, where two Mysteres caught fire and were destroyed. Two pilots who had a particularly close call during the raid were 'Jimmy' Bhatia and A.K. Brahmawar, roommates, who had become a tad casual about their air-raid procedures following the numerous false alarms. The pair decided that they were not going to jump into trenches anymore. Then on the night of 15 September, as one of the bombs hit a standby BPI, 10,000 gallons of fuel went up in flames—'daylight at night, perfect for the bomber pilot'. As the fire spread to 32 Squadron's hangars and a Mystere caught fire, 9,000 kilolitres of fuel exploded, setting off rockets on the fully loaded jets. One of these went off as Brahmawar and Bhatia were still in their room. The rocket came through the window, but luckily didn't explode. Thereafter, for every raid, Brahmawar and Bhatia were in the trenches.

More damage was prevented by the timely intervention of Squadron Leader Earle, who took charge of the fire fighting operations to rescue the aircraft of 32 Squadron. In addition, a newly constructed repair and salvage hangar was destroyed, as was the equipment section.

Further attacks came at 0200 hours and 0500 hours, on the morning of 14 September. One bomb fell near an air raid trench, killing five airmen (AC1 Kunju, AC1 Thapa, Cpl. Mathai, LAC Arunagiri and LAC Daniel) and a DSC guard. The raid also knocked out airfield communications. On the request of the station commander, Wing Commander Taneja, 1 Squadron's CO had to personally go to inform Advance HQ at Jullundhur of the raid.

Paddy Earle paid tribute to the unknown Pakistani pilot:

I have the utmost respect for the Pakistani Canberra bloke who loved to ruin the equanimity of our dreary lives! 8-Pass Charlie was an ace, but he had this nasty habit of turning up about 30 min. after moonrise, just as we were downing our first drink! Seriously, he was a cool dude and a professional of the highest order. To disguise the direction of his run, he used to cut throttles before entering a dive and by the time the ack-ack opened up he was beneath the umbrella of fire. After dropping his load he'd apply full throttle and climb out above the umbrella. In effect, he would only have to pass through the fire of one gun. As those in the know will confirm that the chances of that vintage of gun hitting an a/c flying at right angles through its fire was about 5 per cent max. It is only when we got radar guns, that ack-ack crews had any success. With the arrival of the new ack commander we started developing tactics for airfield attacks defended by radar guns. These we refined when we were in Ambala—ask ex-Pursoot guys who served with me if they recall the success of co-ordinated attacks, which we used extensively during interdiction exercises.

No further damage was done. It was noticed that in spite of the numerous raids, not one B 57 was hit when they came over in the night. It was suspected that someone on the ground was tampering with the tracking radar of the L-70 AA guns. All guns were recalibrated by an expert team and rechecked after the raid. A fortuitous decision, for the B 57 raid the next day did not go away unscathed.

Tuskers on the Rampage: The Raid on Peshawar

After the raids of 7 September, the PAF had moved the bulk of its attack force to its rear airfields. Most of the B 57s were withdrawn to Peshawar, 600 km from the Indian border. It would have been suicidal to attack targets at such extended ranges, as no Indian aircraft had the range and endurance to find a target like Peshawar and attack it. They would be sitting ducks in the daylight; finding the target at night would be fiendishly difficult. Unlike the IAF, the Pakistanis had potent night interception capability in their F 104 Starfighters.

As night fell on Peshawar on 13 September, six Canberras

of 5 Squadron made an audacious raid on its airfield. Squadron Leader J.C. Verma, a senior Flight Commander with the Tuskers, led the raid. The pathfinder for the Peshawar raid was Squadron Leader Gautam and Flight Lieutenant Deshpande (Navigator). The other members of the strike were Wing Commander P.P. Singh, Squadron Leaders J.C. Verma, C.R. Mehta, V.C. Goodwin; the navigators were Bansal, Dastidar, Ahluwalia, and S. Kapoor. Peshawar, on the northern border of Pakistan, was at the extreme flying range of the Canberras, which meant payload was kept to a bare minimum. The fuel gave no allowances for tactical routing to avoid the Starfighters. The Canberras had to fly through the heartland of Pakistan, navigating by starlight and any visible landmarks. The typical profile of a Canberra raid was to approach a given target at low level (1,000 ft above ground or lower) at night and, on coming close to the target, to pull up in a steep climb to about 10,000 ft to drop the load and to then descend down to low level, to escape from Pakistani territory.

Verma flew his Canberra with instructions from his navigator. They successfully identified the river to the north of Peshawar and, by fixing their position relative to the bend in the river, started their run. As the bombers rendezvoused before their final pull-up for the attack, the pathfinder aircraft led by Pete Gautam of the JBCU radioed the formation that Peshawar's ack-ack batteries had woken up. He reported AA fire all the way up to 5,000 ft and accordingly the Canberras adjusted their altitude. Gautam was to be the pathfinder during the bombing run, responsible for dropping the target indicator bomb, which served as a beacon for the others at the beginning of the runway. Assessing their positions in relation to the target indicator bomb, the others would than drop their bombload. Gautam did his job perfectly, laying the bomb near the target. The remaining Canberras had a variety of targets to choose from, including a bulk petroleum installation, aircraft and other PAF ground facilities.

Verma began his bombing run, judging his approach and making corrections as required. As the navigator gave his signal, he released his bomb-load. The aircraft lurched upwards, 8,000 lbs lighter as the bombs tumbled out of the bomb bay. Verma turned hard port and headed north for the hills. The Canberras following Verma confirmed that the bulk petroleum installation had been hit and was burning furiously. Gautam in turn managed to damage the runway with his payload. Verma was flying full throttle to the hills, when he heard the dreaded message: 'Boss! Bandits on our tail!'

A Starfighter launched prior to the attack had started vectoring on to the retreating bomber force. In daytime it would have been a massacre but, at night, the darkness was the Canberra's ally. As Goodwin reported the Starfighter on his tail, Verma called out for an evasive manoeuvre to shake it off. Gautam saw a streak of flame appear in the darkness and make its way towards the Canberra. The Starfighter had launched a Sidewinder missile. The other pilots of the formation saw a huge fireball as the Sidewinder exploded. As they despaired at what they thought was the destruction of one of their aircraft, the jubilant Canberra pilot announced over the R/T that the Pakistani pilot had missed. The Sidewinder had exploded prematurely, missing the Canberra. The Canberras returned safely to Agra. The raid was successful, without any losses for the IAF. The encounter reported by the IAF was the same as reported by PAF Squadron Leader Mervyn Middlecoat, flying a Starfighter. He had managed a lock on one of the Canberras near Sargodha. Middlecoat fired his missiles and claimed one Canberra destroyed, and despite the lack of any photographic or wreckage related evidence, was awarded the kill.

It was the first time in the war that Peshawar had been raided. The runway and the petroleum installations had been damaged, as had some aircraft hangars and the PAF headquarters building outside the airfield. Even the PAF's commissioned hagiographer was moved to an effusive turn of phrase in describing the raid as, 'the most effective Canberra attack of the war'.[8] In the trenches, PAF pilots had the privilege of seeing a Canberra drop flares to illuminate the airfield and then thunder down the main runway at 200 ft, before pulling up at its end to turn back and drop its bomb load at the end of a dispersal of parked aircraft. The single 4000-lb bomb looked certain of totalling the entire force of sixteen B 57s, lined up wingtip to wingtip. Had luck favoured the Tuskers, they would have wiped out the entire strategic attack component of the PAF with a single blow. Unfortunately for the IAF, the bomb hit soft soil and its explosive force was dissipated. An ATC building that stood between the line of B 57s and the path of the explosive force of the bomb took most of the impact. The impact showered fragments and shrapnel over the line of B 57s, but no severe damage was inflicted. It is not known which pilot was responsible for this particularly scary bomb delivery. A plausible candidate is Squadron Leader P. Gautam of JBCU, who was dropping the TI bombs. Two factors suggest this. Firstly, the main force dropped their bombs from a higher altitude and secondly, only Gautam claimed bombing and damaging the runway that night. Ironically, Sikand's Gnat had been flown to Peshawar from Pasrur and was stationed at the airfield during the time of the attack; it escaped being damaged.

The raid shook the PAF out of its complacency. No airfield or town was out of range for Indian bombers. No one in Pakistan had thought that the IAF would bomb Peshawar with impunity. The significance of the raid was a symbolic gesture, less of material damage.

The United States Air Force maintained a full-fledged Signal Intelligence base at Badaber, about 20 miles south of Peshawar. Badaber housed the 6937th Communications Group, specializing in radio interception and eavesdropping. Nearly 600 personnel and their families were housed on the airbase as well as neighbouring areas; a large contingent was based near the Peshawar airfield itself. The bombing of Peshawar forced the Americans to evacuate all families through Iran. A number of C 130 flights were flown from Iran to Peshawar and almost all families and personnel were evacuated over the next few days, returning only after hostilities ended.

14 SEPTEMBER

2 Squadron Hits Back

On 14 September there was a small spurt in the air activities of both the sides, with a few incidents involving air combat. The first occurred over Lahore.

A strike mission of Canberras, tasked for rail yard targets, was scheduled to rendezvous with a formation of Gnats of 2 Squadron, operating from Halwara. Wing Commander Bharat Singh, CO 2 Squadron led the formation. An experienced flyer, Singh had served as a member of 7 Squadron's nine-Hunter aerobatic formation. Taking over the Gnats in April 1963, he was a 'flying hog', taking the juicy missions for himself and leaving the routine missions, like combat air patrols, to the relatively inexperienced pilots. He absolutely detested training flights that involved bringing new pilots to operational level. If cornered into a 'training flight', he would finish the training part within five minutes of getting airborne and lead the other pilot on an unending tail chase! Naturally, all escort missions over enemy territory involved Bharat Singh.

Arriving at the rendezvous point, the leader of the Canberras sighted Sabres as they began their attacking run on the bombers. Singh had sighted the attackers earlier but had not been sure whether they were Mysteres or Sabres. The Sabres had pulled up and dived to attack the Canberras, when Singh came in to disrupt the attack. The Sabres broke off, with Singh in chase. The PAF pilot got down to the deck, with the Gnat in hot pursuit. Singh stayed behind the Sabre through every evasive manoeuvre the hapless Pakistani pilot executed. In the end, the Sabre's frantic evasion of Singh's bullets proved its undoing as, during its manoeuvres, the Sabre flew into the ground. The Gnats had scored again, without incurring any loss.

2 Squadron however suffered their first fatality of the war. While returning with Gnats on an escort mission to Hunters over Khem Karan, Squadron Leader N.K. Malik, who was involved in air combat with the Sabres the previous day, flew into the ground near Halwara and was killed. His No. 2 Flight Lieutenant 'Kamli' Khanna saw Malik's Gnat hit the ground about 15 miles from the Halwara airfield. The crash was suspected to have been caused by the 'trim overflow' problem that plagued the Gnat fleet. In these cases, the elevator set itself to excess trim, forcing the nose down. Tragically, Malik's low altitude rendered a recovery from the aircraft's sudden loss of altitude impossible.[9]

From Adampur, 8 Squadron launched a pair of 2-Mystere

strikes, using 1,000-lb bombs (referred to as 'Dam Buster strikes' because of the 'high' tonnage of the ordnance delivered). Squadron Leader Jatar and Flight Lieutenant Patney, escorted by Gnats, carried out an attack against targets along the Lahore-Gujranwala railway lines. Unfortunately, the damage could not be assessed. Then, Flight Lieutenants B.I. Singh and Pramod Chopra attacked targets in the Lahore-Pasrur sectors. On account of faulty equipment, flight plans and briefings didn't always work out. Patney commented on a mission where the most harm was caused to the Indian jets themselves: 'On the 14th I flew a sortie with B.I. we were supposed to attack this bridge between Lahore and Gujranwala. There was supposed to be a delayed fuse on the bombs. B.I. went in first and pulled up, there was no delayed fuse and his jet was almost damaged by the explosion.'

Jubilation at Adampur

PAF B 57s, dispatched to attack Indian targets, now made their appearance over Adampur. Having recalibrated their guns, the anti-aircraft gunners put up a huge barrage that hit one of the attacking bombers on its second run. As a huge plume of flame shot out of its starboard wing, a great roar of cheering went up from the officers and men of the airfield. As Flying Officer Rajkumar records in the Tigers' war diaries: 'The roar which came up from all personnel as they leapt out of the trenches must have been heard as far as Amritsar and if not there, at least in Jullundur. There was undisguised glee and the dancing and drinking near the trenches in the moonlight was indeed a sight to behold!'

Such overt expression of their feelings by the pilots and ground crew on the shooting down of a single aircraft is better understood in the context of their experience on the ground. The night-raids were a deadly nuisance: a lucky strike could wipe out a significant number of pilots. To reduce the risk of getting caught in one of the PAF night raids, on most nights, pilots dispersed and slept in individual civilian billets, with orders to assemble in the morning. Many pilots will testify that they knew the true meaning of fear while taking cover on the ground in the trenches rather than flying missions in the air, as there was nothing the pilots could do but curse the enemy. Squadron Leader A.S. Lamba remembers the frustration of the B 57 raids over Halwara and the ineffectiveness of AA fire: 'We used to pull out our service pistols and take pot shots at the aircraft, more out of frustration than with any hope of hitting it.'

The stricken B 57 dropped its load on the airfield perimeters, flew for some distance and plunged into the ground near the village of Alwalpur. The PAF crew, Flight Lieutenant Altaf Sheikh and his navigator Flying Officer B.A. Choudhary, both ejected safely. They evaded capture till morning, at which time a group of irate villagers of Madhar rounded them up. They were the first PAF personnel to be taken POW in the 1965 war. At Halwara, the B 57s were successful. Earlier in the day, the airmen and technicians of 7 Squadron noticed a Starfighter make a recce sortie over the airfield and immediately guessed they were due for a raid that night. One B 57 approached Halwara at low levels, in the dark hours. Without much advance warning, it popped up to medium altitude and dropped a stick of 500-pounders near the 7 Squadron hangars. As soon as the raid warning was given, the airmen had jumped in the trenches close to the hangars. The B 57 dropped five of its 500-pounders; the first fell near the air raid trench and the last one just missed the hangar. The near miss was enough: with two fully armed and fuelled Hunters inside, the building caught fire and the aircraft were gutted. Taking shelter in the Officers Mess was Flying Officer Kondiah. As the all-clear sounded, he rushed to the airmen in the trenches. The bomb had missed the trench but had raked up lot of dirt and mud that fell on the men. Though they were covered in dirt and shaken by the close shave, none of them were injured seriously.

The B 57 raids ensured that the day went badly for the IAF. At Halwara, besides the two Hunters destroyed, an early morning raid damaged two of 27 Squadron's Hunters. Pathankot suffered the loss of a Dakota and the complete destruction of its still-under-construction ATC building. Jodhpur was attacked and numerous bombs were dropped on

Plate 44: The cockpit canopy of the B 57 shot down over Adampur on the night of 14 September. The Repair and Salvage Section at Halwara organized a display at the end of the war, of wreckage gathered from the various encounters during the war. The twisted metallic parts in front of the canopy are the .50 caliber Browning machine guns of PAF Sabres.

the airfield. The most damage was done at Jamnagar: the B 57s destroyed two Vampires, a Dakota and a Hunter. It was a very successful 30-hour period for the B 57s of the PAF. They had managed to destroy almost nine aircraft, with the loss of only one of their bombers.

Thus ended the second week of the air war. One significant change in operations was fewer encounters of the opposing forces. Both sides concentrated in attacking ground targets and avoided flying against each other. Other than the raids by Canberras of both sides, which flew by night, raids on Pakistani airfields were not undertaken during the day, nor did the PAF undertake any daylight raids on major IAF bases, except for the Baghdogra attack.

NOTES

1. Famous for their Second World War campaigns—in Eritrea, North Africa and Italy. At the time of Indian Independence it was one of the only six infantry divisions with the army.

2. John Fricker, *Battle for Pakistan*, London: Ian Allen, 1979; D.R. Mankekar, *Twenty-two Fateful Days*, Bombay: Manaktalas, 1996.
3. IAF Hunters seem to specialize in close brushes with the ground. Alfred Cooke's Hunter brought back tree leaves and scrapes on its wings after its dogfight, and pilots at Longewala in 1971 brushed sand dunes, as they carried out low-level rocket attacks on Pakistani tanks.
4. Interview with D.M. Conquest.
5. As Parulkar landed he remembered the previous day's events. The night before Parulkar had just then carried out a Combat Air Patrol, when the air raid siren sounded. The pilots who were lounging near the crew room dived into a nearby trench, with Parulkar landing on a glass cup and breaking it. He picked up the glass pieces from the trench and threw them out, the pieces shattering further after falling on the ground. Nimmi Suri who was watching the incident told Parulkar, 'Dilip, this is not a good sign; its bad luck to break glass twice. You should break it seven more times if you don't want anything bad to happen.' Needless to say, with a B 57 roaming overhead, Parulkar did not feel like getting out of the trench and breaking the glass further.
6. Parulkar was to later comment, 'If I had taken the advice and ejected, I would have been a goner. They would have written me off as an unsuccessful ejection case! They would have said, "We told him to eject, and he must have ejected by the time it was too late. Blame it on pilot error".'
7. The PAF pilot who did the raid on 6 September evening was Squadron Leader Najeeb Ali Khan, CO of the PAF B 57 squadron.
8. John Fricker, op. cit., pp. 131-2.
9. Interview with AVM Viney Kapila.

CHAPTER 8

The End of the War: 15-23 September

15 SEPTEMBER

As the war entered its third week, the Indian and Pakistani armies renewed their efforts to capture territory in the Sialkot sector. In the Chamb and Lahore sectors, their ground positions had stabilized and hardened into a deadlock. But in the Sialkot sector, both sides continued to utilize heavy armour formations—consisting of close to 200 tanks each—and infantry support in trying to capture key towns and villages. The Indian Army's 1st Corp took Phillora on 11 September. It planned to carry on and capture its next strategic objective, the small town of Chawinda.

Chawinda, 5 km south of Phillora, near the Narowal-Sialkot railway line, was an important communications centre for the Pakistani Army. The Indian Army's 1st Armoured Division[1] was entrusted to take Chawinda and committed no less than three armoured regiments and an infantry brigade to the effort.[2] The attack commenced on 14 September, but Pakistani artillery and the PAF constantly harassed Indian armoured columns and gun positions. Chawinda remained in Pakistani hands.[3] But two other key positions, the village of Wazirwali and the railway station at Alhar, were taken.

The battle resumed on 15 September, with the 1st Armoured Division again grinding into action. There was much harassment from the air. The PAF's Sargodha strike wing, led by Wing Commander Shamim, flew numerous interdiction sorties and was met with intense ground fire from Indian Army formations.[4] Most Sabres were hit and damaged but were repaired and put back in the air. In spite of repeated attacks and counter-attacks, Chawinda eluded the 1st Armoured Division, convincing its commander of the need to first establish positions at the villages of Jasoran and Butur Dograndi.

On 15 September, the IAF only received a few calls for close support from the army. Consequently, most IAF units took a breather. Hunters from Halwara, however, saw some action. A two-aircraft mission flown by 'Dice' Dhiman (7 Squadron) and A.S. Khullar (20 Squadron) destroyed a pontoon bridge on the Ichogil Canal in their single sortie for the day.[5]

One accident at 27 Squadron claimed a fatality. During a scramble at Halwara, Flying Officer T.K. Chaudhuri's Hunter suffered a bird hit while taking off. As Chaudhuri decided to turn back and attempt a landing, the Hunter started streaming fuel. As Chaudhuri made his approach, his No. 2 saw fire break out on Chaudhuri's Hunter and called for him to eject. Chaudhuri continued with his approach. The No. 2 called out for an ejection again. Chaudhuri responded and ejected, at low altitude. Though the ejection was successful and his parachute had deployed fully, he drifted into the burning wreckage of his Hunter and suffered severe burn injuries. Chaudhuri was moved to base hospital for intensive care but succumbed to his injuries later in the day.[6]

Plate 45: Flight Lieutenant Thapen Kumar 'Chau' Chaudhuri, 27 Squadron.

At Adampur, Wing Commander Taneja had assumed *de facto* command of all Mystere squadrons. Adampur's 18 Wing flew no sorties on 15 September. With retaliation expected for the downing of the B 57 on the previous night, most of Adampur's Mysteres were withdrawn to Ambala on 15 September. With the ferrying complete, Ambala received 22 serviceable Mysteres from Adampur's three squadrons. Taneja and Squadron Leader Earle went to Advance HQ to get briefed on operations for the next day. The night of 15 September was spent planning the next day's strike missions for 1 and 8 Squadrons.[7]

That night PAF C 130s made another appearance after the Kathua raid, intending to attack Indian tank and troop concentrations near Ramgarh in the Sialkot sector. Two C 130s dumped nine tons of bombs each, in a random and uninspired bombing pattern. The next day a lone C 130 came over to release its load. Both raids had little effect on their intended targets. On the Indian side, the lack of night interception facilities prevented the interception of these huge lumbering transports.

THE LAND BATTLE RAGES ON

Jassoran was taken on 16 September by the 17th Poona Horse and the 9th Dogra Battalion. Another infantry battalion, the 8th Garhwal was tasked to assault and capture Butur Dograndi; its assault route lay through Jassoran. Running into heavy shelling, mortar fire and Pakistani infantry defences, the battalion suffered heavy casualties. Only one platoon managed to reach Butur Dograndi, but was thrown back by a Pakistani counter-attack. However, by evening the battalion recouped and attacked again, retaking Butur Dograndi. The battalion suffered a loss of 129 men, including five officers. Its commanding officer, Lieutenant Colonel Jhirad, and his deputy were killed in the battle.

This sudden spurt in ground offensives, as planned by the 1st Corps, was not accompanied by air support by the IAF, apparently 'because it was not asked for'. The Pakistanis found the lack of air support for the ground offensive surprising.[8] The PAF Sargodha strike wing managed to fly some sorties in the sector, but due to the lack of a clearly defined bomb-line, and the difficulty of distinguishing between the two opposing sides, did not do much damage on the battlefield. Air support was used more effectively against rear formations.

Similarly, away in the south-western sector, in the Thar Desert, Pakistani Army formations moved around unhampered from the air. On 16 September, the Pakistani Army advanced into Indian territory and occupied Munabao, a small village situated a few kilometers from the border. An Indian counter-attack, mounted to repulse the advancing unit, suffered heavy losses.[9] The absence of IAF operational bases in Rajasthan was sorely felt. With no combat aircraft stationed in Rajasthan, air defence, reconnaissance or close support to the army did not materialize. The low priority given to this area in the Indian Army's planning, in turn influenced the IAF's plans. No major operations were planned here even though opposing Pakistani forces were stretched thin. Towards the end of the war some IAF combat aircraft were moved to Jodhpur. But it was too little, too late.

16 SEPTEMBER: PINGALE'S POUND OF FLESH

The next day, 16 September, 7 Squadron went into action against the Sabres on the Amritsar front. Hunters from Halwara had not seen air combat since the evening of 6 September, but that was soon to change.

Late in the afternoon at Halwara, Flying Officer P.S. 'Pingo' Pingale of 7 Squadron was on ORP duty, along with Flying Officer Farokh Dara 'Bunny' Bunsha. Pingale had returned from a medical checkup in Delhi a couple of days earlier—necessitated by his ejection over Halwara—and had since flown a couple of interdiction strikes across the border. Bunsha, originally from 20 Squadron, had been deputed to 7 Squadron for the war. Suddenly, the scramble order was given and both pilots took off in their Hunters. Once airborne, the fighter controller Flying Officer R.C. Mahadik gave Pingale an initial vector in a north-westerly direction, towards Jullundur. They were flying at 20,000 ft altitude at high speed, nearly .9 Mach, looking for intruding aircraft.

The intruders were two Sabres led by Squadron Leader M.M. Alam with Flying Officer M.I. Shaukat, a young pilot with 80 hours on the Sabre, as his wingman. The Sabres were on a baiting mission and were warned about the approaching Hunters by PAF GCI at Sakesar. Alam was looking to enhance his score; an eager Shaukat was set to support him.

The Indian pilots were flying the 'loose deuce' or 'fighting' formation, with Pingo leading the formation and Bunsha following to his left, about 200 yds to the rear. The 'loose deuce' was a well-established battle formation for air combat—the US Navy would put it to particularly effective use over the skies of North Vietnam. It was easy to maintain and track. Bunsha could not only cover Pingale's rear but also watch out for any threats from his rear.

Pingale spotted a single aircraft going in the opposite direction at a lower altitude. It looked like a Mystere. As it flew on almost directly beneath them, Pingale recognized the green and white PAF roundels on the aircraft. It was Alam's Sabre. Pingale called Bunsha on the R/T to announce an attack. Both Hunters peeled off and turned around in a dive. With the Hunters in a turn, the Sabre leisurely put in a turn from its south-eastern direction to south. As both the Hunter pilots approached the Sabre from the rear, it was still flying straight, maintaining constant altitude and speed and not doing any evasive manoeuvring. A puzzled Pingale rapidly closed in with his Hunter.

As he did so, he instinctively looked to his right and, at approximately 4 o'clock, saw another Sabre—flown by Shaukat Ali—at 800 yds and rapidly closing in, ready to fire. Pingale decided to take on the Sabre coming in behind, as it would be easier for him to engage rather than Bunsha, who was much closer to it. Bunsha was in a better position to continue the attack on the Sabre ahead. Pingale called out on the R/T to Bunsha 'Bunny, go after the bogey ahead; I'll tackle this bogey coming from the rear.' 'Roger!' Bunsha replied, and went after Alam's Sabre.

As Pingale put in a steep turn to fly head on to Ali's Sabre, both passed each other at a distance. Pingale reversed into another turn and before Ali could try and turn, Pingo was behind him. Shaukat frantically pulled up the Sabre into the sun, hoping that he would lose the Hunter due to the glare, but Pingo was ready: 'We had practised this many times earlier. You can't go forever into the sun because you don't have the energy. The speed will decay and you will fall off, so I had to just wait and keep looking at the sun, hoping to see him when he comes out of somewhere, either to the left or to the right of the sun.'

Sure enough, as its speed bled off, the Sabre fell. Pingo saw the Sabre coming out of the sun from the right and immediately increased power. Even as the Hunter's powerful Rolls Royce engines kicked in, the Sabre continued to fall. Ali jettisoned his drop tanks and snapped the aircraft into a slow turn, expecting Pingale to overshoot. Pingo could see the Sabre's leading edge slats open and knew the aircraft was going to turn tightly. As the Sabre's speed bled off, in anticipation of stalling Ali probably panicked. He once again straightened out and pulled up: a common mistake in air combat, made by pilots not comfortable with pushing their aircraft to its limits. It was a crucial error, for it allowed Pingale to stay behind the Sabre.

Pingale's first burst at the Sabre had been a wildly aimed shot. The pipper was not properly placed on the Sabre and there was no damage to the aircraft. But now, Pingale had closed in to around 250-300 yds—his training took over as he prepared for the second burst and set the correct parameters for the radar ranging gunsight. He manoeuvred the Hunter to get the pipper positioned just ahead and above the Sabre's cockpit. A single burst from his Aden gunpack would have placed a deadly salvo of 30 mm cannon shells right into the cockpit, but Pingo hesitated, thinking, *'Saala mar jayega, rahne do'* (the poor bugger's going to die, let him be).[10] He eased back on his joystick so that the pipper moved from the Sabre's cockpit to the centre of the fuselage and pressed the gun button at 300 yds.

It was a short burst. No more than a quarter second long—but it was enough. The Sabre exploded in a massive ball of flame. The exploding debris was so close to the Hunter that Pingale would have flown through it but for the fact that he was already putting his Hunter in a turn, heading for Alam.

In the meantime, Bunsha was chasing Alam who started

jockeying his Sabre in turns. Pingale, who was chasing Ali, had kept an eye on Bunsha and his target. Seeing the Sabre start to manoeuvre, he called out a warning to Bunsha, which the latter acknowledged. The chase transformed into a horizontal scissors fight, with both the Sabre and Hunter cutting speed and turning inside into each other, in an effort to get behind each other. This was a particularly dangerous manoeuvre with which to fight a Sabre whilst one was flying a Hunter, especially if not supplemented by vertical breakouts by the latter. Pingale once again called out, 'Bunny be careful, you're losing your advantage, he's getting behind you'. Bunsha again acknowledged.

But the fight was uneven. Man-to-man, Alam had more experience on the Sabre with nearly 1300 hours flying it. He knew the Sabre's quirks inside out; Bunsha, one of the most junior pilots of 20 Squadron, had less than two years of service and about 250 hours on the Hunter. Alam cut inside Bunsha's turn and was able to take a good shot at the Hunter. As Pingale was about to deliver the *coup de grace*, he noticed Bunsha's predicament. After firing at Ali, Pingale instantly put his Hunter in a turn towards Alam.

But it was too late. Pingo noticed Bunsha's Hunter in a very gentle turn; it seemed to have been damaged by gunfire, and Bunsha did not appear to be engaging in combat any longer. Alam, on Bunsha's tail, continued firing. As he closed in, Alam gave up firing at Bunsha's Hunter and turned his aircraft straight towards Pingale. Perhaps he was responding to a call of help from Ali. As both the Hunter and Sabre closed in rapidly, head on, Pingale noticed the gunports of the Sabre twinkling with fire. In a feeble attempt to hit him, Alam had opened fire head-on. Pingale held his fire. It was poor judgement to open fire in a head-on course, the chances of hitting your adversary were slim and besides, Pingo wanted to conserve his ammunition. The lessons from a course in armament training at ATW, Jamnagar, completed a month ago, were still fresh in his mind.

The Hunter and the Sabre crossed over at high speed. Pingale immediately reversed course, hauling the Hunter almost on its wingtip, half expecting to find the Sabre doing the same and coming back at him. But he was in for a surprise.

After turning back, he could see the Sabre flying away at a high speed away from the fight. Obviously, Alam had given up on the fight and was heading for home. An indignant Pingale recollects his feelings at the moment:

> My impression was that this Alam fellow tried to get out of the fight. You know when you are young and you are in a fight and all gung ho, you want the other fellow to put up a fight, you don't want him to run away from you at the slightest hint of trouble. That is where the mettle of a fighter pilot comes in. It is like playing chicken, you are going head to head on with some fellow on a road, which is narrow. You will wait for the other guy to give way first. It all depends on to who hangs onto longer, but surely when you cross each other, then you expect both to turn around and face each other again. I found out that when I turned around, this fellow (Alam) just had not turned around and lot of distance was put in between us. So he ran away from the fight. I still recollect my thoughts at that moment, 'This is not right; look at this fellow he's gone away!'

Pingale started chasing the Sabre. Alam then put the Sabre into a near vertical dive to get out of range of the Hunter. The manoeuvre worked. Pingale put the Hunter on the Sabre's tail, but almost blacked out trying to pull out of the dive. The Hunter clocked almost 9 to 10 G during the pullout. Pingale was already suffering from pain from the back injury sustained by the ejection over Halwara on 6 September. As he eased the pullout, he got his vision back. But there was no sign of the Sabre. Alam had made good his escape. The fighter controller also lost contact with the Sabre at low level.

Satisfied at shooting down Ali, but sad at losing his wingman, Pingale flew back to base. He had not seen Bunsha after the last gentle turn he was putting in. He hoped that Bunsha had ejected and was safe, but it was not to be. Bunsha's Hunter was later found, completely wrecked. Bunsha had not ejected. Surprisingly, even though Pingale saw his target explode in front of him, Ali had ejected in time near Tarn Tarn, unaware that a fellow pilot's benevolence had saved his life. As he was descending in his parachute he came under fire from villagers and suffered a .303 bullet wound and some shotgun pellet injuries. Shaukat was handed over to the troops of the 4th Division and moved to a field hospital, where an Indian Army surgeon removed the bullets and pellets from his body. Shaukat spent the rest of the war in an Indian POW camp. It had been a classic air-battle. The inexperience of the Indian and Pakistani wingmen had been their undoing. Both had failed to exploit the particular strength of their aircraft.

Pingo's second adversary, Alam, flew back to base, after which an unrelated version of the aircombat emerged from the Pakistani side. Alam claimed that Shaukat and himself were bounced by two Hunters, attacking in a yo-yo manoeuvre. It was claimed that Alam not only shot down one Hunter with guns but, after an intense dogfight in which the second Hunter tried to 'run away', he shot down the second one with a sidewinder. Alam received credit for 'downing' two Hunters in this fight, taking his total tally to 'nine kills'.

Pingale doesn't agree with Alam's description of the fight: 'No missiles were fired—first he opened up with the guns and when we crossed over and I turned, he was already flying straight and away trying to get out of the fight.'

Back at the base, Pingale's gun camera footage came out

Plate 46: Air Marshal Arjan Singh meets *Sabre Slayer* Flying Officer PS 'Pingo' Pingale during a visit to Halwara just after the war. Pingale's aircombat with the Pakistani Sabres remains one of the lesser known tales of the war.

perfectly. He had used just half a second worth of ammunition in both his bursts. The first burst was a quarter second long. The subsequent burst, which was more devastating, was another quarter second. Pingale received the VrC for downing Shaukat Ali's Sabre. It was poetic justice for Pingale. After his early exit from combat with Rafique's Sabre over Halwara on 6 September, he had extracted his pound of flesh from the PAF.

Bhattu's 'Kill'

Further to the north in the Chawinda sector, the newly promoted Wing Commander S.K. 'Bhattu' Bhattacharya of 3 Squadron was leading a Mystere sortie against Pakistani Army targets. Bhattacharya was scanning for targets across the horizon, when a slow moving aircraft that was directly in his path, caught his attention. The propeller-driven aircraft was a Cessna L-19 of the 1st Airborne Observation Post (AOP) Squadron of the Pakistan Army, piloted by Captain Hidayatullah. Bhattacharya instinctively put his gunsight on the Cessna. Between the Mystere flying at nearly 400 knots and the slow moving Cessna, there was no time for Bhattacharya to make gyro or gunsight (gravity drop) adjustments. He fired a salvo of rockets from his 68 mm SNEB pods, as he crossed over the Cessna. He observed the rocket's trajectory taking them below the Cessna before he lost sight of his putative target; he thought he had missed. The rockets exploded on the ground below the Cessna, showering it with shrapnel, damaging it badly and injuring the co-pilot Captain Akhtar. Hidayatullah flew the struggling aircraft back to Sialkot and made a forced emergency landing. The Cessna was written off. Back at Pathankot, Bhattacharya met Squadron Leader Tony Mousinho, the flight commander of 31 Squadron. Bhattu laughed off his encounter and what he thought had been a miss. Since he thought he had missed the Cessna, and since it was not his assigned target, he did not report it officially in his combat report to the squadron. Mousinho made a mental note of the incident but soon relegated it to the back of his mind.[11]

Meanwhile, 8 Squadron's Mysteres were engaged in attacking

targets around Pasrur. As Squadron Leader Jatar led Flight Lieutenant Jimmy Bhatia into attacks, using T.10 rockets and guns on Pakistani Army gun positions, the two were warned of the presence of a PAF Starfighter. Another pair of 8 Squadron

Plate 47: Wing Commander S.K. 'Bhattu' Bhattacharya.

pilots in the vicinity had had to abandon their strike—the F 104 was carrying Sidewinders as usual. Undeterred, the pair continued strafing and rocketing even as the Starfighter closed to within 6 miles, before finally deciding to make a run for it. Clearly, Jatar and Bhatia had their minds on the job immediately at hand! The other two members of the 'Black Formation', Flight Lieutenants Pramod Chopra and Vinod Patney, were sent on a bombing strike. Using 1,000-lb bombs, the pair obliterated several Pakistani gun positions in the Lahore sector. The formation returned safely to Ambala.

B 57s Again

Since the B 57's night attacks on Pathankot and Adampur were rapidly proving to be a nuisance for the IAF, all strike aircraft were withdrawn from forward air bases to Ambala. By nightfall on 17 September, all aircraft from Adampur were flown to Ambala to avoid B 57 raids. From Pathankot, 3 and 31 Squadrons also flew their Mysteres to Ambala for safe dispersal.

Apparently Pakistani intelligence on these aircraft movements was accurate—whether through agents on the ground or through photo-recce sorties—for Ambala was the target for a B 57 raid that night.

The only aircraft in the air when the B 57s attacked were Vampires from 45 Squadron, which had withdrawn to Ambala earlier, and were flying night combat air patrols over Ambala and Palam. Flight Lieutenant K.D. Mehra was flying one of these, having taken off from Ambala earlier. His routine entailed a circuit over Palam, before returning to Ambala. As he came overhead Ambala at 0200 hours, he called for permission to land. Flying Officer P.K. Jain, the ATC Officer answered with an emergency call, denying Mehra permission to land. The airfield was under attack. Two B 57s had struck, dropping 1,000 lb bombs on the airfield. Most of the bombs fell outside the airfield perimeter. Though the airfield was bristling with Hunters, Mysteres and Gnats, no damage was done. The IAF pilots on the ground, previously caught in the middle of the bombing, were able to see the B 57 attack in a detached manner, as their billet positions were located well away from the main airfield. The bombs missed the airfield's major installations; some though, hit the base military hospital, causing several casualties. Mehra, unable to see the attacking aircraft in the dark, flew back to Palam.

The PAF planned further raids on Ambala, but they were foiled when, just before they could take-off from Sargodha, they came under attack from 5 and 16 Squadron's Canberras. For 16 Squadron, after its mission against Chittagong in the eastern sector this was its first mission in the western sector. The second mission—mounted from Bareilly, against Sargodha, on the night of 16 September—was carried out by five Canberras. Wing Commander Peter Wilson, the CO, flew the lead aircraft again, with Squadron Leader Shankaran as his navigator. Shankaran not only had to navigate but also mark the target with 2,000-lb target indication bombs, dropped at low level in a shallow glide attack. This was to be followed up by the other four aircraft, which would drop six thousand-pounders each on the target indicators.

As he arrived over the target at 500 ft AGL, Wilson could

not spot the runways or the airfield structures till anti-aircraft fire opened up. He would later remark, 'I did not find Sargodha that night; Sargodha found me!' The target indication bombs were dropped from that level. The high-explosive bombs followed these from the other four aircraft, flying at 7,000 ft. After dropping their bomb-loads, all five aircraft climbed back for the return trip to base. On the return trip, a PAF Starfighter chased Wilson's Canberra. On being warned by the Orange Putter radar, Wilson took rapid evasive action by putting the aircraft into a spiraling dive down to 1,000 ft AGL. The Starfighter, carrying out the interception entirely on radar, was unable to follow through and lost its prey. The only casualty was the PAF pilot's ego.[12]

The second raid on Ambala came on 20 September, when PAF bombs hit and destroyed St. Peter's Cathedral outside the airfield. The B 57 pilots probably mistook GT Road for the runway and dropped their bombs along it, wiping out the cathedral in the process. To this day, the cathedral survives in its bombed-out state.

18 SEPTEMBER

Sandhu's Sabre

On 18 September 23 Squadron planned an offensive strike, to carry out strafing of Pakistani ground troops and concentrations near Lahore. Sqn. Ldr. Amarjit Singh 'Kaala' Sandhu VM, a senior flight commander, was detailed to lead the mission. Sandhu's flying skills were common knowledge in the IAF. His career had started shakily, when he was almost shunted out of flying school for 'lack of officer-like qualities'. Sandhu's determination and drive helped him overcome these assessments and he was commissioned with wings. He stepped into the limelight of the pilot's grapevine in 1964, when he was posted to 23 Squadron, which by then was the prime unit involved in ironing out the bugs in the still-pesky Gnat. On a routine sortie, as he made a final approach to land, the Gnat's unreliable engine flamed out. Sandhu, while well aware of earlier occasions when pilots flying the Gnat came to grief trying to land the aircraft after engine failures,[13] decided not to eject and successfully dead-sticked the aircraft onto the tarmac safely. This feat helped the ground crew to assess the cause of the engine failure. A laconic report assessees damage to the tune of 'Rupees Ten'. Sandhu's successful landing earned him the Vayusena Medal.

This time around, Sandhu had seen action from the get-go, starting from the opening air battle of the war (with Johnny Greene, Trevor Keelor and V.S. Pathania) on 3 September against the Sabres. He had even damaged a Sabre in the first battle. But a confirmed 'kill' eluded him.

On 18 September, four Gnats took off and headed south of Lahore. Sandhu and his formation were warned of approaching Sabres by the Amritsar radar control. Moments later, six Sabres were noticed at a slightly higher altitude. Sandhu put his formation in a climbing turn, to engage the Sabres and went after the lead Sabre that was flying at an altitude of 20,000 ft. An experienced pilot was flying the Sabre; both the Gnat and the Sabre engaged each other in a series of descending turns and climbs. Sandhu relentlessly stuck to the Sabre's tail. Finally at 3,000 ft, the Sabre pilot decided to do his vanishing trick. He did a split-S, half rolled the Sabre onto its back and pulled into a vertical dive.

Sandhu was in a fix. He knew that the Gnat would require a safety cushion of 4,000 ft to pull out of such a manoeuvre, but faced with the prospect of letting his opponent escape, Sandhu followed suit. With incredible skill and endurance, he recovered from the near suicidal dive and shocked the Sabre pilot, who pulled out at near ground level to find the Gnat still glued on his tail. Now in perfect position, Sandhu let off a well-aimed burst with his cannon to shoot down the Sabre, notching up 23 Squadron's third kill. The remaining Sabres and Gnats disengaged from the combat. The Sabre pilots claimed two Gnats shot down, but no losses occurred on the Indian side.

An Indian Army attack on Chawinda was scheduled for the early hours of 17 September, at 0300 hours, but was called off following deficiencies in troop build-up. The Indian Army had suffered heavy losses, including Lieutenant Colonel Tarapore of the Poona Horse, who was killed at Butur Dograndi when his tank suffered a direct hit on 17 September. Tarapore had led his regiment throughout the battle, accounting for 60 Pakistani tanks, with a loss of nine of his own. He was posthumously awarded the Param Vir Chakra, the second and last of the war.

The Corps Commander Lieutenant General P.O. Dunn now gave the task of taking Chawinda to an infantry formation, the 6th Division led by Major General S.K. Korla who scheduled the attack for 18 September. However Butur Dograndi and Jassoran had to be evacuated due to Pakistani Army pressure.

Plate 48: The best place for a pilot on the ground is a 4 ft deep trench! – Wing Commander S. Raghavendran, CO, 23 Squadron (later VCAS) along with, unidentified, Flight Lieutenant S. Krishnaswamy (later CAS), Flight Lieutenant V.S. Pathania and Flying Officer Tejwant Singh check out one of the air raid trenches at Ambala.

The daylight attack of 18 September was thus called off. A night attack on 18/19 September failed to take the town again. Two infantry companies made it into the town but, facing a stiff counter-attack by the Pakistanis, had to withdraw. At daybreak on 19 September, 6th Division stabilized its position, but the attack on Chawinda was never executed.

The Indian Army's employment of tanks and artillery was much more judicious than the Pakistani Army, which sent in tanks without infantry support, adequate camouflage and preparation. Both sides suffered huge casualties in the tank battles. But it was the PAF that had managed to make its presence felt on the ground rather than the IAF.

Civilian Interlude

Down south, a tragic series of events culminated in the death of a prominent Indian politician. On 18 September, PAF Sabres shot down a civilian Beechcraft aircraft of the Gujarat State Government, carrying the Chief Minister Balwant Rai Mehta, his wife and several state administration officials. The Beechcraft's pilot was Jehangir M. Engineer, one of the four Engineer brothers to have served with the IAF in the Second World War. While his three brothers had stayed on with the IAF after the war, Jehangir had moved on to civil aviation. He had on his plane, besides the CM's entourage (including his personal assistant), three crew members, a security guard and a reporter from a local newspaper. The aircraft was on its way to reach Mithapore by 1600 hours but never arrived. At about 1550 hours, the residents of Suthali village heard the drone of a low-flying aircraft mingled with the noise of jets. They looked up to see the Beechcraft being chased by two Sabres. A series of staccato bursts from the Sabres' guns brought down the Beechcraft between Suthali and Nalia village, just off the coast of the Arabian Sea, about 25 km north-west of Mandvi.

At 1635 hours the first reports of the crash of an unidentified aircraft reached the Bhuj control room. Nalia's Tehsildar and Sub-Inspector were sent to the crash site and found the newspaper reporter's burnt ID card. This confirmed the identity of the aircraft. There were no survivors. Questions flew. Why was the aircraft allowed to fly unescorted in a combat zone? Why was clearance given by the IAF? Did the aircraft proceed without the IAF's knowledge? Why did PAF pilots fire on a civilian aircraft?

Four months later, an inquiry was completed. According to its findings, the IAF authorities at Bombay had refused flight permission to the Chief Minister. When the Gujarat Government pressed for clearance, the IAF gave clearance for the pilot to proceed 'at his own risk'. Engineer was told of the clearance and took off for Mithapore. It was deduced from eyewitness accounts that Engineer tried to land the aircraft, but either because of uneven ground, the presence of the Sabres and damage from their gunfire, or the strain he was under, he lost control of the aircraft and crashed. All nine aboard were killed. This was the first time a civilian aircraft had become a target in the hostilities between the two countries. Balwant Rai Mehta became the first Indian politician to die on the frontline due to enemy action.

19 SEPTEMBER

The Wolfpack in Action

Hunters and Mysteres flew more interdiction sorties in the Chawinda area, on the morning of 19 September. One of the Mysteres of 1 Squadron, flown by Flying Officer Rajkumar, lost its undercarriage in mid-flight and had to abandon its strike.

That afternoon, a flight of four Mysteres of 1 Squadron led by Flight Lieutenant J.P. Singh was detailed to carry out an offensive sortie in the Chawinda-Pasrur sector. Gnats escorted the Mysteres.[14] By this time, the IAF had immense confidence in the Gnat's ability to face up to the Sabre. 9 (*Wolf Packs*) Squadron was given the task of providing escort to the four Mysteres. The Gnats consisted of two sections. The first was led by Squadron Leader Denzil Keelor with Flying Officer 'Munna' Rai, who was on his first operational mission of the war, as his wingman. Flight Lieutenant Viney 'Kaddu' Kapila, with Flight Lieutenant Vijay Mayadev as No. 4, led the second section. The formation went up in the air to rendezvous with the Mysteres. Denzil was Trevor Keelor's elder brother, the 23 Squadron pilot with the IAF's first combat kill against the Sabre on the third day of the war. Uniquely for the IAF, two brothers were in combat together, flying the same aircraft type.

The Mystere and Gnat formation made its way to the target area at Chawinda at low-level and was greeted with anti-aircraft fire. As the aircraft were at a very low level, the AA shells exploded above them. Spotting a formation of four Sabres ahead and above at 2,000 ft, Kapila called out his sighting to Keelor and J.P. Singh on the R/T. Singh decided to make a single pass over the target area and exit quickly, without hanging around for a second pass. About this time, Mayadev, the No. 4 in the formation, also called out a warning on the R/T about the four Sabres. Keelor put the formation in a shallow climbing turn to bring the Gnats in a favourable position.

The four Sabres were from Sargodha's 17 PAF Squadron and were being led by their CO, Squadron Leader Azim Daudpota. Neither Daudpota nor his wingmen noticed the four Gnats come in at low level behind them. As Keelor began manoeuvring the Gnats behind the Sabres, they were noticed and a quick call put the latter into a defensive break. The Gnats split up in two sections. Keelor and Rai went after one pair of Sabres, and Kapila and Mayadev after the other.

When Keelor followed the first pair of Sabres in a tight turn, Rai found it difficult to cope up with his leader. As he completed his turn, he lost visual contact with both Keelor and the Sabres. Keelor instructed Rai on the R/T to set course for Adampur and to get out of the fight, which Rai complied with immediately. This left Keelor tangling with the first section of two Sabres.

Meanwhile, Kapila and Mayadev got behind the second section of the Sabres, which then reversed their turn and broke into the attackers. By the time the Gnats recovered from this manoeuvre Kapila found himself at a very low altitude, less than 100 ft from the ground and flying at tree-top height. However, he still had one of the Sabres in his gyro sight. The Sabre tried to shake off Kapila by first engaging into a steep turn starboard and then again in the opposite direction to port. By this time Kapila had jettisoned his drop tanks, which gave him a slight edge in manoeuvrability. He accelerated and opened fired with his cannon at 500 yds, scoring direct hits on the Sabre. The Gnats had met the Sabres at an altitude of 1,500 ft, and now the Sabre, damaged by Kapila's first burst, fell back. He fired a second burst from 300 yds and again the cannon shells tore into the Sabre. Its pilot though, still executed turns and breaks to shake off Kapila who, in quick succession, let off two more bursts. As he finished the third burst, scoring more hits on the Sabre, he noticed the Sabre begin to roll over. Kapila broke off the attack and hauled his Gnat vertically upward, as he heard Keelor's call on the R/T, 'Kaps you hit him! And most likely he's ejecting'. Kapila banked his aircraft and saw the Sabre hit the ground, but neither he nor Keelor saw the pilot ejecting.

Keelor, meanwhile, was not only keeping an eye on his two adversary Sabres but also on Kapila's section, giving them periodic 'tail clear' messages. He missed seeing the No. 4 Sabre from the PAF formation, flown by Flying Officer Saif-ul Azam, sneak in behind Kapila's section and get on Mayadev's tail. Mayadev's tail and elevator surfaces were riddled with .50 caliber bullets by Azam's gunfire. He ejected barely 500 ft above the ground from his stricken Gnat and floated down on his chute, to be captured by Pakistani troops. He had to spend the next five months as a POW.[15] Azam scrambled out of the combat area, a satisfied man.[16]

Having lost contact with Mayadev's Gnat, Kapila looked around to spot Keelor's Gnat and turned around to join him. By that time Keelor had observed another Sabre break out of the melee and head for safety. He put his Gnat into pursuit. The Sabre failed to notice the Gnat and did a hard turn to the right, which bought it within range of Keelor's guns. The Sabre was hit and started streaming smoke and losing altitude. Keelor pulled out of the attack as his closing speed was high and he had lost enough altitude to be skimming the tree-tops. As the Sabre started moving away, Kapila came into deliver the *coup de grace* with a well-aimed cannon burst. However, once again, Kapila's guns jammed after the initial burst and he had to pull out of the attack. His gun camera film clearly showed Keelor's smoking target in his sights.

The Sabre was last seen streaming smoke as it headed towards Sargodha. Its pilot, Flight Lieutenant S.M. Ahmed crashed just short of the runway at Sargodha and was extricated amidst flames and exploding ammunition.[17] Kapila rejoined Keelor and both made their way back to Adampur base. The excitement hadn't ended for Kapila yet as Keelor's Gnat suffered a tyre burst as he landed, bringing the jet to a skidding halt and blocking the runway. Kapila diverted to Halwara, where he landed on the last remaining reserves of fuel.

Subsequent analysis of gun camera film and combat reports at Halwara and Adampur resulted in both Keelor and Kapila being awarded air combat kills and the VrC at the end of the war. The Sabre kill by Denzil earned the Keelor family a unique distinction. Both the brothers now had Sabres to their credit and both earned the VrC, making it the first time brothers had won the VrC for identical feats.[18]

3 Squadron, which had moved the bulk of its aircraft to Ambala, mounted a strike in the Pasrur area. Four of its

Plate 49: Sabre slaying runs in the family:
Squadron Leader Denzil Keelor joined his brother Trevor,
in claiming a Sabre in aircombat.

Mysteres, armed with SNEB pods and front gun ammunition, mounted a rocket attack on a Pakistani Army convoy, destroying it. On their return to Ambala, they stumbled onto Pakistani Army tanks moving out of their harbours. Flight Lieutenant C.S. Doraiswami was one of the pilots:

We were returning from a successful sortie on that day, and were near Pasrur, when we saw tanks that had just come out of their harbour. I had already expended my rockets in the earlier attack on the convoy and had nothing else but the front guns. I went into the attack with just the guns, and perhaps got a lucky hit or something. Since the tanks are lightly armoured on the rear, where the engine is mounted and also due to the fact that they had ventilation grills and carried additional fuel drums there, the target that I attacked burst into flames. I think my full burst of ammo went into the rear portion and it just blew up! The one and only successful tank attack that I had done using just the guns and the results were so clearly perceptible because in a rocket attack, even though you know that you have hit a target, you can hardly see anything in the dust and smoke kicked up by the rockets. But here you can clearly see it getting hit and assess the damage yourself. It just burst into flames.

It was during the attack, as we started rolling into it, that my Mystere was hit by small arms fire. I must have been around 800 or 900' above ground level. One of my instruments got shattered, but I had pressed on with the attack.

Doraiswami's No. 2, Flight Lieutenant Prem Ramchandani was also hit. A bullet entered his cockpit and hit the instrument console directly on the Mach meter, spraying the cockpit with tiny glass pieces. Ramchandani, who had his mask on and the visor down, luckily escaped with minor injuries to his neck. V.R. Nair's aircraft also suffered minor damage.

The Pakistani Sabres had some success when one PAF raid on the Jammu Signal Unit put it out of commission. PAF strikes had forced the 230 SU Mobile Unit at Amritsar to change its location after having had 5-inch holes punched in its antenna. However, it remained in the vicinity of Amritsar.

When night fell, the PAF's converted C 130 Hercules bombers went into action again.[19] Two sorties were flown against Indian Army concentrations in the vicinity of Rurki and Pagowal. As C 130 bombing tended to be blind bombing without much accuracy, it had little effect. Against strategic targets like factories and marshalling yards, it may have been effective but proved useless against tactical targets like infantry concentrations. The next night a C 130 dropped 10 tons of bombs on India artillery positions, 4 miles south-east of Jallo; another dropped 9 tons of bombs on Indian artillery positions at Valtoha. Both raids had minimal effect. Further south, B 57s attacked Jamnagar again at night, and despite heavy ground fire, suffered no losses—a feat repeated on the night of 20 September as well.[20]

20-21 SEPTEMBER

The Last Encounter

The next day, on the evening of 20 September, Amritsar radar control detected an intruding flight of Sabres over Khem Karan.[21] Two Hunters from 7 Squadron were scrambled, along with two Gnats from Halwara. Squadron Leader D.P. Chatterjee and Flight Lieutenant S.K. Sharma were the Hunter pilots. 2 Squadron's Flight Lieutenant A.K. 'Mazi' Mazumdar and Flying Officer 'Kamli' Khanna were the Gnat pilots. As the IAF's Command Headquarters was using new tactics to bait the Sabres, it was the first time a mixed formation was employed to engage them. IAF ground control failed to pick up the Sabres. The formation then split and was directed by ground control to turn left from Amritsar and head west. Even after arriving over Lahore, the Hunters failed to pick up the Sabres.

As Majumdar in the lead Gnat called on his wingman to turn for home and came out of his turn, four Sabres pounced on the Hunters. The lead Sabre, flown by Squadron Leader S.A. Changezi, went after the Hunter flown by Chatterjee and shot it down. It crashed in Pakistani territory, killing Chatterjee. The second Hunter, being flown by Flight Lieutenant S.K. Sharma was also hit. He disengaged and ejected near Katron, just across the border in Indian Territory. Flight Lieutenant Jilani of the PAF was credited with the kill.

The Sabres hardly had time to rejoice at their good fortune, as Mazumdar and Khanna joined the fray. After a few minutes of intense dogfighting, Mazumdar managed to bring down a Sabre near Kasur. The PAF pilot Flight Lieutenant A.H. Malik ejected,[22] and landed inside Pakistani lines. Meanwhile the other Sabres disengaged. The Gnats flew back to Halwara, with the last air combat kill of the war against fighters. The engagement had proved costly for the Hunter pilots who had allowed themselves to be caught offguard.

After the failure of the attack to take Khem Karan on 12 September, both sides engaged in numerous small actions. There was a lull in close support operations flown by the fighters. 3 Squadron did launch yet another four-aircraft strike led by Sqn. Ldr. S.K. Bhattacharya, with Squadron Leader J.F. Josephs as No. 4. The strike was successful, destroying a number of tanks.[23] Josephs was the only pilot on the strike to carry SNEB rockets, which were slung into a pod, 19 on each side, as opposed to the open wing 60 lb rockets carried by the others. The SNEBS had such a small gravity drop that the pilots could see them hitting the target.[24] Josephs remembers going around for multiple runs through heavy ground fire. The targets, a group of tanks taking cover in trees, made the mistake of poking their heads out. Joseph's first salvo took care of one of the tanks and, as he went around, he noticed yet another tank emerge from cover. This tank too, bore the brunt of his SNEBS. The rest of the tanks wisely stayed under cover.

A last ditch attempt to take Khem Karan was planned by the Indian Army's 4th Division and executed on 21 September. The Pakistani Army put up stiff resistance and only marginal gains were achieved by the 4th Division. Khem Karan eluded recapture. A subsequent plan to attack the next day was dropped in view of the ceasefire declaration by both sides. AA fire mounted by 4th Mountain Division claimed three Sabres shot down in the Khem Karan area.

Contrary to Pakistani claims that IAF Vampires were withdrawn from frontline action after the disaster at Chamb on the first day of the war, these cocoon shaped fighters with twin booms were employed with caution and used when air opposition was not expected. Some Vampires from the amalgamated 45/220 Squadron flew tactical reconnaissance missions to Gadra and Naya Chor to support 11th Division's advance. Ground fighting in the south-western sector had been intense for a few days. The previous day Indian ground forces had advanced in the Gadra Bulge till Dali.[25] In the Rajasthan sector, the amalgamated 45/220 Squadron's Vampires flew a low-level strike to hit targets at Arifwala and Montgomery. At Arifwala, the Vampires attacked and destroyed a railway train carrying supplies. Two senior pilots of the squadron who had participated in the first flights of the war, F.J. Mehta and K.D. Mehra, flew on these missions as well.[26] Mehta led a four-aircraft formation, detailed to hit a power station at Montgomery. Taking off from Ambala, K.D. Mehra's Vampire suffered a bird hit. He found that the aircraft was responding well in spite of the hit but called Mehta on the R/T and informed him in any case. Mehta asked Mehra what he proposed to do. Mehra laconically replied, 'If you want me to go back I will, if you want me to come along I will. What do you want me to do?' Mehta replied, 'I didn't hear anything.' The Vampires went ahead and completed their mission, successfully rocketing the power station. All four Vampires returned safely to base. Mehta later told Mehra, 'If I had used the rule book, I would have had to send you back. I let you be the judge. If the aircraft was OK, I knew you would complete the mission.'

The Canberra's Last Missions

The Canberra force of the IAF had had an excellent record since commencement of operations. Not one aircraft had been lost to hostile action in fifteen continuous days of operations. It was only a matter of time before the law of averages caught up with them.

5 Squadron detailed four Canberras to carry out a hi-lo-hi raid on Sargodha on the night of 20/21 September. The Canberras would follow the usual pattern of flying low as soon as they entered hostile territory, then pulling up to 14,000 ft to carry out the attack on the blast pens north of the intersection of Sargodha's runways. The TOT was given as 0415 hours IST. The Pathfinder aircraft was to be flown by Flight Lieutenant V.C. Goodwin. Goodwin's radio beacon, however, became unserviceable and he called out to the main force to carry out the bombing visually, without any target indication.

Flying as No. 2 in the formation was Flight Lieutenant M.M. Lowe, with Flying Officer Kewal Krishan 'Raj' Kapur as his navigator. Lowe had pulled up to the bombing height, about 10 miles ahead of his target. As he approached the target, the entire sky was lit up by ack-ack fire. It was Lowe's third mission over Sargodha and he noticed that the AA fire was denser than it had been on previous missions. Kapur went down to the bomb aimer's position in the nose and as soon as he gave the 'bombs gone' call over the R/T, Lowe held course for about 15 seconds before closing his bomb doors. He was directly over

Sargodha, making a starboard turn for home when he heard a 'thud'—AA hitting his aircraft. Since there was no handling or visual indication of damage, Lowe proceeded to dive down to lower level and started his return leg.

Having settled down at 1,000 ft AGL, he switched off his tail warning radar as it was beeping away annoyingly due to ground clutter. Five minutes into his flight, Lowe noticed that his No. 1 fuel tank was almost empty. This was strange and he surmised it must have been due to the damage inflicted by the AA fire over the airfield. A quick calculation indicated that there was not enough fuel to continue the trip at low level. If he could manage to climb to a higher altitude, he would just about make it to Chandigarh for an emergency landing.

Lowe then informed Kapur, still in the nose, that he was climbing. As he reached 8,000 ft, he switched on his tail warning radar. Unknown to Lowe, as he climbed, he was being pursued by an F 104 Starfighter. The GCI at Sakesar had directed Wing Commander Jamal Ahmed Khan, the Starfighter pilot, within close proximity of Lowe's Canberra. On approaching the Canberra, he utilized the Starfighter's own radar to close in on the aircraft. Surprisingly the Canberra's tail warning radar failed to detect the PAF fighter.

Lowe had now reached 13,000 ft altitude. Kapur, who had by now come back to his navigator's station, decided to get a fix on their position. He was sure the aircraft was within 20 miles of the border, but he needed a visual sighting of the Sutlej River to be sure. He told Lowe that he was going down to the nose to get a visual fix. The Canberra was by now flying at 18,000 ft and gradually climbing. As soon as Kapur moved into the nose position, there was huge explosion on the right side of the aircraft. Lowe felt the aircraft lurch and the lights go out.

A few seconds earlier, after the distinctive audio tone of a 'lock-on', Jamal Khan had launched a Sidewinder. He never saw the aircraft till the missile impacted the starboard engine of the Canberra. He now stared in awe as the Canberra rolled lazily to its right, with flames shooting off its wings and fuselage. He caught a brief glimpse again as the light from the flames reflected off some clouds, briefly illuminating the Canberra.

Inside the stricken aircraft, everything was dark. Lowe announced over the R/T, 'I have been hit, we are going down.' As he took stock of the situation, he felt both engines cutting out with sparks coming out of the jet pipes of both the engines. A blue cone of flame was spreading from his wings to the fuselage. As the starboard wing dropped, Lowe tried to arrest it by moving the control column to the left. This had no effect. Trying to arrest the starboard side drop by the rudder also did not work out. He knew that abandoning the aircraft was inevitable. There was no response when he pressed the fire extinguisher buttons and pulled the HP cocks back. The aircraft electrical system appeared to have gone dead. Lowe put on the emergency lighting system in the Canberra. The nose had dropped down by this time and his airspeed was increasing as the aircraft plummeted towards the ground.

Lowe's first concern was to communicate to Kapur in the nose to bale out of the aircraft. The internal communication system too had gone kaput. Lowe banged his right foot on the floor hoping that Kapur would respond. Not hearing anything, Lowe took out a torch from the top of the navigator's station seat and flashed it towards the nose position. He bent over and tried to look as far as he could inside. He noticed that the entrance hatch had already been jettisoned and that the fire on the wings illuminated the inside of the nose. The gushing wind stream rendered impossible any further communication between Lowe and Kapur. By this time the aircraft had lost considerable altitude and was in a fast spiral towards starboard. There was no time to lose and Lowe threw the torch away and snatched the ejection lever between his legs. The control column pulled away and the canopy ejection bolts fired. But the canopy did not separate from the aircraft. Lowe tried the ejection handle-cum-blind on top of the seat. As he pulled it the seat fired and he found himself tumbling in the pitch dark of the night. His parachute deployed at about 12,000 ft. He noticed a flash as the Canberra impacted the ground not far away and lit the skies.

As he touched down on the ground, Lowe felt a sharp stab of pain in his back. He could hear people running down towards the wreckage and towards him. As he stood up, two men with rifles shouted at him to raise his hands. Soon a mob surrounded Lowe, searched him, took away his wallet and identity card and repeatedly asked him which country he belonged to. Lowe didn't answer but asked them, 'Am I in Pakistan?' Unsurprisingly, he heard the reply, 'This is very much Pakistan.' Pakistani Army regulars had captured Lowe.

Lowe hoped that Kapur had baled out of the aircraft, but he came to know later in the POW camp that Kapur was not able to get out in time. The Pakistani Army found his body in the wreckage.

Lowe's Canberra was the only one of the IAF that failed to return from a mission during the 1965 war.

The Canberra's Last Strike: the Badin Raid

As the war drew to a close, 16 Squadron's Canberras carried out a raid that made it to the history books.[27] The squadron had moved from Kalaikunda to Bareilly. After the raid on Sargodha, the squadron flew a one-aircraft recce mission to Chak Jhumra and seemed destined to have a lacklustre record compared to the Tuskers, but its final strike became a legend.

Badin was home to the PAF's second FPS-6 and FPS-20 Radar Unit, which provided coverage for air operations in the south-western sector. This particular site had been proving a veritable pain in the neck for the IAF, just as Amritsar radar was to the Pakistanis. 16 Squadron was detailed to attack Badin and destroy the unit. Wing Commander Peter Wilson was briefed, using photographs taken on Squadron Leader Jaggi Nath's daylight photo-recce runs. Badin's two radars were housed in two mushroom-shaped domes, both on towers about 80 ft high.

As the first four aircraft dropped their bombs from an altitude of 7,000 ft, Wilson flew in his rocket pod-equipped Canberra[28] from the east to make a pass at the Eastern Tower, believed to house the FPS-20 Azimuth radar. On his first low-level pass, he thought he glimpsed the tower, but on making a run in, found out that it was not the intended target. He had to make a second pass immediately, and wound up attacking the towers from

Plate 50: Wing Commander Pete Wilson (*centre*) from his earlier days as a Flight Commander with Tuskers. Two places to his right is Flight Lieutenant Padmanabha Gautam.

the south. This time he spotted the target, as the Canberra approached the radar dome at an altitude of 30 ft! Wilson fired the rockets *upward* at the dome and pulled out. Here too, snags accompanied the Canberras. One of the rocket pods refused to fire and only the rockets from the other pod fired. These were enough as they slammed into the base of the tower, destroying it. Wilson recounts the raid in his own words:

The fourth and last mission flown by the Squadron was against Badin on the 21 September and mounted from Agra. There were no staging airfields though the aircraft landed for fuel on the way back. The mission consisted of six aircraft and was mounted at 1000 hours on target, with no escorts of any description.

The aim of the mission was to destroy the eastern dome of the S.U., which was wrongly thought to be the azimuth radar, and to damage supporting installations. Since level bombing was not accurate enough to destroy the dome, it was decided to use 68-mm rockets, which had sufficient velocity to approach the accuracy of gunfire. The plan of attack required one aircraft to climb to 10,000', 80 miles short of target to act as a decoy in case of fighter pressure over target. This aircraft returned to base after a brief exposure.

Four aircraft at 2-minute intervals approached at very low level and then climbed to 7,000' AGL for bomb runs. The first two aircraft carried 2 x 4,000-lb bombs (World War II Vintage) and the next two aircraft 6 x 1,000-lb bombs each. The ballistics of the 4,000-lbs bombs was unknown and the first two bombs fell short and called the correction. The second aircraft was more accurate and the other two aircraft had no problem.

The rocket firing aircraft carrying 2 x 19/68 mm pods approached from the south at 30′ AGL and fired upwards at the dome. Only one pod fired and the rockets were seen to splash on the dome. The aircraft exited the area eastward. There was considerable smoke on target and flak bursts were numerous. Since not a single 20-mm round was fired, Badin village could only have been hit by fire from the Pak AA guns.

The combination of high and low altitude attack by the bomb and rocket carrying aircraft got through the defences, and Badin SU bore the brunt of 28,000 lbs of bombs and nineteen 68 mm rockets in a matter of minutes. The raid was a tactical surprise for the PAF, hitting them when least expected. It was confirmed later that the Badin unit was completely destroyed. Luck, an essential ingredient for all successful military operations, also favoured the Canberras. PAF Sabres, returning to Mauripur after a strike on Gadra Road, were alerted by air defense control about the Badin strike, but could not be diverted to intercept the Canberras since they were already low on fuel. Unlike Amritsar, which was raided several times by the PAF, Badin received minimal attention from the IAF, lulling the unit into a false sense of security. It was alleged that the Canberras

Plate 51: Wing Commander Pete Wilson flying a Canberra B(I) 56.

strafed Badin village. This seems highly unlikely however. The only aircraft carrying cannon packs that day were the rocket armed Canberras. Of the two, one was a decoy that did not take part in the actual raid. Wilson, who did not fire his cannons at all, flew the second. The 'strafing' Badin received was perhaps due to shrapnel from Pakistani AA fire. The success of the Badin raid can be assessed from Pakistani accounts, which admit being taken by surprise at the raid. Even Fricker terms the raid a 'resounding success for the Indian Canberras'.

16 Squadron flew four missions and fourteen sorties and, in this brief number, dropped over 50,000 lbs of high explosive bombs, besides employing rockets. For the successful daylight attack on Badin, Wing Commander Peter Wilson was awarded the VrC.

22 SEPTEMBER

Last Day of the War

The bombing did not deter Indian ground troops from fighting their last major battle of the war. The 3rd Jat, under the 15th Division in the Lahore front, planned to attack and take Dograi, on the bank of the Ichogil Canal. After being driven out of the village on 7 September, several efforts to take it had failed. Lieutenant Colonel Desmond Hayde, the doughty Irishman turned Indian, commanded the Jat battalion in this intense battle. By evening, Dograi was under Indian occupation. The Pakistani Army then made several attempts to recapture Dograi. The last one came hours before the ceasefire. But the Jats did not yield.

As the fighting continued at Dograi, with Indian troops in control of the village, four Mysteres from 3 Squadron took off from Ambala to take out targets on the ground around Dograi. In response to a close support request from the army on the previous day, Flight Lieutenant C.S. 'Doru' Doraiswami led the formation (consisting of Doraiswami, Ramchandani, Mistry and Boman Irani), briefed to hit Pakistani Army positions in and around Dograi. By the time the Mysteres arrived, the position on ground had already changed to Indian hands, with no way to communicate this to the strike leader. As Doraiswami and his No. 2 Flying Officer Prem Ramchandani attacked Indian ground positions, the troops retaliated with light machine gun and other anti-aircraft fire. The ground fire was effective. Ramchandani's Mystere was hit and as flames spread through his aircraft, he turned back towards Indian lines and ejected. His parachute deployed and as he descended, he came under small arms fire. Ramchandani was frantically waving his ID card to indicate he was Indian, but was wounded critically. The Jat troops found him still clutching his ID card and lying on the ground with chute still attached. He was quickly moved to an Indian Military Hospital but succumbed to his wounds four days later.

Doru initially believed that he had attacked the wrong position and hit Indian troops. Only later did he find out that he had struck the right target but that the position had already changed hands. The incident was a brutal reminder of the confusion that inevitably accompanied war and a mistake that would be repeated in other conflicts.

Earlier in the day, 27 Squadron was withdrawn to southern India for rest and recuperation, while 20 Squadron raided Pakistani Army positions at Kasur. Flight Lieutenant K.C. 'Nanda' Cariappa, with Flight Lieutenant K.S. 'Kukke' Suresh and Flight Lieutenant A.S. Sehgal as his wingmen, led this mission. The Hunters spotted Pakistani Army positions and launched a rocket attack. At the end of the first run, Sehgal reported his aircraft being hit and pulled out of the mission, heading back for base. Cariappa decided to continue the attack along with Kukke and carried out multiple passes.

As they rolled into their sixth pass over the target, ground fire hit Cariappa's Hunter. Suresh noticed flames streaming out, as Cariappa pulled up in a vain battle to control it. There was no response to Suresh's initial calls for ejection. As Suresh called out for a third time, 'Cary, eject!' he was relieved to see the Hunter's canopy fly off and the seat eject out of the stricken aircraft. As Cariappa's seat cleared, the Hunter blew up in a huge ball of flame and crashed in Indian territory. Cariappa himself drifted over and into Pakistani lines. The ejection had injured his spine and Cariappa fell down as soon as he touched ground. When Pakistani troops surrounded him and commanded him to raise his hands, Cariappa was unable to, for the shock of the ejection had left him temporarily paralysed. He became the seventh and the last IAF POW of the war.

Cariappa was the son of the first Indian Chief of Army Staff, Field Marshal K.M. Cariappa. Aware of this, and given his own personal acquaintance with Cariappa Sr., Field Marshal Ayub Khan offered to treat Cariappa with special privileges, an offer politely declined by him. Cariappa was moved to a Pakistani Military Hospital after a few days of solitary confinement. Though he regained motor function, his ejection injuries left him unfit for fighter flying. He did not know about his Hunter exploding immediately after his exit till he was repatriated. After repatriation, Cariappa switched over to helicopters.

The PAF too was active. Around noon, a workshop company of the EME was rolling out two Centurion tanks after refitting them. PAF Sabres attacked this detachment and one of the tank's engines caught fire and burned. The tank was rolled back in for repairs. Towards the evening, a strike by the some Sabres was called off due to bad weather, which did not deter three C 130s from taking off that night to try and bomb Indian positions by radar. Blind bombing methods dropped some 30 tons of bombs.

Through 22 September, rumours of the impending ceasefire and discussions of politics kept pilots busy in their mess rooms. These were confirmed when Field Marshal Ayub Khan made an announcement accepting the ceasefire, effective from the morning of 23 September.

The last missions flown by the PAF, before the ceasefire became effective, targeted Amritsar radar again, but ended up bombing a residential locality at Cherta on the outskirts of Amritsar. Cherta had no military significance. Fifty-three civilians were killed in the bombing.[29] What made this attack tragic was that the ceasefire was scheduled to be effective six hours later. There was no need for the PAF to have attacked Amritsar radar and no need for this heavy loss of life. Civilian casualties for the war were to total 416, including fire brigade and railway personnel. The last raid on this day in the southwestern sector also hit a civilian target in Jodhpur. Bombs fell on the city jail, killing 30 of the inmates and two other staff, one of the worst civilian casualty incidents of the war.

Hunters from Halwara flew one sortie late in the evening. Wing Commander Zachariah and Squadron Leader Lamba flew to Bhasin village to attack Pakistani Army targets but the results could not be observed in the fading light.[30] Around the same time, Mysteres from 1 Squadron flew the last dusk sortie of the day.[31] A four-aircraft flight led by the CO Taneja, with 'Frisky' Verma, 'Denny' Satur and Philip Rajkumar in tow, took the impending news of the ceasefire as an excuse to do a royal beatup of the Adampur runway at frighteningly low altitude.

In a fitting close to the confusion that characterized life on the airbases, Wing Commander Wollen had the unfortunate experience of being detained as an enemy paratrooper.[32] On the night of the 22 September, Wollen and Flight Lieutenant Sonpar visited the nearby Golf Club for some much needed sleep. The Gorkha guard, suspicious of Wollen's anglicized Hindi, quietly slipped away and alerted a nearby army unit. Both Wollen and Sonpar were woken up from their slumbers by some agitated guards, led by an equally agitated Brigadier who insisted on handcuffing both of them. Only when they were marched to the office of a Major General of the local formation, were matters cleared up. Neither Wollen nor Sonpar were amused by the incident.

The ceasefire was declared at 0330 hours on the morning of 23 September and guns fell silent on both sides of the border.

NOTES

1. The 1st Corps consisted of the 1st Armoured Division and three other infantry divisions.
2. For this attack the three armoured regiments provided weight of the numbers. Usually an armoured div has four armed regiments in one armoured brigade and a lorried infantry brigade. So in this case it had committed 75 per cent of its strength.
3. Major K.C. Praval, *Indian Army after Independence*, New Delhi: Lancer International, 1987, pp. 393-405.
4. John Fricker, *Battle for Pakistan*, London: Ian Allen, 1979, pp. 125-6, 144.
5. Pushpinder Singh, *The Battle Axes 1942-1992*, New Delhi: Society for Aerospace Studies, 1992, p. 143.

THE END OF THE WAR

6. Interview with AS Lamba; 'Official History of the 1965 Indo-Pakistan War'.
7. 1 Squadron's War Diaries—'1965 Operations'.
8. John Fricker, op. cit., pp. 125-6, 144.
9. Major K.C. Praval, pp. 405-6.
10. Conversation with Wing Commander A.C. Chopra and interview with the author.
11. Personal correspondence with Sqn. Ldr. Tony Mousinho. It is entirely possible that to this day, Bhattacharya is unaware of the result, for no combat report was filed for this incident.
12. Correspondence with Air Commodore Wilson.
13. Two pilots—Squadron Leader A. Sudhakaran and Flying Officer R.K. Mehta—earlier tried to dead stick the Gnat after engine flameouts but died in their attempts. Both were awarded the Kirti Chakra Medal posthumously.
14. The other pilots in this mission were Brahmawar, V.K. Verma and Joe Bakshi.
15. Mayadev's capture was never announced by Pakistan nor was it mentioned on the POW list—his fate was cause for anxiety till the exchange of POWs, when he turned up in the list of names to be exchanged.
16. Azam was later to fly with the PAF Detachment in the 1967 Israeli-Arab War. He is credited with the downing of a Super Vautour bomber of the Israeli air force and also the possible downing of a Mirage III fighter while flying an Iraqi Air Force Hunter.
17. Fricker admits the loss of Ahmed's Sabre, states that 'no other Sabre was lost on that day' and fails to give the name of the fourth Sabre pilot or his fate; John Fricker, op. cit., p. 128.
18. The air combat was recounted in the AIR Broadcast as well as *Harvest of Glory*.
19. John Fricker, op. cit., p. 165.
20. Ibid.
21. Pushpindar Singh, op. cit., p. 144.
22. Malik was the same pilot who shot down Babul Guha over Sargodha on 7 September.
23. Interview with Squadron Leader J.F. Josephs.
24. 4 millirads correction on target sight required as opposed to the 6 millirads of the 30 mm cannon fire.
25. At the time of the ceasefire, the Indian Army was in occupation of 150 square miles of territory in the south-western sector, as much as gained in the Sialkot or the Lahore sectors.
26. Interview with F.J. Mehta.
27. Air Commodore Peter Wilson—correspondence.
28. Canberra B(I) 58–IF-963.
29. Interview with Wing Commander Dandapani.
30. Pushpinder Singh, op. cit., p. 144.
31. 1 Squadron's War Diaries—'1965 Operations'.
32. Interview with Wollen by Shiv Sastry.

CHAPTER 9

Ceasefire and Post-mortem

Since the commencement of hostilities on 1 September, the United Nations Security Council (UNSC) had worked feverishly to end the fighting. On 6 September, it passed a resolution asking both nations to call a ceasefire and to withdraw to positions held before 5 August 1965. Still in a belligerent mood, both India and Pakistan rejected the resolution. The Secretary General of the United Nations, U Thant, then visited both countries during the war, first stopping in Pakistan on 9 September and then in India, three days later, in an attempt to convince both administrations to accept UNSC resolutions on ceasefire *without* preconditions. In a cabinet meeting held during Thant's visit on 13 September, the Indian Prime Minister Lal Bahadur Shastri recommended the acceptance of the UNSC resolutions. The Army Chief of Staff, General Chaudhuri disagreed, stating that the Indian Army was on the verge of victory and should be allowed to inflict the maximum damage possible on the Pakistani armed forces. The Chief of Air Staff Arjan Singh too, was not in favour of accepting the ceasefire. The IAF had gained in confidence, its ammunition and fuel stocks were still in good shape and morale amongst the pilots was high. The raids on Peshawar and Kohat had convinced the IAF that strikes could be carried out anywhere in Pakistan. Similarly, other senior members of Indian military staff were in favour of prolonging military action to destroy Pakistani armour and minimize the threat of future attacks by the Pakistani military machine. The Defence Minister Y.B. Chavan supported the army's position. Other cabinet members suggested acceptance of the resolution as a gesture of peace since Pakistan was likely to reject the resolution anyway. The Indian Government was not disappointed as Pakistan made its acceptance subject to conditions that the Kashmir 'dispute' be 'resolved'. So the war dragged on for another week.

As battle in the Sialkot sector intensified, the prospect of a long and bloody war that would result in untenable attrition dampened Pakistani spirits. The UNSC adopted a third resolution on 20 September, demanding the acceptance of a ceasefire on 22 September, by 1230 hours. India accepted. Finally, so did Pakistan, accepting the resolution on 22 September at precisely the UN deadline. Due to delays in Pakistani implementation, the ceasefire time was extended to 0330 hours on 23 September, at which time it became effective.

News of the ceasefire met a mixed response. On the Indian side, there was relief that the slogging match had ended and rejoicing in the fact that the Indian armed forces had performed creditably in a military conflict—for the first time since the disastrous China war in 1962. At ceasefire, India possessed 710 square miles of Pakistani territory. It had lost 210 square miles, mostly in the Chamb sector.

CEASEFIRE VIOLATIONS

There were numerous ceasefire violations after 23 September. Some were exchanges of small arms and artillery fire. Some were brief airspace violations, when aircraft of the opposing airforces inadvertently crossed the borders. Others were deliberate intrusions.

The first of these occurred on 10 October, when a PAF RB 57F was sent to reconnoitre Ambala. The RB 57F, a specially modified version of the B 57 with an enormous wingspan of 124 ft and two auxiliary jet engines, was capable of cruising at over 65,000 ft, well above the ceiling of even the MiG 21. The RB 57's crew expected no surprises on their sortie to Ambala. Unknown to the PAF, the IAF had moved a battery of its SA-2 Guidelines there. When the RB 57F, was detected over Ambala, three Guidelines were fired. The missiles exploded proximal to the RB 57F, causing severe structural damage and shutting down one of its engines. Its pilot, Squadron Leader Rasheed Meer, nursed the heavily damaged aircraft back to Peshawar, its home base. On landing, the nose-wheel failed to extend, damaging the aircraft even further.[1]

The second occurred on 16 December, when a PAF Auster crossed over the Ichogil Canal and flew straight across the Indian border. Two Gnats on air patrol were diverted to intercept the unidentified intruder. The Gnats did so and instructed the Auster to land at Amritsar. When the pilot refused to comply, one of the Gnats fired a cannon burst, bringing down the flimsy aircraft near Boparai village, 8 miles from Amritsar. The pilot, a Pakistani Army Captain, was dead by the time villagers arrived at the wreckage site. Another officer, Major Aftab Haider was rescued from the burning wreckage and admitted to a field hospital with severe burn injuries to his legs. Some official documents and a camera were recovered from the aircraft. The Pakistani Army claimed that the Auster was on a routine administrative flight when it strayed into Indian territory.

Trigger fingers remained itchy after the war. About a year and four months after the ceasefire, on 2 February 1967, a pair of Hunters was scrambled to investigate a slow moving intruder in the Lahore sector. Two Hunters of 27 Squadron, flown by Flight Lieutenant J.S. Sidhu and Flying Officer M.P. Samant, were scrambled out of Halwara by 230 SU at Amritsar. Arriving near the Harike barrage, about 30 km from the international border, they identified a slow moving light plane, flying low and turning from side to side. As visibility was quite poor, it took the pilots some time to visually sight the aircraft. On hearing from the pilots that the aircraft was painted green and resembled a Pakistani AOP aircraft, the GCI officer issued orders for immediate shootdown. Sidhu made the first gun attack but his closing speed was too high. The light aircraft jinked to one side and Sidhu overshot his target. Samant, who was keeping guard on Sidhu's tail, came in behind, saw Sidhu miss the target, and promptly lined up and fired at the Cessna. The tiny aircraft shuddered as it was hit by the 30 mm cannon shells and spiralled down to crash on the ground below. Inspection of the wreckage revealed it to be a civilian flying club plane, lost, disoriented and misidentified due to its paint colour. The pilot did not survive. The speed difference between the Hunter and the Cessna only afforded the pilots a fleeting look at the aircraft in the haze so typical of a north Indian winter.[2]

Plate 52: Pilots of 23 Squadron in their sweaty flight suits after gruelling low level escort mission during the war. *Left* to *right*, Flight Lieutenant V.S. Pathania, Wing Commander S. Raghavendran, CO, Squadron Leader Trevor Keelor and Flight Lieutenant S. Krishnaswamy. Keelor is said to have shot down the intruding AOP aircraft after the ceasefire.

There was a third incident of a light aircraft straying over Indian territory. The precise date of the encounter is not known but this time Mysteres of 3 Squadron were scrambled. Flight Lieutenant Surjit Singh shot down the AOP aircraft using his guns. This was the only other air kill for the Mysteres, besides Devayya's Starfighter.[3]

THE TASHKENT AGREEMENT

On the political front, the Russian Premier, Alexei Kosygin had been in touch with both countries prior to the ceasefire. On 18 September, Kosygin contacted the Indian Prime Minister Shastri and proposed a meeting with Field Marshal Ayub Khan at Tashkent. On acceptance by Shastri the offer was made to Khan. After the ceasefire, and on Ayub Khan's acceptance, the Russians arranged a summit in Tashkent mediated by Kosygin. Six days of hectic bargaining saw the birth of the Tashkent

Declaration on 10 January 1966. Both sides agreed on an immediate exchange of POWs and withdrawal of troops, to positions held before 5 August 1965. The Indian Prime Minister, Lal Bahadur Shastri died in Tashkent of a massive heart attack, sobering an otherwise irate nation, that still angered by the Pakistani attack on Kashmir, might have refused to accept the agreement.

As part of the agreement, establishment of diplomatic relations, halting of hostile propaganda and restoration of economic and social ties were agreed upon. India gained little from the Tashkent Declaration, except for six years of uneasy peace. India was forced to hand over all the captured territory and, besides, its main objective of having Pakistan labelled as the aggressor, was not achieved. The Tashkent Declaration ensured a return to an unsatisfactory *status quo*.

POW exchange took place immediately after diplomatic delegations returned home on 22 January 1966. India received 1083 POWs, including seven IAF pilots. Another 359 missing in action were declared dead. India repatriated 734 Pakistani prisoners, including three PAF personnel. Troop withdrawals proceeded unhampered and by 25 February all occupied territories were returned. India received the Chamb and Khem Karan salient. As confidence building measures, visits by Military Chiefs of Staffs were arranged. General Mohammed Musa, COAS of Pakistani Army, visited New Delhi and was received by General Chaudhuri.

Reciprocating this visit in February 1966, a Tupolev 124 of the IAF carrying Air Marshal Arjan Singh landed in Peshawar, where Air Marshal Nur Khan, the PAF CAS, received him and conducted a tour of the base. Singh noted the damage caused by Canberras in the night raid of 13 September. Singh was no stranger to Peshawar, home of his Second World War training days with 1 Squadron.

The war cost India 3,261 dead and 8,444 wounded, including those lost in the Kashmir counter-insurgency operations from 5 August onwards. The dead included 359 whose fate was never ascertained. Pakistani casualty figures were not given but were estimated to be in the same range for regulars, and nearly 6,000 plus killed for the Mujahid forces of Operation Gibraltar. Both

Plate 53: PAF Chief Nur Khan receives his Indian counterpart Arjan Singh at Peshawar.

sides had engaged half a million troops in battle against each other.

No account of the air war would be complete without a numbers count. Though numbers play little role in deciding the victor or loser of a war, a quantification of the losses of each side can aid us in at least determining whether the objectives of each air force was met.

PAKISTANI CLAIMS

Pakistani claims of losses inflicted on India need to be taken with a pinch of salt. Their considerable exaggerations were clearly intended for public consumption rather than serious analysis. These included claims of 10,000 Indian casualties inflicted or the occupation of 2,000 square miles of Indian territory. Freed from the need to generate wartime hype and hysteria, Pakistan managed to put forward more credible and conservative claims later.

At the end of the war, a Pakistani spokesman claimed the destruction of 104 Indian aircraft against 19 lost by the PAF. The break up of the alleged nineteen losses was thirteen Sabres, two Starfighters and four B 57 Canberras. The losses of the Bell helicopter and the Cessna L-19 were not included and were explained away as those incurred by Army Aviation. Of the 104 Indian aircraft allegedly destroyed, the break up was

35 air-to-air kills, 34 destroyed on the ground and the rest falling to AA fire. Of the air-to-air kills, all but four allegedly fell to Sabres. Starfighters claimed the remaining. These figures require closer examination. Of the latter four claims, only two can be verified through Indian records (Devayya and Lowe). The PAF's claim of force-landing Sikand's Gnat is denied by India, as Sikand is said to have made a navigational error before landing. Later this claim was retracted by the PAF.[4]

A look at the Sabres' claims also produces similar results. Rafiqui's formation over Halwara was supposed to have accounted for five Hunters overall, while only two were lost. Alam's claims of nine Hunters reveal only four losses. The only occasion the PAF came close to estimating correctly was on 20 September, when it claimed two Hunters. Only eighteen air combat losses can be assessed from Indian admissions against a total of thirty-five claims by the PAF. The rest were lost to AA fire or accidents. The PAF got its claim of aircraft destroyed on the ground just about right. Fricker, while estimating Indian figures says, 'Figures of Indian losses were sometimes quoted as high as 75.' We find that the total number of IAF aircraft lost was around 68, but adding the civilian aircraft destroyed and the Navy aircraft that crashed near Santa Cruz, gives us a total of 75.

INDIAN CLAIMS

India admitted a loss of thirty-five aircraft to all causes and claimed seventy-three Pakistani aircraft as destroyed. The break-up for Pakistani air losses was four F 104s (not counting Devayya's Starfighter), eight B 57s, forty-seven F 86s (twelve in air-to-air combat), two C 130 and the rest miscellaneous trainers and transport aircraft. It is believed any exaggeration is due more to the claims of the ack-ack guns than IAF attacks. A rough break-up would be thirteen claimed in air combat (later increased to sixteen), eighteen on the ground and the rest to AA fire. From Pakistani admissions, eight of the air combat kills, a lone Sabre on the ground and five aircraft to AA fire can be verified.

The huge discrepancy in Indian claims and Pakistani

admissions is probably best explained by a combination of over-enthusiastic claims made by the IAF and reluctance to admit combat losses by the PAF. There appears to be little substantiation in Indian claims of over eighteen aircraft destroyed on the ground in Pakistani airfields. The figure is believed to be closer to about half a dozen against one loss admitted by Pakistan. All the kills came on the Sargodha raids.

The main culprit in faulty claims were the anti-aircraft regiments of the Indian Army's Artillery Wing, which overstated the number of PAF aircraft shot down by ground fire and which were liberal in awarding 'kills' without proper verification. Often, aircraft that were victims of air combat were claimed as ground fire 'kills', leading to a few awards to AA guns personnel. A glaring example of this is the Sabre shot down over Kalaikunda, where the army claimed Flight Lieutenant Alfred Cooke's victim as an AA kill. Lance Naik Mudalai Muthu was awarded the VrC for this claim. Without denigrating Muthu's gallantry, it seems clear that the services needed to have better coordination in assessing claims and counter-claims. The same seems to have been the case of the AA kill claimed by Havildar Potharaj at Jammu Bridge. On several occasions, attacking aircraft were claimed as kills after they had been damaged by AA, i.e. observed trailing smoke or fire, but not seen as crashed.

The 'Official History of the 1965 Indo-Pakistan War' claims forty-three PAF aircraft destroyed. Weighing claims, counter-claims and confirmations, it appears that the PAF lost anywhere between thirty to thirty-five aircraft in the war. A tendency observed on the Pakistani side was to cover up combat losses as operational losses, which was a rather transparent attempt to deny the IAF credit. This is best seen in Pakistani versions of the losses of Amjad Hussain's Starfighter because of 'flying through debris of an exploding Mystere', N.M. Butt's Sabre, which was 'shot down by own AA fire', or Alauddin Ahmed's Sabre, which 'flew through the debris of an exploding train'.

India showed a marked reluctance to discuss its losses on ground. Aircraft losses in the air were admitted, as were losses over Pakistani territory and losses relating to incidents in which pilots lost their lives on Indian territory. But losses on the ground were never admitted or acknowledged officially. The losses detailed here were gathered from sundry unofficial publications on the war and personal interviews. The complete extent of IAF losses came to be known after the release of the official IAF history. The Indian Armed Forces had lost a total of 75 aircraft, both in combat as well as operational accidents.

The area where the IAF suffered the most was its losses on the ground, where it lost a total of thirty-five aircraft; ten at Pathankot, eight at Kalaikunda, and four at Jamnagar accounted for two-thirds of the list. Credit for the remaining attacks goes to the PAF B 57 squadrons.

GALLANTRY AWARDS

The IAF received a significant share of the gallantry awards given to the Indian Armed Forces. Most awards were made during the conflict itself. In the IAF's case, these were made to pilots involved in successful air-to-air combat and to air crew, whose contribution was outstanding and immediately perceivable.

The IAF received four MVCs; one awarded to a Mystere pilot, Wing Commander J.M. Goodman, and the rest to Canberra pilots. Forty-two VrCs were also awarded to the air force, seven of them going to navigator crew of the Canberra Squadrons and twelve to Hunter and Gnat pilots with air-

Plate 54: Vir Chakra awardees Denzil Keelor, Alfred Cooke, William Goodman, and Trevor Keelor at a party hosted by the Anglo-Indian Association shortly after the war.

to-air combat kills. Surprisingly, only one VrC was awarded posthumously, to Squadron Leader Jasbeer Singh. Certainly there must have been occasions where pilots who failed to return deserved the awards, such as the three Vampire pilots (Bhagwagar, Bharadwaj, Joshi) lost over Chamb, or the two Hunter pilots (Bhagwat and Brar), who plunged into a scrap with intercepting Sabres to cover the escape of their squadron mates.

Most interdiction awards went to Hunter and Mystere pilots. The solitary VrC given to a Gnat pilot for interdiction and successful leadership, as against an award for an air combat kill, went to Squadron Leader Johnny Greene.

Plates 55, 56: Flight Lieutenant P.C. Chopra and Flying Officer A.R. Ghandhi receive VrCs from the Indian President Sarvepalli Radhakrishnan.

A Kirti Chakra was awarded to Squadron Leader Sawardekar for his gallant retrieval of Squadron Leader Marston from the wreckage of the burning Vampire in Baghdogra. VSM Class I (later PVSM) medals were awarded to two base commanders: Group Captain G.K. John, Station Commander of Halwara and Group Captain Walter Lloyd, Station Commander of Adampur. A VSM Class II (AVSM) was awarded to Wing Commander K. Dandapani, CO 230 SU at Amritsar.

The Chief of Air Staff, Air Marshal Arjan Singh was honoured with the Padma Vibhushan, as was the Army Chief Gen. J.N. Chaudhuri. Arjan Singh's deputies too were honoured with decorations. The AOC-in-C Western Air Command, Air Vice-Marshal Rajaram was awarded the Padma Bhushan. The Vice-

Chief of Air Staff, Air Vice-Marshal P.C. Lal was decorated with the Padma Bhushan. A Staff Officer being given the honour over a field officer pointed to his active involvement in the direction of the war. P.C. Lal was also credited with the successful introduction of the SA-2 SAM missile into the air defence environment of the IAF just before the war.[5]

Seen as being necessary to motivate and preserve the ethos of the Forces, gallantry awards made for a touchy subject. These intentions, as in any other war, were clouded by the smoke of the war and by the use of awards as boosters of the public morale. A major grouse of the Indian Army was that the Air Force received more than it deserved, a complaint dished out in several books published by Indian Army officers, including Major General Sukhwant Singh's *Defence of the Western Border*. The Indian Government was accused of dishing out awards liberally to the IAF in order to achieve two objectives: sustain the IAF's morale in the face of high attrition and score public relations points. Without getting into this particular sniping match, we would like to note that air operations provide unprecedented scope for *individual acts of gallantry* that are not easily ignored or undervalued. Given that awards are made to *individuals*, it was only natural that the IAF would have been awarded a significant percentage of awards.

All this criticism was of little importance to the government or the IAF. In view of the IAF's war effort and its recent expansion, the government upgraded the post of Air Chief to Air Chief Marshal, thus pegging the Air Chief equal to the rank of the Army Chief for the first time since Independence.[6] Accordingly, Air Marshal Arjan Singh became the first Air Chief Marshal of the IAF. All Air ranks previously held by Air Vice-Marshals were upgraded, to be commanded by Air Marshal rank.

PAF GALLANTRY AWARDS

Pakistani gallantry awards are loosely based on the British and Indian systems. The top award is the Nishan-e-Haider, followed by the Sitara-e-Juraat (SJ) and the Tangma-e-Juraat (TJ). The Hilaal-e-Juraat (HJ) is awarded for leadership and direction.

CEASEFIRE AND POST-MORTEM

Plate 57: Chief of Army Staff General J.N. Chaudhuri with IAF VrC awardees. *Left to right*: Flight Lieutenant S.C. Mamgain, Wing Commander Bharat Singh, Squadron Leader A.J.S. Sandhu, Flight Lieutenant A.T. Cooke, General Chaudhuri, unknown, Flying Officer V.K. Neb, Flight Lieutenant Vinay Kapila and Flying Officer Adi Ghandhi.

Plate 58: The Indian Prime Minister Mrs. Indira Gandhi with Air Staff Officers, shortly after the war. *Top left to right* AVM T.S. Virk, AM Y.V. Malse, AVM H.N. Chatterjee, AM O.P. Mehra, AM H.S. Moolgavkar, AM H.C. Dewan. *Sitting left to right*: AM Shivdev Singh, Unidentified, ACM Arjan Singh, Prime Minister Indira Gandhi, Shri Swaran Singh, AM R. Rajaram, AM M.M. Engineer.

Almost all Pakistani pilots killed in action received the SJ, except for those lost in accidents.

Several pilots received double awards. Squadron Leader Rafiqui, killed over Halwara, received both the HJ and the SJ. Squadron Leader Mohammed Alam received a SJ and a Bar. The Chaklala Station Commander, Eric Hall received a SJ. The

CO of the Transport Squadron, Wing Commander Zahid Butt, and six of his pilots were awarded the SJ. Many pilots of the Starfighter squadron, like its CO Squadron Leader Arif Iqbal, Flight Lieutenant Amjad Hussain, and Squadron Leader Mervyn Middlecoat received the SJ. Pilots of the Sargodha Strike Wing, including Wing Commander Shamim, Flight Lieutenants Cecil Chaudhary and Imtiaz Bhatti, received the SJ.

LESSONS OF THE WAR: THE AIRCRAFT

The Gnat was the surprise of the war, emerging with surprisingly low attrition. Three were lost in operations and one to an accident, versus the seven Sabres claimed shot down in air combat. 23 Squadron claimed three, with Nos. 2 and 9 Squadrons claiming two each. All three squadrons lost an aircraft each. The war had strengthened the IAF's belief in the tiny fighter, and subsequently its production was stepped up to equip more squadrons. Air Marshal Janak Kapur expressed the following opinion about the Gnat:

It's like shooting birds. If it's a large size bird, even a near miss will get you, but if it's a small size bird then the hit will have to be dead on the target because a near miss will miss the bird completely. The other thing about the Gnat was it was an extremely manoeuvrable aircraft. Unless you were taken completely by surprise, it wasn't easy to get shot down. People got shot down but because they were in a melee, two vs two, four vs four, you are chasing one, you know that there is somebody at your back but you say alright, five more seconds, ten more seconds and I'll get this chap. So I am not breaking off. I stay with him but the other chap opens fire first.

Kapur's comments are telling in that they point to a healthy aggression in IAF pilots in their encounters with the PAF.

The Mysteres flew with five squadrons; six of them were lost to enemy action, including two in air combat. A further three were lost to accidents. The Mystere though originally a fighter, was employed in a ground attack role; its sluggish dogfighting nature left it at a disadvantage with the Sabre. All Mysteres losses occurred on interdiction missions; none flew air defence sorties. Nine Mysteres were lost on the ground in the Pathankot and Adampur raids.

The Hunters suffered the highest attrition, with fourteen lost to various causes, including ten to enemy action and eight to air combat. Fourteen aircraft out of a total force of forty-eight represented nearly 30 per cent attrition of the entire Hunter force in the west. This would have been a crippling blow but for the fact that, if needed, the IAF would have been able to replenish its fleet with Hunters from the EAC. The EAC Hunters were never needed in the West. All eight Hunters to fall in air combat fell to the Sabre. The Hunters claimed six Sabres in air combat, of which Pakistan admitted four losses. Part of the reason the Hunters suffered was their size. Compared to the Gnat it was larger and offered an easier target. In some cases the Hunters were flying in the ground attack configuration and were easy meat for air the Sabres. Tactically, some Hunter pilots made the mistake of trying to engage the Sabre in the horizontal plane (turns and scissors) where they were outmatched, rather than engaging the Sabre in the vertical plane (climbs), where they would have had the edge. One Hunter pilot that bested his Sabre opponents, Alfred Cooke, agrees: 'Two things saved my life: the Rolls-Royce engine on the Hunter and my training at low level with Piloo Kacker. During my dogfight, whenever I got into trouble and saw the Sabre gaining on me, I would go vertical. He would follow me but have to dive out of the climb since all his speed would wash off and he couldn't follow me.'

The few Gnat pilots, like Kale and Mayadev, who were shot down by the Sabres or damaged by them, like Raina, made the same mistake as the Hunter pilots. As one experienced Gnat pilot remarked:

The Gnat power to weight ratio with an unreheated engine is such that you could get the Sabre into a vertical fight instead of a circular fight, where it had the advantage. As soon as that enemy pilot follows you in the vertical fight then he is at a disadvantage! Simple as that. Because your power to weight ratio in the Gnat and its manoeuvrability is far superior in this the vertical plane, but no one really got down to it. So any fellow who got into a tangle with a Sabre, first thing to do is to drop your tanks and second thing is to pull up. Let the fellow come up and fight you on your terms.

One aircraft that failed to make a good impression on the IAF was the MiG 21. At the time of the ceasefire, 28 Squadron had flown about 80 sorties. Three MiGs were lost in the course of the operations but there were no casualties among the pilots or the ground crew. The MiGs were often used for offensive sweeps to ward off any marauding Starfighters. While no encounters occurred, the sweeps did have the effect of increasing perceived cover for ground attack aircraft, with no aircraft thought capable of taking on the F 104. More than anything else, the sweeps acted as moral boosters for the interdictor missions since the chances of a F 104 slipping through the sweep were limited. In order for the sweeps to be truly effective, total radar cover was required, which was not the case by a long shot in 1965. It was clear by the end of the war that had the MiG squadron had more time to train, both in air combat as well as night interception with the Type 76s, they would have played a significant part. They were the correct aircraft to counter the night raids by the B 57s but with barely four to five months allocated for training, the MiGs could not play a significant role. Moreover, night interception required good radar and ground control infrastructure, the absence of which was felt keenly. Wing Commander M.S.D. Wollen, CO of 28 Squadron, was mentioned in dispatches for his role in operations and, after the war, led a flypast to counter Pakistani claims of the destruction of all the MiGs.

The importance of the role played by the MiG 21 lay in the lacunae it helped identify. The corrections and modifications applied as a result were to pay a rich dividend in the 1971 war. In a candid opinion of the aircraft in the aftermath of the 1965 war, Air Vice-Marshal Harjinder Singh, who retired as AOC-in-C Maintenance Command, felt that the MiG 21 was 'a good for nothing aircraft in combat situations'.[7] Its missiles were useless at tree-top height and the only saving grace was the fitting of a cannon. Perhaps Singh spoke too soon, but in 1965 the MiG 21 was just that. It was hampered by the lack of time to train in specific combat profiles and its contribution to the war-effort left much to be desired.

Another lesson of the war was to decrease the IAF's reliance on the heat-seeker missiles, supplied by the Russians for the MiGs. Post-war trials conducted by 28 Squadron, where the K 13s were launched at para flares, gave unsatisfactory results. Only then did the Russians go back to modifying the missiles for better results. The IAF also got an external 23 mm gunpack fitted to the PF type and a gyro gunsight designed for the MiG. These preparations yielded good results during the 1971 war. The IAF put its faith in the aircraft and used it to equip many squadrons. This faith was repaid in the 1971 war, when the MiG 21 built an envious reputation.

The Canberras flew 196 sorties during the 16 day period from 6-22 September. Almost all major PAF airfields were bombed and over 6,00,000 lbs of bombs dropped. With the exception of 5 Squadron's loss, and the loss of 35 Squadron's Canberra in the landing accident, all other missions returned unscathed. These Canberra losses compare favourably with the four B 57s losses admitted by the PAF. That none of the Indian Canberras were lost to Pakistani AA fire suggests better tactics employed by the bombers. Five Squadron flew nearly 150 sorties against Pakistani targets. When hostilities came to a close, the Canberras took a large chunk of the honours, bagging three out of the four MVCs and eight out of the forty-two VrCs. Six navigators were awarded VrCs. The raids on Peshawar and Badin became part of the Canberra legend. The Canberra was to follow this contribution by its sterling role in the 1971 war, when raids on airfields like Sargodha, Mauripur and the Karachi oil tanks further enhanced its reputation. However, advances in radar and superior air cover led to higher losses. The Canberra went on to complete over four decades of service and currently holds the record for the longest serving aircraft type in the IAF.

The IAF flew a total of nearly 4,000 sorties in the 22-day conflict:

	Sorties	% Effort
Fighter sorties	1,017	26 %
Close support by fighter bombers	696	17 %
Other sorties by fighter bombers	676	17 %
Canberra close support	33	1 %
Canberra night raids	163	4 %
Combat air patrol over IAF airbases	1,352	35 %
TOTAL	3,937	100 %

35 per cent of these were unproductive combat air patrol sorties over airfields. Close support and interdiction accounted for 60 per cent of the sorties. A significant number of sorties were flown in ferrying aircraft to and from Ambala to avoid B 57 night attacks.

The IAF listed 19 officers killed, including one navigator, and 18 airmen lost in PAF raids. Seven officers were taken POW. Pakistan accepted the loss of 10 pilots and 3 navigators. Another two pilots and a navigator were taken POW. Pakistan's losses on the ground are not known.

Pakistan revised its initial figures to claim fifty-four aircraft destroyed in one of their official histories, which may be near the mark. The IAF lost fifty-seven aircraft due to enemy causes. A further 13 were lost in operational accidents (see Appendix).

The details of the 2,363 sorties PAF flew in the 1965 war are as follows:

	Sorties	% Effort
Air Defence	1,303	55 %
Army Support	647	27 %
Day Strike	100	4 %
Night Strike	165	7 %
Photo Recce	148	6 %

The PAF admitted the loss of 19 aircraft, an attrition rate of 0.81 per cent. If we are to believe the figures quoted in (Singh and Rikhye, 1991) of 25 aircraft, the attrition rate is 1.05 per cent, almost the same as the severe Israeli attrition rate of 1.1 per cent during the Yom Kippur War.

War is never so clinical so as to permit the application of facile formulas to assess the damage done to the enemy. To bolster a nation's morale, deliberate untruths are fed to the public, intending to keep both the public as well as the military in high spirits. Admissions of severe setbacks or of inaction against the enemy would invite public anger. Both India as well as Pakistan abide by this style. Thus, the Indian public never hears of the retreat to Jaurian or Khem Karan, while the

Pakistani public never hears of the retreat from Wagah, or the battering its armour received at Assal Uttar.

Pakistan has overdone the propaganda by adding incredible and exaggerated claims to the achievements of the PAF, an issue that with respect to this air war in particular has been examined in numerous writings over the years, most notably in Pushpindar Singh's 'Laying the Sargodha Ghost to Rest'. We will not attempt any systematic debunking except to point the reader to our accounts, in particular of the Halwara and Kalaikunda air battles, and to Sqn. Ldr. M.M. Alam's combats with IAF pilots. The discrepancies are obvious and need little further comment. Fairy tales need not be subjected to systematic refutation. Analysis of the PAF's motivation for including these incredible claims, and of their wholesale consumption by the Pakistani nation, is best left to sociologists and psychologists. However, we will make one comment. The PAF did well in the war. It's a pity that its government and its leadership saw fit to denigrate its achievements by making claims that have ensured that the PAF is associated with bragging as opposed to its actual, praiseworthy achievements.

On the Indian side, Chiefs of Staff did not appear to have had complete access to information. A press conference conducted immediately after the war, on 24 September at New Delhi, is illustrative. Both General Chaudhuri and Air Marshal Arjan Singh participated in it. In the light of newer information released or made available since that time, most claims by the Indian Chief of Staffs during the press conference seem inaccurate. It appears that some information was given off the cuff, probably under journalistic pressure. These included several statements by Arjan Singh. Firstly, the claim that the PAF started the war with about 104 Sabres and twenty-four B 57s in the west, and at least half of the PAF was either knocked out or damaged, remains an unverifiable figure. Singh tacitly admitted the loss of one MiG 21 by inviting reporters to see eight of the original nine IAF MiGs. But the IAF started the war with ten MiGs and had seven left at the end of the war. Secondly, that only aircraft from the western sector were employed in the conflict and that not a single aircraft was withdrawn from the Eastern or the Central Commands to the west. Once again, information on the employment of 16 Squadron's Canberras, which were employed in raids against Sargodha and Badin, does not seem to have been available to Singh. Of course, these aircraft were not as fully employed as those of WAC. 37 Squadron's Hunters too were moved to the western front during the closing days of the war.

AIR COMBAT TRENDS

Since the Korean War, air combat strategists had stressed that the future belonged to the air-to-air missile and interceptors. With the era of gun victories relegated to the past, dogfighting ability and pilot skills were supposed to play a minor role in air combat. This air war proved just the opposite (as would the American experience over the skies of Vietnam). Aircraft relied more on the gun than the missile, and manoeuvrability, turning dogfights and pilot skills played a major role. Most combats took place at low level rather than high altitudes. The air war rewrote the doctrine of how air wars were to be fought in the future in the subcontinent.

Put together, both sides claimed 50 aerial combat victories, 18[8] by the IAF and 35 by the PAF. In reality the actual losses are about half. In about twenty encounters, Pakistan accepted eight losses in air-to-air combat; India had eighteen air combat losses. Pakistani pilots had an edge. Some flew the Sabre against obsolete aircraft like the Vampire, the Canberra or against the Hunter in ground attack configuration. The break-up of Indian air losses was four Vampires, one Canberra, two Mysteres, two Gnats, and two Hunters in the ground attack configuration and six Hunters in the air defence configuration. The Pakistanis accept the loss of one Starfighter and seven Sabres in air combat, though India claims higher figures. Of the Sabres lost, the Pakistanis admit four to Hunters and three to Gnats.

Two Pakistani pilots claimed multiple air combat kills. Squadron Leader M.M. Alam had the most air combat victories, claiming four (Rawlley, Brar, Bhagwat and Bunsha), which can be confirmed on the Indian side, though he claimed a total of nine Hunters. Squadron Leader S. Rafique was the second highest scorer, with two Vampires and one Hunter (Pingale) as his kills. Some Indian losses still retain an aura of confusion. For instance, who actually shot down Flying Officer A.R. Ghandhi? Both Yunus and Cecil Chaudhary were credited with Hunters on that day and ultimately Chaudhary was credited with shooting down Ghandhi. On the Indian side, none of the pilots were awarded multiple air combat kills. Pingale was awarded two kills for his breathtaking aircombat on 16 September, but it is widely accepted that only one is a confirmed kill. Not until the 1971 war did an Indian pilot score his second combat kill. Ironically, though Flight Lieutenant Alfred Cooke put two Sabres out of service during his epic battle with four Sabres over Kalaikunda, formal recognition has not yet been accorded to his feat.

Wartime propaganda suggests to both nations that pilots of the opposing nation fled from air combat. But Indian and Pakistani pilots never shirked combat—except in extreme circumstances when they were short of fuel—whether it was the Vampire pilots on the first day or a rookie pilot like Neb at Halwara. In the Eastern Wing, the Sabre Squadron was instructed to withhold from operations after 14 September, in view of the deteriorating supply condition of Pakistan and the need to conserve their strength.

Pakistani pilots were more experienced in flying and battle tactics with more hours behind them. Since they were operating as close-knit units for quite some time, PAF squadrons were highly optimized. India on the other hand had diluted its pilot strengths during the post-1962 expansion. Many units were bled of expert pilots and commanders to help raise new units. The average IAF unit had a higher percentage of newly inducted pilots, with lesser flying hours than ever. Instead of focusing the Air Force's best pilots to fight against Pakistan, the Air Force had dispersed its strengths throughout its squadrons. Some units like 14, 37 and 17 Squadrons, all equipped with Hunters, wasted their time patrolling against the Chinese during the war.

Plate 59: Air Marshal Arjan Singh visits Halwara air base after the war. *Standing*: Flying Officer A.K. Mazumdar (*1st from left*), Squadron Leader Nimmi Suri (*4th from left*), Dice Dhiman (*7th*) AM Arjan Singh (*8th*), M.M. 'Rusty' Sinha (*10th*) and Wing Commander Bharat Singh (*12th*). *Kneeling*: Ajit Singh Lamba, Unknown, 'Y+H' Behal and Sube Singh 'Chacha' Malik with the exception of Mazumdar and Bharat Singh (*both from No. 2*) all other pilots were from 7 Squadron.

Nor did the Indian and Pakistani Air Forces target civilians on purpose. Arjan Singh pays a compliment to the pilots of both sides: 'Both air forces had an unwritten understanding that civilian targets were to be left alone and not targeted deliberately.'

INDIAN MILITARY PLANNING

The objective of the Indian military plans seemed to be that of inflicting attrition rather than any tangible aims like capture of territory. This could explain the apparent lack of interest in exploiting opportunities during the ground war, like the establishment of a bridgehead over the BRB Canal or the capture of Chawinda. Military planners looked forward to a war lasting a few months, where numerical superiority could be brought to bear on the Pakistani forces. Certainly this was extended to the IAF. In a candid explanation of his approach, Air Marshal Arjan Singh wrote almost after 30 years after the war: 'The IAF was planning its operations on fighting a war lasting at least a few months. However, as we know, the ceasefire was accepted after about 21 days of fighting; that was too short to prove the full capability of the IAF.'

This then, was the core of the IAF's war doctrine: to wage a lengthy war of attrition, in which its opponent would be worn down by sheer weight of numbers. As Vinod Patney would remark dryly years later: 'On the 18th we got sent off for rest and relaxation to Gorakhpur. You see, the Second World War lasted six years; we thought we were going to be fighting this war for 200 years.'

No contingency plan was made for a brief war. The only major war the IAF had participated in after Independence was in Kashmir, which went on for fifteen months. The Hyderabad, Goa or Congo operations were similar to police actions. The China war was unique in the fact that neither side employed strike forces in the air. The 1965 war was a watershed in the IAF's war doctrine, changing it forever.

Another aspect of Indian military planning was the lack of action in the eastern sector. The Indian government had ruled out any land offensive on East Pakistan. Ostensibly, this was done to avoid alienating the sentiments of its people. Political dissonance amongst the Bengalis was already well known, and any attempt to invade East Pakistan would have almost certainly pushed the Bengali East Pakistanis together with West Pakistanis. However, the Indian Government could have used the IAF to destroy the air assets of the PAF, while simultaneously desisting from a land invasion of East Pakistan. Whatever India's reasons, whether it was the foresight of the government or the threat of Chinese, the decision brought results later in the Liberation war of 1971. In 1965, the lack of coordination between the air force and the army was evident in the east. The only day that Central and Eastern Air Commands got involved in the air war was on 7 September: a pitifully low number of sorties, approximately twelve, were planned and executed with the objective of knocking out the Sabres in East Pakistan.

Other lessons of the 1965 war were well imbibed by the IAF. Training facilities were moved south and concentrated in the

Hyderabad area, in bases like Dundigal and Hakimpet. New bases such as Uttarlai and Jaisalmer were activated. Both were not permanent airfields and were to be used as forward bases in times of war. However, an independent air command for the south-western sector was only created in 1981. In 1971, this sector saw more IAF kills than WAC. Aircraft from south-western airfields claimed over fifteen aircraft in the air and on the ground, as opposed to the solitary B 57 in 1965.

ARMY-AIR FORCE COOPERATION

One problem area during the 1965 war was the army-air force cooperation. Neither arm mentioned its plans to the other, making tasks like allocation of sorties for army offensives difficult. More often than not, requests for air support took hours to materialize, if at all. The air force pointed out that the army had kept it in the dark about its plans for offensive action and was referred to only at the last moment, as in the first day at Chamb. Providing close support to the army formations was an area in which the IAF was found wanting. Communication systems required for close coordination between forward troops and the IAF did not exist. In contrast, the PAF had an effective way of coordinating close support and was there on many occasions to provide it. The IAF was not terribly enthused by the quality of the briefings it received from the army's Ground Liaison Officers either. 8 Squadron's war diary contains the following memorable entry: 'GLO briefing is all balls'.

The IAF's Advance HQ WAC was made responsible for close support and Air Defence Centre WAC used to control air defense and counter air sorties. Requests from army formations were channelled through the superior formation till they reached the Corps HQ, where the TAC Commander was appraised. By the time the TAC Commander sorted out his priorities, and the sorties allocation was discussed with the station commanders, nearly a day had passed before the close support sortie was undertaken. 70 per cent of all close support sorties undertaken by the IAF were done on the initiative of Advance HQ, without requests from the army. The army contested the usefulness of these sorties.[9]

The first welcome change was to allocate IAF squadrons to specific sectors on the front line. Each squadron would be responsible for close support activities in its sector and nowhere else. This had two advantages. Firstly, the pilots having operated only in that particular area were well versed with its terrain and landmarks. Secondly, the sector TAC Commanders were well aware of the utilization of the earmarked squadrons and knew which squadron was available for which mission at what time.

The second major change was to improve communication between the Forward Air Controller (FAC), operating with the leading echelons of the army, and the IAF aircraft overhead. During the 1971 war FACs were able to guide these aircraft onto the targets accurately and promptly. Compared to nearly a day or a day and a half taken to respond to a request for close air support in 1965, the IAF took about an hour or an hour and a half to respond to a close air support request during the 1971 war.[10]

THE EYES OF THE ARMY

Besides the AA units, the only army wing to be involved in the air war was the Artillery Regiment, which maintained a small band of army pilots that flew small, light unarmed planes. Known as Air Observation Posts (AOPs), these were employed to direct fire from field regiments onto enemy targets.

The Indian Army maintained one AOP squadron, 659 Squadron, with four flights of Auster light aircraft. These were earlier employed in the 1948 Kashmir war, in both AOP and casevac roles. The AOPs had distinguished themselves in the Rann of Kutch incident, where Major Sushil Kumar Mathur received the Maha Vir Chakra for effectively directing fire against Pakistani targets.

Two AOP Flights were allocated to 11 Corps' thrust towards Lahore and attached to the Divisional Artillery Brigades in the Lahore sector. To make up for the Auster's deficiencies, the army requisitioned light aircraft from flying clubs and employed them in the AOP role. The AOP flights suffered their first loss on the opening day of the Lahore offensive. A HAL Pushpak light aircraft, requisitioned from a flying club, crashed in Indian lines during a misjudged landing, killing the pilot Captain Khurana. Thereafter, the AOPs were employed effectively with 15 Division by directing fire to disperse enemy concentrations and destroy gun positions across the BRB Canal near Lahore. These missions were extremely dangerous, with the flimsy aircraft being very vulnerable to small arms fire from the ground and air interceptors.

This gallant little band of pilots distinguished themselves in the face of extreme danger from air opposition. Three AOP pilots were decorated with the VrC, with one even managing to shake off a couple of Sabres trying to shoot him down during a spotting flight.

PLANNING FOR THE RAIDS

One of the significant decisions taken by the IAF was attacking the Pakistani Defence Complex at Sargodha, an initiative of Western Air command. These raids involved low level attacks at the extreme range of the aircraft involved. In retrospect, the raids appear to have been too piecemeal to have a significant effect. The IAF's losses were not commensurate with the results achieved. Air Chief Marshal Lal offered this opinion on the strikes:[11] 'Many fine men were lost on such sorties, most of which were mounted with insufficient information about targets and the results of which were often impossible to determine. But for the fact that they caused some trouble to the Pakistanis, their value did not, I fear, match the expenditure of life and effort that went into it.'

Lal admits that the IAF relied too much on the concept of the bomber being the main offensive weapon of the war. This thinking went back to the days of Second World War, when the RAF's bomber command was the main show of force in its war against Germany. Perhaps extending this concept, the IAF relied on the Canberra to produce significant results. Unfortunately, the bomber concept was ineffective due to a combination of factors: the small number of aircraft involved (and, concomitantly, the low frequency of raids) and the accuracy of bombings (in itself not surprising, given the lack of guided munitions).

The purported objective of grounding the PAF, or of reducing its ability to fight, was not achieved by the IAF in the limited time available for operations. To make matters worse, weaknesses present in photographic reconnaissance and other intelligence acquisition meant that damage assessment was poor. The lone PR Squadron flying Canberras was an asset, but inadequate to meet the needs of the armed forces. This identified the need to enhance the tactical photo reconnaissance of frontline units by fitting camera pods. Fighters carried gun cameras that supplemented all kill claims (such as those of Sabres by Gnats).

AIRFIELD PROTECTION

Though the abilities of the individual pilots is a topic for endless debate, one area that the IAF needed to address was aircraft protection on the ground, the lack of which was responsible for nearly 50 per cent of all its losses. Two PAF raids on Indian airfields at Pathankot and Kalaikunda accounted for nearly 20 aircraft destroyed. Though they had little effect on the overall combat capability of the IAF, the losses were a definite indicator of poor dispersal and protection practices. In the disastrous Kalaikunda raid, most of the Vampires were parked out on the runway apron while the Canberras were laid out in blast pens, susceptible to rocket and strafing attacks. Little effort was made to camouflage the openly parked aircraft. Since radar warning was either scarce or non-available, aircraft protection and dispersal acquired paramount importance. This led to the development of hard shelters for aircraft, protected with concrete and earth works.

The second visible aspect that was addressed regarding airfield protection was the combat air patrol regimen. Often, potentially ineffective single aircraft CAPs were flown over airfields, leading to the establishment of two-aircraft CAPs as standard procedure during the 1965 war, a practice continued afterwards. On several occasions during the 1965 war, airfield defense guns were asked to hold tight as CAPs were mounted over the airfield, a clear weakness when under attack by multiple aircraft. In order to let air defence guns have a free hand in protecting the airfields, interceptor jets were deputed to patrol a little away from the airfield. Later CAPs were then flown over known ingress points and discontinued over the airfield. For example, rather than carrying out a patrol over Pathankot, Indian interceptors would CAP over the Madhopur Headworks, the ingress point for attacking enemy aircraft.

THE AIR DEFENCE REGIMENTS

The IAF was not alone in fighting the air war. The army pitched in as well, in particular, the Artillery Regiment, which operated the Air Defence Regiments as well as the AOP aircraft. The anti-aircraft guns protecting the airfields and cities were commanded by the Army's Artillery regiment. Unlike today, where the Regiment of Air Defence Artillery takes care of AA defenses, the Regiment of Artillery was directly responsible for Air Defence. The Regiment organized the AA units into Air Defence Regiments, manned entirely by army personnel. In 1947, at Indian Independence, the Artillery inherited one heavy AA Regiment, with 3.7′ heavy AA guns, which were integrated with gun control radar. Accompanying this regiment were six light AA Regiments, with 40 mm L-60 Bofors guns. These were visually aimed and the firing control was manual. The radar cover for necessary warning time was scanty. Several weaknesses were noticed in the air defense exercises with the US in 1963, in which the ground air defences were overwhelmed by the sophistication employed by the Americans. Some early warning radars were procured, but these were not operational during the 1965 war. Defence pacts with the Soviet Union resulted in the induction of the VK-75 (NATO-SA 3 Goa) surface-to-air missile into the IAF. The Artillery and the air force haggled for the control of the SAMs, with the IAF emerging the winner. During the war, however, the SAM batteries were never put into action against the PAF, with the exception of the single missile fired at Delhi.

CEASEFIRE AND POST-MORTEM

The Air Defence Artillery component was largely drawn from the Territorial Army (TA), especially for the defence of the air bases and important rear areas. Normally, the time taken for mobilization of the TA after the outbreak of the hostilities would have caught India napping for the air defence of vital areas but, fortunately, Pakistan's sideshow at Kutch allowed India enough warning and time to keep the TA alerted for mobilization. When war broke out, a screen of AA Defences was quickly established.

The AA regiments were distributed at main airbases, along the entire western border and a few civilian targets like bridges and important railway stations. Major transit points like railway yards and junctions were covered. Border towns like Amritsar, the home of 230 SU's mobile radar unit, and Pathankot were allotted the guns. During the war, AA guns were very effective against PAF aircraft. By one estimate, 90 per cent of aircraft attacking targets in and around Amritsar were hit by AA fire and were damaged. First blood was drawn at Jamnagar, when AA bought down a B 57. The second B 57 was brought down at Adampur, in which the crews were taken POW. AA guns also bought down approximately half a dozen Sabres. An unverified claim for downing a Starfighter was made as well. A detachment of 45 Regiment (Air Defence), responsible for protecting Amritsar and 230 SU, became heroes as the grateful town took a public donation and contributed Rs. 2,00,000 to the regiment. Subedar R.V. Raju of the regiment was the leader of the AA Detachment in Amritsar. The AA Guns did not go unscathed. A gun placement guarding the Beas Bridge received a direct hit, wiping out its crew of a NCO and three gunners. No. 45 lost six of its men to the air attacks.

RADAR COVERAGE

Radar coverage of airfields and other vital areas was found to be extremely deficient. This was a manifestation of old, outdated equipment and its inability to adequately cover the vast geographic areas of the Indian subcontinent. The solitary radar unit at Amritsar (230 SU) was inadequate to provide coverage over the entire western sector. The deficiency of radar coverage was more telling in the eastern sector, where Pakistani Sabres attacked undetected in almost all their raids. The shortage of radar coverage was supposed to be addressed before the 1971 war. However, not much improvement was achieved by that time. The IAF had to employ MiG 21s, flying cabrank in the night, to guide returning aircraft. These aircraft were code-named *Sparrow* and were so successful that the PAF mistook them for AWACS.

INTERNATIONAL SUPPORT TO THE PAF

Had the 1965 war been prolonged, supplies from friendly countries would have beefed up PAF reserves. The ex-PAF Chief Air Marshal Asghar Khan had been appointed as aid mobilizer on behalf of Pakistan by Ayub Khan and made visits to China, Indonesia, Malaysia, Iran and Turkey, requesting direct military aid. Only Indonesia came forward with immediate help, agreeing to supply four MiG 21s and a squadron of MiG 19s and MiG 17s. The utility of the small number of the MiG 21s is doubtful, as PAF pilots would not have had the training to fully exploit its capabilities. The MiG 19 and the MiG 17s would have been an asset but by the time they were to be shipped by sea to Pakistan, the war had ended.

INTER-SERVICE LEADERSHIP RELATIONSHIPS: CHAUDHURI AND ARJAN SINGH

The Army Chief's stature and presence had an overbearing effect on other Service chiefs. General Chaudhuri had been in the limelight for his direction of the Hyderabad operations, in which the Nizam's forces were overwhelmed in four days, and for his handling of the Goa Operations as the Southern Army Commander. After taking over a demoralized army after 1962, and rebuilding its morale and strengths, Chaudhuri maintained a high public profile in order to have convenient access to governmental bureaucracy.

Age played a part in the Chiefs of other arms accepting a

meeker role before the Army Chief. Arjan Singh was hardly 45 when he took over as Air Chief—he was even younger than his deputy P.C. Lal. The Army Chief in contrast was 57 years old. The Naval Chief Admiral B.S. Soman was 52 years old. This disparity in age made the Army Chief look upon them as young and inexperienced. Chaudhuri did not expect much from the other forces, nor did he plan for them. He obviously felt they were not required, but was forced to accept their presence. Chaudhuri claimed later that he had absolute freedom in chalking out plans with the defence ministry, but it was made clear to the IAF that they were not to be privy to any plans drawn up by the army. Air Chief Marshal Lal summed up the Army Chief's attitude as the 'Supremo Syndrome'.

This communication gap probably explains the failure of the IAF to carry out pre-emptive strikes on 6 September, when Indian troops crossed the international border. An obvious move would have been to either to carry out a pre-emptive strike on Pakistani airfields or to provide ground support to Indian troops. Surprisingly the IAF did neither, instead flying ineffective strike sorties against 'targets of opportunity'. The IAF put its contingency plans into action only after it was rudely awakened by Pakistani strikes on the evening of 6 September.

In view of the turbulent times India had gone through in the early 1960s, one cannot, or should not, judge the Service Chiefs in an excessively harsh light. Certainly they acted in the best interests of the services, with the hidden aim of preventing another Chinese-like disaster. The best critique of both the Chiefs of Air and Army Staffs come from the VCAS at the time, P.C. Lal: 'In all fairness to Gen. Chaudhuri and Air Marshal Arjan Singh and the forces that they commanded, it has to be said that while there were failures on points of detail, taking the war as a whole they succeeded in foiling Pakistan's designs on Kashmir. They also restored in good measure to India's armed forces the morale and fighting spirit that had been so severely battered in the 1962 Chinese war.'

The appreciation of the Armed Forces' performance does not mitigate the losses suffered, but is increased by the fact that the objectives of Grandslam and Gibraltar were not met. India remained an integrated nation. While Pakistanis display a strange ignorance and abdication of responsibility towards the grand plans to take Kashmir in the events that preceded the crossing of the international border on 6 September, the fact remained that Pakistan's objective of annexing Kashmir via a proxy war had been shattered.

REFLECTIONS

IAF officers offer candid assessments of the war, sparing no criticism or credit where deserved. Wing Commander Jit Dhawan admits: 'The Pakistanis were on much firmer ground as far as the planning of air operations were concerned. There was lot of confusion and chaos in our higher echelons, this being the first war of major proportions.'

The war prepared Indian forces for further conflicts ahead, and helped to develop and refine its strengths and weed out weaknesses. This showed results in 1971. As Don Conquest, who would go on to play a stellar role in the 1971 war, was to say: 'In 1965, I hadn't seen war before so I couldn't tell the difference. But when I flew again in 1971, the difference was clear.'

It has been claimed that the 1965 war was to the IAF what the 1971 war was to the PAF. Air Commodore Wilson disagrees: 'The 1965 war was a watershed for the Indian Air Force. But the 1971 war was bad news for the Pakistani Air Force.'

Such was the difference between defeat and victory.

NOTES

1. Though the PAF claims this aircraft was ferried back to the US, salvaged, and put back into operations, the damage described makes it most likely that the aircraft was written off.
2. Interview with AM S. Bhojwani.
3. Interview with Squadron Leader J.F. Josephs.
4. Air Commodore Kaiser Tufail—http://www.pafcombat.com
5. The exact role played by these missiles during the war is unknown. It is entirely possible that they were never deployed and fired on any occasion other than the incident over Delhi.
6. This also prompted the first Marshal of the IAF rank to ACM Arjan Singh in 2002.

7. A.L. Saigal, ed., *Birth of an Air Force*, New Delhi: Palit and Palit, 1977.
8. Fifteen aircombat claims can be ascertained through Vir Chakra and Maha Vir Chakra citations; the remaining claims are believed to contain at least two AOP aircraft from post war incidents.
9. Lieutenant General Harbaksh Singh, *War Dispatches*, New Delhi: Lancer International, 1991.
10. Air Chief Marshal P.C. Lal, *My Years with the IAF*, New Delhi: Lancer International, 1986.
11. Ibid.

CHAPTER 10

Epilogue

For most air warriors of the 1965 war, another war waited. The peace that came to the Indian subcontinent at the end of hostilities was an uneasy one. Six years later India and Pakistan drew closer to another war. Most officers who took part in the 1965 war contributed again in 1971. Squadron COs had gone on to become Air Base Commanders; Flight Commanders had gone on to become squadron COs. Each bought to their post their experience of how or how not to fight a war. There would be no repeating their predecessor's mistakes.

ACT II: THE 1971 INDIA-PAKISTAN WAR

Between 1965 and 1971, the IAF undertook another large-scale induction of aircraft. By 1971 the IAF had over seven hundred combat aircraft in frontline service, in spite of the phasing out of the Ouragans in 1967 and the withdrawal of the Vampires from frontline squadrons in 1966. By 1971 only two of the original six Mystere squadrons remained operational. The Vampires, Ouragans and Mysteres were replaced with newer, more potent Russian jets like the MiG 21FL and the Sukhoi 7 fighter-bomber. The induction of the indigenous HAL HF 24 Marut fighter, a product of the design bureau led by the renowned Focke-Wulf designer Dr. Kurt Tank, supplemented this influx. Gnats were manufactured in large numbers and inducted. The PAF was not worse off either. It beefed up its fleet with ninety ex-Canadian Sabres and a hundred F 6s purchased from China. The prize additions for the PAF were twenty-eight French Mirage III Delta wing fighters. These were more than a match for the MiG 21. The PAF Starfighter fleet was bolstered by a detachment of another twelve Starfighters of the Royal Jordanian Air Force 9 Squadron, sent after the 1971 conflict had commenced.

We will not go into the details of the 1971 operations here (that needs a history of its own). It suffices to say that the 1965 operations pale in comparison with the scale of operations in the Bangladesh conflict. Whereas the IAF flew some 4,000 sorties through the twenty-two days of the 1965 conflict, the IAF of 1971 flew 1,000 sorties in the first *two* days of operations. It flew over 7,000 sorties and lost approximately seventy aircraft in the fourteen-day war of liberation for Bangladesh.

In 1971, the IAF's dogged determination in pursuing counter air sorties into West Pakistan paid rich dividends. Its Hunters were pushed to the limit in attacking airfields like Peshawar and radar stations like Sakesar, which previously only the Canberras had attacked in 1965. Faced with a new combination of MiG 19s and Mirage IIIs, armed with better air-to-air missiles, the Hunters suffered heavily (18 were lost in counter air strikes) though they did take their toll in enemy aircraft. Ten PAF aircraft were claimed shot down in air combat. In one encounter, a Hunter of 27 Squadron even engaged a Mirage III and damaged it badly. All six Hunter squadrons from 1965 took part in the 1971 operations. 20 Squadron distinguished itself by its ceaseless strikes on airfields that accounted for more than thirteen PAF aircraft on the ground.

The Canberra too performed well. However, the new Mirage III proved to be its nemesis, causing one Canberra to air and three to AA, as compared to one in 1965. The Gnats maintained their excellent track record and emerged with the lowest attrition rate. The Mysteres were all but withdrawn from service in 1971 and only performed a tactical reconnaissance role. Still, three were lost to AA fire, evidence of the dangerous nature of their work. The MiG 21s and the Sukhoi 7 fighter-bombers were instrumental in taking the war into the PAF's territory. The Sukhoi fleet worked hard to provide close support on the ground and by the end of the war, had done much to be proud of, despite suffering heavy losses. When the PAF sent up opposing fighters, the MiG 21s took a heavy toll, including a winning record against the Starfighter.

The IAF's most significant achievement lay in not the number of Pakistani aircraft destroyed but in its ability to facilitate important tactical and strategic victories on the ground. The blunting of the Pakistani offensive at Longewala; the destruction of armoured reserves in the Changa Manga forest; the raids on the Sakesar and Badin radars; the damage caused to the Pakistani war industry with the raids on the Sui gas plant, the Attock refinery and the Mangla dam; the list goes on.

By the end of the 1971 war, due to the heavy losses suffered on the ground and in the air, the PAF had little to be proud of. The PAF flew 3,028 sorties and lost an estimated minimum of fifty combat aircraft. A confirmed radio intercept after the war put PAF losses at seventy-two. Since nearly twenty aircraft were lost in the eastern sector alone, a figure of fifty plus is not far off the mark. The PAF 'admitted' a loss of thirty-four aircraft, a staggering 1.12 rate. With a conservative estimate of a loss of fifty-four aircraft the attrition rate climbs to 1.78, an unsustainable rate for even a month.

WHERE ARE THE AIR WARRIORS NOW?

As we leave the circumstances and the account of the 1965 war, one inevitably wonders at the fate of the players of the war: the commanders, the pilots, the airmen and the ground crew. Where are they now? What did they achieve subsequently? Were they recognized or just cast away to the bylanes of history?

Several officers at the helm of IAF Operational Commands during the 1965 war played a critical role in the successful conduct of the 1971 war. Some retired. Of these, Air Marshal Shivdev Singh, then AOC-in-C Eastern Air Command, moved on to the VCAS post and retired soon after the 1971 war, receiving the PVSM for distinguished service. The AOC-in-C Western Air Command Rajaram died of leukemia in early 1966, a death as tragic as it was sudden. Air Chief Marshal Arjan Singh, after handing over command to P.C. Lal, led a quiet life serving as the Lieutenant Governor of Delhi and occupying various gubernatorial posts, including an ambassadorial stint to Switzerland. In 2002, Singh was awarded the rank of Marshal of the IAF, the first person to be so recognized.

Air Marshal Pratap Chandra Lal, VCAS during 1965, succeeded Arjan Singh as the Chief of Air Staff in 1967. Lal, a keen strategist and planner, benefited from his first-hand view of the 1965 war and was able to take corrective action to address the IAF's shortcomings. Lal received the Padma Vibhushan to add to his Padma Bhushan from 1965. After retirement he served Indian Airlines and HAL before passing away in 1982, while compiling his memoirs. His book *My Years with the IAF*, a classic in Indian military writing, includes a unique recounting of the IAF's role in the 1971 war.

Air Marshal Minoo Merwan Engineer MVC, DFC, Deputy Chief of Air Staff took over Western Air Command. One of the most highly decorated pilots of the IAF, he led WAC through the 1971 conflict and received the Padma Bhushan to add to his PVSM, MVC and DFC. Engineer was bypassed for the top IAF post when O.P. Mehra became the Air Chief; he accepted the decision and moved on to a retired life at Pune. Air Marshal H.C. Dewan, who flew bombers from England during the Second World War was the AOC-in-C, Eastern Air Command and received the Padma Bhushan for his contributions.

Most Squadron COs of 1965 served as air base commanders or senior staff officers, with important commands/units in the 1971 war and often distinguished themselves in their new capacities.

Wing Commander M.S.D. 'Mally' Wollen, the CO of the MiGs in 1965, handed over his command to Wing Commander S.K. 'Polly' Mehra, went on to become Station Commander of Tezpur and was able to watch his previous command, 28 Squadron, fight another war. Wollen received the PVSM for his role in the 1971 operations, rose to the rank of Air Marshal and, before retiring, served as the Managing Director of Hindustan Aeronautics Ltd.

Wing Commander W.M. 'Jimmy' Goodman MVC, CO 31 Squadron (Mysteres), retired as an Air Commodore and settled in Australia, before passing away early in 2002. Wing Commander O.P. 'Omi' Taneja went on to serve as a Group Captain in 1971 on a staff job with Air HQ. He had an opportunity to meet PAF Squadron Leader Amjad Hussain after

Hussain was shot down over Amritsar and taken POW;[1] 'Omi' retired from the IAF soon after and now lives the quiet retired life in New Delhi. Wing Commander P.P. Singh, CO 5 Squadron, MVC was the Air 1 Officer at Central Air Command and received the AVSM for his part in the 1971 War. Singh retired as Air Marshal.

Wing Commander P.M. Wilson, CO 16 Squadron left the squadron in 1966. On his departure from 16 Squadron (based at Gorakhpur), many of the squadron personnel came to the station to see the family off. But somewhat unusually the aircrew left the station early, making some excuses, even before the train had actually pulled out. Wilson was puzzled and initially even a little hurt, at this apparent discourtesy. However, behind

Plate 60: Chief of Air Staff Arjan Singh visits Jamnagar (*after the war*) with the Station Commander Pete Wilson in tow. A flyer as always, Singh flew in for his visit.

the apparent discourtesy was a plot to pay an unforgettable tribute to a highly regarded departing CO. This became clear shortly into the train journey. The train had not gone very far when six Canberras of 16 Squadron came screaming in over the train at low level, and proceeded to carry out a beat-up to end all beat-ups. Wilson had an eventful stint during the 1971 war. As Station Commander of the Armament Training Wing, Jamnagar, he was responsible for planning strikes on the Karachi oil tanks, Mauripur airfield, Badin SU and the reconnaissance of the Kutch area and desert.

Squadron Leader F.J. Mehta, who took part on the first day of the September war flying Vampires, saw action in the 1971 war flying Hunters with a OCU detachment. Mehta was posted to 20 Squadron as a Flight Commander, under Wing Commander C.V. Parker. In November 1970, he was flying a Hunter T66 trainer at Palam when the engine flamed out at 300 ft AGL. By the time he made his pupil eject and Mehta himself hit the silk, the Hunter was dangerously close to the ground. Mehta hit the ground amidst the burning wreckage of the Hunter just as the parachute blossomed fully; the impact left him with injuries. After recovering at Military Hospital, he was posted to the OCU (commanded by Wing Commander D.M. Conquest). Mehta and his wingman Flight Lieutenant K.S. Suresh both downed Sabres to earn the VrC.[2] Later on in the war, Mehta operated from Jaisalmer where another 1965 veteran, Wing Commander Mian Niranjan Singh, was also based. Singh, who led the disowned raid by 37 Squadron on Kurmitola, commanded 27 Squadron before the war. He had to eject from a Hunter after a bird hit during take-off. The ejection injured his back and he had to spend three months in a plaster cast. Recovering from an ejection at the outbreak of hostilities, he was posted to the Jamnagar detachment as the OC flying during the 1971 war. Fate saw to it that Mehta and Singh flew on an operational sortie in the same aircraft. The pair were on a ground interdiction sortie in a Hunter trainer to Naya Chor area, when a Sabre intercepted them, enabling Mehta and Niranjan Singh to earn the unique distinction of being the only IAF pilots to engage in air combat in a trainer type. During the combat, one of the Sabres crashed trying to follow the Hunter through its evasive manoeuvres. Unfortunately, Singh was not granted the kill after the war even though Mehta's VrC citation acknowledges Mehta's second kill. Singh later retired as Group Captain and migrated to the US.[3] Mehta finished the war and went on to command 27 Squadron. He retired from the IAF in 1979, and in 1982 got caught in another air war while on civilian deputation to Basra as the Iran-Iraq war flared up. Mehta is now settled in Hyderabad.

Mehta's colleague in the Vampire strikes during the 1965

operations, Flight Lieutenant K.D. Mehra flew Hunters during the 1971 war and was shot down by Sabres over Dacca on the very first day. He ejected in hostile territory and, with the aid of the Mukti Bahini, evaded Pakistani forces for over a week before reaching Indian lines. Mehra probably holds the Indian record for being declared missing in action for the longest time before returning to base. His experiences on the ground would take a whole book to fill. The injuries he incurred in the low-level ejection put an end to Mehra's IAF career. Coincidentally his son, an IAF pilot as well, retired prematurely after a MiG ejection made him unfit for fighter flying.[4]

Plate 61: No.1 Squadron after conversion to MiG-21s. *Standing left to right*: Ben Brar, 'Jiggy' Ratnapathi, K.H.S 'Goli' Gill, Seetharam (TO), 'Prabs' Prabhakaran, Tippy Tipnis, Nanda Cariappa, P.S. 'Pop' Pathania, Philip Rajkumar, Lawrie Menezes, S.A.B. Naidu. *Sitting left to right*: O.P. Sharma, Dogi Dogra, W.V.A. Lloyd (*Station Commander, Adampur*), ACM (*Now Marshal*) Arjan Singh, Boss Taneja, Madhav Rao.

Squadron Leader S.K. 'Marshal' Dahar, the CO of the Vampire squadron that flew the first sorties of the 1965 war, went on to become a Wing Commander and took over from 'Omi' Taneja as the CO of 1 Squadron, which had already converted to the new MiG 21. He was awarded the VrC for his leadership on the first day of the war, becoming only the second Vampire pilot to receive the award. He could not take part in the 1971 war; sadly, a MiG crash claimed his life.[5] On returning from a Republic Day Flypast in 1967, Dahar suffered from disorientation in cloud cover and was killed in the subsequent crash.

Wing Commander D.A. La Fontaine, CO 14 Squadron went on to become a Group Captain, serving as the Chief Instructor Flying at Dundigal. As the 1971 war began, he was posted to Bombay to help civil airliner operations. Later, he succeeded Air Chief Marshal L.M. Katre as the CAS of the IAF and was responsible for induction of the state of the art MiG 29 and Mi 35. During his tenure, the IAF found itself supporting army operations in Sri Lanka and the Maldives. The retired Air Chief Marshal now lives a quiet life at his farmhouse in Medak in Andhra Pradesh.

Of the gallantry award winners of the 1965 conflict, four earned a Bar or further decoration in the 1971 conflict. Three VrC awardees earned a Bar in 1971, and one MVC awardee (Gautam) earned a Bar, till date and probably for a long time to come the only double MVC in combat against Pakistan.

Flying Officer V.K. 'Beaky' Neb VrC, the 7 Squadron pilot who shot down the Sabre over Halwara, added another Sabre to his tally in the skies over Kurmitola in December 1971. Serving with 17 Squadron, his Hunter formation's strike on Dacca airport was intercepted by Sabres. In the ensuing dogfight, Neb shot down one of the Sabres and earned another VrC. He retired as a Wing Commander.

Keeping Neb company over the skies of Tejgaon and Kurmitola was Squadron Leader B.K. Bishnoi VrC, formerly of 20 Squadron Hunters, and subsequently CO of 28 Squadron, by then an all Type-77 MiG 21 FL squadron. Bishnoi took over command from S.K. 'Polly' Mehra, the pilot who escaped the bombs of the B 57 by jumping into a pond, and who went on to become the OC Flying of Tezpur during the war. Later Mehra would rise to become Chief of Air Staff, completing his tenure in 1991. Bishnoi led the first raid on Tejgaon, tangled with Sabres, rocketed transport aircraft on the ground, flew the famous 'runway busting' missions and the legendary strike on the Government House at Dacca, which forced the resignation of Governor Malik. Bishnoi received his second VrC and went on to become an Air Vice-Marshal.[6]

Flight Lieutenant V.K. 'Jimmy' Bhatia VrC of 8 Squadron,

graduated to flying the newly acquired Sukhoi 7s with 32 Squadron. As a Squadron Leader in 1971, he led a devastating attack on Shorkot Road air base in West Pakistan on the first day of the war. His formation of four Sukhois destroyed two Sabres, two Canberras and a Mirage III in one of the most successful counter air strikes of the war. Bhatia pushed himself into flying four attacks on Shorkot in two days, evading Sidewinders from Sabres and MiG 19s, and ended the war with an impressive tally of sorties and a Bar to the VrC. Subsequently, 'Jimmy' went on to MiGs, commanded a MiG 23 squadron and climbed up the command ladder to become the AOC-in-C Central Air Command and Western Air Command as an Air Marshal. In 2002, Bhatia was flying an An 32 on an inaugural flight to Kargil airbase, when he inadvertently strayed across the Line of Control into Pakistani territory. A shoulder-fired surface to air missile knocked out one of the engines of the An 32, which detached and fell in Indian territory. Flying the aircraft on a single engine, Bhatia landed safely at Leh airfield. He retired later the same year and is now living the retired life in Gurgaon. His golf partners include his formation mate from the 1965 war, Air Marshal Vinod Patney.

Squadron Leader Padmanabha 'Bob' Gautam MVC earned a Bar to the MVC in the 1971 war. Promoted to command 16 Squadron, Gautam was again in the thick of the action in the liberation war, leading his Canberra formation in night raids on Tejgaon, Chittagong, Jessore and even attacking main airbases in the west, like Mianwali and Murid. He received the second Bar to a MVC awarded to the IAF. Gautam was probably the only Canberra pilot to be decorated in operations thrice. His first decoration was a VM for flying in the Congo, where flying as No. 2 to Wing Commander A.I.K. Suares he destroyed a Fouga Magister at Kolwezi. After the 1971 war, Gautam took over as OC Flying 2 Wing, Air Force Station Pune, home to 8 Squadron flying MiG 21 FLs, 35 Squadron flying Canberras B (I) 58s, 6 Squadron flying L 1049 Super Constellations & Canberras and a SA-2 squadron. On 25 November 1972, Gautam took off in a MiG 21 FL. Immediately after take-off the engine flamed out due to a malfunction. An ejection was out of the question as the seat needed at least 425 ft to deploy successfully. Gautam decided to force land the MiG. The fact that he had managed to successfully deadstick a MiG 17 during his deputation to the Egyptian airforce gave him the much-needed confidence. Gautam skilfully landed the MiG in the fields past the runway. The aircraft landed level and skidded along the soil. But there was an irrigation bund across its path, which the MiG struck head-on, collapsing the airframe. When the rescue crew reached the site, they found Gautam dead due to massive internal hemorrhaging, with his body intact without any disfiguration. The IAF had suffered a great loss. Gautam's loss was deeply felt in the IAF. His funeral attracted a large number of flights into Pune by Canberras and other aircraft from across the country, piloted by officers coming to pay their last tributes—leaving a high ranking officer complaining about the high number of 'unauthorized diversions'.[7]

The only other pilot to get a Bar to the MVC in the IAF, Squadron Leader J.M. Nath, took over command of 106 SPR Squadron in December 1965. However, Nath took premature retirement in 1968 and missed out on the 1971 war. Nath's Bar to the MVC brought with it a strange assertion from the Ministry of Defence that it was the equivalent of a 'half an MVC' and hence the perks that went along with the second award would be calculated accordingly. What prompted this strange logic of comparing a Bar to the MVC as half an award is not known, but to this day Nath has not received in full the land promised by the government, as the standard package for MVC awardees from the wars.[8]

Squadron Leader V.B. Sawardekar KC, who rescued Squadron Leader M.J. Marston from the burning Vampire during the PAF attack at Baghdogra, was the CO of No. 29 'Scorpios' during the 1971 war. He was awarded the AVSM for his leadership of the squadron during the war. His unit claimed three F 104 Starfighters and an F 6 as air combat kills during the war, and became the squadron with the highest number of air combat kills in 1971. However, once again the rigours of peacetime flying claimed a pilot's life. In 1972, Sawardekar's aircraft suffered a bird hit over Delhi during an exercise. Gallantly, Sawardekar chose to stay with the aircraft, to fly it away from a populated area. As he had delayed his ejection, he died in the crash.[9]

Other decorated members from 1965 found themselves on the frontline again in 1971. Foremost among them were the 'Sabre Slayers'. Squadron Leader J.W. 'Johnny' Greene VrC led 2 Squadron without any loss through the conflict. He was involved in action again, including a futile chase of a Starfighter on the second day of the war. Greene received the Vayusena Medal (VM) for his part and became an Air Marshal, subsequently earning a PVSM and an AVSM. His wingmen too graduated to commanding squadrons. Greene's colleague and the first Indian pilot to be credited with an air combat victory, Trevor Keelor, retired as a Wing Commander from the Air Force, before passing away in 2002.

His brother Denzil led an eventful life as well. Going on to 45 Squadron flying the MiG 21 during the 1971 war, Denzil took off from Pathankot on a strike to Chamb. After being hit by AA fire, he had to eject, injuring his spine in the process. He fell in no man's land and, lying on his back and unable to move in a marshy area, could do nothing but wait for help to come from either the Indian or Pakistani armies. A patrol from a Kumaon battalion got to him first.[10] After the war he commanded 4 Squadron, flying MiG 21s at Tezpur. His adventures did not end there. In 1978 as he flew a MiG 21U, the canopy of the aircraft flew off in mid-flight. He quickly regained control and landed, after which he vowed never to fly again with his helmet visor raised. For this effort, he earned the Kirti Chakra, the MVC equivalent for gallantry not in the face of the enemy. Denzil rose to the rank of Air Marshal before retiring.

Denzil Keelor's compatriots with 45 Squadron MiGs in 1971 included one Gnat veteran of the 1965 war, Flight Lieutenant Janak Kapur. He had finished training on the MiGs in Russia after the war and had been sent on detachment to Keelor's unit. On 9 December, Kapur survived a strafing while taking off in his MiG 21 and ended the war with twenty sorties. He went on to become an Air Marshal, commanding Eastern Air Command.[11]

Denzil Keelor's wingman during the 1965 war, Viney Kapila,

flew with 47 Squadron in 1971, which had sent a detachment of six MiG 21s to Jamnagar under Group Captain Peter Wilson. Kapila flew a number of missions, one of which intercepted F 104 Starfighters over the Rann of Kutch. This was the first encounter between the Mach 2 rivals; Kapila's wingman Flight Lieutenant B.B. Soni bought down a Starfighter. Kapila also flew missions to Badin and targets in Sind, during which his CO Wing Commander H.S. Gill was shot down and killed. On another occasion he found himself behind a Sabre at close range. Unfortunately his MiG was carrying two rocket pods and a centreline drop tank, and hence was without a cannon. Kapila took a shot and fired the rockets at the Sabre. However, the lucky Sabre pilot escaped as the rockets missed due to gravity drop.[12] He too rose to a rank of Air Vice-Marshal, going on to serve as CO 108 Squadron, AOC-Ambala and commanding the College of Air Warfare before retiring with an AVSM under his belt.

Flight Lieutenant Virendra Singh 'Pat' Pathania, now posted to 18 Squadron (*Flying Bullets*—Gnats) as one of its flight commanders, was in the thick of action against Sabres over Srinagar. He managed to damage one of the raiders severely over the Kashmir valley and added more shine to his 'Sabre Slayer' title. One of his pilots was Flying Officer N.S. Sekhon, who won his PVC tangling bravely with Sabres over Srinagar. Pathania retired as a Wing Commander.

Squadron Leader Amarjit Singh Sandhu VrC, the first pilot to do a deadstick landing in a Gnat, was posted to 28 Squadron flying MiG 21s. As a senior section leader to Bishnoi, he was a pioneer in training the squadron in its new geographical setting in the east. Identified as leadership material, he was given command of the squadron where he earned his spurs, 23 Squadron flying Gnats at Pathankot in June 1971. However, one September day in 1971, four months before the war, Wing Commander Sandhu VrC VM, took off in Gnat IE1045 from Pathankot. The Gnat's engine flamed out and Sandhu was killed in the crash. The pilot who was marked 'Lack of OLQ' during his training days and subsequently rose to an 'Excellent' grading in his ACR, was now another fallen bird. Ironically, the Gnat in which Sandhu had carried out his dead stick landing, IE1202, which had flown with 2 Squadron in 1965 and scored a Sabre kill, was lost a year before when Flight Lieutenant K. De ejected after a systems malfunction. Sandhu's exploits in peace and in war are his legacy to the IAF and the country.

Flying Officer M.R. 'Manna' Murdeshwar, Johnny Greene's wingman, was a Squadron Leader on the staff of Eastern Air Command during the 1971 war. Intensively involved in planning for the air offensive in the eastern sector, 'Manna' went on to fly MiG 21s and command 108 Squadron before retiring as a Group Captain from Staff College.

A 23 Squadron pilot who certainly had his revenge was Squadron Leader B.S. Sikand. After repatriation from the Pakistani POW camp, he was reinstated after the war and given command of 22 Gnat Squadron on the Eastern Front. The ignominy of letting his Gnat be captured intact by the Pakistanis was wiped off the slate in 1971, when on 22 November 1971, 22 Squadron's Gnats intercepted and shot down three Sabres over Boyra on the East Pakistani border. Two of the Pakistani pilots were captured, including a future PAF Air Chief. 22 Squadron subsequently lent a hand in the fighting, coming out with flying colours, and Sikand started off with a clean slate. He later became an Air Marshal, earning an AVSM.

Sikand's POW mate in 1965, Flight Lieutenant K.C. 'Nanda' Cariappa of 20 Squadron, also served in the eastern sector. Due to his injuries from the ejection, he moved to flying helicopters, earned the distinction of commanding 111 Helicopter Unit during the 1971 war and came out of the war unscathed. His unit flew in the officials for the ceasefire talks and Cariappa had the privilege of witnessing the surrender ceremony. Cariappa became an AOC-in-C before finally retiring as an Air Marshal.

Another pilot who had experienced Pakistani hospitality was Squadron Leader O.N. 'Piloo' Kacker of 27 Squadron. After his expletive ridden departure from his Hunter near the skies of Sargodha, Kacker spent four months in captivity before repatriation. Later he was posted to 10 Squadron (*Flying Daggers*), flying the HF 24 Marut as a Section Leader. He took over command of 10 Squadron in 1971, a pioneer squadron involved in flying the Marut and growing up with it in its evolutionary stage. The squadron moved to Uttarlai, a new airfield activated to make up for the lack of airfields in Rajasthan. After a few days of operations, the runway started to break up; 10 Squadron ceased operations. Two Air Marshals sent by Air HQ to inspect the airfield declared it fit for flying and insisted that Kacker should resume operations. Known for his short temper, Kacker walked off in a huff saying, 'The Air Marshals are talking through their hats. If they want me to fly . . . then I will fly.' Kacker's wingman recalls him being in a rage as the two Maruts lined up for take-off. Kacker's nose-wheel burst on take-off and he decided to carry out an emergency landing. Then, due to rubber ingestion one of the Orpheus' engines shut down and, after failing to recover from the sudden loss of power, the aircraft struck the top of the dune surrounding the runway. 'Piloo' Kacker too, was destined not to take part in the 1971 war. Exactly five years after the start of the 1965 war, the Wing Commander died in his gleaming Marut at Uttarlai. The circumstances behind his last flight would be farcical were they not so tragic.

Wing Commander R. 'Jit' Dhawan, earlier with No. 2 Gnats at Halwara in 1965, was witness to Kacker's unfortunate demise. Dhawan was the CO of 220 Squadron, the other squadron at Uttarlai flying the Marut. By the time Dhawan raced to the crash site in a jeep, it was all over. Later during the war, Dhawan successfully led 220 Squadron in the 1971 war. Part of Dhawan's team flying the Maruts was Squadron Leader K.K. 'Joe' Bakshi, who flew Mysteres with 1 Squadron in 1965. Bakshi distinguished himself by shooting down an F 86 Sabre in the war and earning a VrC. To date it is the only air combat victory claimed by an Indian pilot flying an indigenously made fighter.

Another Mystere pilot with 220 Squadron was Squadron Leader M.S. 'Mickey' Jatar, leader of 8 Squadron's raid on Sargodha on 7 September. On 11 December 1971, as he rolled into a take-off run with Flight Lieutenant Sidhu, a Starfighter flown by Wing Commander Amanullah strafed his Marut on the runway. Jatar stopped his burning aircraft, opened the cockpit and jumped the 6 ft to the ground. The strafing had caused jet fuel to spill into the cockpit and Jatar's flying suit became drenched in it and caught fire. Jatar rolled in the desert sand to put the fire out. But the damage was done. He suffered severe burns from the burning G-suit, which was made of nylon.[13] Jatar went on to retire from the IAF and passed away in November 1985.

'Mickey' Jatar and 'Jimmy' Bhatia's formation mates in the Black Formation went on to further laurels. Pramod 'Chopi' Chopra went to Russia with the second batch of IAF pilots to train on the Sukhoi 7. Chopra later flew with 108 Squadron out of Halwara during 1971, flying many tank-busting missions in Sukhoi 7s as the Deputy Flight Commander. Chopra retired in 1976 as a Squadron Leader, after serving as Flight Commander of 20 Squadron at Hindon. He passed away at home in 1979. In 1986 Chopra's son, Ashutosh, was commissioned in the 138th pilots' course (exactly 69 courses after his father's, the 69th Pilots' Course) joined the IAF and, after converting on Hunters, went on to serve as Commanding Officer of 16 Squadron, flying Jaguars. Chopra's wingman in the 1965 war, Flight Lieutenant Vinod Patney, flew Sukhoi 7s with TACDE during the 1971 operations and carried out some of the most difficult missions of the war: night strikes on Pakistani airfields. Patney went on to become an Air Marshal, serving as C-in-C of Western Air Command during the Kargil Operations in 1999.

Plate 62: Black Formation members P.C. Chopra (*then OC Flying—first from right*) and 'Jimmy' Bhatia (*fifth from right*) meet again—this time at 47 Squadron at Hashimara. L.M. Katre, Station Commander is at centre.

EPILOGUE

He became only the second officer in the Indian armed forces, the first in the IAF, to be decorated with the Sarvottam Yudh Seva Medal (SYSM).

Among the Hunter pilots from Halwara, Flight Lieutenant D.N. Rathore VrC became an Air Marshal and retired as AOC-in-C of Central Air Command. So did two of the 'victim' pilots on Alam's 'legendary' sortie, Squadron Leader M.M. 'Rusty' Sinha and Squadron Leader A.S. Lamba VrC. Lamba had a miraculous escape when he was forced to eject while testing a Gnat in the Srinagar valley. After retiring from the IAF as an Air Vice-Marshal, he was once pulled up by a DGCA official for flying a Pushpak at low-level over an airfield at the breakneck speed of 100 mph. The official in question was probably unaware that Lamba had flown jet aircraft six times that speed at low level in hostile territory.

Flying Officer A.R. Ghandhi VrC of 7 Squadron too rose to high rank. After a stint in Iraq, where he had the opportunity to meet one of his opponents, Cecil Chaudhary, Ghandhi returned to become the Station Commander of Gwalior, when 7 Squadron—now equipped with Mirage 2000s—came under his command. His wingman Flight Lieutenant Prakash 'Pingo' Pingale VrC rose to the rank of an Air Marshal, commanding Air Force Station Hakimpet for a brief period. Fate found the old friends together again in 1998. Air Vice-Marshal A.R. Ghandhi was posted to Air Headquarters to take over as Director Personnel (Officers), where his post was handed over by Air Marshal P.S. Pingale. Pingale went on to the post of Senior Air Staff Officer (SASO) at Southern Air Command; Ghandhi went on to head the College of Air Warfare at Secunderabad, becoming the SASO of Western Air Command and finally the AOC-in-C Western Air Command.

Ghandhi's companion among the AOC-in-Cs as the SWAC Commander was McMahon, the rookie pilot who was flying the single CAP over Pathankot during 'Nosey' Haider's strike. McMahon, who had been a member of the first batch of Indian pilots to train on the Su 7 in Russia, flew Sukhoi 7s with 101 Squadron during the 1971 war and earned a VM. He also earned the distinction of being the CO of the first Jaguar

Squadron in India. In 2003, McMahon became VCAS of the IAF.

Another 7 Squadron pilot to make his mark in the new war was Flying Officer D.K. Parulkar, who after receiving the VM for his service in the 1965 war had moved on to fly Sukhoi 7s with 26 Squadron. During the 1971 war, Parulkar was hit by AA fire over Zafarwal and ejected over Pakistani territory to be taken POW. The adventure didn't end there for this restless character. Not fancying a long stay in a Pakistani POW camp, Parulkar escaped with two other POWs, Flight Lieutenants M.S. Grewal and Harish Singhji. After nearly ten hours and within sight of freedom at the Pakistan-Afghanistan border, some alert frontier guards captured Parulkar and his friends. After completing the mandatory solitary in the clinker, Parulkar was repatriated to India after more than a year in Pakistani prisons.

Sqn. Ldr. Madhabendra Banerji, OC of 24 Sqn in the 1965 war, went on to distinguish himself for his work in the 1971 war. After converting to Sukhoi 7s, he became senior flight commander of 101 Squadron, and earned a Maha Vir Chakra for his leadership during the squadron's dogged support of the Indian Army during the Pakistani Army's counter-offensive in the Chamb. Banerji went on to command 9 Squadron and served as CO of FIS, Tambaram, before finally retiring as Air Vice-Marshal.

S.K. 'Pandit' Kaul, 3 Squadron's flight commander, who had distinguished himself by flying the most strike sorties in the squadron, became the commanding officer of 37 Squadron flying Hunters during the 1971 war. For flying several photo-recce sorties prior to the conflict and for the raids on Tejgaon, Kaul was awarded the MVC and went on to a long and distinguished career, which finally culminated in his becoming Chief of Air Staff.

Other pilots found themselves heading to foreign lands as their families migrated. Wing Commander Paddy Earle went on to command 8 Squadron after the war, before migrating to Australia. Following him on flights to the southern hemisphere were Flight Lieutenant Alfred Cooke, the hero of Kalaikunda, and Squadron Leader J.F. 'Joe' Josephs, who migrated to

Australia and settled down, with memories of the war relegated to IAF reunions and interviews by pesky amateur historians. Cooke tried his hand at flying a Cessna but, 'after you have had a Hunter light up your ass, a Cessna just doesn't cut it', turned to racing boats as his hobby instead. Josephs put up with many jokes from his IAF mates as they noted his car's license plate: PAF 173.

Cooke's coursemate, the Gnat pilot 'Kicha' Krishnaswamy, whose momentary admiration of the Starfighter cost him a kill, completed a long and distinguished career with the IAF, including a tenure as a senior test pilot, culminating finally as Chief of Air Staff, a post that he rose to in 2001.

The man whose voice was familiar to all the Indian pilots flying sorties in the western sector, as he provided directions and warnings about Pakistani air activities from the GCI centre in Amritsar, Wing Commander K. Dandapani retired in 1971. He still has one of the Pakistani folding fin aerial rockets on display in his front room, as is a photograph of the Tamil Nadu Chief Minister Kamaraj on a visit to 'Fish Oil' during the war.

THE PAF PILOTS

Pakistani pilots and personnel too wore warpaint six years later and fought for their nation. Some fought for a second time while others were not allowed to. Many pilots who had fought for the PAF in 1965, with determination and fervour, were Bengali in origin. However, after the brutal military crackdown in East Pakistan and attempts by the Bengali air crew to sabotage PAF equipment or defect to India, the PAF grounded Bengali pilots. This roughly accounted for 10 per cent of the PAF. Bengali ground support crews were withdrawn from service. Led by Air Marshal Rahim Khan, the PAF that went to war in 1971 was already internally crippled.

The Starfighter pilot who shot down Devayya, Flight Lieutenant Amjad Hussain, a Sitara-e-Juraat recipient, again flew Starfighters in 1971. During a strike on Amritsar airfield, his F 104 was downed by AA fire. Hussain ejected for the second time in combat with India. This time he was destined to spend more than a year as a POW. After repatriation, Hussain went on to become an Air Vice-Marshal.

Squadron Leader Mervyn Middlecoat, another recipient of the Sitara-e-Juraat, was promoted to Wing Commander and was on deputation to Egypt when the 1971 war broke out. Middlecoat was recalled to Pakistan, and hastily deputed to a detachment of Jordanian Starfighters operating out of Karachi. On 12 December, on a strike to Jamnagar, Middlecoat's F 104 was shot down by Flight Lieutenant B.B. Soni, flying a MiG 21. He ejected over the Arabian Sea, but was never found. Some pieces of his Starfighter were recovered from the sea twenty-five years later, but Middlecoat had already become a *shaheed*, though of a different faith.

The Squadron Leader who led the daring attack on Pathankot, Sajjad 'Nosey' Haider, was a Group Captain in 1971. Though stuck with a desk job, he could not resist operational flying. He tried his hand in flying the newly acquired Mirage IIIs and, in one sortie, got involved in air combat with a Hunter near Narowal and claimed a kill with a Sidewinder. No such loss occurred on the Indian side.

Cecil Chaudhary led a charmed life. His escape from the ill-fated Halwara mission and numerous combat missions in 1965 did not deter him from flying operationally in 1971. This time around, the AA gunners made no mistake: Indian ground fire damaged his Sabre badly, forcing him to eject in no-man's land in Chamb. He made it back to Pakistani lines and was up and flying the very next day, claiming a Sukhoi 7 in air combat. After the war, Chaudhary was deputed to Iraq as an instructor. He retired as a Group Captain because his promotion beyond the rank was termed not possible, as he was a Christian.

For reasons best known to the PAF, its 'ace in a day', Mohammed Alam did not fly in 1971 though he was in the flying cadre. Alam served till 1982, when he retired from the PAF as an Air Commodore. His crusade to make the PAF alcohol-free was well known throughout the services. He was simultaneously respected and despised for his convictions. Today, Alam lives a quiet life in Karachi; some describe him as a practising mullah, others as a reserved withdrawn pilot.

Alam's ill-fated wingman, Mohammed Shaukat, was repatriated to Pakistan but, being a Bengali, did not fly in 1971. Shaukat elected to join Bangladesh after the war and flew with the lone fighter squadron, flying Sabres with the Bangladesh Air Force (BAF). Shaukat was deputed by the BAF to attend the Junior Command course with the IAF, giving him another opportunity to enjoy Indian hospitality, but this time as an invited guest. Shaukat retired from the BAF and served as Managing Director of Biman Airways, the national airline.[14]

Flight Lieutenant Syed Saad Hatmi became a Wing Commander of a MiG 19 squadron in 1971. He scored a confirmed kill this time, shooting down a Hunter over Sakesar on the second day of the war. He went on to claim additional kills that put his 'total' at five, a tally just as dubious as Alam's 'nine kills'.

Eric Hall, Station Commander Chaklala, went on to become an Air Vice-Marshal and VCAS of the PAF, the only Christian to rise to such a high rank in the PAF. Hakimullah, credited by the PAF for force-landing Sikand and his Gnat went on to become the Chief of Air Staff. Wing Commander Mohammed Anwar Shamim, the OC of the no. 32 Sabre wing at Sargodha, leader of the abortive raids on Amritsar, went on to a controversial stint as Chief of Air Staff of the PAF during General Zia-ul-Haq's tenure.

FORGOTTEN VALOUR

The memories of 1965 soon faded away, remembered only by the soldiers and airmen who participated directly in the conflict. Fresh memories of the jubilant victory of 1971 soon dominated the Indian population's mind and 1965 was relegated to the backburner. It took a commissioned chronicler's version of the 1965 air war to rejuvenate interest for quite unusual reasons.

Interest in the 1965 air war was reborn when the Indian government announced the award of a posthumous MVC to Squadron Leader A.B. Devayya in January 1988, almost a quarter century after his loss over Sargodha. The investigation prior to the announcement stirred quite a few memories. IAF officers like Omi Taneja were interviewed, Pakistani sources cross-checked and the truth ascertained.

In 1979, John Fricker brought out *Battle for Pakistan*, published by Ian Allan, a book unique in that it was the only book dedicated to telling the story of the air war of 1965. Fricker was invited by the PAF to write the history and though he had finished in 1970, the book had to wait for a publisher for almost nine years. The IAF neither brought out its own account nor denied any of the extravagant claims put forward by Fricker's fawning, hagiographic ode to the PAF. Fricker's book, however biased, made an important contribution to the IAF's legacy.

Even though Pakistan admitted the loss of a Starfighter over Sargodha, it was explained away as an accident. In 1972, PAF officials told John Fricker that a Mystere had shot the Starfighter down and it was not as earlier claimed, an 'accident'. Fricker reported the incident as a loss to a Mystere. There lay a mystery. None of the Mystere pilots that day had reported air combat and certainly not with a Starfighter. But two Mysteres were lost over Sargodha. The one lost in the morning, roughly coinciding with the timing reported by Fricker, was Devayya's. After receiving letters of confirmation from Omi Taneja the Indian Government came to the conclusion that Amjad Hussain was shot down by Devayya, who himself crashed soon after. Devayya's widow Mrs. Sundari Devayya received the fifth and the last MVC awarded to the air force for the 1965 war in April 1988, almost 23 years after the event. If Devayya's valour had come to light during the war, it could well have resulted in the first PVC to the air force.

CODA

Almost 40 years on, the war continues to raise passions. Pilots recount the terrible conditions in which they operated, the kills they got and the comrades they lost. Ground crews talk about the brutal pace of work on the ground. Soldiers mention the harassment from the air or the thrill of destroying an enemy tank. There are remnants to remind people of the conflict, like the desolate M 48 Patton lying at the corner of a perimeter at

Hyderabad's EME Centre, or the lone Gnat at the PAF's Karachi Museum. Rafiqui's Sabre's wreck still lies exposed to the elements in one corner of the IAF Museum; faded photos and clippings recount those heady days in the visitor's gallery. As do the etched names on the memorial outside the Museum, reminding the visitors of the nineteen daring fliers and the eighteen airmen who gave their lives for an integrated India that distant September, almost four decades ago.

NOTES

1. Interview with Group Captain O.P. Taneja.
2. Interview with Wing Commander F.J. Mehta.
3. Interview with Group Captain M.N. Singh.
4. Interview with Squadron Leader K.D. Mehra.
5. Ibid.
6. B.K. Bishnoi, 'Thunder over Dacca', *Vayu Aerospace Journal*, I, January 1997.
7. Correspondence with Group Captain Kapil Bhargava.
8. Interview with Wing Commander J.M. Nath.
9. Correspondence with Flight Lieutenant S.B. Shah; siafdu.tripod.com.
10. Major K.C. Praval, *Valour Triumphs*, New Delhi: Thomson Press, 1976.
11. Interview with Air Marshal Janak Kapur.
12. 'Supersonic Combat', *Vayu Aerospace Journal*, VI, November 1997.
13. Interview with Wing Commander Jit Dhawan.
14. John Guttman, 'Pakistan's Sabre Ace', *Aviation History*, vol. 9, no. 1, Washington: Primedia Publishers, September 1998.

APPENDIX A

PAF Air Combat Claims *versus* Actual IAF Losses

TABLE A: LIST OF AIR KILLS CLAIMED BY THE PAF

Date	Aircraft Claimed		Type	Sqn.	Rank	Name	Location
1 Sept.	2	Vampires	Sabre	5	Sqn. Ldr.	S. Rafiqui	Chamb
1 Sept.	2	Vampires	Sabre	15	Flt. Lt.	Imtiaz Bhatti	Chamb
3 Sept.	1	Gnat	Starfighter	9	Flt. Lt.	Hakimullah	Pasrur
6 Sept.	1	Mystere	Starfighter	9	Sqn. Ldr.	Aftab Alam Khan	Rohri
6 Sept.	2	Hunter	Sabre	11	Sqn. Ldr.	M.M. Alam	Tarn Tarn
6 Sept.	1	Hunter	Sabre	5	Sqn. Ldr.	S. Rafiqui	Halwara
6 Sept.	3	Hunter	Sabre	5	Flt. Lt.	Cecil Chaudhary	Halwara
6 Sept.	1	Hunter	Sabre	5	Flt. Lt.	Yunus Hussain	Halwara
7 Sept.	2	Mystere	Starfighter	9	Sqn. Ldr.	Amjad Hussain Khan	Sargodha
7 Sept.	5	Hunter	Sabre	11	Sqn. Ldr.	M.M. Alam	Sargodha
7 Sept.	1	Mystere	Sabre		Flt. Lt.	A.H. Malik	Sargodha
7 Sept.	1	Hunter	Sabre	14	Sqn. Ldr.	S.H. Syed	Kalaikunda
7 Sept.	1	Hunter	Sabre	14	Flt. Lt.	Tariq Habib Khan	Kalaikunda
10 Sept.	1	Gnat	Sabre	19	Sqn. Ldr.	Muniruddin Ahmed	Kasur

(*contd.*)

APPENDIX A (*contd.*)

Date	Aircraft Claimed	Type	Sqn.	Rank	Name	Location
10 Sept.	1 Gnat	Sabre	5	Flt. Lt.	Cecil Chaudhary	Kasur
13 Sept.	1 Gnat	Sabre	11	Flt. Lt.	Yusuf Ali Khan	Amritsar
14 Sept.	1 Canberra	Starfighter	9	Sqn. Ldr.	Mervyn Middlecoat	Sargodha
15 Sept.	1 Canberra	Sabre	5	Flt. Lt.	Cecil Chaudhary	Lahore
16 Sept.	2 Hunter	Sabre	11	Sqn. Ldr.	M.M. Alam	Halwara
18 Sept.	1 Gnat	Sabre		Flt. Lt.	Saad Hatmi	Tarn Tarn
19 Sept.	1 Gnat	Sabre		Flt. Lt.	Saif-Ul-Azam	Sialkot
20 Sept.	1 Hunter	Sabre		Sqn. Ldr.	Changezi	Lahore
20 Sept.	1 Hunter	Sabre		Flt. Lt.	S.N.A. Jilani	Lahore
20 Sept.	1 Auster	Sabre	18	Flg. Offr.	Qais	Badin
21 Sept.	1 Canberra	Starfighter	9	Wg. Cdr.	Jamal Ahmed Khan	Sargodha
Total Claims	36	Actual Losses	16			

APPENDIX B

Official List of Indian Armed Forces Aircraft Losses

The IAF has never released an official list of aircraft losses. The tables presented here have been compiled from various sources, including retired officers and unclassified documents. Though the figures for air-to-air combat and AA losses are accurate, we missed out on figures for operational accidents and those destroyed on the ground. The 'Official History of the 1965 Indo-Pak War' has set right these anomalies.

Aircraft	Air Action	Accidents	On Ground	Aircraft
INDIAN AIR FORCE: 71				
Vampires	4	-	6	10
Mysteres	7	3(1)	9	19
Hunters	10	4(1)	3	17
Gnats	2	3(1)	2	7
Canberra	1	-	4	5
MiG 21	-	-	3	3
Packet	-	-	3	3
Dakota	-	-	5	5
Auster	1(1)	1	-	2
INDIAN NAVY: 1				
Sea Hawk	-	1	-	1
CIVILIAN/OTHERS: 3				
Dakota	-	-	1	1
Caribou	-	-	1	1
Beechcraft	1	-	-	1
TOTAL	26	12	37	75

Note: Figures in parentheses denote that details not available in these tables.

AIRCRAFT LOST BY THE INDIAN AIR FORCE IN THE AIR DUE TO ALL CAUSES

Date	Aircaft	S.No.	Sqn	Rank & Name	Location	Cause	Fate
1 Sept. '65	Vampire		220	Fg. Offr. S.V. Pathak	Chamb	AAA (Anti Aircraft Artillery)	B/O
1 Sept. '65	Vampire		45	Flt. Lt. S. Bharadwaj	Chamb	SD by Squadron Leader S.A. Rafiqui, F-86	Killed
1 Sept. '65	Vampire		45	Flt. Lt. A.K. Bhagwagar	Chamb	SD by Squadron Leader S.A. Rafiqui, F-86	Killed
1 Sept. '65	Vampire		220	Fg. Offr. V.M. Joshi	Chamb	SD by Flight Lieutenant I.A. Bhatti, F-86	Killed
3 Sept. '65	Gnat	IE-1083	2	Sqn. Ldr. B.S. Sikand	Pasrur	Landed at Pasrur	POW
6 Sept. '65	Hunter		7	Sqn. Ldr. A.K. Rawlley	Tarn Tarn	Crashed in AA Combat, S/L M.M. Alam,	Killed
6 Sept. '65	Hunter	BA-289	7	Fg. Offr. P.S. Pingale	Halwara	SD by Squadron Leader S.A. Rafiqui, F-86	E/S
6 Sept. '65	Hunter	BA-251	7	Fg. Offr. A.R. Ghandhi	Halwara	SD by Flight Lieutenant C. Chaudhary, F-86	E/S
7 Sept. '65	Mystere		1	Sqn. Ldr. A.B. Devayya	Sargodha	SD by Flight Lieutenant Y. Hussain, F-104	Killed
7 Sept. '65	Hunter	BA-330	27	Sqn. Ldr. O.N. Kacker	Sargodha	Booster pump failure	POW
7 Sept. '65	Hunter		7	Fg. Offr. J.S. Brar	Sargodha	SD by Squadron Leader M.M. Alam, F-86	Killed
7 Sept. '65	Hunter		7	Sqn. Ldr. S.B. Bhagwat	Sargodha	SD by Squadron Leader M.M. Alam, F-86	Killed
7 Sept. '65	Mystere		3	Sqn. Ldr. Jasbeer Singh	Rahwali	Hit ground after raid on Rahwali	Killed
7 Sept. '65	Mystere		1	Flt. Lt. U.B. Guha	Sargodha	SD by Flight Lieutenant A.H. Malik, F-86	Killed
7 Sept. '65	Auster		659	Captain S. Khurana	Lahore	Crashed while landing	Killed
8 Sept. '65	Hunter		7	Fg. Offr. M.V. Singh	Kasur	AAA	POW
9 Sept. '65	Hunter	BA-236	27	Fg. Offr. G.S. Ahuja	Halwara	Crashed after MAC with a Hunter.	Killed
9 Sept. '65	Mystere		-	Fg. Offr. I.F. Hussain	Lahore	Shot down by AA	E/S
10 Sept. '65	Mystere		31	Fg. Offr. D.P. Chinoy	Chawinda	AAA	E/S
11 Sept. '65	Mystere		1	Sqn. Ldr. R.K. Uppal	Lahore	AAA	Killed
13 Sept. '65	Gnat		2	Flt. Lt. A.N. Kale	Ferozepur	SD by Flight Lieutenant Yusuf Khan, F-86	E/S
13 Sept. '65	Mystere	IA-1049	31	Flt. Lt. T.S. Sethi	Pasrur	AAA	Killed
13 Sept. '65	Mystere		8	Flt. Lt. L. Sadarangani	Kasur	AAA Lahore	POW

Date	Aircraft	Serial	Sqn	Pilot	Location	Cause	Fate
14 Sept. '65	Gnat	IE-1206	2	Sqn. Ldr. N.K. Malik	Halwara	Crashed due to technical failure	Killed
15 Sept. '65	Hunter	BA-207	27	Flt. Lt. T.K. Chaudhari	Halwara	Flameout due to bird hit	Killed
16 Sept. '65	Hunter		20	Fg. Offr. F. Dara Bunsha	Halwara	SD by Squadron Leader M.M. Alam, F-86	Killed
18 Sept. '65	Sea Hawk	IN-185	300	Sub. Lt. K.P. Verma	Bombay	Crashed after take off	Killed
19 Sept. '65	Gnat		9	Fg. Offr. V.M. Mayadev	Kasur	SD by Squadron Leader Saif-ul-Azam, F-86	POW
20 Sept. '65	Hunter		7	Sqn. Ldr. D.P. Chatterjee	Lahore	SD by Squadron Leader Changezi, F-86	Killed
20 Sept. '65	Hunter		7	Flg. Offr. S.K. Sharma	Lahore	SD by Squadron Leader Jilani, F-86	E/S
21 Sept. '65	Canberra	IF-970	5	Fg. Offr. M.M. Lowe (P)	Fazilka	SD by Wing Commander J.A. Khan, F-104	POW
				Fg. Offr. K.K. Kapur (N)			Killed
22 Sept. '65	Hunter		20	Flt. Lt. K.C. Cariappa	Lahore	AAA	POW
22 Sept. '65	Mystere	IA-1339	3	Flt. Lt. P.R. Ramchandani	Lahore	Own AAA Lahore	Killed
Unknown	Auster		-	-	-	AAA	-

AIRCRAFT LOST BY THE INDIAN AIR FORCE ON THE GROUND

Date	No. Lost	Type	Squadron/Unit	Cause	Remarks
6 Sept. '65	2	MiG-21	28	PAF attack on Pathankot	Flight Lieutenant M.R. Murdeshwar's Gnat (IE 1112) lost. Flight Lieutenant Tirlochan Singh, Flying Officer Russell Montes (3 Squadron) and Squadron Leader A.L. Mousinho (31 Squadron, IA-1007) lost their Mysteres.
6 Sept. '65	6	Mystere	3 and 31		
6 Sept. '65	1	Gnat	23		
6 Sept. '65	1	C-119	-		
6 Sept. '65	1	MiG-21	28	B 57 Raid on Adampur	-
7 Sept. '65	2	Canberra	16	First PAF attack on Kalaikunda	Wing Commander Wilson's (IF-916) and Squadron Leader Karve's aircraft destroyed in raid Vampires lost include IB-344 and IB-614
7 Sept. '65	4	Vampire	24		
7 Sept. '65	2	Canberra	16	PAF Raid on Kalaikunda	-
7 Sept. '65	1	Dakota	-	PAF Raid on Srinagar	-
10 Sept. '65	1	C-119	-	PAF Raid on Baghdogra	Squadron Leader MJ Marston died of wounds. Vampire was BY-413
10 Sept. '65	1	Vampire	10	B 57 Raid on Pathankot	IA-1028 Destroyed
12 Sept. '65	1	Mystere	3	B 57 Raid on Adampur	-
13 Sept. '65	2	Mystere	32	B 57 Raid on Jammu	-
13 Sept. '65	1	Dakota	-		
14 Sept. '65	1	C-119	-	PAF Raid on Barrackpore	

14 Sept. '65	1	Dakota	-	B 57 Raid on Halwara
14 Sept. '65	2	Hunter	7	
14 Sept. '65	1	Dakota	-	B 57 Raid on Pathankot
14 Sept. '65	1	Vampire	-	PAF attack on Jamnagar
14 Sept. '65	1	Dakota	-	
14 Sept. '65	1	Hunter	-	
20 Sept. '65	1	Gnat	2(?)	B 57 Raid on Halwara
	35			

CIVILIAN AIRCRAFT LOSSES:

Date	Type	Pilot Name	Owner/Unit No.	Cause	Fate	Remarks
7 Sept. '65	Dakota	-	Indian Airlines	PAF Raid on Srinagar	-	Destroyed
7 Sept. '65	Caribou	-	UNMOGIP	PAF Raid on Srinagar	-	
21 Sept. '65	Beechcraft	J.M. Engineer	Gujarat Government	SD by F-86	Killed	Unknown

SUMMARY:

Total Aircraft Lost in Air (including 1 Civilian, 2 Army, 1 Navy)	38
Total Aircraft lost on ground (including 2 Civilian)	37
TOTAL AIRCRAFT LOST IN THE CONFLICT	75

Note: POW—Prisoner of War, E/S—Ejected Safely, B/O—Baled Out.

APPENDIX C

IAF Claims *versus* Official List of Pakistani Losses

The PAF admits the loss of 19 of its aircraft: 13 Sabres, 2 Starfighters and 4 B 57 Canberras. There were losses from other Armed Forces wings of which positive proof in terms of wreckage was recovered. These include a Bell Helicopter and a Pakistani Army Aviation Auster AOP aircraft. Recent Pakistani writings also admit the loss of an L-19 AOP aircraft to Mysteres. Another civilian Cessna and an AOP aircraft were shot down after ceasefire.

TABLE A: INDIAN AIR FORCE CLAIMS IN THE AIR (AS ON 23. SEPTEMBER 1965)

Date	Victim Type	Pilot	Aircraft and Squadron	Location
3 Sept. '65	F 86	Sqn. Ldr. Trevor Keelor	Gnat No. 23 Squadron	Over Chamb
4 Sept. '65	F 86	Flt. Lt. V.S. Pathania	Gnat No. 23 Squadron	Over Chamb
6 Sept. '65	F 86	Fg. Offr. A.R. Gandhi	Hunter No. 7 Squadron	Halwara
6 Sept. '65	F 86	Flt. Lt. D.N. Rathore	Hunter No. 27 Squadron	Halwara
6 Sept. '65	F 86	Fg. Offr. V.K. Neb	Hunter No. 27 Squadron	Halwara
7 Sept. '65	F 104	Sqn. Ldr. A.B. Devayya	Mystere No. 1 Squadron	Sargodha
7 Sept. '65	F 86	Flt. Lt. A.T. Cooke	Hunter No. 14 Squadron	Kalaikunda
7 Sept. '65	F 86	Fg. Offr. S.C. Mamgain	Hunter No. 14 Squadron	Kalaikunda
14 Sept. '65	F 86	Wg. Cdr. Bharat Singh	Gnat No. 2 Squadron	Lahore
16 Sept. '65	F 86	Fg. Offr. P.S. Pingale	Hunter No. 7 Squadron	Khemkaran
18 Sept. '65	F 86	Sqn. Ldr. A.S. Sandhu	Gnat No. 23 Squadron	Lahore
19 Sept. '65	F 86	Sqn. Ldr. Denzil Keelor	Gnat No. 9 Squadron	Sialkot
19 Sept. '65	F 86	Fg. Offr. Viney Kapila	Gnat No. 9 Squadron	Sialkot
20 Sept. '65	F 86	Fg. Offr. A.K. Mazumdar	Gnat No. 2 Squadron	Kasur

TABLE B: INDIAN AIR FORCE CLAIMS ON THE GROUND

Date	Victim Type	Destroyed by Aircraft	Pilot/formation leader name	Location
7 Sept. '65	C 130 Hercules	Mystere IVa (1 Sqn)	Wg. Cdr. O.P. Taneja	Sargodha AFB
7 Sept. '65	F 104 Starfighter	Mystere IVa (1 Sqn)	Sqn. Ldr. D.E. Satur	Sargodha AFB
7 Sept. '65	F 86 Sabre	Mystere IVa (8 Sqn)	Sqn. Ldr. M.S. Jatar	Bhagtanwala AFB
7 Sept. '65	F 86 Sabre	Hunter (27 Sqn)	Flt. Lt. D.N. Rathore	Sargodha AFB
7 Sept. '65	F 86 Sabre	Hunter (27 Sqn)	Flt. Lt. D.N. Rathore	Sargodha AFB
7 Sept. '65	F 86 Sabre	Mystere IVa (1 Sqn)	Sqn. Ldr. S. Handa	Sargodha AFB
7 Sept. '65	F 104 Starfighter	Mystere IVa (1 Sqn)	Flt. Lt. D.M.S. Kahai	Sargodha AFB
7 Sept. '65	F 86 Sabre	Mystere IVa (1 Sqn)	Flt. Lt. D.M.S. Kahai	Sargodha AFB
7 Sept. '65	F 86 Sabre	Mystere IVa (1 Sqn)	Flt. Lt. D.M.S. Kahai	Sargodha AFB

India initially claimed a total of 18 aircraft destroyed on the ground. The above nine are the only claims that could be compiled from various sources. The PAF admits the loss of one F 86, probably the aircraft by Sqn. Ldr. S. Handa.

TABLE C: OFFICIAL FIGURES OF PAKISTANI LOSSES

Date	Type	pilot/Crew Name	Cause		Target
4 Sept. '65	F 86	Fg. Offr. N.M. Butt	SD by Gnat flown by Pathania	BO	Chamb
6 Sept. '65	F 86	Sqn. Ldr. S. Rafiqui	SD by Hunter flown by Gandhi/Rathore	Killed	Halwara
6 Sept. '65	F 86	Fg. Offr. Yunus Hussain	SD by Hunter flown by Neb	Killed	Halwara
6 Sept. '65	F 86	Flt. Lt. A.T.M. Aziz	Unknown	Killed	Tejgaon
6 Sept. '65	B 57	Sqn. Ldr. S.A. Siddique; Flt. Lt. A. Qureshi	AA	Killed	Jamnagar
7 Sept. '65	F 104	Flt. Lt. Amjad Hussain Khan	SD by Mystere flown by Devayya	BO	Sargodha

(contd.)

TABLE C (*contd.*)

7 Sept. '65	F 86	Flt. Lt. Sikander Azam	Destroyed on Ground	BO	Sargodha
7 Sept. '65	F 86	Flt. Lt. Afzal Khan	Crashed during night landing	Killed	Lahore
7 Sept. '65	F 86	Flt. Lt. Sadruddin	SD by Hunter flown by Cooke	Killed	Kalaikunda
8 Sept. '65	F 86	Sqn. Ldr. Muniruddin Ahmed	AA	Ejected	Amritsar
11 Sept. '65	F 86	Sqn. Ldr. Mohammed Iqbal	AA	Killed	Amritsar
11 Sept. '65	RB 57	Flt. Lt. Saifuddin Lodhi			
13 Sept. '65	F 86	Sqn. Ldr. A.U. Ahmed	Own AA	Killed	Amritsar
14 Sept. '65	B 57	Flt. Lt. Altaf Sheikh; Flt. Lt. B.A. Choudhary	Damaged in Train Blast AA	Killed	Ferozepur
16 Sept. '65	F 86	Fg. Offr. Shaukat	AA	POW	Adampur
17 Sept. '65	B 57	Flt. Lt. M.A. Butt; Fg Offr. Khalid-ul-Zaman	SD by Hunter flown by Pingale	POW	Halwara
17 Sept. '65	F 104	Fg. Offr. G.O. Abbassi	Undershot Runway Crashed	Killed	Risalpur
19 Sept. '65	F 86	Flt. Lt. S.M. Ahmed	Crashed after Air Combat	Ejected	Sargodha
20 Sept. '65	F 86	Flt. Lt. A.H. Malik	SD by Gnat flown by Mazumdar	Ejected	Sargodha
				Ejected	Khem Karan

APPENDIX D

Gallantry Award Winners (IAF) in the 1965 Air War

The Indo-Pak War of 1965 saw the IAF involved in the heaviest fighting since Second World War. A trend in the awards was noticeable. All fighter pilots with air-to-air victories were awarded the Vir Chakra. Most Commanding Officers of attack squadrons were decorated too. Of the 44 Vir Chakras awarded to air force personnel, one was for the Kutch operations in April, well before the start of full-fledged hostilities. One MVC was awarded 23 years after the conflict.

MAHA VIR CHAKRA: 5

1.	Wing Commander	W.M. Goodman	31 Squadron	Mystere
2.	Wing Commander	P. Singh	5 Squadron	Canberra
3.	Squadron Leader	P. Gautam	JBCU	Canberra
4.	Squadron Leader	A.B. Devayya*	1 Squadron	Mystere
5.	Squadron Leader	J.M. Nath	106 SPR	Canberra

VIR CHAKRA: 44

1.	Wing Commander	Bharat Singh	2 Squadron	Gnat	Sabre Kill
2.	Wing Commander	O.P. Taneja	1 Squadron	Mysteres	Sargodha Raid
3.	Wing Commander	S. Bhattacharya	3 Squadron	Mysteres	Interdiction Raids
4.	Wing Commander	P.M. Wilson	16 Squadron	Canberra	Badin Raid
5.	Squadron Leader	Trevor Keelor	23 Squadron	Gnat	Sabre Kill
6.	Squadron Leader	M.S. Jatar	8 Squadron	Mysteres	Sargodha Raid
7.	Squadron Leader	S. Handa	1 Squadron	Mysteres	Sargodha Raid
8.	Squadron Leader	A.S. Sandhu	23 Squadron	Gnat	Sabre Kill

(*contd.*)

APPENDIX D *(contd.)*

	Rank	Name	Unit	Aircraft	Action
9.	Squadron Leader	D. Keelor	9 Squadron	Gnat	Sabre Kill
10.	Squadron Leader	A.L. Mousinho	31 Squadron	Mysteres	Interdiction Raids
11.	Squadron Leader	S.K. Dahar	45 Squadron	Vampire	Chamb Raid
12.	Squadron Leader	S. Malik	7 Squadron	Hunter	Interdiction Raids
13.	Squadron Leader	A.S. Lamba	7 Squadron	Hunter	Interdiction Raids
14.	Squadron Leader	J.W. Greene	23 Squadron	Gnat	Combat Leadership
15.	Squadron Leader	S.K. Singh		Accounts	Paratroopers Roundup
16.	Squadron Leader	B.K. Bishnoi	20 Squadron	Hunter	Raiwind Train Attack
17.	Squadron Leader	Jasbeer Singh*	3 Squadron	Mystere	Rahwali Radar Raid
18.	Squadron Leader	S.N. Bansal	5 Squadron	Navigator	Peshawar Raid
19.	Squadron Leader	C. Mehta	5 Squadron	Canberra	Bhagtanwala Raid
20.	Squadron Leader	Tej Prakash Gill	31 Squadron	Mystere	Interdiction Raids
21.	Squadron Leader	I.J.S. Parmar			
22.	Flight Lieutenant	V.S. Pathania	23 Squadron	Gnat	Sabre Kill
23.	Flight Lieutenant	Tirlochan Singh	3 Squadron	Mystere	Interdiction Raids
24.	Flight Lieutenant	D.N. Rathore	27 Squadron	Hunter	Sabre Kill
25.	Flight Lieutenant	A.T. Cooke	14 Squadron	Hunter	Sabre Kill
26.	Flight Lieutenant	H.S. Mangat	5 Squadron	Navigator	
27.	Flight Lieutenant	P.S. Pingale	7 Squadron	Hunter	Sabre Kill
28.	Flight Lieutenant	V. Kapila	9 Squadron	Gnat	Sabre Kill
29.	Flight Lieutenant	A.K. Mazumdar	2 Squadron	Gnat	Sabre Kill
30.	Flight Lieutenant	S.N. Deshpande	5 Squadron	Navigator	
31.	Flight Lieutenant	C.S. Doraiswami	3 Squadron	Mysteres	Rahwali Radar Raid
32.	Flight Lieutenant	D.M.S. Kahai	1 Squadron	Mystere	Sargodha Raid
33.	Flight Lieutenant	C.K.K. Menon	20 Squadron	Hunter	Raiwind Train Attack
34.	Flight Lieutenant	A.S. Khullar	20 Squadron	Hunter	Raiwind Train Attack

VIR CHAKRA: 44

35.	Flight Lieutenant	V.K. Bhatia	8 Squadron	Mystere	Interdiction Raids
36.	Flight Lieutenant	P.C. Chopra	8 Squadron	Mystere	Interdiction Raids
37.	Flight Lieutenant	Vinod Patney	8 Squadron	Mystere	Interdiction Raids
38.	Flight Lieutenant	G.K. Garud	106 SPR	Navigator	Photo Recces with Nath
39.	Flight Lieutenant	G.R. Railkar	106 SPR	Navigator	Photo Recces with Nath
40.	Flight Lieutenant	P. Dastidar	5 Squadron	Navigator	Peshawar Raid
41.	Flying Officer	A.R. Gandhi	7 Squadron	Hunter	Sabre Kill
42.	Flying Officer	V.K. Neb	27 Squadron	Hunter	Sabre Kill
43.	Flying Officer	S.C. Mamgain	14 Squadron	Hunter	Sabre Kill
44.	Flying Officer	U. Barbara	101 Squadron	Vampire	Kutch Operations

Note: * Posthumous.

APPENDIX E

IAF Order of Battle in the 1965 War

The following is an indicative IAF order of battle for the 1965 war. Only combat units are included in the list. 'Dett' refers to a detachment of four to six aircraft. The names of the Commanding Officers are provided in parentheses.

- *Western Air Command* (Air Vice-Marshal R. Rajaram)
  - *Pathankot* (Group Captain Roshan Suri)
    - No. 28 MiG-21 (Wing Commander M.S.D. Wollen) >>> Moved to Ambala
    - No. 45/No.220 Vampire (Squadron Leader S.K. Dahar) >>> Moved to Ambala > Palam
    - No. 23 Gnat (Wing Commander S. Raghavendran)
    - No. 31 Mystere (Wing Commander W.M. Goodman)
    - No. 3 Mystere (Wing Commander Paul Roby and Wing Commander S. Bhattacharya)
  - *Halwara* (Group Captain G.K. John)
    - No. 7 Hunter (Wing Commander A.T.R.H. Zachariah)
    - No. 27 Hunter (Wing Commander G.D. Clarke)
    - No. 20 Hunter (Dett: 8 attached to No. 7)
    - No. 2 Gnat (Dett.8)
    - No. 9 Gnat (Dett.4)
  - *Adampur* (Group Captain W.V.A. Lloyd)
    - No. 1 Mystere (Wing Commander O.P. Taneja)
    - No. 32 Mystere (Wing Commander E.R. Fernandez)
    - No. 8 Mystere (Wing Commander Milikins)
    - No. 9 Gnat (Dett.4)
  - *Ambala* (Group Captain D.E. Bouche)
    - No. 2 Gnat (Main Dett 8) (Wing Commander Bharat Singh)
    - No. 28 MiG-21 (Wing Commander M.S.D. Wollen) (After 7 September)
    - No. 9 Gnat (Main Dett) (Wing Commander R.J.M. Upot)
  - *Hindon* (Group Captain T.S. Brar)
    - No. 20 Hunter (Main Dett.) (Wing Commander Amrit Lal Bajaj)
- *Central Air Command* (Air Vice-Marshal Shivdev Singh)
  - *Agra* (Group Captain C.S. Marathe)
    - No. 5 Canberra (Wing Commander P.P. Singh)
    - No. 106 Canberra (Wing Commander M.R. Agtey)
    - JBCU Canberra (Squadron Leader P. Gautam)
    - No. 15 Gnat (Wing Commander M.J. Dhotiwala)
    - No. 2 Gnat (Dett.4) >> Ambala / Halwara
  - *Kalaikunda* (Group Captain M.B. Naik)
    - No. 14 Hunter (Wing Commander D.A. La Fontaine)

APPENDIX

- No. 16 Canberra (Wing Commander P.M. Wilson) >>> Moved to CAC Agra
- No. 24 Vampire (Squadron Leader M. Banerji)
- No. 221 Vampires (Squadron Leader Rebello)
- *Baghdogra* (Wing Commander M.B. Singh)
  - No. 101 Vampire
- *Poona* (Group Captain R.M. Engineer)
  - No. 35 Canberra (Wing Commander A.S. Bakshi)
- *Eastern Air Command* (Air Vice-Marshal Y.V. Malse)
  - *Hashimara*
    - No. 4 Ouragan (Squadron Leader M.M. Singh)
    - No. 47 Ouragan (Dett: 1) >>> Moved to Tezpur/Gauhati
  - *Tezpur*
    - No. 29 Ouragan
    - No. 47 Ouragan (Squadron Leader P. Venugopal)
    - No. 17 Hunters Dett
  - *Jorhat*
    - No. 17 Hunter
  - *Chabua* (Group Captain E.J. Dhatigara)
    - No. 37 Hunter (Wing Commander I.N. Bysak) >>> Moved to WAC Hindon
  - *Gauhati* (Wing Commander FD Irani)
    - No. 37 Hunter (Dett: 4) (Squadron Leader M.N. Singh) >>> Moved to WAC Hindon
    - No. 47 Ouragan (Dett: 4)

Notes: 1. No. 45/220 Squadron was an amalgamated unit with 16 Vampires commanded by a Squadron Leader.
2. No. 28 MiG-21 Squadron had only ten aircraft as establishment.

APPENDIX F

IAF Canberra Operations

The following table summarizes the daily raids sent out by the Canberra units against the PAF airfields.

Date	Units	Targets and Sorties	Remarks
6/7 Sept.	5 Squadron	Sargodha	Blind bombing done
7 Sept.	16 Squadron	Chittagong 0500 (2 sorties)	Runway and ATC Building bombed
8/9 Sept.	5, 35 Squadrons, JBCU	Chak Jhumra, Sargodha, Gujarat, Akwal Dab Gujarat	Damage to installations at Sargodha and
9/10 Sept.	5, 35 Squadrons	Sargodha, Wagowal, Risalawala, Chak Jhumra (PAF claim 7 sorties)	Dispersal area at Chak damaged
10/11 Sept.		Chak Jhumra, Risalawala, Sargodha (6 sorties), Wagowal	
11/12 Sept.		Nawabshah, Multan	44,000 lbs dropped
12/13 Sept.	5, 35, JBCU	Chota Sargodha, Sargodha, Risalawala, Wagowal	SE portion of CS damaged, Runway 22 at Risalawala hit
13/14 Sept.	5 Squadron, JBCU	Kohat (2 sorties) Peshawar (6 sorties)	12 x 1,000 lbs dropped 8 x 1,000 lb 6 x 4,000 lb
14 Sept.		Kasur RS	16 x 1,000 lb 4 x 4,000 lb

14/15 Sept.	35 Squadron	Sargodha, Chak Jhumra	Damage caused to runway
15/16 Sept.	35 Squadron	Peshawar	8 x 1,000 lb 2 x 4,000 lb
16 Sept.		Ugoke (Close support)	
16/17 Sept.	5, 16 Squadrons	Chak Jhumra, Akwal and Sargodha	
17/18 Sept.		Chak Jhumra	Poor visibility
18/19 Sept.		Sargodha	Dropped bombs high
		Sakesar (2 sorties)	Target not sighted
19/20 Sept.		Sargodha and Chawinda RS	
20/21 Sept.	5 Squadron	Sargodha	
21 Sept.	16 Squadron	Badin (6 sorties)	Destroyed Radar dome
21/22 Sept.	5 Squadron	Sargodha, Chawinda	One Canberra Shot down

Source: Table compiled from 'Indian Armed Forces—Official History of the 1965 War'.

APPENDIX G

IAF Strength: Reported *versus* Actual

TABLE A: ESTIMATE OF IAF STRENGTH ACCORDING TO (FRICKER, 1979)

Type	Unit	U/E Total
MiG-21s	1 Squadron	10
Hunters	6 Squadrons	118
Mysteres	5 Squadrons	80
Gnats	5 Squadrons	80
Ouragans	3 Squadrons	56
Canberras	5 Squadrons	60
Vampires	8 Squadrons	132
TOTAL		536

TABLE B: ACTUAL STRENGTH OFFICIAL IAF HISTORY

Type	Unit	U/E Total
MiG-21s	28	10
Hunters	7, 14, 17, 20, 27, 37	108
Mysteres	1, 3, 8, 31, 32	80
Gnats	2, 9, 15, 18, 23	80
Ouragans	4, 29, 47	48
Canberras	5, 16, 35, JBCU, 106 PR	70
Vampires	24, 45/220, 101PR, 108PR, 221	64
TOTAL		460

Note: All PR Squadrons were equipped with eight aircraft. Thus the lone Canberra PR Squadron and the two Vampire PR Squadrons had only 8 aircraft each.

TABLE C: ACTUAL STRENGTH OF AIRCRAFT EMPLOYED IN WESTERN SECTOR

Type	Unit	U/E Total
MiG 21	28	10
Hunters	7, 20, 27	48
Mysteres	1, 3, 8, 31, 32	80
Gnats	2, 9, 23	48
Ouragans	None with WAC	-
Canberras	5, 16, 35, JBCU, 106 PR	70
Vampires	45 /221	20
TOTAL		276

Note: The above total does not take into account that one flight of 20 Squadron of 8 aircraft did not take part, being stationed throughout the war at Hindon, and that No. 32 did not take part actively as it was under conversion.

APPENDIX H

Interviewes

We are grateful to Dr. Shiv Shankar Sastry, Mr. Gus Sheridan, Ms Linda Sheridan, Mr. Anandeep Pannu, Mr. Sanjeev Sharma, Mr. Ashit Chakraborty, Mr. Amit Javadekar, Mr. Sree Krishan Kumar, Mr. Kapil Chandni and Mr. Pushpindar Singh Chopra for helping us in arranging interviews or correspondence with them. We would also like to thank several serving IAF officers for their help.

Name	Then
Marshal of the Air Force Arjan Singh DFC	Air Marshal, Chief of Air Staff
Air Chief Marshal (Retd.) I.H. Latif, PVSM	Air Cmde. Air 1 EAC
Air Chief Marshal (Retd.) D.A. La Fontaine PVSM	Wing Commander, OC of No. 14 Hunters
Air Marshal (Retd.) V.K. Bhatia PVSM AVSM VrC Bar VM	Flight Lieutenant, No. 8 Mysteres
Air Marshal (Retd.) Pratap Rao PVSM AVSMVM	Flight Lieutenant, No. 3 Mysteres
Air Marshal (Retd.) Vinod Patney SYSM PVSM VrC VM	Flight Lieutenant, No. 8 Mysters
Air Marshal (Retd.) Y.V. Malse PVSM	Air Vice-Marshal, AOC-in-C EAC
Air Marshal (Retd.) A.R. Pandit, PVSM AVSM DFC	Air Cmde, SASO EAC
Air Marshal (Retd.) Janak Kapur PVSM	Flight Lieutenant, No. 23 Gnats
Air Marshal (Retd.) M.S.D. Wollen PVSM	Wing Commander, OC of No. 28 MiG 21s
Air Marshal (Retd.) M.S. Bawa, PVSM, AVSM	Squadron Leader, No.14 Hunters
Air Marshal S. Bhojwani, PVSM, AVSM VM	Flying Officer, No. 27 Hunters (1966)
Air Vice-Marshal (Retd.) M. Banerji, MVC	Squadron Leader, 24 Vampires
Air Vice-Marshal (Retd.) C.V. Parker, MVC, VM	Squadron Leader on deputation to US

(contd.)

APPENDIX H *(contd.)*

Name	Then
Air Vice Marshal (Retd.) Viney Kapila VrC VM	Flight Lieutenant, No. 9 Gnats
Air Vice Marshal (Retd.) A.S. Lamba VrC	Flight Lieutenant, No. 7 Hunters
Air Vice-Marshal (Retd.) R. Kondaiah VSM	Flying Officer, No. 7 Hunters (Technical Officer)
Air Vice-Marshal (Retd.) C.S. Doraiswami VrC	Flight Lieutenant, No. 3 Mysteres
Air Vice-Marshal (Retd.) S.A.B. Naidu	Flying Officer, No. 2 Gnats
Air Commodore (Retd.) P.M. Wilson, PVSM, VrC,	Wing Commander, OC of No. 16 Canberras
Air Commodore (Retd.) K.A. Hariharan, AVSM VM	Flight Lieutenant, Armament Training Wing
Group Captain (Retd) O.P. Taneja VrC	Wing Commander, OC of No. 1 Mysteres
Group Captain (Retd.) D.M. Conquest AVSM, VrC	Squadron Leader, No. 27 Hunters.
Group Captain (Retd.) M.R. Murdeshwar VM	Flight Lieutenant, No. 23 Gnats.
Group Captain (Retd.) M.N. Singh VM	Squadron Leader, No. 37 Hunters
Group Captain (Retd.) D.K. Parulkar VM VSM	Flying Officer, No. 20 Hunters
Group Captain (Retd.) H.M.P.S. Pannu	Squadron Leader, TTW, Dakotas
Wing Commander (Retd.) J.M. Nath MVC Bar	Squadron Leader, No. 106 Canberra
Wing Commander (Retd.) P.R. Earle, VM	Squadron Leader, No. 1 Mysteres
Wing Commander (Retd.) R. Dhawan AVSM, VM	Squadron Leader, No. 2 Gnats

(Contd.)

APPENDIX H *(contd.)*

Name	Then
Wing Commander. (Retd.) G.V. Kuriyan	Wing Commander, OC (Flying) Pathankot Air Base
Wing Commander. (Retd.) Krishna Dandapani, AVSM	Wing Commander, OC of 230 SU, Amritsar
Wing. Commander. (Retd.) F.J. Mehta, VrC.	Flight Lieutenant, No. 45 Vampires
Wing Commander K.S. Suresh VrC	Flight Lieutenant, No. 20 Hunters
Wing. Commander. (Retd.) D.P. Soni.	Flight Lieutenant, No. 5 Canberra
Squadron Leader (Retd.) K.D. Mehra	Flight Lieutenant, No. 220 Vampires
Squadron Leader (Retd.) A.L. Mousinho VrC	Squadron Leader, No. 31 Mysteres
Squadron Leader (Retd.) J.F. Josephs	Squadron Leader, No. 3 Mysteres
Flight Lieutenant (Retd.) Alfred Tyrone Cooke VrC	Flight Lieutenant, No. 14 Hunters
Flight Lieutenant (Retd.) Samar Bikram Shah VrC, VM	Flying Officer, No. 220 Vampires
Flight Lieutenant (Hon. Retd.) G.C. Chakraborty	Corporal, ADC, Jaffarpur

Bibliography

Ahmed, Brigadier Gulzar, *Pakistan meets Indian Challenge*, Natraj Publishers, 1995.
Bhargava, Group Captain Kapil, *Suranjan Das: The man and the professional*, *Indian Aviation*, September 1999.
Bishnoi, B.K., 'Thunder over Dacca', *Vayu Aerospace Journal*, I, January 1997.
Chatterjee, Admiral A.K., *Indian Naval Aviation*, New Delhi: Allied Publishers, 1990.
Chaturvedi, Air Marshal M.S., *History of the Indian Air Force*, New Delhi: Vikas Publishing House, 1978.
Chinna, R.T.S., 'The IAF Memorial Book' (unpublished).
Dalvi, J.P., *Himalayan Blunder*, Bombay: Thacker & Company, 1969.
Fricker, John, *Battle for Pakistan*, London: Ian Allan, 1979.
Galbraith, J.K., *An Ambassador's Journal*, Boston: Houghtan Mifflin, 1969
Gandhi, S.S., ed., *Encyclopedia of Soldiers with Highest Gallantry Awards*, Indian Defence Review, 1980.
Chakravarty, B.C., ed., *Indian Armed Forces—Operation Vijay—Official History of the 1962 Goa Operations*, New Delhi: Government of India, 1974.
———, 'Indian Armed Forces—Official History of the 1965 Indo-Pakistan War', New Delhi: Government of India (unpublished).
Government of India, *Defending Kashmir*, 1949.
———, *Harvest of Glory*, 1965.
———, *Gallantry Award Winners 1995 Edition*, Indian Defence Review
Guttman, John, 'Pakistan's Sabre Ace', *Aviation History*, vol. 9, no.1, September 1998, Washington: Primedia Publishers.
Hali, Group Captain Sultan M., 'The Air War of 71 Remembered', *Defence Journal*, 1998.
———, 'The F 104 Starfighter in the PAF', *Defence Journal*, May 2000.
———, 'The Tail Choppers—PAF No.14 Squadron', *Defence Journal*, December 1998.
Hiranandani, Vice-Admiral G.M., *Transition to Triumph: The Indian Navy 1965-1975*, New Delhi: Lancer International, 1999.
Iqbal, Wing Commander Arif, 'Eye Witness Account to M.M. Alam', *Defence Journal*, 2000.
Kaul, Lieutenant General B.M., *Confrontation with Pakistan*, New Delhi: Vikas Publishing House, 1971.
Khan, Air Marshal Asghar, *The First Round*, New Delhi: Vikas Publishing House 1979.
Khan, Brigadier Zahir Alam, *The Way it Was*, Karachi: Ahbab Publishers, 1998.
Khan, Farhat, 'Bombs Away', *SUN* (dates not available, out of print).
———, 'The Fighting Five Raid Peshawar', *SUN* (dates not available, out of print).
———, 'We Are Under Attack', *SUN* (dates not available, out of print).

Khan, Major General Fazal Maqueem, *Pakistan's Crisis in Leadership*, New Delhi: Alpha and Alpha, 1981.
Khan, Squadron Leader Shauib Alam, 'The Fighter Gap', *Defence Journal*, May 1998.
Khan, Wing Commander Aftab Alam, 'F-104 Starfighter at War in 1965', *Defence Journal*.
Lal, Air Chief Marshal P.C., *My Years with the IAF*, New Delhi: Lancer International, 1986.
Mankekar, D.R., *Defending Kashmir*, Ministry of Defence, 1949.
———, *Twenty two Fateful Days*, Bombay: Manaktalas, 1966.
Musa, General Mohammed, *From Jawan to General*, New Delhi: ABC Publishing House, 1985.
———, *My Version*, New Delhi: ABC Publishing House, 1985.
Nayar, Admiral K.K., *Amar Jawan*, Bombay: India Book House, 1997.
Pradhan, Y., *From Debacle to Revival: Y.B. Chavan as Defence Minister 1962-65*, Hyderabad: Orient Longman, 1998.
Praval, Major K.C., *Indian Army after Independence*, New Delhi: Lancer International, 1987.
———, *Red Eagles*, New Delhi: Vision Books, 1977.
———, *Valour Triumphs*, New Delhi: Thomson Press, 1976.
Sabharwal, Wing Commander D.P., *No. 3 Squadron—The Cobras 1941-2001*, No. 3 Squadron, 2002.
Saigal, A.L., ed., *Birth of an Air Force*, Dehra Dun: Palit and Palit, 1977.
Salik, Siddik, *Witness to Surrender*, New Delhi: Oxford University Press, 1979.
Sen, Lieutenant General L.P., *Slender Was the Thread*, Hyderabad: Orient Longman, 1969.
Shah, Air Commodore Mansoor, *The Gold Bird: Pakistan and its Air Force*, Karachi: Oxford University Press, 2002.
Singh, Air Marshal M.M., 'Gnats Over Bangladesh', *Air Forces Monthly*, November 1991.
Singh, Lieutenant Colonel Bhupinder, *Role of Tanks in the 1965 War*, Patiala: B.C. Publishers, 1982.
Singh, Lieutenant General Harbaksh, *In the Line of duty—A Soldier Remembers*, New Delhi: Lancer International, 2000.
———, *War Dispatches*, New Delhi: Lancer International, 1991.
Singh, Major General Sukhwant, *Defence of the Western Border*, New Delhi: Vikas Publishing House, 1981.
Singh, Pushpindar, *Aircraft of the Indian Airforce 1933-1973*, New Delhi: New English Book Depot, 1973.
———, 'Laying the Sargodha Ghost to Rest', *Vayu Aerospace Review*, November, 1985.
———, *The Battle Axes—1942-1992*, New Delhi: Society for Aerospace Studies, 1992.
———, W. Green and G. Swansborough, *The IAF and its Aircraft 1932-1982*, London: Ducimus Books, 1982.
Singh, Pushpindar and Ravi Rikhye, *Fiza'ya: The Psyche of the PAF*, New Delhi: Society for Aerospace Studies, 1991.

Singh, Rear Admiral Satyindra, *Blueprint To Bluewater: The Indian Navy 1951-65*, New Delhi: Lancer International, 1992.
Singh, Roopinder, *Marshal of the Air Force Arjan Singh*, Rupa Charitravalli Series, New Delhi: Rupa, 2002.
Slim, Field Marshal W.J., *Defeat into Victory*, London: Cassell, 1961.
'Supersonic Combat', *Vayu Aerospace Review*, VI / 1997 (November 1997).
Tanham, George K. and Agmon Marcy, *The Indian Air Force: Trends and Prospects*, The Rand Corporation, 1995.
Tufail, Air Commodore Kaiser, 'Alam's Speed Shooting Classic', *Defence Journal*, September 2001.
——, 'Mystery of the Downed Mystere', www.pafcombat.com.
——, 'Run . . . it's a 104', www.pafcombat.com.
——, 'Speed shooting classic', www.pafcombat.com.
——, 'Squadron Leader S.A. Rafiqui', *Defence Journal*, September 1998.
Wollen, Air Marshal M.S.D., 'No. 28 Squadron—First Supersonics in 1965', *Indian Aviation*, Bombay, 1992.

Published Interviews

Air Marshal (Retd.) Denzil Keelor (*Times of India*)	Squadron Leader, No. 9 Gnats Squadron
Air Marshal A.R. Ghandhi (*Probe Magazine*)	Flying Officer, No. 7 Hunter Squadron
Air Marshal (Retd.) M. Sinha (*My Years with IAF*)	Squadron Leader, No. 7 Hunter Squadron
Wing Commander (Retd.) T. Keelor (*Harvest of Glory*)	Squadron Leader, No. 23 Gnats Squadron
Air Marshal (Retd.) P. Rajkumar (*Times of India*)	Flying Officer, No.1 Mysteres Squadron
Air Marshal (Retd.) K.C. Cariappa (*The Week*)	Flight Lieutenant, No. 20 Hunter Squadron

Index

Abassi, G. (Fg Offr) 93, 350
Abdul Hamid CQMH 221
Adampur 35, 53, 98, 108; attacked by B-57s 113-17, 241-2; interdiction strikes 247-8, 250, 254, 284; retaliates against Sargodha 127-9, 133, 143, 217, 221, 232, 235, 239; SSG Paradrop 119, 124
Agra 50, 68, 239
Agtey, M.R. (Wg Cdr) 50, 88, 354
Ahamed, S.M. (Flt Lt) 270
Ahluwalia (Flt Lt) 244
Ahmed, A.U. (Sqn Ldr) 108; shot down 236, 293, 350
Ahmed, Muniruddin (Sqn Ldr), chased by MiG 87, 93; shot down 220, 341, 350
Ahmed, Nisar (AC1) 200
Ahuja, Gurbux Singh (Flt Lt) 70; killed in crash 213, 214, 215, 344
Akhnur 79, 84, 94
Alam, M.M. (Sqn Ldr): Adampur combat 108-9, 112; Halwara combat 256-60, 292, 297, 303-4, 336-7, 341-2, 344-5; Sargodha claims 142
Alize, Dassault-Breguet 158
Ambala 34, 36; Gnats 77-8, 100; Gnat operations 238-40; raid by PAF 262-4, 287, 329, 354; SSG Para Scare 120, 206
Amritsar 75, 79, 113; radar under attack 217-20, 248, 313
Anderson, T.L. (Wg Cdr) 150
Antonov (An)-12 29; bomb training 149-55
Antonov (An)-32 326
Ashoka Chakra 236
Augier, D.A. (Sqn Ldr) 150-1, 154, 160

Auster 288, 342-5
Azam, Saif ul (Flt Lt) 127; shoots down Sabre 270, 285, 342, 345, 350
Aziz, A.T.M. (Flt Lt) 169; killed 193, 201, 202, 349

B 57, Martin: raids 108; attacked at Peshawar 245-6; attacks Adampur 129; attacks Amritsar Radar 217-21; attacks Jamnagar 156; damaged over Ambala 287; destroys MiG 114; 8-Pass 241-2; raids Halwara 137; shot down at Jamnagar 115-16
B-24 Liberator 25, 26, 46, 151
Badhwar, Ravi (Sqn Ldr) 237
Badin 57, 90, 218; attacked 278-81, 301, 304, 320, 322
Baghdogra 196, 197, 199
Bains (Fg Offr) 196
Bajaj, Amrit Lal (Wg Cdr) 207, 354
Bakshi, K.K. (Flt Lt) 127, 285, 331
Bal, C.N. (Flt Lt) 76, 237
Balachandani (Sqn Ldr) 100
Banerjee, P.K. (Sqn Ldr) 201
Banerji, Madhabendra (Sqn Ldr) 163; Jessore raid 173-6; wins MVC 334, 354, 360
Bansal, S.N. (Sqn Ldr) 244, 352
Barbara, Utpal (Fg Offr) 61, 91, 353
Barrackpore 163, 173, 175, 180; attacked by Sabres 200, 201; false alarm 193-6
Bawa, M.S. (Sqn Ldr) 198, 199, 201, 360
Beechcraft 267, 343
Begumpet 154, 195
Behal, S.K. (Flt Lt) 306

INDEX

Bell 47 234, 291
Bhagwagar, A.K. (Flt Lt) 69, 70, 72, 344
Bhagwat, S.B. (Sqn Ldr) 137, 138, 139, 344
Bharadwaj, S. (Flt Lt) 72, 344
Bhatia, V.K. (Flt Lt) 33, 121; attack Baghtanwala 133-4; first mission 125-6; VrC announced 210-11, 226, 230, 236, 242, 262, 325-6, 332, 353, 360
Bhattacharya, S. (Wg Cdr) 74, 92, 261, 274, 351, 354
Bhatti, Imtiaz (Flt Lt) 70-2, 240, 298, 341
Bhojwani, S. (Air Marshal) 316, 360
Bishnoi, B.K. (Sqn Ldr) 207-10, 213-15, 325, 329, 339, 352
Bouche, David (Gp Capt) 120, 354
Brahmawar, A.K. (Flt Lt) 127, 129, 229, 242, 285
Brar, D.S. (Flt Lt) 33, 96, 127, 140, 233, 238, 354
Brar, J.S. (Fg Offr) 137-9, 344
Brar, P.S. (Flt Lt) 238, 324
Bunsha, F.D. (Fg Offr) 255-9, 345
Butt, N.M. (Flt Lt) 84, 93, 293, 298, 349
Bysak, H.N. (Wg Cdr) 355

C-119 Packet, Fairchild: damaged at Baghdogra 197; damaged at Barrackpore 201; destroyed at Pathankot 108; in the East 163, 166, 177, 194, 195
C-130 Hercules, Lockheed: as bombers 231-2; destroyed at Sargodha 142; drops Paratroopers 116; supplies to infiltrators 64
Canberra, English Electric: attacks Chittagong 172-3; attacks Karachi 127; destroyed on ground at Kalaikunda 179-80;

eastern sector 163-5; induction into IAF 46-50; J.M. Nath's sorties 88-90; raid on Badin 278-81; raid on Peshawar 244-7; raid on Sargodha 263-4; shot down 49; shot down by Starfighter 275-8
Cariappa, K.C. (Flt Lt) 229; taken prisoner 282-3, 324, 330, 345
Central Air Command 35, 37, 50, 162-5, 170, 307, 326
Cessna 288, 291, 335
Chak Jhumra 138, 139, 229
Chaklala 223, 231
Chakraborty, G.C. (Cpl) 200, 362
Chaman Lal (Fireman) 236
Chamb 66, 75, 77, 79, 84, 91, 94, 104, 352
Chandigarh 35, 54; An-12 operations 149, 150, 152
Changezi, S.A. (Sqn Ldr) 273, 342, 345
Chatterjee, D.P. (Sqn Ldr) 273
Chatterjee, H.N. (Air Marshal) 297, 345
Chatwal, H.P.S. (Sqn Ldr) 216
Chaudhuri, J.N. (General) 67, 286, 295, 297, 314-15
Chaudhuri, T.K. (Flt Lt) 135, 137, 249; dies 253, 345
Chavan, Y.B. 63, 67, 116, 286
Chertta 220, 283
Chinoy, D.P. (Fg Offr) 224, 225, 344
Chittagong 165; attacked by Canberras 171, 172
Chopra, A.C. (Wg Cdr) 332
Chopra, P.C. (Flt Lt): first mission 125, 126, 158; VrC announced 211, 226, 230, 248, 262, 295, 332, 353
Choudary, Cecil (Flt Lt) and Halwara battle 110, 112, 298, 305, 333, 336, 341-4
Clarke, G.D. (Wg Cdr) 99, 100, 233, 354

INDEX

Gnat 240-1; shoots down Vampires 70-3; shot down 212; shot down by Cooke 186-93, shot down by Hunters 110-12; shot down by Keelor 80-2; shot down by Majumdar 273; shot down by 9 Sqn Gnats 268-71; shot down by Pathania 84-5; shot down by Pingale 255-61; shot down by Sandhu 265

Fernandez, E.R. (Wg Cdr) 354

Garud, G.K. (Flt Lt) 353
Gauhati 167
Gautam, P. (Sqn Ldr) 50, 126, 159; and Peshawar raid 244, 246; at Congo 279; killed in crash 325-7, 351, 354
Ghadiok, T.N. (Gp Capt) 149, 150
Ghandhi, A.R. (Fg Offr) and Halwara air battle 110, 112, 122, 226, 295, 297, 305, 333, 344, 348, 353
Ghuman, G.S. (Flt Lt) 238
GIBRALTAR 64, 66, 315
Gill, H.S. (Wg Cdr) 329
Gill, P.S. (Fg Offr) 79, 80
Gill, T.P.S. (Sqn Ldr) 352
Gnat, Folland: A.K. Majumdar's kill 273; Bharat Singh's kill 246-7, 263; detachment at Pathankot 77-86; induction 40-6; Kale's loss 240-1; Kapila's combat 216-17; Keelor's kill 80-1; lands in Pakistan 82; Pathania's kill 84; 9 Squadron's kills 268-71; Sandhu's kill 264-5
Goa 27, 156, 223, 307, 314
Gocal, Keki (Air Commodore) 77, 96, 150, 153
Goodman, W.M. (Wg Cdr): awarded MVC 91, 107, 216, 226, 294, 321, 351, 354; first mission to Chamb 68, 73, 76
Goodwin, V.C. (Sqn Ldr) 244, 245, 275

Goraya (Sqn Ldr) 166
Greene, J.W. (Sqn Ldr): air combat 84-5, 91, 239, 241, 265, 295, 328, 352; move to Pathankot 78-80
Grewal, M.S. (Fg Offr) 334
Guha, U.B. (Flt Lt) 141, 142, 285, 344

Haider, S.S. (Sqn Ldr) 102, 103, 121, 146, 333, 336
Hakimpet 68, 96, 154, 155, 308, 333
Hakimullah (Flt Lt): as Air Chief 337, 341; escapes MiGs 229; intercepts Gnat 82-3; recce sortie 102
Halwara: 35, 42, 77, 79; attacked by Sabres 108-17, 124, 127; Birdhit to Hunter 253; first day missions 99-103; intercept incoming raid 255-61, 303; missions against Sargodha 135-7, 139, 148, 206-7, 213-16, 223-5, 231-2, 240-1, 249
Handa, S. (Sqn Ldr) Sargodha raid 127-8, 130; second raid on Sargodha 139-41, 211, 226, 233, 349, 351
Hariharan, K. (Gp Capt) 361
Harishsinji (Flt Lt) 334
Hatmi, Saad (Flt Lt) 82, 108, 337, 342
HF-24 Marut 318, 330, 331
Hindon 36, 152, 221
HS 748 26
Hunter, Hawker: air Battle 247; air combat with Sabres 109, 255-60; attack Kurmitola 169; attack Sargodha 135-9; Cooke's battle 180-91; first day strikes 99-101; Halwara Air Battle 110-13; in eastern sector 163-201; induction into IAF 42-3; Lahore Air Battle 273; last sorties 282-4, losses 142; lost to

INDEX

Conquest, D.M. (Sqn Ldr) 100, 232, 251, 316, 323, 361
Cooke, A.T. (Flt Lt) 166, 172, 176-7; air combat 180-91, 203, 226, 251, 294, 297, 299, 305, 334, 335, 348, 350, 352, 362

Dabolim 156, 223
Dacca 168, 170, 176, 177
Dahar, S.K. (Sqn Ldr), killed in crash 82, 324, 352, 354; leads Chamb mission 68-72, 73
Dakota C-47, Douglas: at Jammu 241; damaged at Barrackpore 201; destroyed on ground at Srinagar 147; shot at by Hunters 195-6
Dandapani, K. (Wg Cdr) 75, 83, 92; PAF raids 122, 217-22, 285, 335, 362; warns Pathankot 103-4
Dange, S.S. (Flt Lt) 96, 129
Daniels, G.G. (Sqn Ldr) 99
Das, Suranjan (Wg Cdr) 46, 58
Dass, Pushy (Flt Lt) 114
Dastidar, P. (Flt Lt) 244, 353
Datta, P.K. (Flt Lt) 150, 152
Deshpande, S.N. (Flt Lt) 244, 352
Desoares, B.K. (Sqn Ldr) 150, 152
Devayya, A.B. (Sqn Ldr) and Sargodha battle 96, 130-3, 289, 292, 335; awarded MVC 337-8, 344, 348, 351
Dewan, H.C. (Air Marshal) 297, 321
Dhatigara, E.J. (Gp Capt) 167, 355
Dhawan, Gags (Sqn Ldr) 237
Dhawan, Ranjit (Sqn Ldr) 238, 239, 241, 316, 331, 339, 361
DHC-3 Otter 28, 29, 65
DHC-4 Caribou 30, 147, 241, 343, 347
Dhiman, D.K. (Flt Lt) 101, 147, 148, 229, 232, 253
Dhotiwala, M.J. (Wg Cdr) 239, 354
Doraiswami, C.S. (Flt Lt): attack Indian position 361; attack Rah attack tanks 271 mission to Cham
Dum Dum 166, 177, 196, 198-9, 202
Dwaraka 156, 157

Earle, P.R. (Sqn Ldr) a raid 96-8, 127, 129 3, 233, 242-3, 334,
Eastern Air Command 3 162, 165, 167, 198,
Engineer, A.M. (Air Mars 32, 34, 37
Engineer, J.M. 267, 268, 2
Engineer, M.M. (Air Marsh 321
Engineer, R.M. (Gp Capt) 3

F-6, Shenyang 318
F-104 Starfighter: air combat Chamb 80-3; air combat Devayya's Mystere 130-3; destroyed on ground 140 intercepts Hunters 148; intercepts Mysteres 97-8; intercepts Peshawar raid 24 outruns MiG-21s 229; shoot down Canberra 276
F-86 Sabre: at Badin 280; at Sargodha raids 134-9; attack Adampur 109; attack Amritsa 217-22; attack Baghdogra 19 attack Barrackpore 200-3; attack Chertta 283; attack Pathankot 105-8; attack Srinagar 147-8; attack train at Gurdaspur 235-6; chased by MiG-21s 86-7; destroyed on ground 141; in combat with Gnat 216-17; in eastern sector 163-9; in PAF service 57; shoots down civilian aircraft 267; shoots down Indian Canberra 49-50; shoots down

INDEX

AA 212; lost to Birdhit 253; mid air collision 214-15; procurement 25-7; shoots down Cessna 288; shot down by Sabres 110-13

Hussain, I.F. (Flt Lt) 344

Hyderabad 51, 154, 155, 307, 308, 314

IAF, Units of
1 Squadron 41, 92; at Ichogil 233-4, 238, 243, 248; at Kasur 221-3; first ope-rations to Rahwali 96-9, 119, 121, 123; Mystere lost 227-9; second and third raid on Sargodha 139-41, 160; strike at Kasur 268-9, 284-5, 290, 321, 324, 348, 351-2; strike on Sargodha 127-33

2 Squadron 44, 206; first operations 238-41; Sabre downed 246-7, 273, 298, 306, 328, 330, 348, 351-2

3 Squadron 41, 68, 72, 74, 76; aircraft lost to ground fire 281-2; attack on Rahwali radar 143-6, 216, 234; during Pathankot raid 103-6; intercepts Cessna; 261-2, 271-4; intercepts civil aircraft 289, 334, 351-2

4 Squadron 39; at Lal Munir Hat 166-7, 171, 328

5 Squadron 47, 50, 126; loses Canberra 275-8, 301, 322, 351-3, 356-7; Peshawar raid 244-5, 263

7 Squadron air combat with Sabre 255-61; attack Sargodha 137-9, 142; first day operations 99-101; intercept Starfighter 229-30, 247, 249; intercepts Adampur and Halwara raids 108-13; in 1947-8 Kashmir operations 23-5, 42; interdiction sorties 147, 206; Lahore attack 214; lose Hunter to Birdhit 253; loses Hunter 212; mid air collision 215, 223; probe over Lahore 273; with Arjan Singh 306, 334, 348, 352-3

8 Squadron 41, 96, 99; after the war 325-6, 334, 351, 353; awarded VrC 210-11, 222; black formation 226, 230; first mission 124, 128; lose Mystere to AA 236-7, 247, 261-2, 308; raid on Baghtanwala 133-4

9 Squadron 44, first Combat 206, 216; shoots down Sabres 268-70, 298, 334, 348, 352

14 Squadron 42, 78; CAP over Barrackpore 198-9, 305, 325, 348, 352-3; first day operations 176-89, 194; in eastern sector 162-4, 172

16 Squadron 47, 50, 162; after war 322, 332, 351, 356-7; aircraft lost in PAF raid 179-80; attack Badin SU 278; attack Chittagong 171-2; attack Sargodha 263

17 Squadron 42; in eastern sector 162-3, 195, 305

20 Squadron 42; air combat 255; in 1971 war 319, 323, 332, 352, 359; interdiction strikes 206-10, 253; last mission 282

23 Squadron 44; after a sortie 289; analysis 298; during Pathankot raid 104-6, 120, 217; escort Mysteres 234; former members, 329-30, 348, 351-2; Keelor's kill 79-82; move to Pathankot 77-8; Pathania's kill 83-5; Sandhus combat 264-5

24 Squadron 39; attack on Jessore 173-6, 179-80, 334; in eastern sector 162-3

25 Squadron 149, 150

27 Squadron 42, 99; Halwara air combat 111-13; intercepts civil

INDEX

aid 288, 319, 330, 352-3; mid air collision 212-15, 221, 229-30, 249, 282; raid on Sargodha 135-7, 142, 164, 167, 206
28 Squadron induction of MiGs 52-4, 59; move to Pathankot 77; intercept Sabre 85-6, 93; Pathankot raid 108; analysis 300, 321, 329
29 Squadron 39, 68, 167, 327
31 Squadron 41, 68; after the war 321, 351-2; first mission over Chamb 72-3; loses Mystere 224, 237, 262; Mystere lost at Pathankot 107, 173, 216; recce mission 76, 91, 103
32 Squadron 41, 129, 133; loses Mystere to B-57 raid 242, 359
35 Squadron 47, 50; raid Karachi 127, 223, 301, 326, 356, 357
37 Squadron 42; attack Kurmitola 166-71, 195, 304-5, 334; in eastern sector 162-3
41 Squadron loses Otter 65
44 Squadron 149, 150
45 Squadron 39; first mission over Chamb 68-72, 109, 173, 352
47 Squadron 39, 167, 329, 332
48 Squadron 200
101 Squadron 39, 61; Baghdogra raid 196-7, 334, 353
106 Squadron 47; loses Canberra 49-50; recce by Nath 88-9, 327, 351, 353, 356
108 Squadron 39, 329-30
220 Squadron 39; first mission over Chamb 68-72; mission 274-5
221 Squadron 39, 166-76
230 Signal Unit 36, 75; raids by PAF 217-22, 272, 288, 313, 335; Pathankot raid 103, 114, 146; Sabre baiting 79, 83, 90, 101
300 Squadron 155, 157
310 Squadron 156, 157

411 Signal Unit 163, 181-3, 188-9
Ichogil Canal 95, 209, 210, 233
INS Talwar 157
INS Vikrant 156
Iqbal, Arif (Sqn Ldr) 298, 331
Irani, B.R. (Flt Lt) and Chamb recce 74, 76; Rahwali raid 143-6, 281
Irani, F.D. (Wg Cdr) 355
Ivelaw-Chapman, R. (Air Marshal) 22

Jain, P.K. (Flt Lt) 263
Jammu 65, 241, 293
Jamnagar 37, 103; B-57 attack 114-15, 155-6, 235, 272, 313, 322
Jatar, Dinky (Flt Lt) 74; Pathankot raid 104, 106
Jatar, M.S. (Sqn Ldr) Baghtanwala raid 134, 226, 230, 236, 248, 262, 331, 332, 349, 351; first mission 124, 125
Jayakumar, Pondy (Flt Lt) 238
Jayal, B.D. (Flt Lt) 51
Jessore 166, 174, 177
Jet Bomber Conversion Unit 47, 50; Peshawar raid 244, 246, 351, 356, 357
Jilani, Flt Lt 342, 345
Jodhpur 37, 235, 249
Jog, D.S. (Sqn Ldr) 135-7
John, G.K. (Gp Capt) 99, 100, 232, 233, 354
Josephs, F.J. (Sqn Ldr) interdiction 274, 285, 316, 334, 362; 69, 92; Peshawar raid 104, 105, 122, 146
Joshi, V.M. (Fg Offr) 69, 72, 344

Kacker, O.N. (Sqn Ldr) ejects near Sargodha 135, 136; in eastern sector 164, 181, 185, 299, 330, 331, 344
Kahai, D.M.S. (Flt Lt) 127, 130, 140, 229, 233, 349

INDEX

Kalaikunda 50, 98, 163, 165-6, 171; air combat 189, 190, 192-4, 198, 293, 303, 305, 334; mission flown 175-80, 182-3

Kale, A.N. (Flt Lt) 238-41, 299, 344

Kapila, Viney (Flt Lt): awarded VrC 297; first air combat 216, 251; in 1971 war 328-9, 348, 352, 361; shoots down Sabre 268-71

Kapur, Janak (Flt Lt) 59; comments on Gnat 298; in 1971 war 328, 339, 360; Pathankot raid 104-6

Kapur, K.K. (Fg Offr) 238; 275-8, 345

Karachi 127, 223, 301

Karve (Sqn Ldr) 171, 172, 179, 346

Kasur 94, 205

Katre, L.M. (Wg Cdr) 100, 325, 332

Kaul, S.K. (Sqn Ldr): missions at Chamb 74, 234; MVC in 1971 war 334

Keelor, Denzil (Sqn Ldr): in 1971 war 328, 348, 352; shoots down Sabre 268-71, 294

Keelor, Trevor (Sqn Ldr): at Pathankot 78; shoots down Sabre 80-1, 91, 226, 265, 289, 294, 328, 348, 351

Kewal Ramani (Sqn Ldr) 74, 76

Khan, Aftab Alam (Flt Lt): intercepts Mystere 97, 98, 131, 145, 341

Khan, Afzal (Flt Lt) air combat at Kalaikunda 183-6, 188, 190, 192-3, 201, 350

Khan, Amjad Hussain (Flt Lt) intercepts Mystere 97; shot down by Mystere 131-3, 159, 293, 298, 321, 335, 341, 349

Khan, Asghar (Air Vice-Marshal) 58, 62, 63, 91-2

Khan, J.A. (Wg Cdr) 276, 342, 345

Khan, Najeeb (Wg Cdr) 251

Khan, Nur (Air Vice-Marshal) 63, 92, 102, 290, 291

Khan, Shoaib Alam (Sqn Ldr) 91

Khan, Tariq Habib (Flt Lt) and Kalaikunda raid 186; Sabre damaged 190-1, 201, 341

Khan, Yusuf Ali (Flt Lt) hit by Gnat 93; Sabre damaged 240, 342, 344

Khanna, Kamli (Fg Offr) 238, 247; air combat 273

Khem Karan 205, 208, 221, 235

Khullar, A.S. (Flt Lt) and Raiwind attack 208-10, 253, 352

Khurana, S. (Capt) 310, 344

Kirti Chakra 198, 295, 328

Kondaiah (Fg Offr) prepares for strikes 99, 100, 137, 249, 361

Krishna, I.G. (Flt Lt) 240

Krishnaswamy, S. (Flt Lt) and Chamb air combat 79, 80, 81, 85, 266, 289, 335

Kuriyan, G.V. (Wg Cdr) 68, 74, 75, 92; and Pathankot raid 103-5, 121-2, 362

Kurmitola 167, 169

Kutch 36, 60, 61, 353

La Fontaine, D.A. (Wg Cdr) 163-6, 172, 176-8, 189, 192, 194-5, 202-3, 325, 354, 360

Lal, P.C. (Air Marshal) 20, 31-2, 43, 59, 68, 91, 118, 122-3, 159-60, 220, 296, 310, 315, 317, 320-1

Lamba, A.S. (Sqn Ldr): after war 306, 333, 352, 361; first missions 99-101, 121; last missions 284-5; Sargodha raid 137-9, 147, 160, 249

Latif, I.H. (Air Chief Marshal) 360

Law, R.D. (Wg Cdr) 165, 188, 190, 192

Leh 65, 146, 326

Lloyd, W.V.A. (Gp Capt) 295, 324, 354

Lodhi, Saifuddin (Flt Lt) 350

INDEX

Lowe, M.M. (Flt Lt) 275-8, 292, 345

Maha Vir Chakra 24, 33, 88, 90, 226, 294, 301, 309, 317, 325, 334, 337, 338, 351
Mahadik, R.C. (Flt Lt) 255
Malik, A.H. (Flt Lt) shoots down Mystere 141-2; shot down by Gnat 273, 341, 344, 350
Malik, N.K. (Sqn Ldr) 238, 240-1; killed in accident 247, 345
Malik, Sube Singh (Sqn Ldr) 99, 101, 147, 229, 306, 352
Malse, Y.V. (Air Vice-Marshal) 37, 297, 355, 360
Mamgain, S.C. (Fg Offr) 166, 172, 176-7, 180, 182-3; air combat 187-8, 190-1; awarded VrC 226, 297, 348, 353
Mangat, H.S. (Flt Lt) 352
Marathe, C.S. (Gp Capt) 354
Marston, M.J. (Sqn Ldr) 196, 197, 327, 346
Mauripur 223
Mayadev, V.M. (Fg Offr) 268-70, 285, 299, 345
Mazumdar, A.K. (Fg Offr) 238, 239; shoots down Sabre 273, 306, 348, 352
McMahon, M. (Fg Offr) 32, 73, 107, 333, 334
McNeil, W.D. (Wg Cdr) 167, 170
Meer, Rasheed (Sqn Ldr) 287
Mehra, K.D. (Flt Lt): CAP over Ambala 263; first missions 69; in 1971 war 324, 339, 362; searches for Gnat 82; Vampire sortie 274-5
Mehra, S.K. (Sqn Ldr) 51; bombed by B-57s 114, 321, 325
Mehta, Balwant Rai 267, 268
Mehta, C.R. (Sqn Ldr) 244, 352
Mehta, F.J. (Flt Lt): first mission over Chamb 69, 72, 87; in 1971 war 323, 339, 362;
Vampire sortie 274-5
Mehta, R.K. (Flt Lt) 285
Menon, C.K.K. (Flt Lt) and Raiwind attack 208-10, 352
Michael, P.S. (Wg Cdr) 149
Middlecoat, M. (Sqn Ldr) 245, 298, 336, 342
MiG 21: analysis of role 299-301; bombed by B-57s 114; destroyed on ground 106; encounter with Starfighter 229; first combat action 85-8; in 1971 war 318-19; induction into IAF 51-4
Mil Mi 4 26, 28, 241
Milikins (Wg Cdr) 354
Mirage III 51, 318, 319, 326
Mohla (Fg Offr) 196, 197
Moolgavkar, H. (Air Cmde) 43, 44, 68, 150, 297
Mousinho, A.L. (Sqn Ldr): mission over Chamb 73; Pathankot raid 107, 122, 261, 346, 352, 362
Mukherjee, A.K. (Sqn Ldr) 51, 53; at Pathankot 77; chases Sabre 85, 86
Mukherjee, S. (Air Marshal) 19, 25, 27, 34
Murdeshwar, M.R. (Flt Lt): first air combat 78-80; Pathankot raid 104-6, 120, 122-3, 330, 346; second air combat 84-5
Mystere IVa, Dassault: attack Baghtanwala 133-4; attack Rahwali 144-6; attack train at Rahwali 97-8; destroyed by B-57s 242; Devayyas combat 130-3; during Pathankot raid 106-8; 8 Sqn missions 210; 8 Sqn strikes 125-6; first sorties 72-6; induction into IAF 38-40; interdiction strikes 221-30, 233-6, 268-74; lost to AA fire 237-8; raids on Sargodha 128-31, 139-42; Sabre baiting 79-

INDEX 375

80; shoots down Cessna 261; shoots down stray aircraft 289; shot down by own fire 281-2

Naidu, S.A.B. (Fg Offr) 238, 324, 361
Naik, M.B. (Gp Capt) 165, 166, 178, 354
Nath, J.M. (Wg Cdr): Badin recce 278; Lahore recce sortie 88-90; retirement 327, 339, 351, 361
Neb, V.K. (Fg Offr): awarded VrC 226; in 1971 war 325, 348, 353; shoots down Sabre 111-13; with army chief 297, 305
Negi, D.S. (Flt Lt) and Raiwind attack 208-10

Ouragan, Dassault 25, 27, 37-9, 43, 55, 63, 68, 167, 171, 318, 358

Padma Bhushan 295, 296, 321
Padma Vibhushan 295, 321
Palam 54, 100, 151, 153, 221, 263, 354
Pandit, A.R. (Air Commodore) 34, 167, 170, 360
Pandiya, C.G. (Fg Offr) 99, 100
Pannu, H.M.P.S. (Flt Lt) 195, 196, 361
Param Vir Chakra 23, 221, 266, 329, 338
Paranjpe (Sqn Ldr) 208
Parihar, P.S. (Fg Offr) 135
Parker, C.V. (Sqn Ldr) 323, 360
Parmar, I.J.S. (Sqn Ldr) 352
Parulkar, D.K. (Fg Offr) 207, 208; injured in sortie 213-15, 251, 334, 361
Pathak, S.V. (Fg Offr): mission to Chamb 70; shot down 72, 344
Pathania, V.S. (Flt Lt): after sortie 289; awarded VrC 226, 265-6; first air combat 79-81; in 1971 war 329, 348, 352; shoots down Sabre 84-7, 91, 93, 120
Pathankot: 35, 36; B-57 attack 262, 275, 312; first missions over Chamb 66-9, 73-4, 76-9, 82, 85, 87-8, 90, 95, 100, 102, 105; interdiction missions 234-6; launches Rahwali attack 143, 145-6, 152, 216, 225, 232; under PAF attack 107-8, 113, 116-17, 122, 126
Patney, V. (Flt Lt) 125, 126, 158, 211, 230, 236, 248, 262, 307, 326, 332-3, 353
Peshawar 21, 57, 102-3, 114, 146; attacked by Canbarras 243, 244, 301
Pingale, P.S. (Fg Offr) 101 as Air Marshal 333, 344, 348; shot down Sabre 110, 255-61
Poonch 65, 66
Potharaj, Hav 87, 91
Potnis (Fg Offr) 234
Prasad, Niranjan (Maj Gen) 94, 204-5
Pune 326
Puri, P.S. (Flt Lt) 192
Purushotam (Gp Capt) 150, 153
Pushpak 309, 333

Qais (Sqn Ldr) 342
Qureshi, Aslam (Sqn Ldr) 115

Rafique, S.A. (Sqn Ldr): killed over Halwara 109-10, 112, 261, 297, 305, 339, 341, 344, 349; shoots down Vampires; 70-2
Raghavendran, S. (Wg Cdr) 58, 77, 78, 234, 266, 289, 354
Rahwali 57; Mystere attack 96, 98, 143-5
Rai, G.S. (Fg Offr) 268-70
Railkar, G. (Flt Lt) 353
Raina, P.R. (Sqn Ldr) 238, 241, 299
Rajaram, R. (Air Vice-Marshal) 20, 34-5, 37, 153-4, 295, 297, 320, 354

Raje 127, 129
Rajkumar, P. (Fg Offr) and Sargodha raid 127, 130, 140, 159, 160, 248, 268, 284, 324
Rajwar, G.C.S. (Fg Offr) 171
Ram, P.V.S. (Gp Capt) 154
Ramchandani, Prem (Flt Lt) attacks tanks 272; shot down by own fire 281-2, 345
Rampal, S.N. (Flt Lt) 49, 50
Rao, Dopey 238
Rao, Pratap (Air Marshal) 360
Raphael, Dickey (Flt Lt) 152
Rathore, D.N. (Flt Lt): as Air Marshal 333, 348-9, 352; attack on Sargodha 135; awarded VrC 226 shoots down Sabre 111-13
Rawlley, A.K. (Sqn Ldr): shot down by Sabres 109, 113, 122, 344
Risalpur 21
Roby, P.C. (Wg Cdr) 68, 74, 354
Rufus, R.A. (Wg Cdr) 149-55

Sadarangani, Lal (Flt Lt) 96; shot down 236, 344
Sadruddin, S. (Fg Offr) 212, 350
Sahay, Sanjeev (Flt Lt) 70
Sakesar 57, 97, 218, 276, 320
Salins, E.G. (Sqn Ldr) 96, 230
Samant, M.P. (Fg Offr) 288
Sandhu, A.J.S. (Sqn Ldr): awarded VrC 297; first air combat 84; killed in Crash 329, 348, 351; shoots down Sabre 264-6
Sandhu, I.S. (Sqn Ldr) 237, 238
Sanyal, A.N. (Flt Lt) 173-6
Sapru, Ajay (Sqn Ldr) 74
Sargodha 57, 103, 119, 124, 128; Canberra raid 223; 275-6, 301, 310, 330, 349, 351-2; IAF raids 130-7, 139-42, 148, 153, 159-60, 180
Sarvottam Yudh Seva Medal 333
Satur, D.E. (Sqn Ldr) 96, 128, 130, 228, 229, 238, 284, 349
Sawardekar, V.B. (Sqn Ldr) 196-8, 327
Sea Hawk, Hawker 41, 155-8, 343, 345
Sekhon, N.J.S. (Fg Offr) 329
Sen Gupta, J.C. (Sqn Ldr) 49, 50, 57
Sen, Tushar (Fg Offr) 120
Senapati (Wg Cdr) 194, 195
Sethi, T.S. (Flt Lt) 237, 238, 344
Shah, S.B. (Flt Lt) 339, 362
Shamim, Anwar (Wg Cdr) 252, 298, 337
Shankaran, O.N. (Sqn Ldr) 171, 238, 263
Sharma, C.P. (Flt Lt) 238
Sharma, S.K. (Fg Offr) 109; aborted mission 137; ejects 273, 345; mid air collision 213-15
Shaukat, M.I. (Fg Offr) shot down by Hunter 256-61, 337, 350
Sheikh, Altaf (Flt Lt) 249, 350
Shekaran (Sqn Ldr) 237
Siddique, S.A. (Sqn Ldr) 349
Sidhu (Fg Offr) 288, 331
Sikand, B.S. (Sqn Ldr) 77; air combat 79-80; as Air Marshal 330, 344; lands at Pasrur 82-3, 246, 292
Sikka, R.L. (Flt Lt) 63, 64, 92
Singh, Arjan (Air Chief Marshal) as CAS 31-5, 58; awarded Padma Vibhushan 295-7, 303, 306, 315-16, 320-1, 324, 360; Chamb fighting 67, 88, 92, 116, 122, 162, 191, 202, 260, 286; during Kutch fighting 62-3; in WW II 20; with Nur Khan 290-1
Singh, B.I. (Flt Lt) 96, 248
Singh, Bakshish (Wg Cdr) 355
Singh, Bharat (Wg Cdr) 238-9; shoots down Sabre 247, 297, 306, 348, 351, 354
Singh, Dilbagh (Gp Capt) 51-4, 153
Singh, Dushyant (Flt Lt) 200

INDEX

Singh, Harbaksh (Lt Gen) 35, 120, 123, 317
Singh, Harjinder (Air Vice-Marshal) 300
Singh, J.P. (Flt Lt) 129; Sargodha raid 141, 228, 233-4, 268, 269
Singh, Jasbeer (Sqn Ldr) 143-6, 295, 344, 352
Singh, K.Y. (Flt Lt) 216
Singh, M.M. (Sqn Ldr) 43, 58, 167-8; Lal Munir Hat sortie 170-1, 355
Singh, M.N. (Sqn Ldr) 93, 212, 323, 339, 355, 361
Singh, M.V. (Fg Offr) 344
Singh, Murat (Air Commodore) 178
Singh, N.B. (Wg Cdr) 355
Singh, P.P. (Wg Cdr) 50, 126, awarded MVC 226; Peshwar raid 244, 322, 351, 354
Singh, Pushpindar 33, 92, 159, 160, 284, 285, 302, 303
Singh, Shivdev (Air Vice-Marshal) 37, 162, 165-6, 173, 178, 297, 320, 354
Singh, Sree Krishna (Sqn Ldr) 117, 352
Singh, Surinder (Gp Capt) 151, 154-5, 289
Singh, Trilochan (Sqn Ldr): awarded VrC 226, 346, 352; first missions over Chamb 74, 76; Pathankot raid 104, 106, 143-4, 216
Singha, B.K.(Flt Lt) 150, 152
Sinha, M.M. (Sqn Ldr) 99, 101, 109, 137, 229, 306, 333
Soman, B.S. (Vice-Admiral) 315
Sondhi, W.M. (Fg Offr) 72
Soni, B.B. (Flt Lt) 329, 336
Soni, D.P. (Flt Lt) 362
South Western Air Command 36
Special Services Group (SSG) 116
Srinagar 64-5, 147, 241
Suares, A.I.K. (Wg Cdr) 50, 326

Sudhakaran, A. (Sqn Ldr) 285
Sukhoi Su-7 318, 319, 326, 332, 333, 336
Suresh, K.S. (Flt Lt): comments on MiG 54; in 1971 war 323, 362; last sortie of war 282
Suri, N.C. (Sqn Ldr) 208, 229, 251, 306
Suri, R.L. (Gp Capt) 43, 44; first mission over Chamb 68, 69, 74, 75, 95; Pathankot raid 103, 104, 144, 354
Syed, Shabbir (Sqn Ldr) 115

T 33, Lockheed 114
Tactical Air Center (TAC) 227, 228, 308, 309
Takle, M.M. (Flt Lt) 50
Taneja, O.P. (Wg Cdr): first missions 96-98, 100, 121-2; Sargodha raid 127-30, 133, 159-60, 222, 227, 238, 243, 254, 321, 324, 338-9, 349, 351, 354, 361
Tarapore, A.B. (Lt Col) 265, 266
Tejgaon 166, 168
Tipnis, A.Y. (Flt Lt) 53, 324

Upot, R.J.M. (Wg Cdr) 240, 354
Uppal, R.K. (Sqn Ldr) 228, 344
Uttarlai 330, 331

Vampire, De Havilland: introduction 37-9, 24; Sqn 173-6; analysis of role 295; at Barrackpore 200; first strikes from Pathankot 68-70; hit by B-57s at Jamnagar 115; in the East 163; recce sortie 82; shot down by Sabres 72; sortie over Palam 263; strafed at Baghdogra 196-7; strike mission 274-5
Vayusena Medal 265
Venugopal, P. (Sqn Ldr) 355
Verma, J.C. (Sqn Ldr) 244, 245

Verma, K.P. (Sub Lt) 158, 345
Verma, V.K. (Flt Lt) 127, 129-31, 159, 222-3, 233, 284-5
Vir Chakra, 117, 126, 210, 226, 230, 261, 281, 294-5, 297, 301, 310, 317, 323, 324-6, 351
Virk, J.S. (Sqn Ldr) 194
Virk, T.S. (Air Vice-Marshal) 297
VK-750 Surface to Air Missile 211, 212, 312

Western Air Command 35, 36, 51, 77, 95-6, 103, 151, 153, 156, 158, 207, 226, 227, 304, 308, 310, 326, 332
Wilson, P.M. (Wg Cdr) 48, 50, 58, 162; Badin SU raid 278-81, 285; Chittagong raid 164-5, 171, 179; Sargodha raid 263-4; in 1971 war 322, 329, 346, 351, 354, 361
Wollen, M.S.D. (Wg Cdr) 51; arrested by police 284-5, 300; chases Sabre 85-7, 90; in 1971 war 321, 354, 360; induction of MiGs 53-4, 59; move to Pathankot 77; Pathankot raid 107, 122, 220

Yunus, M. (Fg Offr) and Halwara raid 111, 112, 305, 341, 344, 349

Zacharaiah, A.T.R.H. (Wg Cdr): first missions 99-101; intercepts Adampur raid 109; last sortie of war 284, 354; Sargodha attack 137-9, 212